Walter Stuart White

The register book of christenings, weddings, and burials,

Within the parish of Leyland: in the county of Lancaster, 1653 to 1710 - Vol. 2

Walter Stuart White

The register book of christenings, weddings, and burials,
Within the parish of Leyland: in the county of Lancaster, 1653 to 1710 - Vol. 2

ISBN/EAN: 9783337724368

Printed in Europe, USA, Canada, Australia, Japan

Cover: Foto ©ninafisch / pixelio.de

More available books at **www.hansebooks.com**

Report for the Years 1888-9 and 1889-90.

Read at the Annual Meeting, held in the Audit Room of the Chetham Hospital, Manchester, November 5th, 1890.

THE members of the Society are aware that last year, owing to various causes, no Meeting of the Society was held. The present Report has, therefore, to deal with the proceedings of the two years, 1888-9 and 1889-90.

Since the last Annual Meeting, held on the 31st October, 1888, four volumes have been delivered to the members; two volumes are now in the printers' hands, and two others are very nearly ready for the press. Of the volumes delivered to the members, Vol. XVII., Lancashire Inquisitions, Stuart Period, Vol. III., 1622 to 1625, and Vol. XVIII., Index to the Wills at Chester, 1681 to 1700, were fully described in the last Report. The remaining volumes, XIX. and XX., are the two volumes for the year 1888-9, and were issued some months since. Vol. XIX. is entitled:—'Memorials of the Civil War in Cheshire and the adjacent counties,' by Thomas Malbon, of Nantwich, gent., and 'Providence Improved,' by Edward Burghall, Vicar of Acton, near Nantwich, edited by Mr. James Hall, author of 'A History of Nantwich.' This is a most interesting volume, and a valuable historical record of one of the most eventful periods in the history of England. The origin of the two MSS. here printed is not a little curious. In the year 1778, Burghall's "Providence Improved" was printed for the first time at the end of the second of two miscellaneous volumes relating to Cheshire, rather absurdly entitled "The History of Cheshire." It was afterwards reprinted in 1819 by Dr. Ormerod in his "History of Cheshire," and again in 1855 by the late Mr. T. Worthington Barlow at the end of his book entitled "Cheshire: its Historical and Literary Associations," but in none of these was it accurately done. In each case the first version, which was full of errors, was copied. From its first publication it was recognised as an extremely important addition to Cheshire history, and has been freely

quoted by all writers on Cheshire, from Dr. Ormerod down-
wards. A few years ago, however, a MS. was referred to in
the fifth Report of the Royal Historical MSS. Commission as
being in the possession of Reginald Cholmondeley, Esq., at
Condover Hall, near Shrewsbury, which, on being examined
by Mr. Hall, was found to be a very full contemporary account
of the Civil War in and around Nantwich, drawn up by
Thomas Malbon, a resident in that town. This MS. is now
here printed in its entirety for the first time, and it is perfectly
clear that it has been the source from whence the Rev. Edward
Burghall compiled his "Providence Improved" about the
year 1660. Malbon's "Memorials" only relate to the period
1642 to 1648, and Burghall has added a number of so-called
"providences" referring to a period of twelve years or so before
and after Malbon. In order to show the correlation of these
two MSS. they have been printed in this volume in close
juxtaposition the one to the other, Malbon's "Memorials," as
being the more valuable, as well as the fuller, being in larger
type than Burghall's.

As printed in this volume (XIX.) these two MSS. will be
found full of very interesting reading and they are simply
invaluable for the history of the period to which they relate.
Instead of a dry record of the action of the various com-
manders on either side during the Civil War in Cheshire and
the adjacent counties, they are crowded with incidents of
much local and general importance, which help to bring the
character of that struggle and its chief actors before us in a
very graphic manner. Mr. Hall has edited this volume with
much care; and, in addition to a very full introduction, he has
printed a "Chronological Table of Contents," which will be
found very useful, and has added several Appendices con-
taining much matter of importance.

Volume XX., which is the Index to the Wills and Inven-
tories now preserved at Chester from 1701 to 1720, has, like
the previous Lists of Wills at Chester, been edited by Mr.
J. P. Earwaker. The Council can only re-iterate what was
stated in the last Report, and express their gratification that
there has now been placed in the hands of the members the
complete list of all the wills relating to Lancashire and
Cheshire, known to be preserved at Chester, from the earliest
date, 1545, to the year 1720, as well as those which were
proved in London between the years 1650 and 1660, when
the Diocesan Courts of Probate were closed. The total
number of wills calendared in the *five* volumes now printed,
embracing the periods, 1545 to 1620, 1621 to 1660, 1660 to
1680, 1681 to 1700, and 1701 to 1720, cannot be far short

HAROLD B. LEE LIBRARY

of 90,000 ! As the names are arranged in strictly alphabetical order, it is now possible for any one to ascertain, with little or no trouble, what wills belonging to any particular Lancashire or Cheshire family, down to the year 1720, are now preserved at Chester, and this too without the necessity or expense of a visit to Chester and a special search through each year's Index in the Probate Registry there. It is, therefore, not surprising that these volumes have been the most frequently consulted of any printed by the Society, and that the example which the Record Society has set, with regard to the wills at Chester, has been and is being followed by other Societies in various parts of England. The Council hope to continue the printing of these lists from time to time down to the year 1780 or possibly 1800.

The two volumes for the year 1889-90 will probably be (1) the " Register of Leyland, co. Lancaster," 1653 to 1710, edited, with a careful Introduction and an account of the church and parish, by the Rev. W. Stuart White, M.A., Curate of Leyland, and (2) a further volume of the Index to the Wills at Chester, 1721 to 1740, edited by Mr. Earwaker. Of these the first volume is already in the press and the second will be sent to press shortly. The two volumes for the current year, 1890-91, will consist of a " Miscellaneous Volume" (the second volume of that character issued by the Society) and the first volume of the " Lancashire Royalist Composition Papers" (arranged alphabetically, A to F), edited by the Rev. J. H. Stanning, M.A., Vicar of Leigh. This latter volume is now ready for the press and the former will be ready next year. The Council propose to print in this Miscellaneous Volume several records of much local value, to be selected from a number of documents, such as Subsidy Rolls, Lists of Papist Recusants, &c., now in the hands of the Hon. Secretary. The Council hope that these volumes will be issued to the members before the next Annual Meeting.

The following is the complete list of the Society's publications already printed or arranged for, up to the present time :—

1878–79. {
I. Commonwealth Church Survey.
II. Index to the Wills at Chester, 1545 to 1620.

1879–80. {
III. Lancashire Inquisitions. Stuart Period. Part I. 1603 to 1613.

1880–81. {
IV. Index to the Wills at Chester, 1621 to 1650.
V. The Register of Prestbury, co. Chester, 1560 to 1636.

The last four volumes are those now in hand.

Two volumes have been issued in each year, except on two occasions, when a single volume of more than average thickness was substituted for the two volumes.

In previous Reports attention has been directed to the various volumes which the Council hope to be able to issue in future years. Of these, perhaps the most important is the Index to the Raines MSS., now in the Chetham Library, Manchester, and to the Piccope, Palmer, Barritt, and other local MSS. there, which will form the first of a series of volumes, describing the contents of the various MSS. relating to Lancashire and Cheshire, now preserved in the different public libraries in the two counties. Since the last Report, Mr. J. E. Tinkler, recently Librarian at the Chetham Library, has completed the Index to the 45 folio volumes of the Raines MSS., and this is now ready for the press. It is not, however, quite sufficient to make a volume, and the Council hope to be able to include the Indices to the other MSS. in the Chetham Library, so as to form a complete record of the valuable MS. material for local history there preserved.

Mr. J. A. C. Vincent has made considerable progress with his Report on the Lancashire Lay Subsidy Rolls, but the Council regret that the volume is not yet fully printed. When completed it will be found full of original information of much local value.

As announced in the last Report, the important Court Rolls of the great Honor of Clitheroe, co. Lancaster, have during the past few years been carefully examined by two members of the Society, Mr. A. J. Robinson, of Clitheroe Castle, and Mr. W. Ecroyd, of Burnley, who have kindly agreed to allow the results of their labours to be printed by this Society. The great quantity of material, and the trouble of making such selections as will show the true value of these ancient Rolls, are difficulties which the Council trust these gentlemen will be able to overcome, so that their account of them, with copious extracts from the Rolls, may be printed before long.

The Council hope to obtain permission to print the Early Marriage Licences relating to Lancashire and Cheshire, preserved in the Bishop's Registry, Chester, which begin in 1608. These Marriage Licences contain information of great genealogical value, which well deserves to be placed on permanent record. They are also of use in supplying the names of the local clergy who were licensed to celebrate these marriages.

Since the last Report, full abstracts of all the *Cheshire* Royalist Composition Papers have been made at the Record Office, London, and the Council hope to print these documents at no distant date. The method of arranging, and the value of this class of local records were described in the Report for 1887 in the following terms, which may be repeated here: "The simplest arrangement will probably be an alphabetical one, as that will bring the many scattered documents together under the name of the person to whom they relate. Much light is thrown by these records on the tyrannical and arbitrary means employed by those in authority in confiscating the property of the Royalists, and the hardships that the latter had to undergo. These Royalist Composition

Papers, relating as they do to a period (1644 to 1652) of very great public interest, will make singularly valuable volumes for the history of both Lancashire and Cheshire, and will supply a mass of information entirely new, the very existence of which, up to a few years ago, was unsuspected."

Several important MSS. have recently been offered to the Council for publication, such as the "Plundered Ministers' Accounts" for Lancashire and Cheshire during the Civil War and Commonwealth period, to be edited by Mr. W. A. Shaw, M.A.; the early Registers of Whalley, co. Lancaster, commencing 1538, to be edited by Mr. W. A. Abram; and the Roll of the Freemen of the City of Chester, to be edited by Mr. T. Cann Hughes, B.A. These are before the Council, whose desire is to print such records as will be found of interest to the great majority of the members of the Society, rather than those which are likely to be of service to a few members only.

The death of Mr. Thomas Hughes, F.S.A., of Chester, who was a member of the Council from the commencement of the Society, has caused a vacancy in the Council, which has been filled by the appointment of Mr. Henry Taylor, F.S.A., of Chester, Town Clerk of Flint.

The Council wish to direct special attention to the fact that the number of members is now much below the 350 names, to which the Society is limited, and they are most anxious that this should be remedied. The volumes issued by the Society are of great value for the history of Lancashire and Cheshire, and the Council think it cannot be a difficult matter for the present members to interest their friends in a Society, which has done and is doing such good work.

☞ The Council must again refer to Rule 5, under which no volume can be delivered to any member whose subscription is in arrear.

The Balance-sheets, showing the receipts and expenditure of the Society for the years 1888-9 and 1889-90, will be found on the next pages.

RECORD SOCIETY—LANCASHIRE AND CHESHIRE.

Receipts and Expenditure from 1st July, 1888, to 30th June, 1889.

Dr.

	£	s.	d.
Balance (Bank-book), June 30, 1888	428	17	5
Subscriptions received, July to December, 1888 ...	214	4	0
Subscriptions received, January to June, 1889 ...	36	15	0
Books sold	28	13	4
Bank Interest	8	0	3
Subscription overpaid (Rev. C. B. Norcliffe) ...	0	10	6
	£717	0	6

Cr.

	£	s.	d.
Insurance of Stock of Books	1	0	0
Mr. Bradbury, Rent of Stock-room	11	14	0
Mr. Mason, Arranging Stock, taking care of same, and sending out sundry volumes	4	3	10
Amount overpaid (Rev. C. B. Norcliffe)	0	10	6
Messrs. Wyman and Sons, Printing	150	0	0
Mr. E. R. Morris, Transcribing Royalist Compositions, &c.	40	9	0
Hon. Secretary, Checking and Arranging List of Wills (vol. 18)	10	18	4
Hon. Secretary, Arranging Royalist Compositions, &c. ...	2	6	0
Hon. Treasurer, Postages, &c.	3	15	0
Bank Commission	1	16	8
Balance (Bank-book), June 30th, 1889	490	7	2
	£717	0	6

Audited and found correct,

(Signed)   ANDREW E. P. GRAY, } *Auditors.*
            JAMES E. WORSLEY, }

(Signed)   J. PAUL RYLANDS,

                  Hon. Treasurer.

13th July, 1889.

RECORD SOCIETY—LANCASHIRE AND CHESHIRE.

Receipts and Expenditure from 1st July, 1889, to 30th June, 1890.

Dr.	£	s.	d.	Cr.	£	s.	d.
Balance (Bank-book), June 30, 1889	490	7	2	Mr. Bradbury, Rent of Stock-room	5	17	9
Subscriptions received, July to December, 1889	76	13	0	Mr. Fourness, Rent of Stock-room	6	0	0
Subscriptions received, January to June, 1890	34	13	0	Insurance of Stock of Books...	0	12	0
Books sold	17	17	0	Cheque Book	0	5	0
Bank Interest	8	15	3	Messrs. Wyman & Sons, Printing, &c.	88	7	2
				The Manchester Press Co. Limited, Printing	97	11	4
				Mr. Pearse, Receipt-books	0	17	6
				Miss Walford, Collating Burghall's Diary	3	7	2
				Mr. Dooley, Transcript of Prestbury Registers, 1637-1685	4	4	0
				Mr. Morris, Transcribing Royalist Composition Papers ...	25	16	0
				Messrs. Mason & Beard, removing stock to new rooms ...	1	0	0
				Mr. Mason, taking care of stock and sending out volumes	2	2	0
				Hon. Secretary, checking and arranging Lists of Wills ...	13	17	0
				Ditto ditto ditto			
				Ditto copying Leyland Transcripts, Church Papers, &c.	9	0	0
				Bank Commission	4	5	0
				... ...	1	1	0
				Balance (Bank-book), June 30, 1890	364	2	6
	£628	5	5		£628	5	5

Audited and found correct,

(Signed)   JAMES E. WORSLEY, } Auditors.
           ANDREW E. P. GRAY, }

19th July, 1890.

(Signed)   JOHN PAUL RYLANDS,
           Honorary Treasurer.

THE RECORD SOCIETY

FOR THE

𝔓ublication of Original Documents

RELATING TO

LANCASHIRE AND CHESHIRE.

VOLUME XXI.

1890.

COUNCIL FOR 1889-90.

The Register Book

of

Christenings, Weddings, and Burials,

within the

Parish of Leyland,

In the County of Lancaster,

1653 to 1710.

(With a few earlier "Transcripts," 1622-1641.)

Edited,

WITH AN INTRODUCTION AND NOTES,

BY THE

REV. WALTER STUART WHITE, M.A.,

Senior Curate of Leyland.

PRINTED FOR

THE RECORD SOCIETY.

1890.

MANCHESTER:
EXAMINER PRINTING WORKS,
PALL MALL.

INTRODUCTION.

THIS volume had its origin in a desire to provide a duplicate copy of the Registers of the parish of Leyland, so that research¡might be facilitated, the originals saved from wear and tear, and the important matter contained in them safeguarded from accidental loss through fire or other mishap. The first portion of the Register was copied whilst waiting for funerals, which, in this parish, are frequent and sometimes unpunctual. The idea of publication, which was an afterthought, supplied the incentive for completion. The offer of the Lancashire and Cheshire Record Society to include a transcript of the earliest volume of the Registers amongst its publications, afforded an opportunity which was gladly embraced. The genealogical and other notes which have been appended to most of the important entries in the following pages are intended to serve merely as indications of the value of these entries to those who are unaccustomed to the scientific use of such sources of information. It is hoped that the care bestowed upon them will have insured a large measure of accuracy.

The Historical Introduction, with which it was intended to furnish this volume, has had to be put aside, owing to the unforeseen length to which the transcript of the Register, with its notes, has grown. The material, which has been accumulated for that purpose, may possibly see the light at some future time in a different form. A brief survey of the parish and church of Leyland, with a list of the Vicars (so far as they are at present known), must on the present occasion suffice.

The parish of LEYLAND is of considerable extent, and has a history of something like a thousand years. It is situated in that part of Lancashire which lies between the Ribble and the Mersey, and *may* originally have been co-extensive with the hundred of Leyland. There have always been, however, within historic memory, as many as six ancient parishes within that hundred: Leyland, Penwortham, Croston, Eccleston, Standish, and Brindle. These parishes, with the forty townships of which they consist, are constantly mentioned in the Leyland Registers. The parish of Leyland is bounded on the east by the parish of Blackburn, on the north by the parish of Penwortham, on the west by the parish of Croston, and on the south by the parish of Standish, while the parish of Bolton-le-Moors touches it at the south-eastern corner. The extreme measurement is (roughly) nine miles from east to west and five miles from north-west to south-east.

There are nine townships within the parish of Leyland, which have from time immemorial been grouped as follows:—Leyland and Euxton have invariably been the first and second quarters; Whittle-le-Woods, Clayton-le-Woods, and Cuerden have together formed the third quarter; Heapey, Wheelton, Hoghton, and Withnell have always been known as the fourth, or Moor quarter.

There are good grounds for supposing that Leyland dates back far into the Saxon era as an ecclesiastical centre, but there is no direct historical evidence to prove its existence till the reign of William Rufus. Although the Domesday Book does not speak of the church of Leyland, yet it does mention a priest resident there, and it is surely no unfair inference that he had a church and an altar for his ministry. The Chartulary of Evesham Abbey (Worcestershire) and the private deeds of the local families supply us with the information that a donation of the churches of Leyland, Penwortham, the chapel of Meols, and other appurtenances of his lordship, was made by Warin Bussel, a comrade and adherent of Roger of Poictou, soon after the Conquest. (See Hulton's *Priory of Penwortham*, Chetham Society, vol. xxx.) The connection of Matilda, the wife of Warin Bussel, by association and ownership with the town of Evesham suggests a motive for his gift of Lancashire territory, &c., to the Worcestershire monastery. This donation was confirmed and added to by successive members of the same family, so that the Abbot and Convent of Evesham continued to enjoy the whole of the great tithes of the district and the advowson of the church until the suppression of the Abbey in 1536. A special provision for a perpetual vicar was made in 1331, under the licence of the King and the sanction of the Bishop of the diocese (Lichfield). A papal bull given on the occasion is also in existence.

No considerable change took place in the state of the parish or the position of the vicar until the era of the Reformation saw the patronage transferred to the family of Fleetwood, which had become possessed, by purchase from the Crown, of the neighbouring priory of Penwortham. The disturbed period from 1645 to 1660 left fewer marks upon the parish than might have been expected. Vicar Langley, who was growing old when the Presbyterian system was adopted, sat as a prominent member of the sixth Classis. His successor, Rothwell, was not sufficiently puritanical for the zealots, and so he was driven into hiding until "the King enjoyed his own again," when he reassumed the duties of his office. In 1690 the Crown conferred upon "the poor Vicar of Leyland" a confiscated estate which had been assigned to "charitable uses." The sale of the Fleetwood property in 1748 led to the transfer of the advowson of Leyland Church to the Baldwin family, which has supplied seven of its members as vicars of the said church. The Rev. Thomas Baldwin, M.A., the first of these, was also one of the co-rectors of Liverpool, succeeding the Rev. Henry Richmond in 1721.

The fabric of Leyland Church as at present standing is worthy of inspection, although it cannot compare with many other buildings of the same date. The western tower (which is about twenty-four feet square) and the chancel are the only parts which are ancient, the nave having been destroyed and rebuilt in 1816. The date assigned to these existing portions is about A.D. 1350. From some fragments which were removed from the foundations of the south-west wall, it is evident that a church of Norman construction stood on the same site. The interior of the chancel has some features of special interest. The three sedilia form an arcading under a simple roll moulding, a fourth arch covers a double piscina. Opposite to these, in the thickness of the north wall, is one of those curious openings known as low-side windows, the middle point of which is in a direct line with the centre of the altar. Upon one of the window ledges rest six chained books (popularly supposed to be Bibles), of which one is a black-letter copy of Foxe's *Book of Martyrs.* The south-west corner of the nave is occupied by the ffarington Chapel, the right to which was confirmed by Bishop Chadderton, in 1591. It represents the ancient chantry chapel of S. Nicholas, founded sometime in the fourteenth century by the lord of the manor. The tower has a peal of six bells, dating mostly from 1722. The churchyard possesses some ancient and curious memorials of the departed. There are no less than twenty-five rude incised crosses in different parts of the yard, and some of them plainly show the chalice and book of the ecclesiastic. Most of these are said to be as early as the fourteenth century. One stone dated 1558 is well worth attention.

The Communion plate is comparatively modern, but one cup looks as though it had been remodelled. Two pattens, each with a foot, were given by Mrs. Elizabeth ffarington, widow, in 1716. Two tall flagons and a cup were the gift of Samuel Crook, gentleman, in 1759. Besides these there is a small patten, a salver, and a double-handled (pint) cup.

Chantries or Oratories existed at Euxton and at Heapey in the sixteenth century. Within the present century churches have been built and districts assigned to Heapey, Hoghton, Whittle, and Withnell. Euxton is an endowed curacy; but whether a separate parish or not, does not clearly appear. The church of St. James, Leyland, built and endowed by the liberality of the ffarington family, has, since 1855, supplied the necessities of the western portion of the parish. St. Ambrose Church (at present a chapel of ease) stands on the northern boundary of the parish. The late vicar and his wife contributed very largely towards its erection.

The following is the list of the Vicars of Leyland as far as their names have been at present traced. It was originally intended to have given particulars of most of them, collected

from original deeds, wills, the parish registers, &c., but the space
at my disposal does not now permit of this.

THE VICARS OF LEYLAND, 1220 to 1891.

1220 (4 Henry III.)	THOMAS DE BUSHELL.
1303, 18 Kal. Feb.	WILLIAM DE CRINEBOYS instituted.
1332 and 1337.	JOHN LE WHITE.
1359—1366 (?)	ADAM DE MELYS.
1366—1392.	JOHN LE SERJEANT.
1409.	JOHN ALSTON (but ?)
1434 (dead in)	JOHN DE WALTON.
1434—1450 (?)	RALPH DE FFARYNGTON.
c. 1450.	THOMAS BANASTRE.
1457.	HUMFREY FFARINGTON presented.
1488—1516.	SETH WOODCOCK.
1516—1535.	EDWARD MOLYNEUX, B.D.
1540—1546.	ADAM BECKENSALL.
1546—1562-3.	CHARLES WAINWRIGHT.
1562-3—1570.	THOMAS BULKELEY.
1570—1595.	JOHN SHERBURNE, B.D.
1595—1604.	JOHN WHITE, M.A.
1604—1611.	THURSTAN BRERES, M.A.
1611—1650.	JAMES LANGLEY, M.A.
1650—1675.	WILLIAM ROTHWELL, M.A.
1675—1684-5.	JOHN RISHTON, M.A.
1685—1689.	GEORGE WALMESLEY, M.A.
1689—1719.	THOMAS ARMETRIDING, M.A.
1719—1733.	CHRISTOPHER SUDELL, M.A.
1733—1748.	EDWARD SHAKESPEAR, M.A.
1748—1753.	THOMAS BALDWIN, M.A.
1753—1802.	THOMAS BALDWIN, M.A.
1802—1809.	THOMAS BALDWIN, LL.B.
1809—1824.	NICHOLAS RIGBYE BALDWIN, M.A.
1824—1852.	GARDNER BALDWIN, M.A.
1852—1891.	THOMAS RIGBYE BALDWIN, M.A.
1891.	OCTAVIUS DE LEYLAND BALDWIN, B.A. (The present vicar.)

I very sincerely regret that the Rev. T. Rigbye Baldwin,
Vicar of Leyland, who gave his sanction to this publication,

has not lived to see its issue and to receive the befitting acknowledgment of the favour thus granted. Without the kind encouragement, assistance, and counsel of the Hon. Secretary of the Record Society, J. P. Earwaker, Esq., M.A., F.S.A., I should not have been able to present the work in the form which it now assumes. To the same gentleman my thanks are also due for supervising the proof sheets and for many suggestions, &c. Valuable assistance has also been received from Miss ffarington, of Worden Hall, Leyland, W. A. Abram, Esq., of Blackburn, and W. Brown-Clayton, Esq., of Brown's Hill, Ireland.

An apology is offered to the members of the Society for the unavoidable delay which has attended the completion of this book.

W. STUART WHITE.

LEYLAND,
OCTOBER, 1891.

ADDENDA ET CORRIGENDA.

Page 9, line 4 from bottom, "Henry Courtnay" became Roman Catholic, 1600;
received minor orders in English College at Rome; received into the
Society of Jesus in *Articulo Mortis*, September 29th, 1603.

,, 17, among the Marriages, "Ann" Eastham, which is so written in the
Transcript, should probably be "John."

,, 97, note 1, read "hamlet" for "township;" also p. 103, note; p. 134, note 1;
p. 178, p. 223.

,, 109, note 1 is incorrect, see p. 277 note.

,, 114, note 3. The report in 1554 was that of the Commissioners for the
restoration of Chantries by order of Queen Mary.

,, 212, note line 7 from bottom, for "Goderstaffe" read "Toderstaffe."

,, 281, note 1. The Ambrye Meadows are by the banks of the Lostock, and
belong to the Vicars of Leyland.

N.B.—The Transcripts of Marriages and Burials are extant at Chester for
the same years as those of the Baptisms, which find acknowledgment in the notes.

The Registers of the Parish of Leyland (co. Lanc.).

THE earliest Register of the parish of Leyland, now extant, commences in 1653, those of prior date being unfortunately lost. It has therefore been thought desirable to print here the few "Transcripts" of the entries in these Registers, which are now preserved at the Bishop's Registry at Chester. Every clergyman was directed to forward to the Bishop of the diocese a copy of the entries of Baptisms, Marriages, and Burials made in his parish Register during each year, and such copy had to be certified as correct by himself and the churchwardens. Much irregularity prevailed in the sending of these "Transcripts," as they are technically called, and much laxity was shown in their safe preservation, even when they reached the custody of the Bishop's officials. Hence it is that there are now only *seven* documents of this class relating to Leyland prior to the year 1653, namely, those for the years 1622, 1629, 1630, 1637, 1639, 1640, and 1641, each comprising the entries for a single year only. As the legal year then began on the 25th March, the entries run from that date till the 24th March following.

1622.

A Register of all the names and sirnames of all and every psonn and psonns which haue beene baptized, maried, or buried at the pishe Church of Leyland In the yeare of our lorde god One Thousand sixe hundreth Twentie and two, viz.

Imprimis de baptizatis.

Margerie Dawsonne, fil Hugh, baptized March xxviij[th], Anno p[r]dict.

Margret Leyland,[1] fil Thurstan, baptized the xv[th] of Aprill.

---

[1] A person of this name, John de Leyland, tailior, was admitted a Foreign Burgess of Preston at the Guild of 1397. He appears again in 1415. Sir Wm.

B

Ann Grundie, fil Jacobi, baptized the xix[th] of Aprill.

John Tompsonne, fil Joĥis, baptized the xxvj[th] of Maye.

Ann Charnocke, fil Rogeri, baptized the xx[th] daye of June.

John Hodsonne, fil Richardi, baptized the xxviij[th] daye of Julie.

Ann Shorrocke, fil Thomæ, baptized the third day of August.

Elizabeth Dewhurst, fil Joĥis, baptized the xxvj[th] day of December.

Marie Nelsonne,[1] fil Ricardi, baptized the xxvij[th] of December.

Ann Clayton, fil Willimi, baptized the xx[th] daye of Januarie.

Elline Slater, fil Willimi, baptized the xxiij[th] daye of ffebruarie.

Richard Jacksonne,[2] fil Gylberti, baptized the vij[th] daye of Marche.

De nupt'.

William Morresbie & Jonie Lyptrott, maried the xx[th] daye of Maye, Aõ p[r]dict.

Richard Boulton and Alice Boardman, maried the first day of December, Aõ p[r]dict.

William ffarrington[3] and Alice Somner, maried the xxiij[th] daye of January, Aõ p[r]dict.

William Worsley and Elizabeth Peareson, maried the xxiiij[th] day of ffebruarie.

Richard Bannester and Alice Blackborne were maried the same daye.

Raphe Cowp[4] and Alice Bushell,[5] maried the same daye Aõ p[r]dict.

Leyland, of Morleys, a reputed manor situated in Astley (near Bedford, co. Lanc.), was the son of John Leyland, who married Eleanor, d. of Sir Ric: Molyneux. As the Molyneux family owned the lordship of Euxton, this may suggest a connection. A family of Leylands, of yeoman rank, was resident for many years in Clayton. Representatives of the original stock settled in West Derby, Kellermergh (in Kirkham parish), &c. The founder of the eminent Liverpool firm seems to have sprung from Preston, and so of course originally from this parish.

[1] The local seed plat of the Nelsons was in Mawdsley township in Croston parish.

[2] Is not this the baptism of the celebrated Dr. Kuerden? In the pedigree which he entered in 1664 he gave his father's name as Gilbert, and his own age as 41 years. The family appears to have been called Jackson *alias* Kuerden. There is a tombstone in Leyland churchyard to the memory of "*Gilbert Jackson, alias Kuerden.* Deceased 17 day of Oct., 1662, æt. 70. Ex sumpt: Alisiæ, ux: ej:"

[3] There are numberless offshoots from the old stock, descendants of younger sons in early generations. It must not, therefore, be concluded that any individual bearing this name was related, except in a very remote degree, to the family in possession of the lordship.

[4] This is doubtless intended for Cowper, but Cowpe is a common name in Cuerden, and there are people so called in Leyland at this present date. Was not a "cowpe" a primitive sledge used for agricultural purposes?

[5] Probably of Cuerden, d. of Edm: Bushell (cf. Pedigree, 1664).

De sepultis.

Rob[ert] Cocker, b[uried] the xvth daye of Aprill, Aõ p^{r}dict.
David [. . . .]res, [bu]ried the xixth day of Aprill.
John Whittl [buri]ed the xxiijth daye of Aprill.
Elizabeth,the [?wife of] Thomas ffishwicke,buried the xthof Maye.
Ann Walmysley, [fil] Christopheri, buried the sixteenth day of Maye.
Eline, fil Joĥis [? Brad]shey, buried the xxxth daye of Maye.
William Beardsworth, buried the xiijth daye of June.
Eline Worden, buried the xxth daye of June.
Richard Singleton, buried the xvth daye of Julie.
John Allinsonne, buried the xxth daye of Auguste.
Thurstan Pi^1 [torn] ryed the xxvth day of Auguste.
Thomas Leyland, [burie]d the xxixth day of Auguste.
Thomas Cliffe, [buried] the xth day of September.
John Blackborne, [buried] the xvth day of September.
Elizabeth, the wiffe of Roger Cliffe, buried the seacond day of October.
Mr Thomas ffarrington,^{2} buried the xiiijth day of October.
Robert Clayton, buried the xxvth daye of October.
Ann Blackborne, buried the vth day of Nouember.
Peeter Somner, buried the xxth day of Nouember.
William Myller, buried the third of December.
Thomas Anthonies, buried the xiijth of December.
Mrs Ann ffarrington,^{3} buryed the xxvijth day of December.

[1] Almost certainly Pincock. The family was of yeoman rank and for centuries resident in Euxton township.

[2] The eldest son of Willm. ffarington, Esq. (who died in 1610). His father disinherited him on account of his spendthrift habits, and settled the estates upon William, the son of this Thomas. There is a portrait of this gentleman, dated 1593, now at Worden Hall [formerly Shaw Hall], the present seat of the family. He was Constable of Lancaster Castle and Steward of the Queen's lands in Lonsdale. His wife (married 3 Aug., 1581, at Beetham) was Mabel, one of the daughters and coh: of George Benson, Esq., of Hugill, Westmoreland, and widow of John Preston, of Holker. He had two sons besides William (the Royalist) and four daughters. He is believed to have re-married some one of inferior position. Mr. Thomas ffarington is entered on the Preston Guild Rolls for the years 1582, 1602, 1622.

[3] This appears to be the mother of Mr. Thomas ffarington just noticed. She was the daughter of Sir Thos: Talbot, of Bashall, and brought as her dower the lease of Blackburn rectory estate, &c. It was her husband who was the first of the ffaringtons to dwell at Worden. He also repurchased the manor of Leyland, which had passed away, through the female line, to the Huddlestons. He obtained, per Lawrence Dalton, Norroy King-at-Arms in 1560, a patent authorizing him to make a change in the family crest, which was henceforth to be "A wivern tail nowed, argent, collared gules, the chain reflexed, or." William ffarington, Esq., died before his wife, on July 3, 1610, directing by his will that he should be buried "within the Chappell erected in the Southe syde of the Parish Church of Leyland." Portraits of this lady and gentleman are now in the collection at Worden Hall, formerly Shawe Hall.

Margrett, the wiffe of Raph Johnsonne, buried the fifth of
January.
William Cawsey,[1] buried the xth day of Januarye.
William Euxton, buried the xv[th] day of Januarye.
John Tompsonn, buried the xxiij[th] day of January.
Ann Cawsey, wiffe of William, buried the vij[th] of ffebruarie.
Katerine Somner, wiffe of Ellice, buryed the tenth of ffebruary.
Richard Leyland, buried the xij[th] of ffebruary.
Ann Watsonne, fil Henrici, buryed the xxvij[th] of ffeb:
Sicely Waterworth, buried the third of March.
Roger Ayscowe, buried the v[th] of March.
Jane Leyland, buried the xvij[th] of March, Aõ p[r]dict.

finis anni 1622.

(Not signed.)

[On parchment.—Torn in places.
Length, 22 inches; width, 9 inches.   Writing good.]

1629.

A Regist[r] for Leyland parish, Anno Dñi 1629.

Bapti3at'.

Raph, sonn of Rich: Pemmerton, of Eccleston, bapt: the 19 of
Aprill.
Rob: sonn of Raph Pilkington, of Leyland, bapt: the 3 of May.
Jo: sonn of Thom: Godman, of Leyland, bapt: the 3 of May.
Rob: sonn of Will Maudesley, of Leyland, bapt: the 5 of June.
Edw: sonn of Geo: Houghe, of Leyland, bapt: the 8 of June.
Will, sonn of Rich: Ballshaw, of Euxston,[2] bapt the 22 of June.
Jane, daught[r] of [blank] Hodsonn, of Euxston,[2] bapt the 28 of
June.
Margarett, daugt[r] of Jo Shorrock, of Cuerden, bapt the 24 of
Aug:
Hen: sonn of Will Westby, of Cuerden, bapt the 13 of Septem:
Alice, daught[r] of Will Hugh, bapt the 20 of Septemb:
Jennett, base daught[r] of Rog: Pincock, bapt the 27 of Septem:
James, sonn of Will Crichlow, of Euxston, bapt the 2 of Octob:
Margery & Chat[h]erin, twins, children of Will Kellett, of
Clayton, bapt the 16 of Octob[r].

---

[1] Will at Chester.   Is there called "of Heapey."
[2] Formerly spelt Eukeston; pronounced at present Exton.

Rob: sonn of Rob: Blackledge,[1] of Whittle, bapt the 26 of Octob:

Rich: sonn of Jo: Estham, of Whittle, bapt the 4 of Nouemb:

Rob: sonn of Wiħ Taylior, of Whittle, bapt the 12 of Nouemb.

Ann, daught[r] of Rob: Parkinson, of Euxston, bapt the 8 of Decemb.

Rich:[2] sonn of M[r] ffleetwood, of Penortham,[3] bapt the 13 of Decemb.

Rob: sonn of Tho: Godman, of Leyland, bapt the 10 of January.

Thom: sonn of Raph Clough, of Leyland, bapt the 17 of January.

Henry, sonn of Jo Dewhurst, of Leyland, bapt the 31 of Jan.

Alice, bastard daught[r] of Tho: Sharples, of Plessington,[4] bapt the 8 of ffebr:

Wiħ, sonn of Jo Thornley, of Cuerden, bapt the 11 of ffebr.

Elizab: bastard daught[r] of Tho: Bannest[r], of Cuerden, bapt the 11 of ffebr:

₥upt'.

Wiħ Blackledge married Chaterin Willkinson the 7 of Aprill.

Rich: Maudsley married Alice Ellery the 13 of Aprill.

Rog: Sharples married Margarett Edge the 2 of May.

Tho. Vgnall married Margarett Shaw the 6 of June.

Rich: Hamson married Margarett Clayton the 22 of June.

Tho: Harrison, de longton,[5] married Margarett Woodes the 22 of Aug:

Jo Wallmesley married Margarett Garstange the 19 of Septemb:

Ja: Boulton married Jennett Sudall the 3 of Octob:

Wiħ Euxston married Alice Aspden the 26 of Jan.

Ja. Pilkinton married Ciceley Garstange the 28 of Jan.

[1] This name is variously spelt Blakeleach, Blacklach, Blakelidge, Blacklidge. Lach = a soft, muddy place.

[2] Son of John ffleetwood, Esq., and Anne, his wife (who was the daughter of William ffarington, of Worden, Esq., High Sheriff 1636). The marriage entry would be found among those for the year 1627, as it took place at Leyland on Sept. 25 (cf. Hulton's *Penwortham*, p. lxiv.). John ffleetwood, Esq., was a collector with his brother-in-law [? father-in-law], Wm. ffarington, Esq., of the subsidy granted at Preston, 10 Dec., 1642, to raise 4,000 foot and 400 horse for the King. £8,700 was the amount of the levy on the county (*ibid.*). He was a Guild-Burgess of Preston 1622 and 1642. In 1645 he compounded for his estates at £641 : 3 : 4. His will is dated 20 Mar: 1651, and he was buried at Penwortham 4 Feb., 1657. Richard, the son here mentioned, died unmarried 16 Feb: 1647. This Richard is also entered on the Preston Guild Rolls for 1622 and 1642.

[3] For Penwortham, a parish bounded on the north by the Ribble. Locally pronounced Penwerum, Penerdum, or Penortham.

[4] In Blackburn parish.

[5] A township in the parish of Penwortham.

Sepult'.

Alice Kent, of Leyland, buried the 27 of March.
[Blank], fil: Ja: Garstange, de Owswallton,[1] buried the [torn] Aprill.
Jennett Parke, of ffarington, buried the 11 (?) of Aprill.
Elizab: daught[r] of Hugh ffarnworth de Wheelton, buried 20 of Aprill.
the wife of Thom Moore, of Euxston, buried 24 of Aprill.
Jo Hudson, of Euxston, buried the 2 of May.
Ja: the sonn of Rob: Sumner, of Owswallton,[1] buried [blank].
Rob: the sonn of Will Maudsley, of Leyland, buried the 5 of June.
Will Euxston, of Clayton, buried the 19 of June.
M[rs] Orwell,[2] of ffarington, buried the 1 of July.
[Blank] fil: Geo Benton,[3] of Leyland, buried the 2 of Aug.
Rob: Chadwicke, of Euxston, buried the 26 of Aug:
the wife of Henry Whittle, of ffarington, buried the 15 of Septemb:
Will Wallmesley,[4] of ffarington, buried the 24 of Septemb:
Ja. Garstange, of Owswallton, buried the 13 of Jan.
the wife of Rich: Occleshaw, of Euxston, buried the 2 of ffebr.
Chaterin, daught[r] of Tho: Tysinge, of ffarington, buried 12 of ffeb:
Rich: Cowper, of Euxston, buried the 18 of ffebr.
Jennett, daughter of Jo Stanworth, of Cuerden, buried 28 of ffeb:
Will, the sonn of Jo Wignall, buried the 3 of Marche.

(Signed) JA: LANGLEY,
    [5]vic de Leyland.   [6]gardian[i] { EDM: BALLSHAW, EDW: WOODCOCKE, RICH: STONES, WILL GABBOTT. [Not signatures.]

[On parchment. All in the handwriting of James Langley.
Slightly torn.
Length, 19 inches; width, 6 inches. Writing good.]

[1] For Ulnes-walton, in Croston parish. It is locally pronounced Ouse-warton or Ouse-walton. Is sometimes printed Oveswalton.
[2] ? Ann Orrell, of Farrington, widow, whose will (dated 1629) is at Chester. Richard Orrel, gent., who compounded for his estate in 1645, was probably her son.
[3] More probably Benson.
[4] Will at Chester. Is there described as a "miller."
[5] See "List of Vicars" in the Introduction for all that is known of him.
[6] Churchwardens for the four quarters: 1. Leyland. 2. Euxton. 3. Whittle, Clayton, and Cuerden. 4. Heapey and the rest of the moor quarter.

1630.

A register of those yᵗ haue beine baptiz: married, or buried att the parish ch: of Leyland, Anno Doñi 1630.

[Torn]

[Impri]mis baptiȝati.

Jo: fil: Wiłłmi ffarington, de Snubsnape,¹ bapt: 4° Aprilis.
Elizab, fil Johannis Wright, de Leyland, bapt 12 Aprilis.
Jane, fil: Rich: Maudsley, de Cuerden, bapt 18 Aprilis.
Jennett, fil: Thom: Buttler, de Clayton, bapt 21 Aprill.
Ellin, filia Wiłłmi Holland, de Shevington, bapt 16 Maij.
[Blank] Cowper, de Cuerden, bapt 1° Junij.
Ann, fil. Jacobi Langley,² de Leyland, bapt 6 Junij.
Ann, filia Joh: Sumner, de Hollins,³ bapt 13 Junij.
Grace, filia Wiłłmi Dandie, de Cuerden, bapt 27 Junij.
Ciceley, filia Wiłłmi Dallton, de Whittle, bapt 6 Julij.
Wiłł: fil. Henr: Winnell, de Withnell, bapt 8 Julij.
Jenett, fil. Tho: Sumner, de Leyland, bapt 18 Julij.
Thom: fil. Joh: Peeterson, de Euxston, bapt 28 Julij.
Thom: fil. Thom: Clayton, de Crooke,⁴ bapt 15 Augusti.
Thom: fil. Richardi Hall, de Euxston, bapt 18 Aug.
Alicia, fil Wiłł: Eaues, de Leyland, bapt 19 Septem:
Jacob, fil. Joħ: Jamson [Jameson], de Cuerden, bapt 26 Septemb:
Alice, filia Wiłłmi Corner, bapt 10 Octobris.
Ann, fil: Wiłł Euxston, de Leyland, bapt 27 Octob:
Ellin, fil: Joħ: Leaver, de Leyland, bapt: 31 Octob:
Wiłł, fil. Thom: Waringe, de Euxston, bapt 9° Nouemb.
Isabella, fil. Wiłł Mutton, de ffarington, bapt 14 Nouemb.
Joh: fil. Thom: Allison, de Euxston, bapt 22 Nouemb.
Edw: fil: Wiłł Holmes, de Leyland, bapt 28 Nouemb.
Jeneta, fil. Joħ: Tomson, de Euxston, [bapt] 27 Decemb.
Henr. fil. Mʳ Adami Morte,⁵ bapt 16 Januarij.

¹ There is a farm of this name at the S.W. corner of Leyland township.
² ? The Vicar of Leyland.
³ The Hollins farm is not far from Snubsnape, but nearer to Eccleston.
⁴ This may be the Crook in Whittle, which was a well-known estate of the Clayton family. If so, the child here baptized was probably the son of Thomas Clayton, by his wife Ann, d. of Robert Blundell of Ince, Esq. He afterwards became the "Merchant Thomas Clayton," of whom Dr. Kuerden speaks in his Itinerary; and finally the founder of the family of "Clayton of Adlington." He married Ann, d. of John Atherton, Esq. By the tablet in Standish Church he died 1721, aged 91 years. His elder brother was Robert Clayton of Fulwood, gent.
⁵ This is probably the second son of Mr. Adam Mort, by his second wife. The name occurs in the Preston Guild Roll of 1642. The Morts belonged to the neighbourhood of Bolton, and held the estates of Dam House, Highfield Hall in Farnworth, Smith Fold in Hulton, &c. The gentleman here mentioned was the third son of

Ann fil: adulter. Elizab. Eaues, bapt 16 Jan.
Maria, fil. Thom. Dewhurst, de Leyland, bapt 23 Jan.
Jenett, fil. Rich. Loxham, de ffarington, bapt 23 Jan.
Kath[erine], fil: Rich: Nellson, de Leyland, bapt 30 Jan.
Thom: fil: adulter. Jenett Wearden, bapt: 21 ffebr.
Margareta,[1] fil. M^r fflcetwood, de Penortham, bapt 3 Martij.
Jenett, fil: Geo: Hodgkinson, de Whittle, bapt. 4 Martij.

Nupt' apud Leyland, Anno 1630.

— Elizeus Hoogh,[2] duxit Katherin Pincocke, 1° Maij.
Lawrence Tumlinson, duxit Margaret Dollton, 22 Maij.
Will Low, duxit Jenett [O]cclcshaw, 5 Julij.
Jo. Wildinge, duxit Margret Broxopp, 30 Julij.
Thom: Hunt, duxit Elizabeth Leyland, 18 Septemb:
Rich: Horrobin,[3] duxit Elizab: Hodgson, 21 Septemb.
Robert^s Rimmer, duxit [A]licia[m] Whittle, 29 Nouemb.
Will Miller, duxit Ann Sumner [blank].
Joh: ffarrer, duxit Graceiam Hesketh, 17 Januarij.
Will Abbott, duxit Ann fleacher, 19 ffebr.
Thom: Leyland, duxit Aliciam Letherburrow, 21 ffebr.
Thom: Smith, duxit Ann Holmes, 21 ffebr.

Adam Mort, sen., of Bolton, and Jennet, d. and h. of Thomas Mort, of Dam House.
He became a burgess of Preston, and married firstly, Elizabeth, d. of Seth Bushell
of Preston, gent., by whom he had one son (Seth Mort, born 1624) and a daughter
Jennet. For his second wife he married Elizabeth, d. of Sir Thomas Tildesley, knt.,
by whom he had five sons and a daughter, all of whom were young children in 1642.
This alliance may perhaps explain the very prominent part taken by him on the side
of the King when most of his fellow-citizens inclined towards the Parliamentary side.
He was elected Mayor of Preston in Oct., 1642, but seems to have been too busy
mustering men for the King to be able or willing to attend to civic affairs. Upon
his refusal to repair to the town to take the necessary oaths the Council declared him
"contumacious," and imposed a fine of 100 marks to be forthwith levied on his goods.
Mr. Mort seems to have assumed the position of Mayor while the King's party was
in temporary ascendancy. The Parliamentary forces, however, succeeded in carrying
the town by assault in February, 1642-3, and in gallantly opposing their entrance
Mr. Mort was slain. In a letter addressed by the Rev. John Tilsley, pastor of Dean
(who was present on this occasion), to "an eminent Divine in London," we find him
saying : "And as if men must have been singled out for slaughter we could scarce
have picked out better, the Major [*i.e.* Mayor] . . . that was resolute to desperateness
in this cause, that had oftentimes been heard sweare *He would fire the town ere he
gave it up, and beginne with his own house,* &c., &c." (Cf. Abram's *Memorials of
Preston Guilds,* &c., &c.) The funds obtained by the subsidy granted on Preston Moor
(£8,700) were to have been entrusted to the High Sheriff, Adam Mort, and others.

[1] This child's name does not appear in the pedigree given by Mr. Hulton
(*Penwortham Priory,* page lxv.), but another Margareta is mentioned as having been
baptized 11 Aug., 1633, and entered in the Penwortham Register. Perhaps this
infant died, and another received the same name.

[2] A variation from Hough or Haulgh.

[3] A name uncommon in this parish, but of frequent occurrence in the Bolton
district.

Sepult' apud Leyland, 1630.

vx[r] Cristoph: Wallmesley, de Heapey, sepult 13 Junij.
Ann filia Will ffarington, de Moss, sepult 25 Junij.
relicta Thom: Smith, de Leyland, sepult 27 Julij.
Jo Lucas, de Withnell, sepult 18 Augusti.
Robert Harrison, de Clayton, sepult 24 Septemb.
Robert Clayton,[1] de ffarington, sepult 9 Octob.
Lawrence Dewhurst, de Radlesworth, sepult 15 Octob.
Alicia Winnell, sepult 15 Octob.
M[r] Ja: Anderton,[2] de Clayton, sepult 9 Nouemb.
vx[r] Jacobi Pilkington, de Whittle, sepult 18 Nouemb.
Mary, filia Joh: Woodcocke, de Cuerden, sepult [blank].
Robert Brodeston,[3] de Cuerden, sepult 11 Decemb.
vx[r] Jo: Winckley, de Leyland, sepult 3º Januarij.
Will, fil: Thom. Woodcocke, de Leyland, sepult 7 Jan.
vx[r] Radulphi Cowper, de Cuerden, sepult 8 Jan.
Will Euxston, de Leyland, sepult 15 Jan.
Jo: Knowle, de Whittle, sepult 12 ffebr:
Euan Browne, de Whittle, sepult 15 ffebr.
Henr. Knowle, de Cuerden, sepult 27 ffebr.
Maria, filia Rich: Jackson, de Cuerden, sep: 4 Martij.
vx[r] Joh: Crichlow, de Wheelton, sepult 7º Martij.
Peter Blackhurst, de Leyland, sepult 10 Martij.

(Signed) { JA: LANGLEY, vic[s] de Leyland. }   WILLM FFARINGTON, OSKELL SOMNER, JAMES MARTIN, WILLM BANCROFTE, } gard.
[Not signatures, but in a different handwriting.]

Endorsed on back,
"A regist[r] for Leyland."

[On parchment. All in the handwriting of James Langley except the wardens' names. Slightly torn. Writing good. Length, 19 inches; width, 5 inches.]

[1] Will at Chester, described as "Linen Weaver."

[2] This appears to be James Anderton, the son of Hugh Anderton, who purchased the different portions of the Leycesters, Orrells, and Huddlestons (inheritors as co-heirs of John Clayton, Esq.), and thus became sole lord of Clayton. With his cousin James Anderton, of Lostock, this James was farmer of the goods of outlaws and receiver of the Duchy for sundry Ports. He was an active propagandist for Rome. His son Hugh, born 1579, was known in religion as Father Henry Courtnay. He entered himself and his sons at the Preston Guilds of 1582-1622.

[3] Is not this a curious rendering of "Balderstone," which is derived from the township of that name in Blackburn parish?

1637.

Ḿomina eorum qui baptisati fuerunt Eccles': Leyland: Ano Doni 1637.

Alice, filia John Clayton,[1] off ffarrington, baptized the 16th off Aprill.
Alice (?), fil: Evan Whitle, off farringtō, baptized the 30th off Aprill.
Henry, fil Robt Cocker, bapt 4th off June.
Alice, fil Richard Balshaw, de Euxtō, bapt: 13 August.
Wiłłm, fil Wiłłm Sumer, de Leyland, baptized the 3d off Sept:
[? Jane] fil John Woodcocke, de Leyl: baptized the 17 Sept:
Adam, fil: Edmund Bushell,[2] de Curden, bapt: the 24 Sept:
Alice, fil: Wiłłmi Cooper, de Cureden, bapt: 24 Sept:
Ann, fil: Henery Nelson, de Leyl: bapt: 29 Sept:
Roger, fil: James Pilkinton, de Whitle, bapt: 11 October.
Wiłłmi, fil: George Bolton, de Leyl: bapt: the 12 November.
Margary, fil John Jackson, de Leyl: bapt: the 12 off November.
Katherin, fil: Richard ffarringtō, de Leyl: bapt: 19 November.
Jane, fil John Leaver, de Leyl: bapt: 20 Novēber.
Elin, fil: John Blackburne, de Curden, bapt: 23 Novēber.
Alice, fil: John Cooper, de Cuerden, bapt: 19 Decēber.
Margarett, fil: Wiłłm Jackson, de Cuerden, 31 Decēber.
Anne, fill Robt Walmesley, de Whittle, bapt 8 Jan:
Wiłłmi, fil Alex: Chesnall, de Euxtō, bapt: 15th off Jan:
Richard, fill: Wiłłmi Leyland, de Heapy, bapt: 21 Jan:
Anne, fill Roger ffarringtō, bapt: 21 Jan:
Andrew, fil: Wiłłm Dandie, de Curden, bapt: 22 Jan:
Elin, fil Richard Callerbancke, de Euxtō, bapt: 28 Jan:
Margarett, fil: John Garstange, de Whitle, bapt: 30 Jan:
Wiłłm, fil: Wiłłm Jackson, de Leyland, bapt: 14 ffebr:
Wiłłm, fil: Hugh Johnson, de Leyl: bapt: 15 ffebr:
Richard, fil: Tho: Balshaw, de Leyland, bapt: 8 Marcij.

Ḿomina eorum qui Matrimonium Contraxerunt Jbid: eodemq₃ Ano.

John Leyland, duxit Elinā Pope, 27 Sept.
Elis Sumer, duxit Margeriā Walton, 28 November.
Isaac Shorrocke, duxit Jenetā Stones.

---

[1] There has been a branch of the family of Clayton resident in Farrington from remote times (cf. Hulton's *Penwortham*, p. 53).

[2] *Vide* Pedigree of Bushell family given in Fishwick's *History of Goosnargh*.

Nomina eorum qui sepulti fuerunt Jbid: eodemq; Ano.

vx: John Croston, buried the 25th off March.
Thomas Walmesley, bur: 7 off Aprill.
vx: Tho: Liuesey, de Withnell, 10 Aprill.
George Brining, bur: the 11 Aprill.
Elin, vx: Tho: Dewhurst, 12 Aprill.
Christopher Walmesley, bur: 13 Aprill.
Alice, vx: Tho: ffarringtō, de Leyl: bur: 14 Apr:
Edward Crooke,[1] bur: the 14 Apr:
Mary Barker, bur: 18 Apr:
Agnes Tasker [of] ffarringtō, 28 Aprill.
Eliz. vx: John Cooper, 28 Aprill.
Robt Lucas, bur: 30 Apr:
Margery Sumer, bur: the 8th off May.
Añe, vx: Will: Heald, 13 May.
Willm ffarringtō, fil: Will: ffarringtō, Esq: buried the 3 May.[2]
Elin Dobsō, bur: 27 May.
Alice Blackburne, de Cuerdū, 28 May.
Tho: Claytō, de Euxtō, bur: 28 May.
Robt Cocker, bur: 2 June.
Alice Eastam, [of] ffarringtō, 4 June.
Isabell Walmsley, [of] ffarringtō, 5 June.
Margrett Barker, bur: 7th June.
Agnes Roskow, bur: 11 June.
Christopher Euxton,[3] bur 14 June.
Willm Pilkingtō, bur: 9 July.
Elin, vx: Richard Stones, bur: 13 July.
Richard Ocklshaw, bur: 6 August.
Tho: Claytō, de Euxt: bur: 9 August.
Raph Beatson,[4] bur: 18 August.
Robt Sumer, bur: 19 August.
Raph Chrichlow, 19 August.
Henery Harrison,[5] 21 August.
John Eastam, bur: 21 August.
Mary, vx: Richard Beardsworth, 24 August.

[1] Will of Edw: Crook, yeoman, of Clayton, at Chester, 1637.

[2] Probably the eldest son of Wm. ffarington, Esq., and Katharine [ffleetwood], his wife. If so, he does not appear in the pedigrees. Henry ffarington, who married Susan, d. of Diggory Wheare, D.D., succeeded his father in possession of the Worden estates.

[3] Inventory of goods at Chester of Christopher Exton, 1637.

[4] Representatives of this family hold land in Euxton, &c., by strict entail. Ancient deeds are in their possession which go back to a remote period.

[5] Will of Henry Harrison, of Clayton, husbandman, 1637 (at Chester).

Alice, fil: Thurstan Chrichlow,[1] bur: 9 Sept:
Jenet Wiggans, bur: 26 Sept:
Elizabeth Wash, bur: 10 October.
Peeter Langtō, bur: 15 October.
Wiłłm ffauster,[2] bur: 20 October.
Jenet, vx: Tho: ffarringtō, bur: 26 October.
Jane, vx: Raph Winell, bur: 6 Novēber.
Elin, fil: John Blackburne, bur: 8 Novēber.
Wiłłm Bolton, fil: George Boltō, bur: 18 Novc̄b:
James Suṁer, bur: 25 Novēber.
Jane ffowlbie, bur: 28 Decēber.
Elizabeth ffisher, bur: 30 Decēber.
Añe, vx: Robt Dandie,[3] bur. 31 Decēber.
Wiłłm Garstange, bur: 24 Jan:
Elizabeth, fill: Wiłłm Euxton, bur: 28 Jan:
Elin Withnel, bur: 31 Jan:
Wiłłm Tootall, bur: 12 ffebr:
John Chrichlow, bur: 13 ffebr:
Margery, fil: Wiłłm Chrichlow, bur: 15 ffebr:
Richard Shorrocke, bur: 1 March.
Elizabeth, vx: Richard Ocklshaw,[4] bur: 5 March.
Alice Hesketh, bur: 11 March.
Thomas Shorrocke, bur: 12 March.
Margrett, fill: Edward Sherley, bur: 15 March.
Elizabeth Asley, bur: 17 March.
Agnes Waring, buried the 17 March.
Wiłłm Dickenson, bur: 18 March.

(Not signed.)

[Three pieces of parchment sewn together.
Writing fair.   Torn and illegible in places.
Length, 38 inches; width, 5 inches.]

[1] There is also the variety Critch-ley, which is the more common form at the present day.

[2] Will at Chester.   Is there described as "yeoman" and "of Farrington."

[3] Probably of Lostock (in Cuerden).   See stone slab in Leyland churchyard.

[4] One of the ancient houses in the Towngate, Leyland, is called Occleshaw House.

1639.

Nomina baptizatorum Ecclesia Leyland, Ano Doni 1639.

Edward, fil: Richard Hodgson, baptized 19 May.
Margrett, fil: Wiłłmi Watterworth,[1] baptized 19 May.
Thom: fil: Henery Bryning, baptized 26 May.
Jane, fil: of Seth Langton, baptized 26 May.
Ciseley, fil: Roger Claytō, de Curdē, bapt: 26 May.
Margret, fil: Wiłłm ffarringtō, bapt: 2 June.
Tho: fil: Robt Walsh, de ffarrington, bapt: 9 June.
Richard, fil: Edward Sherdley,[2] de ffarrintō, bapt: 9 June.
Richard, fil: Tho: Godman, de Leyl: bapt: 21 July.
Daniel, fil: Willm Dandy, bapt: 25 August.
John, fil: John Low, de Euxton, bapt: 10 September.
Tho: fil: Wiłłmi farrington, de Snubsnape,[3] bapt: 16 Sept:
Wiłłm, fil: Richard Gray, bapt: October 4th.
Anne, fil: Elis Hough, de Whitle, bapt: 6 December.
Alice, fil: Wiłłm Sargeant, bap: 3 December.
Margery, fil: John Clayton, de farringtō, bapt: 5 Novēber.
Elizabeth, fil: John Sumer, bapt: 22 Octobris.
Margrett, fil: John Dawson, de Leyl: bapt: 21 January.
Thomas, fil: Jacobi Pilkintō, de Whitle, bapt: 26 Jan:
Mary, fil: of Mr Willm farringtō,[4] bapt: 30 January.
Elizabeth, fil: Richard Armettryding,[5] bapt: 9 ffebr:
Elizabeth, fil: Jacobi Cooper, de Cuerdē, bapt: 9 ffebr:
Richard, fil: Roger Eaves, de Leyland, bapt: 21 March.
Alice, fil: Edmund Pickles, bapt: 1 March.
Añe, fil: Evan Whitle, baptized 1 March.
Robt, fil: Robt Cocker, de Leyl: bapt: 8 March.
John, fil: adulter: Robt Hesketh, bapt: 8 March.
Jane, fil: Wiłłm Sumer Junior, de Leyl: bapt: 8 March.

---

[1] The Waterworths were yeomen and connected with the Robinsons, of Buck-shaw. There are two farmhouses known by this name. 1st. The ancient house in Towngate, Leyland, opposite to the village Cross. 2nd. The farm situated at the top of Sheepbrow, in Clayton-le-Woods.

[2] *Vide* Baptisms, 10 Jan., 1640; also Burials, July 21, 1639.

[3] A farm to the south-west of Leyland township, bounded by the Shaw Brook.

[4] Child of Wm. ffarington, Esq., and his wife, Katharine, d. of Richard ffleet-wood, of Penwortham, Esq. She was afterwards married to William Anderton, of Euxton, Esq., and was buried at Leyland, March 1, 1702.

[5] Richard Armetriding was entered at Preston Guild with his father, John (and brothers), in 1602 and 1622. A full account of the family will be found in the Introduction under the heading of Armetriding, Rev. Thos., vicar of Leyland.

Christian, fil: Wiłłm Dewhurst, de Darley side, bap: 8 March.
Wiłłm, fil: Wiłłm Dolton, bapt: 15 March.
Tho: fil: Isaack Walkden, bapt: 25 March.

Momina Matrimonium contrabentium, ibidem eodemq₃.

George Croston & Elin Sumer, both of this parish, were married
10 of August.
Thomas Garstange & Elizabeth Gerrard, of Brindle, were married
13 ffebr.
[1]Richard Clayton & Mabell ffarrington, both of this pish, were
maried the 17 off September.

[This entry is in a different handwriting.]

Momina sepultorum ibidem eodemq₃ ano.

Añe, fil Robt Lucas, buried 25 March.
John Jameson, buried 26 March.
Elizabeth Sumer, buried 6 Aprill.
Añe, vx Wiłłm Garstange, buried 24 Aprill.
John Whitle, buried Aprill 25.
Wiłłm Bolton, buried 12 May.
Añe ffarrington, buried May 15.
Christopher Walmesley, buried May 29.
Wiłłm ffarringtō, buried May 31.
John Gooding,[2] buried June 4.
Raph Euxton, buried June 10.
Raph Cooper, buried June 20.
Wiłłm Haworth, buried June 21.
John Cooper,[3] buried June 23.

[1] This entry should be noted, for nearly all the pedigrees are incorrect with respect to the marriages of the children of Wm. ffarington (the Royalist). This lady, in particular, is frequently called Ann. Richard Clayton, Esq., of New Crooke in Whittle, was born c. 1617, for he was sworn at Preston as a burgess on Oct. 5, 1638. He actively assisted his mother-in-law (when the Parliamentary colonels sequestered the Worden estates, &c.) by purchasing for her some £80 worth of "goods." In 1643-4, John Fleetwood, Esq., of Penwortham, requests his "loving brother Mr. Richard Clayton" to be one of the overseers of his will. He was buried at Leyland, June 7th, 1659. Having but one child (Margaret), who died an infant, the Crooke estate passed to the Leycesters, of Toft, through his sister, Dorothy Clayton, who had married George Leycester. Mabel Clayton, the wife, afterwards married for her second husband Sir Peter Brooke, of Mere, co. Chester, who had been twice previously married.

[2] A name now generally spelt Goulding, but found in endless variety.

[3] See stone slab in Leyland churchyard, where it says "John Covper, of Curden, aged 62, Buried the twentieth day of June, 1639." The word "buried" has probably been put on the stone instead of "died."

Thomas Livesley, buried June 26.
Richard, fil: Edward Sherdley, buried July 21.
Jenet Darrin,[1] buried July 28.
Richard Sherdley,[2] buried July 29.
Richard Martin, buried August 10.
Lawrence Pincocke, buried Aug: 17.
Henery Chitam, buried Aug: 25.
Thomas Chitham, buried Aug: 31.
James Ashers,[3] buried Septēber 7.
Margrett, vx: Edward Sum̃er, buried Sept: 12.
Grace Hesketh, buried Sept: 21.
Thomas Rivingtō,[4] buried Sept: 30.
Margery, vx: Tho: More buried October 4.
John Nelson, buried October 4.
Elizabeth Pincocke, buried Octob: 13.
Wiħm Hesketh, buried October 17.
Daniel [Andrew crossed through] Dandy, buried Octob: 30.
Robt Ayscough, buried Novēb: 9.
Wiħm Hesketh, buried Novēb: 14.
Elizabeth Millner, buried Decēb: 10.
Edmund Hiltō, buried Decēb: 13.
Jane Burskow, buried Decēb: 13.
Raph Sum̃er, buried Decēb: 24.
James Livesley, buried January 1.
Willm Vgnall, buried Jan: 9.
Thomas ffarringtō, buried Jan: 16.
Elizabeth, vx: Edward farrer, buried Jan: 25.
Alice Euxton, buried ffebr: 1.
Sisley Slater, buried ffebr: 10.
Wiħm Snape, buried March 4.
Richard Boydell, buried March 15.

(Not signed.)

[On parchment.—Slightly defaced.
Two pieces sewn together. Writing fair.
Length, 26 inches; width, 6 inches.]

[1] Probably for Darwen or Darrin as locally pronounced.

[2] Will at Chester. Is there described as "yeoman" and "of Farrington." There is a farm near to Woodcock Hall which is still called " Sherdleys."

[3] Probably Ashworth. There is a will at Chester of a James Ashworth, of Euxton, dated 1639.

[4] Will at Chester. Is there described as yeoman and of Euxton.

1640.

Momina eorum qui baptizati fuerunt in Ecclesia Leylandiensi, Ano Doni 1640.

Richard, filius Samuel Backstonden, de Euxton, baptized Aprill 5th.

Richard, fill Edmund Bushell, de Cuerden, bapt: 12 Aprill.

Katherin, fil: Josiæ Waringe, de Leyland, baptiz: 25 Aprill.

Miles, fil: Henery Nelson, de Leyland, baptiz: 10 Maij.

Alice, fil: John Jackson, de Leyland, baptiz: 14 Maij.

Edward, fil: John Willinge, de ffarringtō, baptiz: 17 Maij.

Margarett, fil: Math. Boydell, de Leyland, baptiz: 24 Maij.

John et Margery, gemelli Tho: Haddocke, de ffarringtō, baptiz: 14 June.

Alice, fil: John Cotton, baptiz: 24 June.

Elin, fil: Will Burskow, de Leyland, baptiz: 5th July.

Tho: fil: Edwardi Woodcocke,[1] de Euxton, baptiz: 26 July.

Margarett, fil: Christopheri Litherland, de Clayton, baptiz: 26 July.

Margrett, fill: Jo: Graistocke, bapt: 9 August.

Ralphe, fil: Richard Jackson, de Cuerden, baptiz: 9 August.

Margarett, fil: Tho: Garner, de ffarringtō, baptiz: 16 August.

Hañah, fil: Tho: Whitle, de Leyland, bapt: 23 August.

Elizabeth, fil Willm Jackson, de Leyland, bapt: 23 August.

Elin, the bastard child of Añe Machan, de Leyland, baptiz: 23 August.

Richard et Raph, gemelli Joħnis Leaver, de Leyland, bapt: 3 September.

Jeñet, fil. Henry Wright, de Leyl. bapt. 13 Septēber.

Willm, fil Robt Walmsley, de Whitle, bapt: 11 October.

Elin, fil: George Woodcocke, de Curden, bapt: 15 October.

Margrett, fil: John Woodcocke, de Leyl: bapt: 8 November.

Thomas, fil. Jo: Asley, baptized 15 Novēber.

Tho: fil: Willmi Willinge, de Leyl: baptiz: 16 Novēber.

John, the bastard son of John Jelly, baptiz: 8 January.

Tho: fil Willmi Jackson, de Leyland, baptiz: 12 Jan:

Richard,[2] fil: Edward Sherdley, baptiz the 10 January.

---

[1] See tombstone in Leyland churchyard of Edw: Woodcock and his wife Mary, both of Euxton. (Cf. Abram's *History of Blackburn*, pp. 733-5, for a carefully worked out succession of the Woodcocks of Cuerden and Walton.)

[2] There is a finely-cut inscription in Leyland churchyard to the memory of Richard Sherdley, yeoman, of Farrington, who died in 1687, in the 47th year of his age.

Tho: the bastard child of Isabell Chrichlow, de Euxton, baptiz: 14 January.
[Blank], fil Jo: Bigans, de Whitle, baptiz: 17 Jan:
Elis, fil: Robt Sumer, de Leyland, baptiz: 17 Jan:
Wiłłm, fil: Roger Southworth, de Leyl: bapt: 17 Jan:
Elizbeth, fil: Tho: Watson, de Leyland, bapt: 20 Jan:
Richard, fil: Jo. Banester, de Curden, bapt: 14 ffebr:
Wiłłm, fil: Jo: Hilton, de Whitle, baptiz: 24 ffebr:
Mary, fil. Wiłłm Dandy, baptiz: 28 of ffebr:
Sisly [Mary crossed through], fil. James Parkinson, baptiz: 28 of March.

Momina eorum qui Matrimonium contraxerunt ibidem eodemq; Ano.

Jo: Soothworth & Ann Wealch were married yᵉ 20 of Ncuemb:
Rob: Blackledge & Jennet Asley were married yᵉ 20 of Nouemb:
Will Cowlinge & Mary Ouerall were married yᵉ 13 of Janua:
Ann Estham & Elizab: Whittle, married Aug: 17.

[The above four entries in a different handwriting, rather shaky (? James Langley's).]

Momina eorum qui sepulti fuerunt ibidem eodemq; Ano.

Mary, fil: John Leaver, buried the 4ᵗʰ of Aprill.
Richard Eastham, buried the 7ᵗʰ of Aprill.
Añe, fil: Richard Shaw, de Prestō, buried 7 Aprill.
Margrett, fil: Richard Tasker, buried 9 Aprill.
Elin Osbaldeston, buried 13 off Aprill.
Thomas Starkey, buried the 23 of Aprill.
Mathew Anderton,[1] buried 29 of Aprill.
Añe, fil: Christopher Litherland, buried 8 May.
Margrett, vx: Robt Wiggans, buried 15 of May.
Elin, vx: John Gerrard, buried 28 of May.
Margrett Cooper, buried the 3º [*sic* for 30] of May.
Adam, fil: Evan Eastham, buried 31 of May.

---

[1] Probably the fourth son of James Anderton, of Clayton, Esq., entered at Preston Guild in 1602, 1622, but not in 1642. There is at Chester a will of Matthew Anderton, gentleman, dated 1640. As there were three different individuals named Matthew Anderton belonging to the Clayton branch of this family, it is difficult to identify them. One Matthew is said to have been killed at Sheriff Hutton about this time. If so, then the one buried on April 29 would be either the *brother* of Father Hugh Anderton, S.J., or a *nephew*, and son of the James Anderton who took such an active part in the Civil War.

c

Elin, vx: Henery Blacklach, buried 1º June.
John, fil: John Willinge, buried 24 June.
John Heald, of Leyland, buried 13 of July.
Peeter Marsden, buried 13 of July.
John Shorrocke, of Euxtō, buried 26 July.
Jenett Wilson, buried 31 of July.
Jane, vx Roger Lockwood,[1] buried 7 August.
Miles, fil: Henery Nelson, buried 9 of August.
Alice Smith, buried the 3º [*sic* for 30] of August.
Katherin Waring, buried the 3ᵈ of Septēber.
Raph Pilkinton, buried the 7ᵗʰ of Septēber.
Mar[gar]ett, vx: Roger Whitle, buried 12 Septēber.
Mar[garett] fil: Thomæ Garner, buried 23 Septēber.
John, fil: Tho: Dewhurst, buried 25 Septēber.
Elin Leyland, off Whitle, buried 25 September.
Jane, vx: John Pincocke, buried 3º [30] of Septēber.
Margrett, fil: Rich: Pincocke, buried 1º October.
Richard, fil: John Leaver, buried 10 October.
Miles, fil: Henery Nelson, buried 12 October.
Alice, fil John Jackson, buried 25 October.
Elin, vx: John Bosse, of Whitle, buried 7 Novēber.
Elin, vx: Willm Cooper, buried 12 of November.
Willm ffarrington, de Leyl: buried 14 Novēber.
Añe Sumer, buried the 20 of November.
[Blank], fil: Thomæ Blacklach, buried 22 Novēber.
Agnes Waring, buried the 28 of November.
Margery Yong, buried the 3ᵈ of Decēber.
Elin, vx: Thomæ Tison, buried 10 of Decēber.
Margrett, vx: Robt Nelson, buried 15 Dēber.
Elin, vx: James Blackburne, buried 3ᵈ January.
[torn] ne, vx: Robt Glasborrow, buried 12 January.
Wiłłm ffletcher, buried 16 of January.
[El]in Tootell, buried the 17 of January.
Wiłłm Haddocke, buried 20 of January.
Edward Snartt,[2] buried the 27 of January.
Raph Smith, buried the ffirst of ffebruary.
John Willing, buried the first of ffebr:
John Sumer, buried the first of febr:

---

[1] Roger Lockwood is named in a series of deeds relating to the transfer of a messuage and land in his tenure and holding from Joseph Huddleston, of Farington, Esq., to Thomas Westbie, of Mowbricke, Esq., and John Ascowe, of Farington, yeoman. The property referred to is situated on what is now called Golden Hill, Leyland. The deeds are dated 1619, 1626, &c.

[2] Tombstone in Leyland churchyard. The name frequently occurs in early deeds, but has been variously mis-read as "Smart," "Suart," or even "Stuart."

Añe Morris, buried the 2d of ffebruary.
Alice, vx: Willm Waring, buried 2d ffebr:
John Bolton, buried the 2d of february.
Letice Pincocke, buried the 13 of ffebr:
Alice, fil: John Jackson, buried 27 ffebr:
Margrett, vx: Henery Banester, buried the 10 of March.
Henery Whitle, buried the 21 of ffebr:

(Not signed.)

[On three pieces of parchment sewn together.   Torn and illegible
in places.   Writing poor.
Length, 41 inches; width, 6 inches.]

1641.

Nomina eorum qui baptiȝati sunt in Ecclesia Leylandiæ, Ano Doni 1641.

Cicily, fil: Jacobi Parkinson, bap: the 28 March.
ffrancis, fil: Robt Blacklach, bap: 4 Apr:
Catharin, fil: Joħnis Leyland, bap. 6 Apr:
Tho: fil: Tho: Philipp, de Vlneswaltō, bap: 11 Apr:
Richard, fil: Rich: Taskar, de ffarringtō, bap. 11 Apr:
James, fil: Pauli Morrey, bap: 22 Apr:
Alice, fil: John Low, bap: 23 Apr:
Tho: fil: Richar: Caltherbancke,[1] 25 Apr.
Tho: fil: Rich: Hodson, 26 Apr:
Richard, fil: Willim Jackson, bap: [blank].
Tho: fil: Rich: Tomlinson, bap: 18 July.
Anne, fil: Tho: Smith, bap. 18 July.
George, fil: James Shorrocke, bap. 28 Octob:
[Blank], fil: Christopher Suṁer, 4 Novēb.
Eliz: fil: Willm Asley, bapt: 28 Novēb:
Elin, fil Richardi Barnes, 28 Novēber:
Mary, fil: Joħnis Suṁer, 25 December.
Alice, fil: Willm Clayton, de farringtō, bap: 14 January.
Oskell,[2] fil: Elis Suṁer, bap: 16 January.
John, fil: Joħnis Jackson, bap: 13 ffebrary.

---

[1] This name is Calderbank, according to the local pronunciation, which sometimes makes it Cawtherbonk.

[2] These two Christian names Oskell and Ellis are common in the Sumner family, but unusual except with them.

George, fil: Joħnis Berry, bap: 24 ffebr:
Seth, fil: Seth Jelly, bap: 6 March.
Edward et [blank], gemelli Edw: Whitle, bap: 6 March.
Thomas, fil. Tho: Whitle, bap: 6 March.
[Blank], fil: Joħnis Garret, bap. 13 March.
Wilħm, fil Wiħm Hornby, bapt: 13 March.

[Marriages.]

Evan Estham & Elizabeth Whitle were married the 17 off
August.
Roberte Wigan & Mary Gorton were married the 14 of ffebruary.

[This entry is in a different handwriting (? James Langley's).]

Nomina sepultorum Ecclesiæ Leylandiæ, Ano Domi 1641.

Alice, fil: Johannis Jackson, March 31.
Willim Chernocke,[1] March 31.
Alice, fil: Robt Lucas, Apr: 1.
John, fil: Thomas Haddocke, Apr: 2.
James Sumer, Apr: 9.
James Tootell, Aprill 9.
Jane, vx: Lawr: Pickhop, Apr: 9.
Jane, vx: Edw: Crooke, 22 Septemb:

[Different hand (? James Langley's).]

Tho: Hodson, October 10.
Richard ffishwicke, Oct: 29.
Grace Clayton, Oct: 30.
Hugh Withnel, November 7.
Eliz: Hilton, Novēber 24.
Thomas Cliffe, Novēber 28.
William, fil. Hugh forshaw, Decēber 3.
Elizabeth Leigh, Decēber 4.
Katherin Cluch [? Clough], December 11.
Lawrence Pickhop, Dec: 11.
Margrett Lucas, January 10.
Jane Smith, January 11.
Edw: fil. Wiħm Shaw, of Prestō, Jan: 13.

---

[1] Possibly the eldest son of Roger and Ann Charnock, of Leyland Hall. He
was entered in the pedigree of 1613, but the property certainly came to a younger
brother Robert.

John Asley, January 17.
Willm Burskow, Jan: 18.
Margrett Dawson, Jan: 18.
Elin, vx Tho: Parr, Jan: 20.
George Hough, Jan: 31.
Elin Blacklach, ffebr: 9.
James, fil. Willmi Hellewell, febr: 12.
Elin, vx: Raph Clayton, March 5.
Jenet Disley, March 7.
Seth, fil: Seth Jolly, March 10.
Jane Garrett, March 10.

(Not signed.)

[On parchment.—Defaced in places.
Two pieces sewn together. Writing fair.
Length, 36 inches ; width, 5 inches.]

The Registers of Leyland.

[The following Memoranda are written on the first page of the fly-leaf, left blank by the person who commenced the Register.]

> This Book contains Baptisms and Burials from 1653 to 1710 inclusive, and Marriages from 1655 to 1708 or 9.
> GARD^R BALDWIN,
> Vicar, 1834.

[This note seems to have been added after making up the return required for the Parliamentary Blue Book of 1833, entitled "A Parish Register Abstract."]

November the 4th 1664.
It is concluded upon by Mr Rothwell vicar and the Churchwardens now in being that the ringers appointed by them shall obserue to ring in due time on Sundaies and take the benefit of ringing at Burialls & other tims to bee diuided amongst them by equall portions & received & distributed by Peter Tootell Clarke or Robert Sargeant & hereunto the ringers doe subscribe their names the day and year aboue written.

PETER TOOTELL	RICHARD BALSHAW
ROBERT SERIANT	JOHN CLOUGH
RICHARD BALSHAW	MATTHEW WILDINGE
(Crossed out)	
THOMAS C	

[The handwriting of this resolution is similar to that of the entries made from August, 1663, to August, 1676. For some account of the Bells *vide* Introduction.]

[i.]

These are to Certifie all whom itt may concerne that uppon ellection made by the Inhabitants of ye Prish of Leyland in the County of Lanc uppon Thomas Walker of Leyland aforesaid yeoman to bee Register for their said parish of Leyland according to the Acte [of Parliament] of the 24th of August last past. I doe therefore allow of him the said Thomas Walker to be Register for the said parish & have according to the terme of the said Act administered the oath of a Register to him and likewise delivered into the hands of the said Thomas Walker the old Register Book (belonging to the said parish) bearing date from the 27th of Aprill 1538 to the 3rd of Aprill 1597. In testimony whereof I have hereunder written my hand the 22nd day of September 1653.

Lancr ff. (Signed) [1]EDWARDE ROBINSONN.

[It is to be noted that the first Register commenced on the 27th Aprill, 1538. This was just after the suppression of the Monasteries (1536) and the collapse of the Pilgrimage of Grace (1537). One of the grievances of the multitude engaged in that insurrection was the order for compulsory registration. It was thought that a tax was to be laid upon the administration of the sacraments. No trace of this " old Register Book " is to be found later than in the certificate (iii.) dated 1656.]

[ii.]

Whereas ye above said Thomas Walker being deceased [cf. Dec. 7, 1655] and ye parish of Leyland being void of a Register ye Inhabitants of ye said prish or ye Major part of yem have att a Gen'all meeting by a Certificate under yere hands ellected and chosen Mr William Rothwell yeir minister to bee Register of ye parish aforesaid with a provisoe yat hee shall relinquish itt when ye parish or ye greater part yereof shall think fitt to conferr itt upon ye Schoole[master]. These are therefore to certifie all whom itt may concerne that ye said Mr Rothwell comeing before mee one of ye Justices of peace for ye said Countie of Lancr and tendered ye said certificate I haue allowed of him to be Register for ye said prish and have tendered and given him ye oth of A Register according to an Act of parliamt of ye 24th of August 1653 in yat case provided And hath also deliud to the safe keepeing of ye said Mr Rothwell ye old Register above mentioned.

Given under my hand att Buckshaw[1] the 25th of Januarie 1655.

(Signed) [1]EDWARDE ROBINSONN.

[1] Mr. Justice Robinson, who here exercises one of the duties of his office, was a somewhat prominent mover in the affairs of Leyland Hundred during the Commonwealth period. The house which he names in Certificates ii. and iii. as his residence, is situated in Euxton, a township of Leyland Parish. A passing view of this old timbered mansion may be obtained from the Lancashire and Yorkshire Railway, for it lies within a few hundred yards of Euxton Junction, on the right going north. It is now called Higher Buckshaw, to distinguish it from a smaller and less important

24   *Leyland Registers.*

[Mr. Rothwell seems to have kept in favour with his parishioners thus far, but, according to the story given in Walker's *Sufferings of the Clergy*, he had to endure much persecution and hardship between this date and that of the Restoration. *Vide* List of Vicars, given in the Introduction.]

A REGISTER FOR THE PARISH OF LEYLAND 1653.

WILLIAM ROTHWELL Vicar.

HENRY HEALD
RICHARD BALSHAW
JAMES BROMILEY
WILLIAM BLAKELEACH
} Church-wardens.

THOMAS WALKER Register.

[iii.]

Whereas Mr Rothwell the late Register being displaced and ye said parishioners of Leyland meeteing att the prish Church of Leyland upon the first day of May 1656 the Major part then p^rsent did ellecte and choose Robert Abbott of Leyland abouesaid yeoman to bee for the tyme p^rsent Register for the said prish and to execute that office till the parish with ye aprobacōn of the next Justice of peace should thinke fitt to conferr ye said office upon some other pson. Theese are therefore to certifie all whom itt may concerne that ye said Robert Abbott comeing

farm called Lower Buckshaw, which is less than a quarter of a mile distant. Until recently it was the property of T. Towneley Parker, Esq., of Cuerden Hall, but he has transferred it to Colonel T. R. Crosse, of Shaw Hill, to whom it now belongs. There is a good illustration of this specimen of domestic architecture in the Chetham Society's Volume (lxii.), from which book also may be obtained information concerning the Robinson family and Mr. Justice Robinson in particular. The plate will be found on the page facing the title and at the conclusion of the introductory chapter. In Dugdale's Visitation of 1664-5 (Chetham Society vol.) Mr. Robinson entered a pedigree of four generations, but no coat of arms was allowed him. His parents were Mr. Richard Robinson, buried at Leyland, 5th March, 1657-8, and Margaret, daughter of Mr. Adam Holland, of Newton, near Manchester. He was born about the year 1610, and married Helen, daughter of John Brown, of Scale Yate in the Fylde. At the outbreak of the Civil War he took the Parliamentary side and served under Colonel Assheton, of Middleton, Colonel Shuttleworth, and Colonel Rigby. In May, 1644, he is described as Major Edward Robinson, and there is strong reason to believe, as Mr. Beamont has pointed out, that he was the author of the anonymous " Discourse of the Warr in Lancashire." At the restoration he appears to have made his peace with the authorities, although he was at first arrested. His wife was buried at Leyland on November 23rd, 1670, and he himself on January 7th, 1680-1. He had two sons and five daughters, whose names are entered in the 1665 pedigree.

that day before mee one of the Justices of ye peace for y^e
said Countie I have approved and allowed of him and hath
administred ye oath of A Register to him according to y^e
Acte of parliam^t in that case provided and also hath deliu'ed
into his safe keeping the old Register Booke menconed in the
first certificate on ye other side.   Given under my hand att
Buckshaw ye 2^d of May 1656.   [1]EDWARD ROBINSONN.

[This, and the two other similar certificates of appointment,
have been written and signed by Mr. Justice Robinson.]

[N.B.—The use of the word "Register" as applied to a
person has a strange appearance to eyes accustomed to the form
"Registrar." The former is, however, strictly correct, while the
latter is merely a maimed Latin word, which has been adopted
through ignorance, or careless inattention to the fact that it was
the abbreviation of Registrarius.]

Nathaneell, son of William Rothwell, vicar, baptised at Leyland,
 June the 20th, 1651, p me.
James, son of William Rothwell, vicar, baptized at Leyland,
 May the 8th, 1653, p me.   WILLIAM ROTHWELL,
                                       vicar.

[N.B.—These entries in the handwriting of Vicar Rothwell
are similar, in general appearance and in the shape of the letters,
to the writing with which the register commences. Hence we
may infer (notwithstanding the appointment of Thomas Walker
to be Register) that the entries of Births and Burials from the
commencement down to ffebruary, 1655-6 are in Vicar Rothwell's
handwriting, especially as the same style is discernible from
August, 1663, to the date of Rothwell's death. The intervening
period is one of bad writing and worse spelling. In comparing
also the Briefs for 1653 and 1671, which are signed "by mee
William Rothwell," the foregoing supposition becomes even
more probable.]

William, son of John Crichlow, of Claiton, baptised Aprill 1st, 1644.
William, son of James Crichlow, of Exton, baptised June 24, 1653.

[These two entries I have placed here because they are
earlier than the date at which the existing Register commences.
They will both be found again entered among the Baptisms in
1655.]

[1] See note, p. 23.

The Birth of Children in this yeare 1653.

Thomas, the son of Edward Robinson,[1] of Buckshaw,
Esq., borne the 7th day of Oct.

Sisley, the daughter of James Garstang, in Whittle[2] ... Oct.   15
Annice, the daughtr of Robert Dandy, in Cuerden   ...   „   18
Margret, daughter of John Jackson, in Cuerden ...   ...   „   19
Annice, daughter of William Sergeant, of Leyland   ... Nov.   9
Margret, daughter of William Haukshead, of Chorley..   „   28
Dorathy, daughter of Lewis Bushell, in Cuerden   ... Dec.   1
Margret, daughter of James Werden,[3] in Claiton   ...   „   9
Alice, daughter of William Gant, in Leyland   ...   ...   „   15
John, son of Peter Rutter, in Ulneswalton[4]... } „ 25
Edward, son of John Holme, in Leyland   ...   ...
Alice, daughter of Lawrence Croft, in Whittle   ...   ...   „   27
Katharin, daughter of Henry Nelson, in Leyland   ... Jan.   15
Henry, son of Henry Heald, of Leyland   ...   ... } „ 29
Antony, son of William Marrow, of Charnock[5] ...
Alice, daughter of William Godman, of Leyland } Feb. 5
Robert, son of William Leauer, of Leyland...   ...
Oliuer, son of James Haddoke,[6] in Whittle...   ...   ...   „   12
Jennet, daughter of Richard Calderbanke, in Exton } „ 13
Margret, daughter of John Naylor, in Charnocke
Henry, son of Henry Marclow, in Ulneswalton ...   ...   „   15
Mary, daughter of Richard Armettriding,[7] in Exton } „ 17
Alice, daughter of William Chritchlow, in Whittle
Anne, daughter of Richard Garner, of Leyland ...   ...   „   19
Isabell, daughter of Thomas Machon, of Leyland   ...   „   21
John, son of Edmund Tasker, of farrington[8]   ...   ...   „   23
William, son of John Darwin, of Cuerden   ...   . March 4
Jane, daughter of John Hilton, in Wheelcton   ... } „ 5
Jane, daughter of Robert Winstanley, in Charnock

---

[1] For some account of Edward Robinson, Esq., and of "Buckshaw," see note on the certificates found on the opening pages of this Register (pp. 23-4). This child "Thomas" only survived to Jan. 6, 1653-4.

[2] Whittle-le-Woods, a township in Leyland parish.

[3] Werden, a thoroughly local name, which may possibly have been derived, at some remote time, from the township of Cuerden.

[4] A township in Croston parish.

[5] Charnock Richard, a township in Standish parish.

[6] More usually "Haydock" or "Heydock," but pronounced as in the text. "Hey"=an inclosure, and dock, which is a diminutive, as hill-ock.

[7] See under Rev. Thos. Armetriding in List of Vicars in the Introduction.

[8] In Penwortham parish.

Richard, son of William Whitehead, in Ulneswalton... March 7
Ashton, son of William Maudesley, of Leyland... ... „ 8
Raphe, Margrett,}twins of John Cowper, in Cuerden[1] ... ... „ 17

[Births in] 1654.

Ellin, daughter of Christopher Wielden, of ffarrington} March 26
Mary, daughter of Thomas Lion, of Wheeleton[2]
Margret, daughter of Robert Parke, of Ulneswalton ... Aprill 2
Annice, daughter of John Sharrocke, of Euxton... ... „ 5
Elizabeth, daughter of John Marsh, of Chorley ... ... „ 9
Sisley, daughter of Richard Norbanke, of Whittle ... „ 10
John, son of Henry Jackson, of Leyland ... ... May 14
Thomas, son of Richard Jones, of Exton ... ... „ 24
Richard, son of William Crooke, of Hesken[3] ... ... June 12
Elizabeth, daught[r] of John Croston, of Chorley ... „ 27
Agnis, the daught[r] of John Garner, of ffarington ... „ 28
Richard, son of John Nickson, of Leyland ... ... }
Alice, daughter of Thomas Jackson, of Ulneswalton } July 8
Isabell, daughter of Alexander fforshaw, of Ulneswalton}
Margret, daughter of William Holme, of Leyland ... „ 13
James, son of Richard Buckley, of Charnocke ... ... „ 23
Richard, son of John Beardsworth, of Leyland ... } Aug. 27
Jennet, daught[r] of Robert Jackson, of Charnock }
Richard, son of Richard Robinson, of Exton ... } Sept. 3
Elizabeth, daught[r] of Robert Whittle, of Claiton }
George, son of John Hilton, of Exton ... ... }
Margret, daught[r] of John Woomell, of Wheeleton } „ 10
John, son of William Asburner, of ffarington ... }
Thomas, son of Thomas Jackson, of Cuerden ... ... „ 24
Raphe, son of Thomas Slator, of Welsh-Whittle[4] ... Oct. 4
Robert, son of John Blakeleach, of Whittle... ... ... „ 8
William, son of Roger Garstang, of Wrightington[5] ... „ 11
Roger, son of Thomas Starkie, of Cuerden ... ... } „ 22
Jane, daughter of Richard Charnock, of Leyland }
Thomas, son of Thomas Hey, of Heapie[6] ... ... }
Sisley, daughter of Gilbert Ugno, of Wheeleton... } „ 25
Alice, daughter of Thomas Cowper, of Leyland ... }
William, son of Robert Dickinson, of Wrightington ... Nov. 2

[1] A township in Leyland parish near to Walton-le-Dale.
[2] Wheelton, a township of Leyland parish. [3] A township in Eccleston parish.
[4] A township in Standish parish.
[5] A township in Eccleston parish. [6] A township in Leyland parish.

Richard, son of John Rotchet, of Leyland ...   ...   ⎫
James, son of Nicholas Bromilcy, of Leyland   ...   ⎬ Nov.   5
Ann, daughter of Robert Eccles, of Exton...   ...   ...   „   19
John, son of Thomas Ryding, of Leyland ...   .   „   23
John, son of Henry Barker, of Charnock   ...   .   „   26
Ann, daughter of William Garstang, of Ulnswalton ...   „   29
John, son of William Norbanke, of Whittle...   ... · ...   Dec.   24
Elizabeth, daughter of William Chisnall, of Heskine...   „   25
Henry, son of John Dawson, of Leyland   ...   .   Jan.   2
William, son of James Holme, of Leyland ...   .   „   19
John, son of Richard Stopworth, of Leyland   ...   ⎫
John, son of John Burscow, in Eccleston   ...   ...   ⎬ „   29
William, son of William Wiggans, of Cuerden   ...   ⎫
Rachel, daughter of John Jolly, of Whittle ...   ...   ⎬ ffeb.   11
John,   ⎫
Robert, ⎬ twins of William Slator, of Leyland   ...   ...   „   15
Henry, son of John Atherton,[1] of Leyland...   ...   ⎫
Edward, son of Henry Bickerstaffe, of ffarington   ⎬ „   25
Jennett, daughter of William Wild, of Claiton   ...   ⎫
Margery, daughter of Lawrance Cliffe, of Whittle   ⎬ March 4
Jennet, daughter of William Harrison, of Charnocke...   „   7
James, son of Thomas Critchlowe, of Leyland   ...   ...   „   14
Anne, daughter of Raphe Gorton, of Winnell[2]   ...   ⎫
William, son of Lawrance Cottom, of Exton   ...   ⎬ „   18

[Births in] 1655.

Lawrance, son of Abraham Holme, of Ulneswalton ...March 25
Anne, daughter of William Martin, of Whittle ...   ... April   1
Ellin, daughter of John Ainscow, of Chorley   ...   ⎫
William, son of Thomas Lowe, of Ulneswalton ...   ⎬ „   2
Henry, son of Thomas Whittle, of Leyland   ...   ...   „   3
Elizabeth, daughter of Roger Sharples, of Leyland ...   „   5
Christoph[r], son of Robert Pilkinton, of Leyland   ...   „   8
Ann, daughter of Thomas Tootell, of Whittle   ...   ...   „   10
Ellin, daughter of Thomas Partington, of Charnock ...   „   17

---

[1] About half a mile due south of Leyland Church there is a fine old farmhouse, apparently at one time of some importance, which bears on the 6in. Ordnance Map the name of Atherton Hall. It is now the property of Miss ffarrington. On the headstone of the principal entrance there will be found deeply cut J. A. 1635. The Athertons, of Atherton, in Leigh parish, made several local alliances with the Claytons, ffarringtons, &c. A branch of the Atherton family occupied a distinguished position in the borough of Preston. There was also a yeoman family of this name resident in the neighbourhood. A certain John Atherton occurs in the list of those wearing the "cloath" of Sheriff ffarington in 1636.

[2] For Withnell, a township in Leyland parish.

William, son of Josiah Waring, of Leyland... ... ... April 22

Henry,}
Mary, } twins of Henry Eastham, of Whittle ... ... „ 23

Alice, daughter of James Cockar, of Claiton ... }
Ann, daughter of Robert Sergeant, of Leyland ... } „ 29

Alice, daughter of James Charnock, of Exton ... ... May 5

William,[1] son of James Crichlow, of Exton, baptised June 24, 1653.

Margery, daughter of James Crichlow, of Exton ... „ 6

Henry, son of Lawrance Croft, of Whittle ... ... }
Mary, daughter of Lewis Bushell, of Cuerden ... } „ 13

Katherin, daughter of Robert ffarington, of ffarington „ 20

Henry, son of Thomas Waring, of Ulneswalton ... ... „ 23

William,[1] son of John Crichlow, of Claiton, baptised Aprill 1st, 1644.

William, the son of Thomas Jackson, of Leyland ... „ 27

Jane, daughter of John Hodson, of Cawbeck[2] ... }
Anne, daughter of Robert Whittle, of Leyland ... } June 10

Mary, daughter of Richard Sharrok, of Cuerden.

John, son of William Ralinson, of Chorley ... ... }
Henry, son of Mr. Henry ffarington,[3] of Shaw-hall }
Edward, son of William Okenshaw, of Exton ... } „ 17
Alice, daughter of Robert Sumner, of Leyland ... }

Raphe, son of William Cowper, of Leyland ... ... July 1

John, son of Robert Walmersley, of Whittle ... ... „ 3

William, son of William Jackson [blank] ... ... „ 8

Henry, daughter (*sic*) of Henry Haydock, of Charnocke „ 22

Lawrance, son of Lawrance Taylor, of Leyland... ... „ 24

William, son of George Johnson, of Ulneswalton ... Aug. 5

Thurstan, son of Raphe Leyland, of Leyland ... }
Anne, daughter of Robert Abbott, of Leyland ... } „ 12

Robert, son of Robert Sibbring, of Charnock ... }
Isabell, daughter John Tomlinson, of Ulnswalton } „ 19

John, son of John Hilton, of Wheeleton ... ... }
Isabell, daughter of Christopher Weilden ... ... } „ 26

[1] These two entries of Baptisms are in the same handwriting as all the rest, and occur as here placed. (See p. 25.)

[2] In Euxton township.

[3] The eldest son of Mr. Henry ffarington and his wife Susanna, daughter of Degony Ware, D.D., Professor of History and Principal of Gloucester Hall, in Oxford University. The Henry whose birth is here noted afterwards married Ann Diconson, of Wrightington, but had no issue. He died before his father. Mr. Henry ffarington, the father, was the son of William ffarington, Esq. (the younger), who took such an active part for the King in the Civil War, and who, at this date (1655), was still living at Worden. Shaw Hall was the residence of the heir presumptive.

Seth, son of Edward Woodcocke, of Exton... ... ... Sept. 3

Alice, ⎫
Elizabeth, ⎬ twins of John Charnock ... ... „ 12

Elisabeth, daughter of William Roscow, of Charnock... „ 14

Thomas, ⎫
Robert, ⎬ twins of John Southworth, of Leyland ... „ 16

Daniell, son of Thomas Bruise ... ... „ 17

Margaret, daughter of William Lowe, of Ulnswalton... „ 23

Adam, son of John Mather, of Croston ... ... Oct. 7

John, son of Thomas Godman, of Leyland ... ... ⎫
Roger, son of Roger ffarington, of ffarington ... ⎬ „ 21

Elizabeth, daughter of Edward Dawson, of Walton ⎫
Elizabeth, daughter of John Warberton, of Charnock ⎬ Nou. 11
John, son of Edward Parker, of Leyland ... ... ⎭

William, son of Thomas Johnson, of Exton ... ⎫
Ellin, daughter of Robert Dandie, of Cuerden ... ⎬ „ 18

John, son of Thomas Towning, of Eccleston ... ... „ 28

Andrew, son of John Cowper, of Claiton ... ... ⎫
Robert, son of Richard Okleshaw, of Eccleston ... ⎬ Dec. 2
Isabell, daughter of William Leauer, of Leyland ⎭

William, son of Robert Smith, of Ulnswalton ... ⎫
Richard, son of William Nickson, of Charnok ... ⎬ „ 5

Alice, daughter of Thomas Bibby, of Charnock ... ⎫
Seth, son of Edward Claiton, of ffarington ... ... ⎬ „ 16

Margaret, daughter of Alexander fforshaw, of Ulneswalton ... ... „ 21

Elizabeth, daughter of John Sharrock, of Exton... ... „ 25

Elizabeth, daughter of John Woodcock, of Leyland ... Jan. 10

B. James, son of James Pilkinton, of Eccleston ... ... „ 24

Agnes, daughter of John ffisher, of Eccleston ... ... „ 26

Grace, daughter of Richard Garnet, of Leyland ... ... „ 27

John, son of John Cubban, of Eccleston ... ... ffeb. 2

Anne, daughter of Henry Heald, of Leyland ... ... „ 6

James, son of Robert Charnock, of Exton ... ... ⎫
Ellin, daughter of William Crooke, of Hesken[1] ... ⎬ „ 10
John, son of John Holme, of Leyland ... ... ⎭

Mary, daughter of Richard Whittle, of Cuerden... ... „ 17

[At this point there is a change in the handwriting.]

Isabell, daughter of Elline Wynnell, of Whitle ... ... „ 29

Alice, daughter of Henry Wynnell, of Whitle ... ... March 2

Elizabeth, the daughter of Anne Hough, of Whitle ... „ 5

ffrances, the sonne of Wm Sergeant, of Leyland ... „ 13

---

[1] A township in Eccleston parish.

Alice, the daughter of Richard Leghe, of Ulneswalton. March 14
Ellin, the daughter of John Nelson, of Ulneswalton ... „ 16
Henry & Mary, twynnes of Henry Eastham, of Whitle „ 18
Anne, daughter of Rich: Chernock, of Leyland ... ... „ 21
Tho: and Margrett, twynns of Robert Dobson ... ... „ 25

[Births and Baptisms] 1656.

[N.B.—The entries on and after July 6th are all of baptisms.]

Anne, the daughter of John Dewhurst, of Curden   ... March 30
Rich: the sonne of Wm Breres, of Euxton ... ... April 25
Mary, the daughter of Ann pepper, of Euxton, hir
 chyld being borne there ... ... „ 27

[From this date nearly all the entries are in this form,
"William, the sonne of Thomas Clough, of Leyland, baptised
the sixt daye of July," but for shortness are printed as here.]

James, the sonne of William Lowe, of Leyland, hus-
 bandman ... ... May 2
Margerye, the daughter of William Holmes, of Whittle June 8
William, the sonne of Thomas Clough, of Leyland
 baptised July 6
Anne, the daughter of James Sumner, of Exton
 baptised „ 7
James, the sonne of William Sumner, of Leyland
 baptised „ 19
Allice, the daughter of Henery Crofton, of Whittle
 baptised „ 20
Grace, the daughter of Gillbert Jacson, of Curden
 baptised „ 20
William, the sonne of John Jackeson, of Curden, baptised Aug. 10
John Woodcocke, the sonne of Rodger Woodcocke, of
 Leyland ... ... baptised Sept. 19
Alice, the daughter of John Garner, of ffarington ... „ 26
Elizabeth, the daughter of George Johnson, of Ulns-
 walton ... ... baptised Oct. 5
Thomas, the sonne of William Mackerell, of Leyland
 baptised „ 19
Ellin, the daughter of James Chrichlow, of Whittell
 baptised „ 26
William, the son of William ffarington, of Snubsnape[1]
 in Leyland ... ... „ last

[1] A farm on the south-west of Leyland township bounded by Balshaw Brook.

Kathrin, the daughter of William Couper, of Curdin,
tayler ... ... baptised Nov. 2
Margrett,[1] the daughter of Master Henry ffarington,
gentleⁿⁿ, of the shaw-hall ... ... „ 14
Ann, the daught^r of John ffiswicke, of Exton, baptised „ 16
Richard, the sonne of Richard Johnnes, of Exton
baptised „ 23
Richard, the sonne of Thomas Whithed, of Leyland
baptised „ 24
Ann, the daught^r of Robert Jackson, of Charnock
baptised „ last
Thomas, sonne of Thomas Ridley, of Exton baptised Dec. 13
John, the sonne of John Beardsworth, of Leyland
baptised „ 15
Thurston, the sonne of William Chrichlow, of Whittell
baptised „ 28
Alice, the daughter of James Coucker, of Clayton
baptised Jan. 4
John, the sonne of William Marton, of Whittell
baptised „ 4
Margret, the daughter of Abraham Houlems, of Ulnes-
walton ... ... baptised „ 4
Ellin, the daughter of Thomas Crichlow, of Leyland
baptised „ 14
John, the son of Peter Moncke, of Chorley ... baptised „ 14
William, the son of Ralph Leyland, of Leyland, baptised „ 20
Hennery, the sonne of Edward Shorroke, of Curden
baptised ffebr. 8
Thomas, the sonne of Thomas Starrkey, of Curden
baptised „ 15
Margret, the daughter of Adam Clayton, of Clayton
baptised March 8

[Baptisms] 1657.

Hugh, the sonne of Thomas Warringe, of Eccleston
baptised March 29
Marcy, the daughter of Lawrance Cotom, of Exton
baptised „ 29
Grace, the daughter of John Shorroke, of Exton
baptised April 5

---

[1] Daughter of Mr. Henry ffarington and Susanah (Weare) his wife, and grand-daughter of William ffarington, Esq. (Knight of the Oak), who was at this time living at Worden. Miss Margaret ffarington became (in 1702) the wife of the Rev. Thos. Armetriding, M.A., Vicar of Leyland (1689-1717).

Alice, the daughter of Richard Stopforth, of Leyland
　　　　　　　　　　　　baptised April 12
Hennery, the sonne of James Weourden,[1] of Clayton
　　　　　　　　　　　　baptised　„　19
Jane, the daughter of Thomas Lowe, of Uleswalton
　　　　　　　　　　　　baptised May　3
Thomas, the sonne of William Clayton, of Cuerden
　　　　　　　　　　　　baptised　„　3
Ellin, the daughter of John Dewerst, of Curden, baptised　„　17
Alice, the daughter of Robert Sarrgant, of Leyland
　　　　　　　　　　　　baptised June 20
Martha, the daughter of Richard Ockleshaw, of Eccles-
ton ... ... baptised　„　20
Alice, the daughter of Robert Abbott, of Leyland
　　　　　　　　　　　　baptised　„　28
Grace Gerard, daughter of James Gerard, of Wthnell
　　　　　　　　　　　　baptised July　5
James, the sonne of Robert Whittell, of Clayton
　　　　　　　　　　　　baptised　„　26
Lawrance, the sonne of Alexander fforeshaw, of Ules-
walton ... ... baptised Aug.　2
Ann, the daughter of Hennery Jacson, of Leyland
　　　　　　　　　　　　baptised　„　23
Hennery Atherton, the sonne of William Atherton, of
Leyland ... ... baptised Oct.　25
Gilbert Jacson, sonne of Thomas Jacson, of Curden
　　　　　　　　　　　　baptised Nov.　8
Katharin, the daughter of Robert Smith, of Ulnswal-
ton ... ... baptised Dec.　13
William, the sonne of Thomas Darwen, of Clayton
　　　　　　　　　　　　baptised　„　13
Richard, the sonne of Robert Ecckeles, of Euexton
　　　　　　　　　　　　baptised Jan.　3
Hugh Armetridinge,[2] the sonne of John Armetriding,
of Euexton ... ... baptised　„　10
Richard Balshaw, the sonne of William Balshaw, of
Euexton ... ... baptised ffeb.　26

[1] For Worden, see Baptisms, 1653.

[2] Tomb in Leyland churchyard. Buried April 23, 1700, in his 42nd year. He was the eldest brother of Vicar Armetriding. His name is found as one of the trustees appointed for the transfer of the Leyland Hall estate from the Crown to the Vicars of Leyland. This matter is referred to at length elsewhere.

D

[Baptisms] 1658.[1]

William Haslom, the sonne of William Haslom, of
Leyland, bastard ... ... baptised June   8

Robert Couper, the sonne of William Couper, of
Leyland ... ... baptised   „   27

John Bannester, the sonne of Lenones[2] Bannaster, of
Curden ... ... baptised   „   27

Rodger Hilton, the sonn of John Hilton, of Euexton
baptised July 11

James Couper, the sonn of William Couper, of Curden
baptised Oct. 22

Ann Adlington, the daughter of James Adlington, of
Curden ... ... baptised Jan.   2

John Garner, the sonne of John Garner, of ffarrington
baptised   „   2

[Baptisms] 1659.

Mary Rouckecrofte,[3] the daughter of John Rouckecrofte,
of Uleswalton ... ... baptised April 10

Richard Jacson,⎱ the sonn of John Jacson, of Curden
baptised May 29

Alice Jacson, ⎰daughter of John Jacson—both twines
of John Jacson, of Curden [no date,
probably same].

Thomas Beardsworth, the sonne of John Beardsworth,
of Leyland ... ... baptised   „   29

Thomas Hoall,[4] the sonne of Thomas Hoall, of Leyland
baptised   „   29

Rodger Worsley, the sonne of William Worsley, of
Uleswalton ... ... baptised June 26

Jane Smith, daughter of John Smith, of Uleswalton
baptised July 24

William Goulden, the sonne of John Goulden, baptised Aug. 11

---

[1] The year is noted in the original after each entry, but is here omitted for the sake of convenience. The extremely small number of Baptismal entries in comparison with the number of Burials for the same year (62) leads us to infer that many have been left unrecorded. There were no transcripts made for diocesan purposes during this disturbed period.

[2] This curious name should be noticed. It is possible that the illiterate scribe intended to write Leoninus, or even Leonard !

[3] Usually spelled Roe-croft or Roocroft. A name well known at the present day in the same township.

[4] Probably derived from the township of Hole or Hool, which was formerly in Croston parish, but made parochial in 1641.

George Munce the sonne [of] Petter Muncke, of
Chorley ... ... baptised Aug. 14
Elizabeth Duckeson, the daughter of William Duckeson,
of Leyland ... ... baptised „ 20
Elizabeth Willden, daughter of William Wilden, of
Leyland ... ... baptised Sept. 4
Ann Martton, daughter of John Marton, of Clayton
baptised „ 11
[1]Elizabeth, daughter of John ffiswicke, of Euexton ... „ 21
Agnes Barker, the daughter of Henery Barker, of
Charnock ... ... baptised „ 24
Robert Doson, the sonne of John Doson,[2] of Leyland
baptised Oct. 2
Jane Roscowe, the daughter of John Roscoe, of Euexton
baptised „ 2
Thurstan Leyland, the sonne of Ralph Leyland, of
Leyland ... ... baptised „ 9
Margrett Torner, daughter of John Tornor, of Curden
baptised „ 16
Jannot ffarington, daughter of James ffarrington, of
Leyland ... ... baptised Nov. 10
Elizabeth Holinerst, daughter of William Holinerst, of
penwortham, Bastard ... ... baptised „ 20
Jane Clayton, daughter of Edward Clayton, of ffarring-
ton ... ... baptised Dec. 4
John Cross, the son of Richard Cross, of Bratherton[3]
baptised „ 18
John Wittell, the sonne of Robert Whittell, of Leyland
baptised Jan. 1
William Mose,[4] the sonne of James Mose, of Clayton
baptised „ 21
Elizabeth Tayler, daughter of John Tayler, of Whittell
baptised „ 21
John Mather, the sonne of Renard Mather, of Leyland
baptised „ 21
[5]Ann Wilden, the daughter of Christoph[r] Wilden, of
ffarington ... ... baptised „ 29
Richard March, the sonne of John Marce, of Leyland
baptised ffeb. 5
[5]Margret, the daughter of Roger Sharples, of Leyland
baptised „ 5

---

[1] This entry has been inserted, but is in the same handwriting as the rest.
[2] For Dawson.   [3] Bretherton, a township in Croston parish.
[4] Moss is the common form of the name.
[5] This entry has been inserted, but the handwriting is the same.

Margrett Stones, the daughter of Andrew Stones, of
   Euexton, bastard... ... ... baptised ffeb.   5
Marie Wackeffild, daughtr of Robert Wackeffild, of
   Leyland   ... ... baptised „ 26
Ann Sumner, daughter of Elish Sumner, of Leyland
                                  baptised March 11
John ffarington, sonne of William ffarington, of Leyland
                                  baptised „ 19

[Baptisms] 1660.

Adam Bushell, the sonne of Mr. Seth Bushell,[1] of
   Euexton, baptised   ... ...March 25

[1] Mr. Seth Bushell, here mentioned, was the son of Adam Bushell and Alice, his
wife, daughter of John Loggan, of Garstang (co. Lanc.). He married, 1st, Mary, d.
of Mr. Roger ffarrington, of Leyland (buried at Leyland, Dec. 26, 1656), and
2ndly, Mary, d. of Mr. Wm. Stanfield, of Euxton (married at Preston, 23 July, 1657),
by whom he had four sons and three daughters. A third wife survived him, and, as
Mistress Elizabeth Bushell, was buried at Preston, 16 July, 1697. Her will was
proved at Richmond. Adam, the son whose baptism is here recorded, was the
second child and eldest son. He was buried at Preston, 15 June, 1696. William,
the next son, was born at Spout House in Euxton, 5 March, 1661, but no entry of
baptism appears in this Register. This William became curate of Goosnargh and
rector of Heysham, and was buried at Goosnargh, 30 April, 1735. By his wife,
Margaret, d. of William Werden, gent., of Preston (who presented him to the rectory
of Heysham), he became the father of a son, William Bushell, M.D., the munificent
founder of Goosnargh Hospital. It is frequently stated that this benefactor lies
interred in Leyland churchyard, but that is not the case. There is a stone placed
over the portion of ground, supposed to appertain to Spout House, which has the
inscription, "Spout House, Euxton, Sacred to the memory of William Bushell,
Esquire, Founder of Goosnargh Hospital." At the lower part of the slab are the names
of Richard Slater, William Porter, Richard Latham, Roger Charnock, trustees, by whom
the stone was in all probability placed there to connect the benefactor with the parish of
Leyland. The doctor died about 10th June, 1735, and is buried at Goosnargh.
Mr. Seth Bushell, the father of the child named in the text and the grandfather of
the benefactor, was born in 1621, and in 1639 became a commoner at S. Mary's
Hall, Oxford. When the civil war turned Oxford into a garrison Mr. Bushell retired
to Lancashire. The name Seath Bushell occurs in the list of schoolmasters of
Longton Free School in a return furnished by William Banester in 1673, and as
Bushell was his immediate predecessor the dates allow of an identification. In the
Church Surveys of 1650 (vol. i., Record Soc. Publications, p. 101), we find the following reference to him: " Mr Seath Bushell is the p'sent Incumbent there [Euxton]
and is a godly p'chinge minister and conformable to the p'sent goverm! and came
into the said place by an order from the Committee of plundered ministers, and hath
ffor his sallery forty pounds p' ann' yssueinge out of the sequestracons of the [great
tythes]." In 1654 Mr. Bushell returned to Oxford and graduated B.A. and M.A.,
at which time he appears to have been minister, probably curate, of Whitby or
Whitley in Yorkshire. On June 10, 1665, he became B.D., and on 27 June, 1672,
he proceeded to the degree of D.D. The exact date when Seth Bushell became
vicar of Preston has not yet been definitely ascertained, but there is an entry in the
Preston Register of the baptism of "Alice, daughter of Seth Bushell, Clerk, Vicar of
Preston," on Dec. 18, 1664. (See Fishwick's *History of Goosnargh*, from which
much of the information contained in this note is derived.) Upon his resignation of
the vicarage of Preston he was instituted vicar of Lancaster, on June 19th, 1682,
upon the presentation of George Toulson. On the north wall of Lancaster Parish

Ann Garston, daughter of James Garston, of Whittell
baptised April 15
Elizabeth Clough, daughter of John Clough, of Leyland
baptised „ 29
Margery Johnson, daughter of George Johnson, of
Uleswalton, baptised ... ... „ 29
Jayne Willson, daughter of William Willson, of Leyland
baptised „ last
Elizabeth Ecckelles, daughter of Robert Ecckelles, of
Euexton, baptised ... ... May · 1
John Weelles, the sonne of John Weells, [of] [1]Whitt-
Chapell, nere olegatto, London, baptised ... ... „ 20
[2]Doratey Woodcocke, daughter of Edward Woodcock,
of Euexton, baptised ... ... June 5
Elizabeth Sargunt, daughter of Robert Sargent, of
Leyland, baptised ... ... „ 11
Susanne Abbott, daughter of Robert Abbott, of Leyland
baptised July 18
Robeart Torner, the sonne of Robert Torner, of Leyland
baptised „ 29
Susanne Holmes, daughter of Abraham Holmes, of
Uleswalton ... ... baptised Aug. 6
Thomas Lowe, the sonne of Thomas Lowe, of Ules-
walton ... ... baptised „ 12
Elin, the daughter of Edward Willien, of Charnocke
baptised „ 26
Thomas D[o]son, the sonne of A[r]thur Doson, of
ffarrington ... ... baptised „ 26
Nicklows Alius Loxom, of ffarrington, b[a]ptised the
sum (*sic*) day.
Elizabeth Crichlow, daughter of Tomus Crichlow, of
Leyland ... ... baptised Sept. 30
Margery Woodcocke, of Uleswalton ... ... baptised „ 30
Thomas Waringe, the sonne of Thomas Waringe, of
Eckeleston ... ... baptised Oct. 8
Thomas Grine, the sonne of Omfre [Humphry] Grine, of
Eckeleston ... ... baptised „ 8

Church is a memorial brass to "Seth Bushell, S.T.P., who died 1684, aged 63"
(*i.e.*, before June 17th, 1684, the date of the next institution). On the Preston Guild
Roll for 1682 we find the name of "Seth Bushell, Theologiæ Professor," together
with four sons, Adam, William, Seth, and Samuel. The first of these sons is the
one whose baptism is recorded in the text.
  [1] "Whitt-Chapell, nere olegatto, London." The exact meaning of this is not
very clear.
  [2] This entry has been written after the one which follows, for the writing overlaps
in several places. It appears, however, to be contemporary.

John fforshaw, the sonne of Alixander fforshaw, of
Uleswalton ... ... baptised Oct. 28
Henery Cottom, the sonne of Lawarance Cottom, of
Euexton ... ... baptised Nov. 11
Elizabeth, the daughter of John Woodcocke, of Leyland
baptised „ 11
Jane, the daughter of James Hand, of Leyland, baptised „ 11
Elin Sumner, daughter of Lawarance Sumner, of Ules-
walton ... ... baptised Dec. 9
Richard Shorroke, the sonne [of] Richard Shorroke,
of Curden ... ... „ 23
Elin, the daughter of John Dewest, of Curden, baptised „ 29
Elizabeth Whittell, daughter of Henery Whittell, of
Clayton... ... ... baptised Jan. 6
William Alius Loxam, of ffarrington ... ... baptised „ 13
Margret, the daughter of Edward Litherland, of Whittell
baptised ffeb. 3
Mary, the daughter of Robert Pilkinton, of Leyland
baptised „ 10
William, the son of Hennery Jacson, of Leyland, baptised „ 10
Hennery, the sonne of Richard Slator, of Leyland
baptised „ 13
John Chittom, the sonne of Richard Chittom, of
ffarrington ... ... baptised „ 17
Adam Wignes, the sonne of William Wignes, of Curden
baptised „ 24
Alice Sumner, the daughter of James Sumner, of
Euexton ... ... baptised March 14
William Milner, the sonne of William Milner, of Ules-
walton ... ... baptised „ 14
Ann, the daughter of George Rocroft, of Euexton,
baptised the same day ... ... „ 14
Doraty, the daughter of Robert Sumner, of Leyland
baptised „ 23
Thomas, the sonne of John Gouldinge, of Leyland
baptised „ 24
Margret, the daughter of John Roucroft, of Uleswalton
baptised „ 24

[Baptisms] 1661.

Margaret Holle, daughter of Robert Holle, of Ecckelston
baptised Mar. last
Edward Atherton, the sonne of William Atherton, of
Leyland ... ... baptised Ap. 14

Margret Burstow, the daughter of John Burstow, of
Leyland ... ... baptised Ap. 14
Elner Couper, daughter of William Couper, of Curden
baptised „ 15
John Crose, the sonne of Oliver Crose, of Euexton
baptised „ 29
Jane Couper, daughter of Robert Couper, of Euexton
baptised May 5
Margret, the daughter of John Hillton, of Euexton
baptised „ 5
Richard, the sonne of Nicklous bromley, of Leyland
baptised „ 12
Richard Rose, the sonne of Thomas Rose, of Euexton
baptised „ 14
James, the son of James Carter, bap. the 27 day of Aprill, 1662.[1]
Ralph, the sonne of Richard Johnes, of Euexton, baptised the
seventinth day of August, 1662.
Adam, the sone of John Cliffe, of Leyland, baptised the seventinth
day of August, 1662.
Jane, the daughter of James Marten, of Heapey, baptised the
ffiftinth day of October, 1662.
James, the son of Edward Woodcocke, of Euexton, baptised [no
date given].
George, the sone of George Muncke, of Leyland, baptised ffortinth
day of September, 1662.
Thomas, the sone of John Nelson, of Uleswalton, baptised the
ffortinth day of September, 1662.
William, the sone of John Jackeson, of Leyland, baptised the
twentith day of December, 1662.
Alice, the daughter of Rodger Worsley, of Whelton, baptised the
26 day of December, 1662.
[2]John Roscow, the sonne of John Roscow, of Euexton, baptised
the twentith seventh day of January, 1661.
[2]Richard, the sonne of Hennery Heald, of Leyland, baptised the
second day of ffebruary, 1661.
[2]Ralph ffidler, the sonne of John ffidler, of ffarington, baptised
the second day of ffebruary, 1661.

[1] It seems probable that this and the following dates should be 1661, unless,
indeed, the entries are all misplaced, and should be 1662.

[2] The last figure of the year has been altered in each of these fifteen entries, which
are printed in full here, exactly as in the Register. Originally 1662, it now appears
as 1661. The person making the entries from the Clerk's book, or from loose papers,
into the parchment Register, seems to have neglected to do so until a large number
had accumulated. This may perhaps account for the confusion of dates. It will
be noticed that the baptism of "John, son of Oliver Cross, Ap. 29, 1661" (and some
others), are repeated. The order as here printed is exactly that of the Register.

[1]Doraty, the daughter of William Willden, of Leyland, baptised the second day of ffebruary, 1661. ·

[1]Hennery, the sonne of Henery barker, of Charrnocke, baptised the sixtenth day of ffebruary, 1661.

[1]Alice, the daughter of Richard Boulton, of Euexton, baptised· the second day of March, 1661.

[1]Ann, the daughter of Richard Godman, of Leyland, baptised· the second of March, 1661.

[1]Thomas, the sonne of Thomas Couper, of Leyland, baptised the sixt day of March, 1661.

[1]Ann, the daughter of Robert Dobson, of Leyland, baptised the sixtinth day of March, 1661.

[1]Ralph, the sonne of Elish Sumner, of Leyland, baptised the sixtinth day of March, 1661.

[1]John, the sonne of John Jackeson, of Curden, baptised the· sixtinth day of March, 1661.

[1]Jane, the daughter of Richard Stopforth, of Leyland, baptised the three & twentith day of March, 1661.

[1]Jannett, the daughter of James Marton, of Leyland, baptised the three & twentith day of March, 1661.

[1]Jane, the daughter of William Leuer, of Leyland, baptised [no date given].

[1]Marie, the daughter of Lawrance Sumner, of Uleswalton, baptised the sixt day of Aprill, 1661.

John, the sonne of Oliver Crose, of Euexton, baptised the twentith ninth day of Aprill, 1661.

Edward, the son of Will: Willden, of Leyland, baptised 13 day of April, 1661.[2]

Jane, the daughter of Robert Couper, of Euexton
                                          baptised Maye 5

Margery, the daughter of John Hilton, of Euexton
                                          baptised „ 5

William ffarrington,[3] the sonne of Henery ffarrington, of worden, gentellman, baptised the   ... ... „ 19

---

[1] See note ([2]), p. 39.

[2] This entry inserted, but same hand.

[3] This entry supplies an item which has hitherto been wanting in all the pedigrees. Probably the irregularities of the Register at this period have caused this baptism to be overlooked. The William ffarrington here mentioned was the son of Henry ffarrington and Susanna, daughter of Digory Weare, D.D. [N.B. In Foster's Lanc. Pedigrees and in Baines (edit. Croston) this marriage is stated to have taken place in 1685; but as both give 1656 for the date of the eldest son's birth, this must be an error for 1655.] Why the father is here described as "of Worden" is not very evident. William ffarrington, Esq., sen. (the proposed Knight of the Oak), was living until after Feb., 1672, and so would properly be "of Worden" at this date. The child whose baptism is here recorded succeeded his father in the possession of

Edward, the sonne of William Atherton, of Leyland[1]
baptised Maye 19
John, the sonne of Hennery Eastom, of Whitell, baptised   „   19
Margret, the daughter of John Burstow, of Leyland[2]
baptised   „   19
John, the sonne of William Sargant, of Leyland
baptised   „   29
Edward, the sonne of Richard Johnnes, of Euexton
baptised June   9
Ralph, the sonne of William Pilkington, of Leyland
baptised   „   14
John, the sonne of John Hodson, of Curden, baptised..   „   23
John, the sonne of Hennery Bickerstafe, of ffarrington,
baptised the ...   .   „   25
Ann, the daughter of William Couper, of Leyland,
baptised the ...   .   „   last
Elizabeth, daughter of Thomas Stanley, of Euexton,
baptised the ...   .   „   last
Elizabeth, the daughter of William Balshaw, of
Euexton, baptized the...   ...   . July   20
John Blackeborne, the sone of William Blackeborne, of
Curden, baptised ...   .   „   21
Margrett, the daughter of William Mackerell, and Thomas, the
sonne, both twins of William Mackerell, of Leyland, baptised
the ffifth day of August.
Marie, the daughter of John Smith, of Leyland, baptised the tenth
day of August.
John, the sonne of William Godman, of Leyland, baptised the
ffiftinth day of August.
Jane, the daughter of John Kneuet, of Charnocke, baptised the
eight day of September.
Jenett, the daughter of Henry tisinge, of Ulneswalton, baptised
the eight day of September.
Elin, the daughter of Richard Charnley, of Curden, baptised
the owne and twentith day of September.
William, the sonne of James ffarrington, of Leyland, baptised
the twentith ninth day of September.

---

the family estates, and in 1714 was High Sheriff. He married Elizabeth, d. of
Edmund Swettenham, of Somerford Booths, co. Chester, Esq., but died s.p. in 1715.
There is a very handsome tablet erected to the memory of this gentleman and his
wife upon the walls of the ffarington chapel, within Leyland Church. The date of
his death (1715) is given, but no age or date of birth. Mrs. ffarington is there said
to have died in 1723.

   [1] Inserted; same hand.

   [2] Inserted. Overlaps last entry, but is in the same hand.

Thomas, the sonne of James Mose, of Clayton, baptised the tenth day of Nouember.

Alice, the daughter, and Elin beardsworth, dougteres of John Beardsworth, both twines, baptised the tenth day of Nouember.

Elizabeth, the daughter of James Holumes, baptised the seuenth day of Nouember.

William, the sone of Rodger South: of Leyl: baptised ye 24th d. of November. [Inserted.]

James, the sonne of James Dandey, of Tarlton, bastard, baptised the eleuenth day of December.

Thomas Clough, the sonne of Thomas Clough, of Leyland, baptised the ffiftinth day of December.

Marie, the daughter of William Willson, of Croston prish, baptised the ffiftinth day of December.

Margret, the daughter of Richard Carter, of Eckelston, baptised the towe and twentith day of December.

William, the son of Roger Southworth, bap: the 24 day.[1]

[Baptisms] 1662.

Jane, the daughter of John Taylor, of Whittell, baptised the fforth day of January.

William, the sonne of John Torner, of Euexton, baptised the fforth day of January.

Jane, the daughter of Ralph Pearson, of Whelton, baptised the eightinth day of January.

Alice, the daughter of Robert Marton, of Oulerton,[2] baptised the eighttinth day of January.

Alice, the daughter of Alixander fforshaw, of Uleswalton, baptised the twentith ffifth day of January.

John, the sonne of Robert Sargant, of Leyland, baptised the thirtith d. of January.

Thomas,[3] the sonne of John Armetrydinge, of Euxton, baptised the eighth day of ffebruary.

Ann, the daughter of William Blackeborne, of Curden, baptised the ffifftinth day of ffebruary.

Elizabeth, the daughter of William Miller, of Uleswalton, baptised the twentith fforth day of ffebruary.

Margret, the daughter of Henry Tisinge, of Uleswalton, baptised the ffirst day of March.

---

[1] No month or year given. See Nov. 24th, which is evidently the same baptism.

[2] Otherwise Ollerton, which is a hamlet in the township of Withnell in Leyland parish.

[3] This is the baptism of the future Vicar of Leyland (1689-1719). For particulars see List of Vicars.

Ralph, the sonne of Thomas Lowe, of Uleswalton, baptised the ffiftinth day of March.

[1]Jane, the daughter of John Slator, of Euexton, baptised the ffiftinth day of March.

[Baptisms] 1663.

John, the sonne of William Garston, of Whittell, baptised the twentith ninth day of March.

Elin and Jenet, daughters of Thomas Jackeson, of Curden, both twines, baptised the nintinth day of Aprill.

Margret, the daughter of William Godman, of Leyland, baptised the third day of May.

Thomas, the sonne of Edward Litherland, of Whittell, baptised the twentith fforth day of May.

Hugh,[2] the sonne of James Aryetmetrydinge, of Whittell, baptised the ffortinth day of June.

Alice, the daughter of William Pilkinton, of Leyland, baptised the eightinth day of Jun.

Annes, the daughter of Richard Tumlison, of Uleswalton, baptised the nintinth day of Jun.

John, the sonne of John Willden, of ffarrington, baptised the owne and twentith day of June.

[Fresh handwriting, very similar to commencement of Register. (?) William Rothwell's.]

Elizabeth, daughter of William Johnson	... Aug.	23
John, son of Richard Slator, of Exton	... „	23
Henry, son of Henry Bickerstaffe, of ffarington ...	... „	30
Elizabeth, daughter of John Cowper, of Clayton	... Sept.	6
John, son of Thomas Walmersley, of Whittle ...	... „	13
Alice,⎫ twins of Nicholas Bromiley ... ... Anne,⎭	... „	16
Robert, son of William Maudsly, supposed	... „	20
Mabella, daughter, of Mr. Thomas Brooke[3] ...	... „	24
Henry, son of Henry Brining, of Whittle	... „	29

[1] This entry is at the top of a new page, over which is written "The Birth of Children, 1662."

[2] Became in 1687 a benefactor to Heapy Chapel, giving (with Thurstan Leyland, of Clayton) his bond for £80 to provide a preaching minister.

[3] Probably Mr. Thomas Brooke, eldest son by the first marriage of Sir Peter Brooke, of Mere, co. Chester, who married Mabel, daughter of William ffarington, Esq. (and widow of Richard Clayton, Esq., of Crooke in Whittle), as his third wife. The Brookes rented Astley Hall about this time, and so were in the immediate neighbourhood.

Sarah, daughter of Richard Broxop, of Exton ... ... Oct. 18
Robert, son of William Bordman, of Winnell ... ... „ 22
Anne, daughter of Arthur Dawson, of ffarington ... Nov. 5
Mary, daughter of Robert Whittle ... ... „ 9
Sisley, daughter of William Welsh, of ffarington ... „ 22
Isabell [Mary crossed out], daughter of John Wielden. „ 29
Alice, daughter of William Garstang, of Whittle ... Dec. 2
Roger, son of John Dewhurst, of Cuerden ... ... „ 3
Thomas, son of John Smith, of Leyland ... ... „ 6
Ellin, daughter of William Rigby, of Charnock ... ... „ 6
James, son of James Sumner, of Exton ... ... „ 25
Ellin, daughter of Thomas Stanley, of Exton ... ... Jan. 3
Anne, daughter of William Sarieant, of Leyland ... „ 10
Margret, daughter of John Jackson, of Ulneswalton ... „ 28
Thurstan, son of Thurstan Sharrok, of Whittle ... ... „ 31
Henry, son of William Wilson, of Leyland... ... ... ffeb. 7
Edmund, son of William Howorth, of Whittle ... ... „ 7
Edward, son of John Beardsworth, of Leyland ... ... „ 21
——, son of Richard Wasley, of Chorley ... ... „ (*sic*) 14
Margrett, daughter of John Clough, of Leyland... ... March 1
John, son of William Cowper, of Cuerden ... ... „ 6
James, son of James Holme, of Leyland ... ... „ 6
Elizabeth, daughter of John Hilton, of Leyland... ... „ 6
Anne, the daughter of James Worden, of Clayton ... „ 10
Elizabeth, daughter of John ffidler, of ffarington ... „ 20

Christnings, 1664.

Katharine, daughter of John Parker, of Chorley... ... Aprill 3
Robert, the son of John Baron, of Exton ... ... „ 10
Richard, the son of Thomas Clough, of Leyland ... „ 10
George, the son of Henry Eastham, of Leyland ... „ 11
Elizabeth, daughter of Richard Carter, of Eccleston... „ 17
Elizabeth, daughter of John Dugson, of Brindle[1] ... „ 17
John, son of Thomas Hilton, of Wheelton ... ... May 8
John, son of Thomas Sumner, of Euxton ... ... „ 15
Mary, daughter of John Pearson, of Wheeleton ... ... „ 22
John, son of Edmund Tasker, of Cuerden ... ... June 5
Isabell, daughter of William Watson, of Whittle ... „ 5
B. Hugh, son of { Hugh Parke, / Alice Whittle, } of Leyland ... ... „ 10
Katharine, daughter of John Bomber, of ffarington ... „ 12
Thomas, son of Thomas Whitehead, of Leyland ... „ 19

[1] Brindle parish adjoins Leyland on the eastern side.

William, son of Lawrance Croft, of Whittle ...	... June	19
Elizabeth, daughter of John Jackson, of Leyland ...	„	19
Thomas, son of Richard Godman, of Leyland ...	... July	9
Thomas, son of Raphe Leyland, of Clayton	„	10
Anne, daughter of John Roscow, of Euxton	„	14
James, son of Thomas Crichlow, of Euxton	„	17
John, son of William Gerratt, of Clayton	... Aug.	7
Henry, son of John Beardsworth, of Leyland	„	9
William, son of John Hodson, of Cuerden	„	14
ffrances, son of Thomas Duteson, of ffarington	„	18
Thomas, son of Edward Sharrok, of Walton	„	28
Margrett, daughter of John Cliffe, defunct: of Leyland.	Sept.	18
Katharine, daughter of John Monke, of Leyland ...	„	19
Richard, son of James Wilson, of Whittle	„	28
Isabell, daughter of William Garstang, of Whittle ...	Oct.	9
Elizabeth, daughter of William Blackburne, of Cuerden.	„	9
Joane, daughter of James Gorton, of Clayton	„	18
Christopher, son of James ffiswich, of Whittle	„	28
Elizabeth, daughter of John Marsh, of Leyland... ...	„	30
Isaak, son of William Sharrock, of Euxton...	„	31
Richard and ⎱ twins, children of Richard Chetam, of		
Elizabeth; ⎰ ffarington	... Nov.	5
Adam, son of Edward Clayton, of ffarington	„	5
Robert, son of Robert Pilkinton, of Leyland	„	27
B. —, daughter of Christopher Newsom, of Ulneswalton	„	28
Oliver, son of Raphe Pearson, of Olivers[1] in Wheeleton.	Dec.	25
Alice, daughter of John Taylor, in Whittle	„	25
Alice, daughter of Richard Gregson, in Euxton... ...	„	25
Anne, daughter of Thomas Rigby, of Charnock... ...	„	28
John, son of Thomas Glaseborow, of Ulneswalton ...	„	29
Robert, son of John Gouden, of Leyland	... Jan.	8
Elizabeth, daughter of Richard Jones, of Euxton ...	„	15
Edward, son of Thomas Parre, of Leyland...	„	17
Jennett, daughter of William Baxenden, of Euxton ...	„	22
Anne, daughter of Thomas Winnell, of Whittle	„	22
Edward, son of Robert Parker, of Leyland...	„	29
Thomas, son of William Leaver, of Leyland ...	... ffeb.	5
Jennett, daughter of William Marsh, of ffarington ...	„	7
Jennett, daughter of James Mosse, of Clayton	„	12
Anne, daughter of James Woodroofe, of (Eux)ton ...	„	12
Richard, son of Roger Southworth, of Leyland... ...	„	15
Christopher, son of Edward Litherland, of Whittle ...	„	19
Alice, daughter of Jeffray Taylor, of Heapy	„	26

[1] A farmhouse.

William, son of William Welsh, of ffarington ... ... March 19
James, son of John Jackson, of Cuerden ... ... „ 19
Isabell, daughter of Christopher Willden, of ffarington. „ 19
James, son of John Dewhurst, of Cuerden ... ... „ 24

Cbristenings, 1665.

Elizabeth, daughter of Robert Lukas, of Leyland ... Aprill 2
Ellin, daughter of Roger Clayton, of Cuerden ... ... „ 5
Roger, son of William Clayton, of Cuerden ... ... „ 5
Mathew, son of John Martin, of Clayton ... ... „ 30
Margret, daughter of William Makerill, of Leyland ... „ 30
Elizabeth, daughter of Adam Blakburne, of Cuerden... „ 30
Richard, son of Thomas Calderbanke, of Leyland ... May 21
Thomas, son of Edward Tilsley, of Euxton ... ... „ 25
Anne, daughter of Thomas Rowes, of Euxton ... ... „(*sic*) 4
John, son of James Holme, of Leyland ... ... „ 28
Ellin, daughter of Robert Turner, of Leyland ... ... „ 28
Theophilus, son of Michael Taylor, of Euxton ... ... „ 31
Jane, daughter of Thomas Machon, of Cuerden ... ... June 11
Jane, daughter of Robert Sumner, of Leyland ... ... „ 18
Thomas, son of Thomas Porter, of Leyland ... ... July 2
John, son of Nicholas Bromiley, of Leyland ... ... „ 2
Hamlett, son of William Holmes, of Whittle ... ... „ 5
Mary, daughter of Robert Sergeant, of Leyland ... „ 13
Mary, daughter of William Pilkinton, of Leyland ... „ 16
[1]Edward, son of Mr. John Robinson, of Euxton, was
 borne the first day of June and baptized the four-
 teenth day, 1665.
Alice, daughter of Henry Allinson, of Euxton ... ... „ 23
Edmund, son of James Garstang, of Whittle ... ... „ 23
Elizabeth, daughter of John Armettriding, of Euxton .(Aug.)[2] 9
Hannah, daughter of Richard Broxop, of Euxton ... „ 27
Mary, daughter of Thomas Bateson, of Leyland ... Sept. 3
Susanna, daughter of William Southworth, of Leyland „ 6
Anne, daughter of Henry Eastham, of Walton ... ... „ 21
Margrett, daughter of Raphe Lowe, of Euxton... ... „ 24
Mary, daughter of William Godman, of Leyland ... „ 24
Ellin, daughter of Richard Tomlinson, of Walton ... Oct. 15

---

[1] See account of the Robinson family at the commencement of this volume, p. 23. This is the grandson of Major Robinson, who afterwards became the owner of "Buckshaw," in Euxton. His name is entered (together with his brothers Thomas, John, and George) on the Foreign Burgess Roll of the Preston Guild in 1682. Mr. John Robinson, mentioned in the text, died in 1676, in the lifetime of his father.

[2] August inserted in later hand—? Vicar Armetriding's.

William, son of Henry Bickarstaffe, of ffarington	... Nov.	8
Martha, daughter of Nathaneel Woodworth, of Euxton,		
baptized July 19, 1665	...[July	19]
Peter, son of Roger Woodcock, of Ulneswalton...	... Dec.	10
John, son of Edward Clough, of Leyland	... „	24
Mary, daughter of John Woomell, of Wheelton ...	... „	24
William, son of Henry Tyson, of Ulneswalton ...	... „	24
Elizabeth, daughter of James Armettriding, of Whittle.	„	30
Richard, son of Edward Shaw, of Ulneswalton ...	... Jan.	14
Ellin, daughter of William Wilson, of Leyland ...	... „	26
William, son of John Sharrock, of Walton	... „	28
Thomas, son of Ellis Sumner, of Leyland	... „	31
John, son of Richard Slator, of Euxton	... ffeb.	11
Jane, daughter of Edward Litherland, of Whittle	... „	18
James, son of John Clough, of Leyland	... „	18
George, son of George Muncke, of Leyland	... March	2
Alice, daughter of Thomas Walmersly, of Whittle ...	„	4
Katherine, daughter of Richard Barnes, of Whittle ...	„	11
Robert, son of Richard Slator, of Euxton	... „	11

[Baptisms] 1666.

Henry, son of William Harrison, of Clayton	...	...March 30
Jennett, daughtr of Richard Loxam, of ffarington	... Aprill	1
George, son of William Boydell, of Euxton	... ...	„ 1
Robert, son of Robert Waring, of Euxton	... „	1
Mary, daughter of Thomas Sumner, of Euxton ...	... „	22
Elizabeth, daughtr of Thomas Winnell, of Whittle	... „	22
Alice, daughtr of William Watson, of Whittle	... ... „	29
Anne,[1] daughter of Mr. Henry ffarington, of Worden...	„	30
Richard, son of William Whitehead, of Leyland	... „(sic)20
Elizabeth, daughter of Joseph Houlden, of Euxton,		
baptized the 20th day of June	...[June 20]
Hugh, son of Henry Smith, of Euxton	... ... May	6
William, son of William Jackson, of Whittle	... ... „	16
William, son of John Wielden, of Leyland ...	... ... „(sic)13
James, son of James Wilson, of Whittle	... ... „	20
Margret, daughtr of Thomas Croston, of Ulneswalton. June	3
Alice, daughter of Raphe Smith, at Lostock-hall[2] ...	„	10

[1] The youngest daughter of Mr. Henry ffarington, and Susanna, his wife (née Weare). She married a Mr. Kelsall, from Ireland. Vicar Armetriding left a legacy of £200 to his "nephew, Mr. James Kelsall," who would, of course, be the son of the lady whose baptism is here recorded.

[2] The River Lostock winds about so much that it is difficult to be quite certain of the locality indicated. Lostock-hall, however, is in Cuerden township.

Thomas, son of Henry Eastham, of Leyland ... ... June 17
John, son of John Baron, of Euxton ... ... „ 17
Anne, daught^r of James Martin, of Leyland ... ... July 15
John, son of William Howorth, of Whittle ... ... „ 22
Henry, son of John Dewhurst, of Cuerden ... ... Aug. 5
William, son of Raphe Johnson, of Whittle ... ... „ 26
Alice, daughter of Thomas Lowe, of Ulneswalton ... „ 26
Katherine, daught^r of Roger ffarington, of ffarington... Sept. 2
Raphe, son of Thomas Clough, of Leyland... ... ... „ 9
Abraham, son of Raphe Johnson, of Cuerden ... ... „ 16
Robert, son of James Martin, of Heapy ... ... „ 30
Richard, son of William Marsh, of ffarington ... ... „ 30
Richard, son of John Blackburne, of Euxton ... ... Oct. 7
Alice, ⎫
Anne, ⎬daughters of John Clayton, in Clayton... ... „ 10
Jennett,⎭
John, son of Thomas Calderbank, of Euxton ... ... „ 18
Margrett, daught^r of James ffiswick, of Whittle ... ... „ 21
Margrett, daught^r of Thomas Glasborow, of Ulnes-
walton ... ... „ 21
Sisley, daughter of John Hodson, of Cuerden ... ... „ 21
Robert, son of William Welsh, of ffarington ... ... Nov. 4
George, son of William Garstang, of Whittle ... ... „ 4
Anne, the daught^r of John Smith, of Leyland ... ... „ 11
Elizabeth, daught^r of Thurstan Heald, of Leyland ... „ 11
Anne, daughter of Lawrance Croft, of Whittle ... ... „ 12
Ellin, daught^r of William Blakburne, of Cuerden ... „ 13
Edmund, the son of John ffidler, of ffarington ... ... „ 18
John, the son of John Armettriding, of Euxton ... ... „ 25
Richard, son of Richard Griffith, of Euxton ... ... „ 25
Margrett, daughter of John Rotchett,[1] of Leyland ... „ 28
Mary, daughter of Christopher Wielden, of ffarington... Dec. 9
John, son of Richard Charnly, of Cuerden ... ... „ (*sic*)3
Lawrance, son of Richard Gregson, of Euxton ... ... „ 16
John, son of John Taylor, of Whittle ... ... „ 25
William, son of Richard Clough, of Leyland ... ... „ 26
[2]John, son of John Dobson, borne in Leyland ... ... Jan. 15
Anne, daughter of John Wright, of Leyland ... ... „ 6
William, son of William Balshaw, of Euxton ... ... „ 25
B. Jane, daught^r of Katharin Hollinhurst, of ffarington „ 29
Elizabeth, daught^r of Thomas Parre, of Euxton ... ... ffeb. 7
Henry, son of Edmund Tasker, of Cuerden... ... ... „ 10

---

[1] An older form (probably the original) of the name now written Rodgett.
[2] This entry is inserted.

William, son of William Dalton, of Whittle ... ... ffeb. 19
Jane, daughter of John Marsh, of Moss-side ... ... „ 24
Elizabeth, daughtr of John Roscow, of Euxton ... ... March 8
Henry, son of John Slator, of Euxton ... ... „ 10

[Baptisms] 1667.

Margrett, daughter of Roger Clayton, of Cuerden ... March 25
Ellin, daughter of Thomas Eastham, of Ulneswalton... „ 31
Esther, daughter of Richard Godman, of Leyland ... Aprill 8
Ellin, daughter of Michaell Taylor, of Euxton ... ... „ 10
William, son of William Sharrock, of Euxton ... ... „ 25
George, son of Thomas Porter, of Leyland ... ... „ 25
Elizabeth, daughtr of Richard Nelson, of Leyland ... „ 26
John, son of William Leaver, of Leyland ... ... „ 28
John, son of Thomas Thornley, of Clayton, borne May the 2: 1667.
William, son of Thomas Cowper, of Leyland ... ... May 9
Anne, daughtr of Richard Jones, of Euxton ... ... „ 12
Anne, daughtr of Alexander fforshaw, of Ulneswalton „ 12
James, son of Henry Bickerstaffe, of ffarington ... ... June 6
Jane & Thomas, } twinns of William Clayton, of Cuerden ... „ 11
Anne, daughtr of John Smith, of Bretherton[1] ... ... „ 11
Richard, son of John Gouden, of Leyland ... ... „ 23
Anne, daughtr of William Whalell, of Standish pish ... „ 23
Roger, son of Roger Woodcock, of Ulneswalton... ... July 7
John, son of Mr. William Cross,[2] of Darwin ... ... „ 10
William, son of John Heskat, of Leyland ... ... „ 14
John, son of Roger ffiswick, of Winnell[3] ... ... „ 21
Jeffrey, son of Jeffry Taylor, of Heapie ... ... „ 21
William, son of William Jackson, of Euxton ... ... „ 21
Mary, daughr of Raphe Leyland, of Clayton ... ... „ 25
John, son of Henry Brining, of Whittle ... ... „ 28
William, son of William Oldham, of Whittle ... ... Aug. 11
Alice, daughr of John Jackson, of Leyland ... ... „ 18
William, son of John Pincocke, of Euxton ... ... „ 25
John, son of William Clayton, of Clayton ... ... Sept. 14
John, son of John Clayton, of Clayton... ... ... „ 22
Thomas, son of William Cowper, of Cuerden ... ... „ 24
Anne, daughter of Thomas Hilton, of Wheelton ... „ 29
Margrett, daughr of Ellis Sumner, of Leyland ... ... Oct. 1

[1] Township in Croston parish now made parochial.
[2] See note on entry for June 21, 1668. [3] For Withnell—written as pronounced.

B. Thomas, son of William Holme, jun[r], of Leyland... Oct. 4
Tomasin, daugh[r] of John Smith, of Ulneswalton   ...   „   6
Margrett, daugh[r] of Edward Langton, of ffarington ... Nov. 10
Elizabeth, daught[r] of William Wilson, of Leyland   ...   „ 17
Jennett, daugh[r] of George Munck, of Leyland ...   ...   „ 23
Alice, daugh[r] of William Clayton, of ffarington ... ... „ 24
John, son of Thomas Horrocks, a passenger   ...   ...   „ 24
Ellis, son of Ellis Sumner, of Leyland ...   . Dec. 5
Richard, son of Robert Parker, of Mosse-side[1] ... ...   „ 15
Edward, son of Henry Barker, of Charnock   ...   ...   „ 29
William, son of William Pilkinton, of Leyland ...   ... ffeb. 9
Alice, daugh[r] of William Harrison, in Walton[2] ... ... „ 20
David, son of William Price, a passenger   ...   . „ 23
Thomas, son of Henry Allinson, of Euxton... ...   ...   „ 23
Ellis, son of William Jackson, of Whittle ...   . March 1
Jennett, daught[r] of John Armettriding, jun[r], of Euxton. „   5
Nicholas, son of Nicholas Bromiley, of Leyland... ...   „ 15
Mary, daught[r] of Richard Broxop, of Leyland ... ...   „ 19
John, son of Alice Parker, of Leyland ...   . „ 22

[Baptisms] 1668.

Richard, son of John Armettriding, of Euxton ...   ... May 3
Thomas, son of Dauid Jones, of Euxton   ...   .   „ 17
Margery, daugh[r] of Ellin Thornton, of ffarington   ...   „ 18
Sisley, daugh[r] of William Roscow, of Charnock...   ...   „ 31
Lawrance-Howorth, son of Thomas Leekas, of Whittle June 7
Mary, daugh[r] of John Clough, of Leyland ...   .   „ 14
Anne, daugh[r] of William Howorth, of Whittle ...   ...   „ 14
John, son of William Shaw, of Leyland   ...   .   „ 14
Anne, daught[r] of William ffarington, of ffarington ... „ 21
Grace, daugh[r] of Mr. William Crosse,[3] of Darwin ... „ 21

[1] The part of Leyland township adjoining Croston parish.

[2] Walton-le-Dale, which adjoins Cuerden township.

[3] Mr. William Crosse here mentioned was the eldest son of John Cross, of Over Darwen, gent., and Millicent, his wife, daughter of Thomas Astley, of Stakes, gent. His first wife was a Mistress Ann Rogers, widow, whose maiden name was Bold. She was sister to Grace Bold, of Carnarvon, a resident for many years at Leyland Hall, first with Lady Tildesley, who rented the estate, and afterwards with Robert Charnock, gentleman, the owner thereof. The marriage of Mr. William Crosse and Ann Rogers took place at Leyland, Aug. 28, 1666. The child whose baptism is here recorded was probably named after her mother's sister. A full account of the great law suit concerning Leyland Hall, in which Mr. Cross and others, the legatees under the will of Grace Bold, were engaged, will be found later on (see Burials, 1670). It was this gentleman who in the year 1687 took the leading part in the contest with the Vicar of Blackburn (Price) for the possession of St. James' Chapel, Over Dawen. He was buried at Blackburn, March 8, 1697-8. (Cf. Abram's *History of Blackburn.*)

Thomas, son of Thomas Sumner, of Euxton, deceased June 24
Thomas, son of Henry Bickerstaffe, of ffarington   ... July   6
Elizabeth, daughter of John Baron, of Euxton ...   ... „   12
Richard, son of Thomas Winnell, of Whittle   ...   ... „   12
Ellin, daught^r of John Browne, of ffarington   ...   ... „   26
Anne, daugh^r of Thomas Pilkinton, of Leyland ...   ... Aug.   2
Margrett, daugh^r of William Walmersley, of Euxton...   „   9
Ellin, daugh^r of Margrett Mayre, of Euxton   ...   ... Sept.   6
Isabell, daugh^r of Roger Brining, of Whittle   ...   ... „   27
B. John, son of Anne Short, of Leyland   ...   . Oct.   12
Ellin, daughter of John Jackson, of Walton   ...   ... „   30
Ellin, daught^r of Thomas Hall, of Euxton ...   . Nov.   1
Anne, daught^r of William Gerratt, of Brindle   ...   ... „   8
Thomas, son of Lawrance Croft, of Whittle   ...   ... „   16
Elizabeth, daughter of William Johnson, of Leyland... „   26
Raphe, son of Richard Sheardley, of Leyland   ...   ... „   26
William, son of William Sergeant, of Leyland ...   ... Dec.   10
Elsabeth, daugh^r of William Baxenden, of Walton   ... „   19
John, son of Adam Blakburne, of Cuerden ...   . Jan.   11
William, son of Thomas Leyland, of Leyland ...   ... „   18
Margrett, daugh^r of Thomas Walmersley, of Whittle... „   24
William, son of Thomas Blakburne, of Cuerden...   ... „   31
Alice, daugh^r of Raphe Johnson, of Whittle   ...   ... ffeb.   7
John, son of Ellis Sumner, of Leyland   ...   . „   19
Alice, daugh^r of John Wielden, of Leyland...   ...   ... „   24
Elsabeth, daugh^r of John Harpur, of Whittle   ...   ... „   28
Margrett, daugh^r of James Holme, of Leyland ...   ... „   28
John, son of William Clayton, of Cuerden ...   . March 7
Thomas, son of John Heskett, of Leyland ...   . „   7
Alice, daugh^r of Roger Dewhurst, of Cuerden   ...   ... „   18

1669. Christnings.[1]

Elizabeth, daugh^r of James ffiswick, of Whittle ...   ... Aprill   1
Hugh, son of James Martin, of Heapie   ...   . „   4
Mary, daughter of Thomas Parre, of Euxton   ...   ... „   11
Ellin, daughter of Thomas Richmond, of Winnell   ... „   17
Raph, son of Henry Smith, of Euxton...   ...   . „   18
Oliuer, son of William Garstang, of Whittle   ...   ... „   25
Thomas, son of Thomas Cowper, of Leyland   ...   ... May   9
James [William erased], son of William Marsh, of
ffarington   ...   . „   16

[1] There is a transcript of this year's entries in the Bishop's Registry at Chester, written on parchment, long and closely written. The writing is fair. It is signed by William Rothwell, the vicar, and the churchwardens.

William, son of John ffidler, of ffarington ... ... May 16
Anne, daugh^r of Richard Clough, of Leyland ... ... „ 25
John, son of John Pincock, of Euxton... ... ... June 27
John, son of Nicholas Bromiley, of Leyland ... ... July 11
Tomasin, daugh^r of Alexander Breres, of Whittle ... „ 11
Elizabeth, daught^r of George Bury, of Winnell ... ... „ 18
George, son of William Dalton, of Whittle ... ... Aug. 8
Agnes, daught^r of Christoph^r Wielden, of ffarington ... „ 8
Mary, daughter of William ffarington, of ffarington ... „ 29
Robert, son of John Blakburne, of Cuerden ... ... „ 29
Mary, daught^r of Edward [Christph^r erased] Lither-
    land, of Whittle ... ... Sept. 5
Thomas, son of Richard Whittle, of Leyland ... ... „ 5
Thomas, son of Thomas Hilton, of Wheeleton ... ... „ 12
Robert, son of Raphe Lowe, of Whittle ... ... „ 12
Thomas, son of Edward Clough, of Leyland ... ... „ 26
Andrew, son William Waterworth, of Leyland ... ... Oct. 17
William, son of Raphe Johnson, of Cuerden ... ... „ 17
Richard, son of John Lee, of Ulneswalton ... ... „ 24
Robert, son of Robert Cockar, of Leyland... ... ... Nov. 7
Ellin, daught^r of Thomas Clough, of Leyland ... ... „ 7
William, son of John Clayton, of Clayton ... ... „ 11
Jennett, daughter of William Clayton, of Clayton ... „ 11
William, son of Mr. William Crosse,[1] of Darwin ... Dec. 3
Richard, son of John Sharrock, of Walton ... ... „ 8
Roger, son of William Howorth, of Whittle ... ... „ 19
John, son of John Tyson, of Ulneswalton ... ... „ 19
John, son of John Slator, of Leyland ... ... „ 28
Richard, son of Richard Nelson, of Leyland ... ... „ 28
Anne, daughter of William Whitehead, of Leyland[2]... Jan. 16
Oliuer, son of Euan Hilton, of Leyland ... ... „ 16
Robert, son of Thomas Jackson, of Leyland ... ... „ 17
Alice, daught^r of Thomas Pilkinton, of Whittle ... ... „ 18
Richard, son of John Whittle, of Longton ... ... „ 29
Jennett, daugh^r of John Blakburne, of Euxton ... ... ffeb. 6
Gilbert, son of John Roscow, of Euxton ... ... „ 13
Elsabeth, daugh^r Thomas Calderbank, of Euxton ... „ 13
John, son of Richard Wigans, of Whittle ... ... „ 20
Thomas, son of John Wielden, of Leyland ... ... „ 27
Elsabeth, daught^r of Thomas Doutson, of Cuerden ... March 4
Henry, son of Henry Eastham, of Leyland ... ... „ 6
Thurstan, son of Edward Hodson, of Leyland ... ... „ 20

---

[1] See note on entry in 1668.   [2] This entry is inserted, but contemporary.

[Baptisms] 1670.[1]

Jane, daught^r of John Smith, of Leyland ... ...March 27
Margrett, daught^r of William Harrison, of Clayton ... Aprill 10
Thomas, son of John Crooke, of Euxton ... ... „ 17
Elizabeth, daughter of Thomas Leyland, of Leyland... „ 17
Roger, son of Dauid Jones, of Euxton .. .. „ 18
John, son of Richard Woodrooffe, of Wheelton ... ... „ 24
Mary, daught^r of Edward Tilsley, of Euxton ... ... „ 24
Henry, son of John Slator, of Euxton ... ...May 1
John, son of Richard Godman, of Leyland... ... ... „ 8
Elsabeth, daught^r of Ellis Sumner, of Leyland ... ... „ 22
Sisley, daughter of Thomas Lowe, of Euxton ... ... „ 22
Elnor, daugh^r of Richard Broxop, of Euxton ... ...July 10
James, son of Mr. James Carter, of Leyland[2] ... ... „ 12
Bartholomew, son of John Taylor, of Whittle ... ... „ 27
James, son of Richard Walton, of Leyland... ... ... „ 31
Thomas, son Edward Tilsdley, of Euxton ... ... „ 31
Katharin, daugh^r of John Walmersley, of Whittle ... „ 31
Alice, daught^r of John Calderbanck, of Mosse-side ... Aug. 19
John, son of William Clayton, of ffarington ... ... Sept. 4
Jennett, daugh^r of Thomas Porter, of Leyland ... ... „ 4
Alice, daught^r of William Pilkinton, of Leyland ... „ 18
Alice, daught^r of Raphe Johnson, of Whittle ... ... „ 25
Thomas, son of Ellis Sumner, of Leyland ... ... „ 25
ffrancis, son of Roger Brining, of Whittle ... ... Oct. 2
Margrett, daught^r of William Baxenden, of Euxton ... „ 6
Miles, son of John Scott, of Whittle ... ... „ xi.
Margrett, daught^r of William Jackson, of Whittle ... „ 13
Margrett, daught^r of Henry Allinson, of Euxton ... „ 16
Alice, daught^r of William Wright, of Euxton ... ... „ 23
B. Anne, daughter of {Richard Parker, / Sisley Baxenden,} of Leyland... „ 31
William, son of John Baron, of Euxton ... ...Nov. 6
Thomas, son of Thomas Leekas, of Whittle ... ... „ 13
Thomas, son of William Shaw, of Leyland... ... ... „ 23
Elizabeth, daughter of John Martinscroft, of Leyland.. „ 28
Alice, daught^r of Robert Parker, of Mosse-side ... ... Dec. xi.
Margrett, daught^r of John Jackson, of Leyland ... ...Jan. 1
John, son of Hugh Duckworth, of Walton ... ... „ 2
John, son of John Park, of Leyland ... ... „ 28

[1] There is a transcript at Chester, written on parchment, in a clear hand. It is signed by William Rothwell, the vicar, and the churchwardens.

[2] Not at present identified.

Hannah, daught[r] of James Holme, of Leyland ... ... ffeb. 2
Jennett, daugh[r] of Edward Clough, of Leyland ... ... „ 5
Thomas, son of Mr. William Crosse,[1] of Darwin ... „ 10
Thomas, son of Roger Horrocks, of Euxton ... ... „ 12
William, son of Adam Blakburne, of Cuerden ... ... „ 22
Andrew, son of Richard Clough, of Leyland ... ... „ 19
Anne, daughter of Christopher Sumner, of Leyland... „ 19
Roger Leyland Sharrok, son of Will: Sharrok, of Euxton. March 16

Christenings, 1671.

Ellin, daught[r] of Richard Whittle, of Leyland ... ... March 30
Ciceley, daugh[r] of Thomas Winnell, of Whittle ... ... Aprill 21
Thomas, son of John Crooke, of Euxton ... ... „ 30
Agnes, daugh[r] of John Armettriding, of Shaw-green[2].. May 14
Edward, } twins of John Clayton, of Clayton ... ... Aug. 20
Elsabeth,}
Anne, daugh[r] of Raphe Lowe, of Whittle ... ... „ 27
Robert, son of William Marsh, of ffarington ... ... Sept. 3
Anne, } twins of Thomas Waring, at Norbrooke[3] ... „ 19
Elsabeth,}
John, son of William Johnson, of Leyland ... ... „ 24
Michaell, son of John Taylor, of Whittle ... ... Oct. 1
William, son of John Cockar, of Mosse-side ... ... „ 8
William, son of Giles Leaver, of Leyland ... ... „ 16
Robert, son of William Welsh, of Eccleston ... ... Nov. 1
Alexander, son of Thurstan Whittle, of Winnell ... „ 2
William, son of Thomas [John erased] Blundill, of
    ffarington ... ... „ 12
Dorathy, daugh[r] of Robert Wielden, of ffarington ... „ 16
Elsabeth, daughter of Lawrance Whittle, of ffarington. Dec. 3
Jennett, daughter of Raph Winstanley, of Euxton ... „ 17
Edward, son of Robert Sergeant, of Leyland ... ... „ 25
Isabell, daugh[r] of Thomas Parre, of Euxton ... ... „ 29
James, son of William Lee, of Euxton ... ... „ 31
William, son of John Okenshaw, of Euxton ... ... Jan. 10
Sarah, daughter of Hugh Crooke, of Whittle ... ... „ 16
John, son of Richard Wigans, of Whittle ... ... „ 28

---

[1] See note in Baptisms for 1668.

[2] In Euxton township. A small area contained by a loop in the direct road from Croston to Chorley, and within a short distance of the junction of that road with Leyland Lane.

[3] Lies to the N.W. of Leyland township by Bannister Brook. Formerly a residence of a younger branch of the ffaringtons. Afterwards pulled down and reduced to a farm. It still continues a part of the estate.

John, son of Thomas Couper, of Leyland ... ... ffeb. 4
Ellis, son of Ellis Sumner, of Euxton ... ... „ 9
Clemence, daugh^r of William Crichlow, of Whittle ... „ 18
Thomas, son of John Smith, of Ulneswalton ... ...March 10
Lucy,[1] daughter of Thomas Walmersley, of Euxton ... „ 10
Thomas, son of Nicholas Bromiley, of Leyland ... ... „ 17

[Baptisms] 1672.[2]

Mary, daughter of William Woodcock, of Leyland ...March 25
James, son of James ffarington, of Leyland... ... ... „ 29
Elizabeth, daught^r of Roger Dewhurst, of Cuerden ... Ap. 5
Elizabeth, daught^r of Thomas Caulderbank, of Leyland „ 14
William, son of William Clayton, of Cuerden ... ... „ 14
Jane, daugh^r of William Monck, of Leyland ... ... „ 15
William, son of William Waterworth, of Leyland ... „ 17
Margrett, daught^r of John Wright, of Leyland ... ... „ 21
Katharin, daughter of William ffarington, of ffarington „ 28
Margrett, daughter of Thomas Winnell, of Whittle ... „ 28
Anne, daughter of John Pincock, of Euxton ... ...May 12
Mary, daughter of Thomas Pilkinton, of Whittle ... „ 12
Richard, son of John ffidler, of ffarington ... ... „ 27
B. Ellin, daugh^r of Thomas Parker, of Leyland ... ... „ 28
B. William, son of William Southworth, of Leyland ... „ 28
Henry, son of Henry Carre, of papermilne[3] ... ...June 2
Anne, daught^r of Raphe Pincock, of Whittle ... ... „ 5
John, son of Lawrance Garstang, of Euxton ... ... „ 6
Roger, son of John Blakburne, of Cuerden ... ... „ 16
Susan, daughter of Roger Cliffe, of Penwortham ... „ 16
John, son of Thomas Leyland, of Leyland ... ... „ 25
Elanor, daughter of John Martinscroft, of Leyland ... July 11
B. Alice, daughter of Alice Longton, of Cuerden ... „ 14
William, son of Thomas Porter, of Leyland ... ... „ 21
Roger [William erased], son of William Garstang, of
    Whittle... ... ... Aug. 4
Jennett, daught^r of William Garstang, of Whittle ... „ 11
James, son of William Clayton, of Clayton ... ... „ 18
Elsabeth,[4] daughter of Mr. George ffarington, of Worden Sept. 5

[1] The first appearance of this name.

[2] The transcript for this year is at Chester. It is signed by William Rothwell, Vicar, and the Churchwardens. The writing is clear, although the lines are close together on a long sheet of parchment.

[3] Paper milne. Perhaps at Withnell, where the same industry now flourishes.

[4] Elder daughter of Mr. George ffarington and his wife Elizabeth, daughter of Valentine Whitmore, of Thurstaston, co. Chester, Esq. She died without issue.

Roger, son of Roger Walton, of Mosse-side... ... ... Sept. 8
Jane, daught^r of Richard Walton, of Leyland ... ... „ 15
Katharin, daugh^r of Thomas Whittle, of ffarington ... „ 22
Margrett, daugh^r of William Chetam, of ffarington ... Oct. 20
Anne, daugh^r of Thomas ffishwicke, of Whittle ... ... „ 20
Thomas, son of James Cowper, of Cuerden ... ... „ 27
Elsabeth, daugh^r of Richard Wigans, of Leyland ... Nov. 13
Margrett, daughter of Adam Blakburne, of Cuerden ... „ 17
Abraham, son of Raphe Johnson, of Cuerden ... ... „ 21
Thomas, son of Charles Whitehead, of Leyland ... ... Dec. 1
Thomas, son of Thomas Woodcock, of Whittle ... ... „ 1
Margrett, daugh^r of John Wielden, of Leyland ... ... „ 8
Margery, daught^r of John Clough, of Leyland ... ... „ 15
George, son of Thomas James, of Leyland ... ... „ 22
Margrett, daught^r of John Bradley, of Leyland ... ... „ 22
B. Thomas, son of Jennett Waterworth, of Ulneswalton Jan. 3
John, son of Euan Garner, borne in Euxton ... ... „ 25
William, son of John Okenshaw, of Euxton ... ... „ 26
William, son of Hugh Mayre, of Leyland ... ... ffeb. 2
William, son of Thomas Atkinson, of Walton ... ... „ 9
William, son of Thomas Jackson, of Leyland ... ... „ 15
Alice, daughter of William Lee, of Euxton... ... ... „ 16
Ellis, son of Thomas Waring, of Norbrooke ... ... „ 19
Margrett, daught^r of John Hesketh, of Leyland... ... „ 21
James, son of Alice Parker, of Mosse-side ... ... „ 22
William, son of John Cockar, of Mosse-side ... ... March 2
Alice, daugh^r of Roger Horrocks, of Euxton ... ... „ 9

[Baptisms] 1673.[1]

Elsabeth, daughter of Henry Brining, of Whittle ... March 30
Amy, daughter of William Muncke, of Leyland... ... „ 31
Esther, daught^r of John Blakburne, of Euxton ... ... Ap. 1
[[2]Lawrance, son of Alexander Breres, of Whittle ... „ 3]
James, son of John Roscowe, of Euxton ... ... „ 13
Alice, daughter of Henry Smith, of Euxton ... ... „ 13
Mary, daughter of Richard Whittle, of ffarington ... „ 13
George, son of George Bury, of Winnell [for Withnell] „ 13
Abraham, son of Richard Clough, of Leyland ... ... „ 27
Thomas, son of Raphe Lowe, of Whittle ... ... May 8
John, son of Christopher Sumner, of Leyland ... ... „ 15

---

[1] The transcript for this year is at Chester. It is signed by William Rothwell, Vicar; and the names of the four Churchwardens are given.

[2] See before Christnings, 1682.

Ellin, daught^r of Richard Jackson, of Cuerden ... ... May 20
Elsabeth, daught^r of Edward Tilsley, of Euxton ... „ 25
Hannah, daught^r of William Miller, of Ulneswalton ... „ 27
Mary, daught^r of Richard Whittle, of Leyland ... ... June 1
William, son of Richard Broxop, of Euxton ... ... „ 22
John, son of John Crooke, of Euxton ... ... „ 22
James,⎫ twins of Richard Nelson, of Leyland ... ... July 7
Ellin, ⎭
Isaack, son of William Sharrok, of Euxton ... ... „ 28
Euan, son of Adam Eastham, of ffarington ... ... Aug. 3
Margery, daught^r of Richard Higgison, of Whittle ... „ 3
Jenett, daught^r of Henry Waring, of Euxton ... ... „ 17
John, son of William Walmersley, of Euxton ... ... „ 17
Richard, son of William Wright, of Euxton ... ... „ 17
Alexander, son of John Parke, of Leyland ... ... „ 24
Margery, daught^r of Richard ffarington, of ffarington... „ 24
Anne, daughter of John Baron, of Euxton ... ... Sept. 7
Elsabeth, daught^r of Thomas Balshaw, of Walton ... „ 7
Richard, son of John Hodson, of Euxton ... ... „ 21
Jeremy, son of Thomas Clough, of Leyland ... ... Oct. 26
William, son of Robert Sergeant, of Leyland ... ... Nov. 2
Jennett, daught^r of John Almon, of Leyland ... ... „ 2
Richard, son of Giles Leauer, of Leyland ... ... „ 2
John, son of Thomas Bowlin, of Charnock ... ... „ 9
John, son of Lawrance Garstang, of Euxton ... ... „ 14
John, son of John Smith, of Whittle ... ... „ 18
Thomas, son of William Whaley, of Euxton ... ... „ 30
John, son of Robert Hunt, of Cuerden ... ... „ 30
Samuell, son of William Baxenden, of Exton ... ... Dec. 25
Thomas, son of Richard Godman, of Mosse-side ... „ 28
Robert, son of Raph Winstanley, of Euxton ... ... Jan. 11
John, son of John Slator, of Euxton ... ... ffeb. 15
Thomas, son of Edmund Balshaw, of Leyland ... ... „ 15
William, son of Mr. John Woodcocke,[1] of Cuerden ... „ 22
Margrett, daught^r of John Wigans, of Cuerden ... ... March 8

---

[1] Mr. John Woodcock was of Woodcock Hall (or Crowtrees as it was called by Dr. Keurden), where his family had been seated for many generations. According to the learned antiquary just quoted, the property in Cuerden had been in the possession of the Woodcocks for "400 or 500 years." The house and land (which lie upon the left hand of the high road between Leyland and Preston) are now owned by T. T. Townley Parker, Esq., of Cuerden Hall. Mr. John Woodcock, here named, was a burgess at the Preston Guilds of 1682, 1702, and 1722. For an account of this family see Abram's *History of Blackburn*, pp. 733-4. Also under "Seth Woodcock," in the list of Vicars of Leyland in the Introduction.

[Baptisms] 1674.[1]

William, son of John Sumner, of Lostock[2] ... ... Aprill	12
James, son of Thomas Couper, of Leyland ... ... „	12
Nicholas, son of Mr. John Rishton, Curate of Eccleston, now living in Leyland[3] ... ... „	27
Robert, Anne, } twins of Thomas Sumner, of Leyland ... ... May	10
Ellin, daught[r] of Thomas Pilkinton, of Whittle ... ... „	17
Elsabeth, daught[r] of Raphe Pincock, of Whittle... ... „	17
Jennett, daught[r] of John Wielden, of Leyland ... ... „	24
[4 Priscilla, daughter of Alexander Breres, of Whittle ... June	6]
Katharin, daught[r] of Henry Waterworth, of Ulneswalton „	7
Elsabeth, daught[r] of Richard Whittle, of ffarington ... „	7
Elsabeth, daught[r] of Robert Harrison, of Leyland ... „	9
Seth, son of Nicholas Bromily, of Leyland ... ... „	14
Elsabeth, daught[r] of Roger ffiswick, of Winnell ... ... „	7
Alice, daught[r] of Raph Walmersley, of Winnell... ... „	16
James, son of Roger Dewhurst, of Cuerden... ... ... „	24
John, son of John Martinscroft, of Leyland... ... ... „	28
Edward, son of Mr. John ffarnworth,[5] of Euxton ... July	4
Richard, son of William Cowper, of Cuerden ... ... „	16
Richard, son of John Crooke, of Euxton ... ... „	19
Thomas, son of Edward Longton, of Whittle ... ... Aug.	2
George, son of William Garstang, of Whittle ... ... „	9
Thomas, son of Thomas Walmersley, of Euxton ... „	16
Anne, daugh[r] of John Clayton, of Clayton ... ... „	16

[1] The transcript for this year is at Chester. It is signed by the Vicar and Church-wardens.

[2] The Sumner family must have been of some consequence, or at least of considerable wealth at this period, for, while William ffarington, of Worden, Esq. (the High Sheriff of 1636), and his son, Mr. William ffarington, were fined for "delinquency," the sums respectively of £536 and £117. 13s. 4d., the Sumners (senior and junior) were fined £805. Among those who wore the "Sheriff's Cloth" in 1636, we find the names of William Somner de Worden [? Steward], William Sumner de Lost: sen., and William Sumner de Lost: jun. These are not included among the "Gentlemen," but probably rank as yeomen or tenant-farmers. In 1622, Wm Sumner (son of John Sumner "de Radom") "servus Willm ffarington Ar" is entered as a foreign burgess at the Preston Guild. In the same year (1622) " Will'm's Sumpner de Lostocke" is sworn and pays a fine of xl. s. upon which his name, together with those of his sons, William and Christopher, are entered.

[3] Vicar of Leyland from 1677 to 1684. See List of Vicars.

[4] See *postea*, Baptisms, 1682.

[5] "Joh'es ffarnworth de Euxton, Gen:" was sworn as a foreign burgess at the Preston Guild of 1662. He appears among the foreign burgesses in 1682 as "Joh'es ffarnworth de Runshaw Gen:" with his sons Edward, John, and Ralph. See also Baptisms, 1676.

James, son of Richard Walton, of ffarington	Aug.	30
Margerie, daughʳ of Ellis Sumner, of Euxton	Sept.	4
Thomasin, daughtʳ of John Bradley, of Leyland ...	„	20
Elsabeth, daughtʳ of John Taylor, of Leyland	„	27
Mary, daughtʳ of John Jackson, of Leyland	„	27
James, son of John Gouden, of Mosse-side...	Oct.	4
Oliuer, son of William Crosse, of Euxton	„	18
William, son of William Winnell, of Whittle	„	25
B. Margrett, daughtʳ of John Blackburne, of Cuerden...	Nov.	11
Martha, daughtʳ of Thomas Holme, of Euxton	„	15
Thomas, son of John Garstang, of Whittle	Dec.	6
Ellin, daughʳ of William Shaw, of Leyland...	„	7
William, son of Wiłł: Clough, of Leyland	„	8
Hannah, daughtʳ of Roger Horrocks, of Euxton ...	„	25
John, son of Henry Eastham, of Cuerden	„	27
Elsabeth, daughtʳ of John Wright, of Leyland ...	Jan.	10
Robert, son of Richard ffarington, of ffarington... ...	„	14
Thomas, son of Euan Garner, of ffarington	„	17
William, son of Thomas Atkinson, of Walton	„	31
William, son of John Cockar, Jun., of Mosse-side ...	„	31
James, son of Roger Walton, of Leyland	ffeb.	2
Roger, son of John Bigans, of Clayton...	„	7
Robert, son of Robert Welsh, of Leyland	„	14
Alice, daughtʳ of William Burscow, of Leyland... ...	„	14
Anne, daughtʳ of Richard Whittle, of Leyland	„	24
Mary, daughtʳ of William Howorth, of Whittle	„	28
Anne, daughtʳ of William Cockar, of Mosse-side ...	March	3
William, son of Richard Jackson, of Cuerden	„	4
Mary, Elsabeth, } twins of William Clayton, of Cuerden ...	„	9
John, son of William Woodcock, of Leyland	„	17
John, son of Richard Hilton, of Euxton	„	21

[Baptisms] 1675.[1]

Christopher, son of Thomas Woodcock, of Whittle	March	25
Ellin, daughtʳ of Thomas Waring, of Norbrook... ...	„	25
William, son of William Clayton, of ffarington ...	April	4
Robert, son of Thomas Martin, of Whittle	„	6
Tomasin, daughtʳ of Raphe Johnson, of Whittle ...	„	18
Alice, daughter of Richard Wigans, of Whittle	„	25
William, son of Thomas Calderbank, of Leyland	May	16

[1] The transcript for this year is at Chester. It is signed by the Vicar Rothwell and the four Churchwardens.

Elizabeth, daught[r] of William ffarington, of ffarington. May 23
Jennett, daught[r] of Thomas Blundill, of ffarington ... „ 23
James, son of John Almon, of Leyland ... ... „ 24
Thomas, son of William Clayton, of Clayton ... ... „ 30
William,[1] son of Mr. George ffarington, of Shawe-hall June 10
William, son of John Smith, of Leyland ... ... „ 27
Margrett, daught[r] of William Parke, of Euxton... ... „ 27
Robert, son of Richard Sumner, of Leyland ... ... July 4
Mary,[2] daught[r] of Mr. Richard ffleetwood, of Leyland „ 12
Mary, daught[r] of Thomas Ditchfield, of Whittle... ... Aug. 22
Margrett, daught[r] of John Hodson, of Euxton ... ... „ 29
Margery, daughter of Roger Cliffe, of ffarington ... „ 29
Thomas, son of Thomas Porter, of Leyland ... ... Sept. 5
Raphe, son of Thomas Longton, of Whittle ... ... „ 5
Elizabeth, daught[r] of John Martinscroft, of Leyland... „ 7
Jane, daught[r] of Lawrance Watmough, of Leyland ... „ 12
Ellin, daughter of William Wright, of Alker[3] in Euxton „ 26
Elizabeth, daughter of William Whaley, in Euxton ... Oct. 3
Anne, daught[r] of John Gerratt, of ffarington ... ... „ 10
Margery, daught[r] of Thomas Sumner, of Leyland ... „ 18
Elizabeth, daught[r] of William Lee, of Euxton ... ... Nov. 7
William, son of Margery Okenshaw ... ... „ 15
Richard, son of William Cowper, of Cuerden ... ... „ 30
Dorathy, daught[r] of William Woodcock, of Euxton ... Dec. 6
William, son of Hugh Waterworth, of Leyland... ... „ 19
John, son of Thomas Sumner, of Leyland ... ... „ 19
William, son of John Wigans, of Cuerden ... ... „ 19
Henry, son of John Okenshaw, of Euxton ... ... „ 25
B. Elsabeth, daught[r] of John Jackson, of Leyland ... „ 26
Anne, daught[r] of George Garstang, of Whittle ... ... Jan. 1
Robert, son of Edmund Balshaw, of Leyland ... ... „ 2
Thomas, son of Edward Sergeant, of Leyland ... ... „ 9

---

[1] William ffarington, Esq., son of Mr. George ffarington and his wife Elizabeth (née Whitmore), succeeded to the Worden estates, in 1715, upon the death of his cousin William (son of Henry ffarington, Esq., "of Worden," Preston Guild Roll, 1682), who had held the headship of the family from March, 1691-2. He married Elizabeth, daughter and sole heir of Dr. James Rufine, of Boulogne, a Huguenot refugee, and became the father of three sons and three daughters. His name is entered as a foreign burgess at Preston Guild in 1682 and 1702.

[2] This lady was buried at Poulton-le-Fylde, November 24, 1698. The father, Mr. Richard ffleetwood, was son and heir of Francis ffleetwood (third son of Sir Paul, of the Rossall line). He married Margaret, d. and h. of Edward ffleetwood, Esq., of Leyland, who was a cadet of the Penwortham family, and settled in Leyland (probably) on account of his marriage with Margaret ffarington. There is an old house near to the Leyland Station which still bears the name of Fleetwood Hall.

[3] A farm just over the Shawe-brook, within a short distance of Shawe-hall (now Worden).

Raphe, son of Roger Brining, of Whittle ... ... Jan. 16
B. Gilbert, son of Gilbert Cowlin & Elsabeth Hough, of
    Whittle ... ... „ 19
[[1]Edmund, son of Alexander Breres, of Whittle ... „ 24]
Margery, daught[r] of William Sharrok, of Euxton ... „ 31
William, son of Richard Higgison, of Whittle ... ... ffeb. 6
Dorathy, daught[r] of William Baxenden, of Euxton ... „ 8
William, son of John Miller, at Werden ... ... „ 12
B. ${Gilbert, \atop Margrett,}$ twins of —— ——, of Euxton ... „ 13
Robert, son of Thomas Cowper, Jun[r] of Leyland ... „ 27
John, son of John Heskett, of Leyland... ... ... „ 26
John, son of John Sumner, of Lostock... ... ... March 2
Abraham, son of William Clough, of Leyland ... ... „ 5
Richard, son of John Parke, of Leyland ... ... „ 12
Vallentine,[2] son of Mr. George ffarington, of Shaw-halle,
    baptized the 26: day of August, 1676.

[This entry is in the handwriting of the person who kept the
Register from Sept. 3rd, 1676, onwards. It has been written at
the bottom of a page where space permitted.]

Cbristenings, 1676.[3]

Elsabeth, daught[r] of William Crooke, of Leyland,
    thatcher... ... ...March 26
Esther, daughter of Robert Garner, of ffarington ... Aprill 2
Roger, son of Hugh Crooke, of Whittle ... ... „ 12
Richard, son of Adam Blakburne, of Cuerden ... ... „ 12
B. Nicholas, son of Nicholas Whittle & Alice Parker, a
    bastard ... ... „ 19
Mary, daught[r] of Raphe Lowe, of Whittle ... ... „ 25
John, son of Richard Nelson, of Leyland ... ...May 1
Sisley, daugh[r] of Christoph[r] Sumner, of Leyland ... „ 11

[1] See *postea*, Baptisms, 1682.

[2] Valentine (younger brother of William ffarington, baptised on June 10th, 1675)
married Agnes, daughter of —— Prickett, of Natland Abbey, co. Westmorland,
by whom he became the father of two sons and two daughters. The eldest son,
Henry, who was Guild Mayor of Preston in 1742, and Alan, who married a daughter
of —— Tyrer, of Liverpool, both died without issue. His eldest daughter, Elizabeth, married Col. Gardiner, of Uttoxeter, co. Stafford, and became the mother of
the first Lord Gardiner. The younger daughter, Sarah, married Nicholas Starkie,
of Riddleston, and had issue. Valentine ffarington was entered with his father and
brother at the Preston Guild of 1682. He is described as M.D. and "of Preston" in
Foster's *Lancashire Pedigrees*.

[3] The transcript for this year is at Chester. It is signed by Edmond Thornley,
p'sent Minister of Leyland.

John, son of Mr. John ffarnworth,[1] of Euxton [Inserted] May ye 30
William, son of Edward Tilsley, of Euxton   ...   ... June   4
Nathaneel, son of Thomas James, of Leyland ...   ...   „   18
Stephen, son of William Tilson, of Euxton...   ...   ... July   9
Margrett, daught[r] of Nicholas Woomell, of Wheelton..   „   15
John, son of William Waterworth, of Leyland ...   ...   „   16
Richard, son of Thomas Winnell, of Whittle   ...   ...   „   16
Richard, son of Richard ffarington, of ffarington   ... Aug.. 20
Cicely, daughter of Richard Jackson, of Cuerden   ...   „   24

[There is a change in the handwriting at this point.[2]]

John, son of James ffiswick, of Whittle...   ...   . Sept.   3
Elsabeth, daught[r] of John Bradley, of Leyland ...   ...   „   17
Francis, daught[r] of John Clough, of Leyland   ...   ...   „   24
A son of Ralph Crichlow, of Euxton ...   . Oct.   8
Mary, the daughter of Will: Cross, of Euxton ...   ...   „   26
Alice, daught[r] of Thomas Pilkinton, of Whitle ...   ...   „   29
John, son of Roger Dewhurst, of Cuerden ...   . Nov.   5
Elsabeth, daughter of John Taylor, of Walton in ley
   dayle   ...   .   „   12
Jane, daughter of Edward Clough, of Leyland ...   ...   „   14
Joh[n], son of John Wright, of Leyland   ...   .   „   19
Robert, son of John Somner, of Cuerden ...   .   „   19
Alice, daughter of John Smith, of Whittle ...   .   „   26
John, son of William Borscow, of Leyland ...   . Dec.   3
Elizabeth, daughter of John ffarington, of ffarington ...   „ 21 (?)
John, son of Richard Sharples, of Leyland...   ...   ... Jan.   7
John, son of John Charnocke, of Cuerden ...   .   „   14
Elsabeth, daughter of Thomas Clithero, of Euxton ...   „   14
Anne, daughter of James Hough, of Leyland   ...   ...   „   16
Thomas, son of John Jackson, of Leyland ...   .   „   28

---

[1] A member of this family, "Mistress Ann ffarnworth, of Euxton," was married at Leyland, on 2 Aug., 1670, to Mr. Thos. Rishton, of Preston. Again, in 1672, July 2, was buried Mr. Raphe ffarnworth, of Euxton. A Mr. John ffarnworth appears as one of the four gentlemen appointed by Commission from the Exchequer Court to take the depositions (at Leyland) of witnesses summoned in the Leyland Hall case (Attorney-General *v.* William Cross, gent., and Gaynor Jones, widow), April 6, 1687. From an entry of a burial in 1692, the ffarnworths (or one of them, Edward) appear to have been resident at Runshaw Hall, in Euxton. Mary, d. of Edw: ffarnworth, of Runshaw, gent., is mentioned in the Patten pedigree as the wife of William Patten (born 1700), who settled in London. Probably this Edward was the son of John named above. In 1715 Edwd. ffarnworth, of Euxton, registered his estate as a Roman Catholic. In the pedigree of Crosse, of Shawe Hill, Dorathy Crosse was married to Edward ffarnworth, and the burial of Dorathy ffarnworth is entered at Leyland on Feb. 18, 1720.

[2] See after March 12, 1675, for a baptism which took place on Aug. 26th of this year.

[Margrett, daughter of John Taylor, Leyland, baptized Jan. 26]
[Written along the inner edge of the page.]

Ellin, daughter of William Cocker, of Leyland ... ... „ 28
Thomas, son of Thomas Somner, of Leyland ... ... „ 30
Alice, daughter of Euan Garner, of ffarington ... ... Feb. 4
Jane, daughter of Thomas Hoome, of Euxton ... ... „ 6
Jane, daughter of Richard Somner, of Mosse-side ... „ 8
William, son of Richard Whittle, of Leyland ... ... „ 18
Bridgett, daughter of Henry Waterworth, of Ulnes-
walton ... ... March 4
William, sone of John Athurick, of ffarington ... ... „ 4
Thomas, } twins of Thomas Whittle, of ffarington,
Katharin, }
March 29 [1677].
Thomas, sonn of John Cocker, Junior, of Mosse-side,
Aprill 1 [1677].

[Baptisms] 1677.[1]

Ann, daught^r of Richard Cliffe, of Leyland ... ... Aprill 1
Richard, son of Thurstan Sharrock, of Euxton ... ... „ 8
Thomas, son of fild, of ffarington ... ... „ 15
[[2]Alexander, son of Alexander Breres, of Whittle ... „ 18]

[There is at this point an entire change in the style of hand-writing. This continues only for the next nine entries, but is observable again in May, 1678, when it goes on for a period of nine months, with one or two exceptional entries. There were evidently two persons registering the baptisms, &c., during the next vicariate, as though there were a curate-in-charge and a vicar occasionally in residence. From an old MS. now in the hands of the Rev. T. R. Baldwin, we learn that the name of the curate in Vicar Rishton's time was Edmund Thornley, and that he was living as late as 1720. Vicar Rishton was certainly resident at Bury at the time of his death, and thus the modern running hand which commences with the next entry may be his. There is a great similarity, however, between this writing and that which occurs during the vicariate of George Walmesley, who was certainly resident during the whole period of his incumbency. The conclusion, therefore, is not very definite.]

Elizabeth, daught^r of Will: Woodcock, of Euxton ... May 10

[1] The transcript for this year is at Chester. It is signed by "Edmond Thornley, Curat," and the names of the Churchwardens are given (not signatures).
[2] See *postea*, Baptisms, 1682.

Helen, daught[r] of Richard Balshaw, of Goldenhill,[1]
carp: ... ... May 10
John, son of John Crook, of Euxton ... ...(*sic*) „ 0:6
Thomas, son of Adam Balshaw, of Euxton... ... ... 0:20
Richard, son of Thomas Martin, of Whittle... ... ... June 0:5
. . . Daught[r] of Thomas ffarington, of ffarington ... July i.
. . . Daught[r] of John Marsh, of Leyland ... ... „ 8
Ellis, son of Robert Sumner, of Ulneswalton 0:25
Mary, daught[r] of Thomas Winnell, of Whittle 0:29
B. James, son of James Pendlebury & Sison Cocker,
a Bastard   ... ... Sep. 30
William, sonn of William ffarington, of ffarington ... Oct. 21
Thomas, sonn of Robert Hunt, of Cuerden... ... ... „ 28
Roger, son of William Clayton, of Cuerden... ... ... Nov. 4
Richard, son of William Wright, of Euxton ... ... „ 11
[[2]Roger Bowlin, son of Thomas, Nov. 20 ... ... „ 20]
Annas, daught[r] of John Tomlinson, of ffarington ... „ 25
James, son of Roger Horrocks, of Euxton ... ... „ 30
Susan, daught[r] of Roger Pilkinton, borne in ye town-
shipe of Leyland, Dec. ye 2 ... ... Dec. 4
William, son of William Wright, of Euxton ... ... „ 5
William, son of Thomas Woodcock, of Whittle .. ... „ 9
Katharin, daughter of Roger Walton, of Leyland
Moss-side   ... ... „ 16
Clamance, daughter of Lawrance Watmore, of Leyland „ 23
Ann, daughter of William Willson, of Leyland ... ... „ 23
Ellin, daughter of William Garrett, of Cuerden ... ... „ 30
Robert, son of Richard Hillton, of Euxton... ... ... Jan. 13
Roger, son of Thomas Bowlin, of Euxton, November
ye 20 ... ...[Nov. 20]
B. Ciceley, daughter of Jane Somner, of Mosside ... Jan. 16
Henry, son of Lawrance Garstang, of Euxton ... ... „ 20
Ellizabeth, daughter of John Somner, of Leyland ... „ 20
William, son of William Clough, of Layland ... ... „ 27
Edward Clayton, son of William Clayton, of Clayton [blank]
Ciceley, daughter of John Jackson, of Cuerden ... ... Feb. 3
John, son of John Hodson, of Cowbick[3] [Cawbeck] in
Euxton ... ... „ 5

[1] Golden Hill was an estate formerly the possession of a family named Worden, and the name was afterwards applied to the whole district lying along the northern boundary of Leyland township, where it touches Farington.

[2] See in January next below.

[3] Cawbeck, primarily the name of a tributary of the River Yarrow, here denotes a farmhouse, &c., which lies about half a mile to the north of the Yarrow and at an equal distance to the south of Runshaw Moor.

Ellizabeth, daughter of Richard Tootell, of Whittle ... Feb. 24
Hugh, son of Hugh Crooke, of Whittle ... ... March 12
Thomas, son of Richard Sharples, of Leyland ... ... „ 24
Ellizabeth, daughter of Thomas Porter, of Leyland ... „ 24
Ann, daughter of John Jackson, of Leyland Lane,
March 29 [1678].

[Baptisms] 1678.[1]

Ann,[2] daughter of John Somner, of Lostock of Leyland Ap. 23
Jane, daughter of John Woodcock, of Cuerden ... ... May 1
Christopher, son of Robert Woodroof, of Wheelton ... „ 12
James, son of Richard Wiggans, of Whitle ... ... „ 19
Ann, daughter of James Clayton, of Clayton ... ... „ 19
Jane, daughter of John fforshaw, of Leyland ... ... „ 26
Margarett, daughter of Thomas ffarington ... ... June 9
Susanna, daughter of Henry ffell ... ... „ 16
Jane, daughter of William Leigh, of Euxton ... ... „ 16
John, son of John Martinscroft, of Leyland ... ... „ 26
Thomas, son of Roger Sharples ... ... „ 30
Richard, son of John March, of Leyland ... ... July 14
Thomas, son of Samuel Hall, of ffarington... ... ... „ 16
Susan, daughtr of Hugh Waterworth, of Leyland ... Aug. 4
Richard, son of James Hall, of Euxton ... ... „ 11
Elizabeth, daughtr of John Blackburn, of Euxton ... „ 11
Hugh, son of Henry Waterworth, of Ulneswalton ... Sept. 1
Jennett, daughter of Will: Woodcock, of Euxton ... „ 8
Richard, son of John Okenshaw, of Euxton ... ... Oct. 16
Isabel, daughtr of Richard Sumner, of Leyland ... Nov. 5
Andrew, son of John Bradley, of Leyland ... ... „ 10
Elizabeth, daughtr of Christopher Sumnr, of Leyland... „ 13
Elizabeth, daughtr of Henry Sydall, of Croston ... Dec. 1
Margaret, daughtr of Rich: Cliffe, of Leyland ... ... „ 1
John, son of Cuthberd Carr, a traveller... ... ... „ 8
Ellin, daughter of John Parke, of Leyland ... ... „ 12
William, son of Thomas Withnell, of Whittle ... ... „ 22
Jennet,[3] daughtr of Richard Jackson, of Kuerden ... Jan. 5
James, son of James Garrett, of Wheelton ... ... „ 13
Margary, daughter of Ralph Lowe, of Whitle ... ... „ 20
Jeffeory, son of John Taylour, of Whittle ... ... „ 26

[1] The transcript for this year is at Chester. It is signed by Edmond Thornley, "Curat de Leyland." The Churchwarden's names are given.

[2] Elizabeth has been erased, and Ann inserted in different coloured ink.

[3] This word is not clear; it may possibly be Ann.

F

Richard, son of Henry Brining, of Whitle ... ... Feb. 2
Ellin, daughter of John Biggens, of Leyland   ... ... „ 9
Ann, daughter of Ewerd Holmes, of Leyland ... ... „ 23
B. Andrew, son of Margrert Somner, of Ulneswalton... „ 26
Henry, son of Thomas Whalch, of ffarington ... ... March 2
Margreat, daughter of Henry Jackson, of Euxton ... „ 2
William, son of William Baxenden, of Euxton ... ... „ 9
B. Richard, son of Alis Parker, on ye Moss-side ... „ 10
B. Ellnor, daughter of Elleanor Ireland, of Leyland... „ 10
Margret, daughter of William Waterwort, of Leyland „ 16
Thomas, son of Robert Somner, of Ulneswalton ... „ 23
Ann, daughter of James Horneby, of Leyland ... ... „ 23
Lawrance, son of Henry Garstang, of Hepey. [Entered
    after] ... ... „ 21

Christnings, 1679.[1]

Thomas, son of Richard Balshaw, of Leyland ... ...March 30
Ralfe, son of Richard Tootell, of Whittle ... ...Ap. 6
Henry, son of Henry Berchall, of Euxton ... ... „ 6
Ellizabeth, daughter of Euan Garner, of ffarington ... „ 6
John, son of Thurstan Shorrock, of Euxton   ... ... „ 13
Agnus, daughter of Lawrance Tomlinson, of ffarington „ 13
James, son of Roger Dewhurst, of Ceuerden   ... ... „ 20
Ann, daughter of Edward Tidesley, of Euxton ... ... „ 23
Robert, son of Rob (*sic*) Thomas ffarington, of ffarington May 1
Elizabeth, daughter of John Smith, of Leyland ... ... „ 1
Thomas, son of Ralph Crichlow, of Euxton   ... ... „ 4
Mary, daughter of Gilbert Cowlin, of Leyland ... ... „ 4
James, son of Richard Higgison, of Whittle   ... ... „ 11
William, son of John Wright, of Leyland ... ... „ 11
[2]Ellizabeth, daughter of Mr. Richard ffleetwood, of
    Leyland   ... ... „ 13
Thomas, son of Thomas Martin, of Heapey ... ... „ 18
James, son of Richard Husband, of Whittle ... ... „ 25
Joney, daughter of Richard Beardsworth, of penwortham „ 25
Mary, daughter of Georg Woodcock, of Euxton... ... „ 25
Ann,
Dorathy, } daughters of Adam Blackborn, of Ceuerden... June 4
James, son of Thomas Pilkinton, of Whittle ... ... „ 8
Margrett, daughter William Burscow, of Leyland ... „ 8
Ellizabeth, daughter of Thomas Stillson, of Leyland... „ 18

---

[1] The transcript for this year is at Chester. It is signed as in the previous year.
[2] See note on entry of baptism July 12, 1675.

Edward, son of William Woodcock, of Leyland ... ... June 22
Robert, son of Adam Balshaw, of Euxton ... ... „ 29
William, son of William Cross, of Euxton ... ... „ 29
Anna, daughter of John Taylor, of Leyland ... ... „ 29
James, son of Thomas Porter, of Leyland ... ... July 6
Ralph, son of Mr. John ffarnworth,[1] of Euxton ... ... Aug. 15
Allis, daughter of John Allmond, of Leyland ... ... „ 17
Ellizabeth, daughter of James Hough, of Leyland ... „ 24
Allis, daughter of James Garstang, of Whittell ... ... Sept. 7
Jane, daughter of Ralph Pincock, of Whitel ... ... „ 7
William, son of Thomas ffarington, of Leyland ... ... „ 25
Ann, daughter of Raph Cooper, a travaler ... ... Oct. 5
Adam, son of Thomas Somner, taylor, of Leyland ... „ 12
Jane, daughter of Thomas Haddock, of Penwortham... „ 12
Anna, daughter of Richard Whittell, of Leyland ... Nov. 2
Ann, daughter of Adam Eastom, of Walton in le dale „ 14
William, son of John Crook, of Euexton ... ... „ 16
William, son of Roger Sharples, of Leyland ... ... „ 30
- Nicholas, son of James Brimala, of Leyland ... ... Dec. 14
John, son of William Bury, a traualer ... ... ffeb. 29
B. Thomas, son of Thomas Southworth, of Leyland ... „ 29
Jane, daughter of Thomas Chrichlow, of Exton ... ... March 7
Margret, daughter of Nicolas Whittle & Ellin, his wife,
   of Leyland ... ... „ 14
B. Ellin, daughter of Allis ffarington and John Hoole,
   both of ffarington ... ... „ 14
John, son of Robert Walsh, of Leyland ... ... „ 21
Gilbert, son of Richard Lancaster, of Clayton ... ... ffeb. 10
[[2]Mathyas, son of Alexander Breres, of Whittle ... „ 24]

[Baptisms] 1680.[3]

William, son of John Garrett, of Leyland ... ... Ap. [blank]
Jane, daughter of William Wright, of Euxton ... „ [blank]
Ann, daughter of James Marsden, of Hepey ... ... Ap. 9
Georg, son of William Shaw, of Leyland ... ... „ 11
B. William, son of Jenat Waterworth, of Ulneswalton.. „ 18

---

[1] This entry is in the modern hand referred to in the note "May, 1677." It has also been written after the following one, for the long strokes overlap in several places. Mr. John ffarnworth probably resided at Runshaw Hall. (See similar entries in earlier years.)

[2] See *postea*, Baptisms, 1682.

[3] The transcript for this year is at Chester. Signed as in previous year, but only three names of Churchwardens given.

Allis, daughter of John Cocker, of Moss-side ... ... May 2
Katerin, daughter of Thomas Longton, of Whittel ... „ 23
Jane, daughter of John Jackson, of Leyland ... ... July 4
William, son of Richard Hilton, of Euxton ... ... „ 25
Eward, son of Thomas Woodcock, of Whittle ... ... „ 25
B. John, son of Andrew Stones, of Leyland, Baptised
ye 24 day of December, 1683.[1]
William, son of William Mackrill, Taylor, of Leyland... Aug. 1
[William, son of John Martinscroft, of Leyland ... ... „ 22]
John, son of John fforshaw, of Leyland ... ... „ 29
Thomas, son of John Atkinson, of ffarington ... ... Sept. 12
Andrew, son of John Hesketh, of Leyland ... ... „ 12
John, son of Edward Sargent, of Leyland ... ... „ 26
Jane, daughter of John Bradley, of Leyland ... ... Oct. 17
[2]William, son of John Martinscroft, of Leyland ... ... Aug. 22
Margrett, daughter of James Cheetham, of ffarington... Nov. 7
Thomas, son of Thomas Cletherro, of Euxton ... ... „ 21
Edmond, son of William Woodcock, of Leyland ... „ 28
Dorathy, ye daughter of James Gibbans, of Leyland... Dec. 12
Margret, ye daughter of John Biggins, of Leyland ... „ 19
Joshaf, son of Jane Craskill, of Longton, a bastard ... „ 22
Ralph, son of Robert Hunt, of Cuerden ... ... „ 25
Georg, son of William Clayton, of Clayton ... ... „ 26
William, son of James Hornby, of Leyland... ... ... Jan. 2
Christopher, son of John Somner, of Leyland ... ... „ 2
Ellizabeth, daughter of John Somner, of Leyland ... „ 2
Mary, ye daughter of William ffarington, of Leyland... „ 9
Agnus, daughter of Edward Holmes, of Leyland ... „ 16
Mary, daughter of Thurstan Sharrock, of Euxton ... „ 25
Henry, son of James Halle, of Euxton ... ... „ 30
William, son of Gilbert Cowlin, of Leyland... ... ... Feb. 6
Elizabeth, daughter of Andrew Stones, of Leyland ... „ 6
Margaret, daughter of John Sumner, of Noock,[3] in
Leyland ... ... „ 13
John, son of James Brimale, of Leyland ... ... „ 27
Mary, daughter of Thomas ffarington, of Leyland ...March 13
Ellizabeth, daughter of John Giller, of ffarington ... „ 20
Ellin, daughter of Timathy Wardle, of Whittle ... ... „ 27

---

[1] Crowded in at the bottom of the page. Entered also in proper place. Hand-writing the same.

[2] Inserted above.

[3] Nook, a farm at the extreme south-west corner of Leyland township, in the angle formed by the Hollins brook and the River Lostock. It is approached from Leyland Lane. A family of this name has held possession until recently.

[Baptisms] 1681.[1]

William, son of Henry ffell, of Leyland	[March]	28
Josaph, son of Robert Boulton, of Winnell ... ... Ap.		1
Georg, sone of William Baxenden, of Euxton	„	3
Richard, son of Ellis Somner, of Leyland	„	3
Ann, daughter of William Lee, of Euxton	„	17
B. Ellin, daughter of John Wiggans, of Heapey ...	[blank]	
William, son of Ralph Chrichlow, of Euxton ... ... May		1
William, son of Roger Walton, of Leyland, Aprill yᵉ 4, 1681 ... ...[Ap.		4]
Robert, son of Thomas ffarington, of ffarington ... ... May		15
Hugh, son of William Woods, of Winnell	„	15
Kattering, daughter of Richard Jackson, of Cuerden ...	„	15
B. William, son of Allis Parker, of Leyland	„	15
Adam, son of Richard Cliffe, of Leyland ... ...June		19
Peter, son of William Shaw, of ffarington	„	29
Ellizabeth, daughter of Richard ffarington, of ffarington... ... ...July		6
Ellin, daughter of William Pincock, of Euxton	„	10
Jane, daughtʳ of Hugh Watterworth, of ffarington ...	„	10
Ann, ye daughter of Lawrance Croft, Juneor, of Whittle	„	13
Christopher, son of Christopher Somner, of Leyland... Aug.		14
B. Josaph, son of Ann Charnock, of Ulneswalton ...	„	14
William, son of William Burscow, of Leyland	„	17
Roger, son of Roger Sharples, of Leyland ... ... Sept.		1
. . . , son of Robert Woodroofe, of Heapy...	„	4
Robert, ye son of Richard Hilton, of Whittle ... ... Oct.		2
Richard, son of Richard Balshaw, of Leyland	„	6
James, son of Hugh Crooke, of Whittle	„	9
Thurstan, son of William Darwin, of Keurden	„	24
Elizabeth, daughter of Lawrance Walmsley, of Whitle	„	24
John, son of John fforshaw, of Leyland	„	16
Allis, the daughter of John Jackson, of Leyland lane... Nov.		13
Allis, the daughter of William Willson, of Leyland ...	„	20
Richard, ye son of John Park, of Leyland	„	24
John, ye son of Adam Balshaw, of Euxton...	„	27
Thomas, ye son of William Jackson, of Whittle... ...	„	27
John, ye son of Thomas Somner, of Leyland, taylor ...	„	28
Thurstane, ye son of Richard Wiggans, of Whittle ... Dec.		4

[1] The transcript for this year is at Chester. It is signed by Edmond Thornley, "Curat de Leyland," and the four Churchwardens.

Ellizabeth, ye daughter of John Garrett, of Leyland ... Dec. 18
Jennet, ye daughter of William Woodcock, of Euxton. „(*sic*) 5

[The above is at the bottom of the page. The next entry is
at the top of the page following, and evidently made long afterwards.—W.S.W.]

Jane, ye daughter of James Hough, of Leyland, ye 19
  ffeb. [no year].
Thomas & Martha, twins of Thurstan fficwick, [*sic*] of
  Withnell, baptised ye 21 May, 1698.

[Here follows the certificate of marriage between Arthur
Ingleby, Esq., and Margerie ffarrington, daughter of William
ffarrington, of Shaw-hall, Esq. This took place, after the civil
form in use at the date of the event (2 January, 1653-4), before
the nearest magistrate, Edward Robinson, Esq., of Buckshaw, in
Euxton. It will be found printed at the commencement of the
entries of marriage.]

Cbrist'ings.

[Irregular entries; probably made in 1681, as the writing
shows no difference in style or appearance. I have inserted each
baptism at the right place in each year. Possibly Alexander
Breres was some official connected with the church, who made
all these entries in 1681.]

Lawrance, son of Alexander Breres,[1] of Whittel... Aprill 3, 1673
Priscilla, daughter of Alexander Breres,of Whittel. June 6, 1674
Edmond, son of Alexander Breres, of Whittle ... Jan. 24, 1675
Alexander, son of Alexander Breres, of Whittle...Aprill 18, 1677
Mathyas, son of Alexander Breres, of Whittle ... Feb. 24, 1679

[Baptisms] 1681 (*continued*).

Richard, ye son of John Hodson, of Euxton   ... ... Dec. 12
John, ye son of Richard Lancaster, of Clayton ... ... Jan. 1
Allis, ye daughter of Richard Balshaw, of Leyland ... „ 8
Georg, son of William Tomson, of Leyland   ... ... Feb. 24
Ellizabeth, daughter of William Cross, Euxton ... ... „ 26
Francis, ye daughter of William Watterworth, of Ley-
  land   ... . „ 26

[1] Entered at the Preston Guild of 1682 as a foreign burgess, "Alex'us Breers, de
Whittle-in-le-Woods, Jur'.," with sons Lawrence, Ed'r'us, Alexander, and Mathias.
He is named as a trustee in the conveyance of Leyland Hall to the Vicars of Leyland,
in 1690. The second son's name is clearly *Edmond* in the Register.

Ann, ye daughter of Edward Tinsley, of Euxton ... March 5
Thomas, ye son of Adam Blackborn, of Cuerden ... „ 18

Cbrist'ings in 1682.[1]

Henry, ye son of Edward Howarth, of Whittle ... ... Ap. 9
Jenet, ye daughter of Nicolas Whittle, of Leyland
Mos-side ... ... „ 9
Ellizabeth, ye daughter of William Willson, a traueller „ 12
Ann & Elizabeth, ye daughters of John Crook, of Euxton „ 16
Ellnor, ye daughter of Richard Nelson, of Leyland ... „ 17
John, son of Henry Chatburn, of Leyland ... ... „ 23
Susan, daughter of Henry Wareing, of Ulneswalton ... „ 27
James, son of William Clough, of ffarington ... ... :, 30
John, son of Thomas Chrichlow, of Euxton ... ... „ 30
Ann, ye daughter of Richard Slaytor, of Leyland ... May 7
Ellin, ye daughter of Lawrance Whittell, of Leyland... „ 16
Ellizabeth, ye daughter of Robert Walsh, of Leyland.. „ 21
Ellizabeth, ye daughter of John Atherton, of Leyland. „ 23
Henry, ye son of Andrew Stones, of Leyland ... ... June 5
Agnus, ye daughter of Thomas Cetham, of ffarington.. „ 18
Susanna, ye daughter of Richard Whittle, of Leyland. July 2
Agnus, ye daughter of Edward Clough, of Leyland ... „ 23
Hugh, ye son of Thomas Morris, of Heapy... Baptised „(*sic*)13
. . . , ye daughter of Thomas Stilson, of Whittell ... „ 30
William, ye son of William Park, of Euxton ... ... Aug. 6
William, ye son of James Low, of Leyland... ... ... „ 20
John, son of James Allon, of Cuerden ... ... Sept. 10
William, son of Robert Somner, of Ulneswalton ... „ 17
Allis, daughter of John Biggans, of Leyland ... ... „ 17

[Bottom of page; next page previously used for Publications
of Marriage, 1655-1656. Also Marriages, 1663. These will be
found printed with the continuous entries of marriages beginning 1664.]

Cbrist'ings, 1682.

Ellizabeth, ye daughter of John Harrison, of Mosside[2]. Sept. 24
Agnus, ye daughter of William ffarington, of Littlewood[3] „ 25

---

[1] Transcript signed as in previous year. Writing poor.

[2] The part of Leyland township west of the River Lostock.

[3] Littlewood, the largest farm in Leyland Hundred. It is situated in the township of Ulneswalton, and is now the property of Miss ffarington, of Worden Hall.
The moiety of Ulneswalton manor has been held by the ffarington family since the
year 1558, when it was purchased by William ffarington, Esq., from Sir Anthony
Browne, his kinsman, who, in turn, had received it in 1551 by grant from the Crown.

Allis, ye daughter of Timothy Wardle, of Whittle ... Sept. 29
Ralph, ye son of Ralph Pincock, of Whittle ... ... Nov. 5
Ellizabeth, ye daughter of James Gibbans, of Leyland Dec. 2
Mary, ye daughter of Charles Cherchin, a trauerler ... „ 10
John, ye son of Thomas ffell, of Whittle ... ... „ 17
Jane, ye daughter of James Hornby, of Leyland ... „ 31
Jane, ye daughter of Ellis Somner, of Leyland ... ... Jan. 11
Robert, ye son of James Cocker, of Clayton ... ... „ 21
Thurstan, son of Thomas Woodcock, of Whittle ... „ 21
Ellizabeth, ye daughter of Lawrance Watmough,
     Leyland ... ... „ 24
Ellizabeth, ye daughter of James Cheetham, of ffarington „ 28
Sarah, ye daughter of Henry Berchall [written thus,
     Berᶜhall], of Exton ... ... ffeb. 4
Ann, ye daughter of William Wright, of Alker[1] in
     Euxton ... ... „ 5
William, ye son of Thomas Porter, of Leyland ... ... „ 18
Ann, ye daughter of John Rachatt, of Leyland ... ... „ 18
William, ye son of John Wright, of Leyland ... ... „ 25
Allis, ye daughter of John Citherro, of Euxton ... ... „ 25
Martha, ye daughter of John Martinscroft, of Leyland March 4
Richard, ye son of Ralph Cross, of Leyland ... ... „ 4
Ellizabeth, daughter of Hugh Woodcock, of Euxton.
     [Bottom of page]... ... ... „(*sic*) 2
Susana, ye daughter of Richard ffarington, of ffarington,
                                        Baptised Jan. 17
Isabell, ye daughter of William Woods, of Winnell ... March 18
Agnus, ye daughter of John Bradley, of Leyland ... „ 18

[Baptisms] 1683.[2]

Edward, yᵉ son of William Woodcock, of Leyland ... March 25
Anna, ye daughter of Thomas ffarington, of ffarington... „ 27
Robert, ye son of Richard Somner, of Leyland ... ... Ap. 1
Edward, ye son of John Berdsworth, of ffarington ... „ 1
Gilbert, ye son of Gilbert Cowlin, of Leyland ... ... „ 8
Richard, ye son of Georg Woods, of Euxton ... ... „ 22
Margaret, ye daughter of Richard Balshaw, senior, of
     Leyland ... ... „ 22
John, son of William Bancks, of Leyland ... ... May 13
Susana, ye daughter of Richard Parker, of ffarington... June 24
Richard, ye son of William Clough, of ffarington ... July 1

---

[1] A farm to the south-west of Shaw Hall, and within a very short distance of it.
[2] No transcript for this year now at Chester.

James, ye son of Thomas Longton, of Whittle ... ... July 29
Allis, ye daughter of John Jackson, of Cuerden ... ... ,, 29
Jeffery, ye son of John Taylor, of Heapey ... ... Aug. 12
Allis, ye daughter of James Garstang, of Whittle ... Sept. 2
Ellin, ye daughter of John Garret, of ffarington ... ... ,, 2
Lawrance, son of Lawrance Croft, of Whittle ... ... ,, 23
Ellizabeth, daughter of Lawrance Croft, [of] Whittle... ,, 23
John, ye son of John Somner, of Leyland ... ... ,, 23
William, son of John Atherton, wheelewright, Leyland ,, 26
Margery, ye daughter of John Johnson, of Hepey ... ,, 30
John, ye son of John Allmon, of Leyland-lane ... ... Oct. 7
Ellin, ye daughter of John Cocker, of Leyland ... ... ,, 14
Allis, ye daughter of Roger Horrocks, of Euxton ... ,, 14
Jennet, ye daughter of Adam Blackborn, of Kuerden... ,, 28
William, ye son of Thomas Bomber, of Euxton... ... Nov. 4
Mary, ye daughter of James Halle, of Euxton ... ... ,, 18
Mary, ye daughter of William Baxenden, of Euxton... Dec. 9
[¹John, son of Andrew Stones, of Leyland, baptised ... ,, 24]
Thomas, ye son of William Burscow, of Leyland ... ,, 25
Thomas, son of Thomas ffarington, of Leyland ... ... ,, 25
Mary, ye daughter of Hugh Watterworth, of ffarington ,, 30
Jane, ye daughter of Robert Walsh, of Leyland ... ... ,, 30
Margaret, ye daughter of Edward Holms, of Leyland.. Jan. 6
John, ye son of William Wilden, of ffarington ... ... ,, 20
Ann, ye daughter of John Cowper, of Leyland ... ... ,, 20
Richard, ye son of Richard Lancaster, of Clayton ... ,, 27
Robert, ye son of Edward Howorth, of Whittle ... ... Feb. 3
James, ye son of John fforshaw, of Leyland... ... ... ,, 10
Thurstan, ye son of Thurstan Sharrock, of Exton ... ,, 24
Margret, ye daughter of Roger Sharples, of Leyland ... March 2
Thomas, ye son of John Park, of Leyland ... ... ,, 9
Samuell, ye son of William garnord, of Kuerden ... ,, 9
Jane, ye daughter of Thomas Jackson, of Kuerden ... ,, 9
Allis, ye daughter of Will: Tomson, of Leyland... ... ,, 9
Thomas, ye son of John Riding, of Leyland ... ... ,, 13
William, ye son of James Clayton, of Clayton ... ... ,, 16
Sissilla, daughter of James Clayton, of Clayton ... ... ,, 16
Mary, ye daughter of James Armariding (*sic*), of Euxton ,, 23
Henry, ye son of Roger Dewhurst, of Cuerden ... ... ,, 23

¹ See p. 68.

[Baptisms] 1684.[1]

Margeret, ye daughter of Richard Nixon, of Leyland...	Ap.	14
James, ye son of William Darwin, of Cuerden	May	4
Mary, ye daughter of John Ratchet, of Leyland... ...	„	11
Danyel, ye son of William Shaw, of ffarington	„	18
Thomas, ye son of Richard Rose, of Euxton	„	18
Robert,ye son of Robert Prescod,a basterd in Standish par.	„	18
Jennet, ye daughter of Richard Jackson, of Kuerden ...	„	29
James, ye son of, & Ellizabeth, daughter of Thomas Martin, Whittle	„	29
Adam, ye son of Richard Cliffe, of Leyland	June	8
Thomas, ye son of Henry Wareing, of Leyland	„	8
Jannet, ye daughter of Thomas Calderbank, of Euxton	„	8
John, ye son of Richard Bromely, of Leyland	„	8
Ellizabeth, ye daughter of Richard Balshaw, o'th goulden hill	„	29
Jane, ye daughter of Ralph Whittell, of Whittle... ...	July	6
Ellin, ye daughter of James Clayton, of ffarington ...	„	6
Thomas, ye son of Henry Eastham, of Leyland... ...	„	20
Ellizabeth, ye daughter of Richard Whittell, of Leyland	„	27
Thomas, ye son of Henry Chatburn, of Leyland ...	Aug.	10
Thomas, ye son of Edward Whittle, of Leyland... ...	„	10
Ellin, ye daughter of William Ashton, of Kuerden ...	„	24
William, ye son of John Atherton, Leyland	„	26
Ellin, ye daughter of Thomas Nowell, of Leyland ...	„	31
Ann, ye daughter of John Garret, of Leyland	„	31
Georg, ye son of Thomas Clitherrow, of Euxton... ...	Sept.	28
B. Ellizabeth, ye daughter of Edward Howorth, of Whittle	Oct.	5
Ann, ye daughter of John Harrison, of Lanckester prish.	„	5
B. Margret,ye daughter of Margret Sharples,of Leyland	„	11
Christopher, son of Thomas Somner, of Leyland, born 6, Baptised	„	12
Ann, ye daughter of William Cowlin, of Leyland ...	„	18
Richard, ye son of William Jackson, of Whittle	Nov.	9
Georg,} Allis, } twins of Richard Hillton, of Whittle	„	16
Ellizabeth, daughter of William Parke, of Euxton ...	„	16
William, ye son of Robert ffoster, of Euxton	„	23
Thomas, ye son of Lawrance Allmond, of ffarington...	„	30
Ellizabeth, ye daughter of John Ockenshaw, of Euxton	Dec.	7

[1] Transcript signed by Geo: Walmsley, Vic: de Leland, and Churchwardens. Writing clear.

William, ye son of William Wilson, of Leyland Mos-side Dec. 14
Mary, daughter of James Hough, of Leyland ... ... „ 14
William, ye son of Thomas Low, of Euxton ... ... „ 21
Robert, ye son of Robert Torner, of Leyland ... ... „ 25
Anna, ye daughter of John Marsh, of Euxton ... ... „ 26
Allis, ye daughter of Robert Somner, of Usewalton ... Jan. 4
. . . , ye daughter of James Bromiley, of Leyland ... „ 11
Roger, ye son of John Woodcock, of Euxton ... ... „ 19
Thomas, ye son of Thomas Darwin, of Cuerden... ... „ 25
Allis, ye daughter of Andrew Stones, of Leyland ... „ 25
Ellin, ye daughter of Thomas Chetham, of ffarington.. „ 25
Prissilla, ye daughter of Richard Balshaw, of Leyland. Feb. 5
Henry, ye son of John Berdsworth, of ffarington ... „ 8
Thomas, ye son of Ellis Somner, of Leyland ... ... „ 19
Ellizabeth, ye daughter of John Stuard, a traveller ...March 29
Mary, ye Daughter of S^r Ch: Hoghton[1] of Hoghton,
Bart., March ye 19th, 1684. [Inserted later.]

Cbrist'ings in 1685.[2]

Kattering, ye daughter of Richard Nellson, of Leyland Aprill 1
Ellizabeth, ye daughter of Henry Croft, of Heapy ... „ 17

[There is a change in the handwriting at this point. The entries which follow are in a small hand, of quite modern appearance, and seem to be the work of a rapid writer. The ink is pale and, in some places, much faded.]

Izabel, ye daughter of James Whitehead, of Macclesfield, in Cheshire ... ... May 17
Thomas, ye son of John Bradley ... ... „ 31
Margaret, ye daughter of Wm Woodcock, of Leland ... June 4
. . . , S: of Tho: ffarington, of Leyland ... ... Aug. 7
Anne, ye D: of John Forshaw, of Leyland Lane ... „ 23

---

[1] Sir Charles Hoghton (4th baronet) was Knight of the Shire for co. Lancaster in the Parliaments of 1679-1681, 1681, and 1688-9. He died at Hoghton Tower, June 10, 1710, aged 66 years, and was buried at Walton. Lady Hoghton was the eldest daughter of John Skeffington, Viscount Massarene. This marriage took place in 1676 and the lady died on the 30th of April, 1732. Some of the children of this family may be conveniently noticed here. On March 19th, 1684-5, was baptised Mary, who died at Chester, Sep. 19, 1710, unmarried. On July 23, 1686, Cordelia, who became the wife of Robert Davie, of York. On Oct. 7, 1687, Skeffington, who died unmarried, Feb. 8, 1768, and was buried at Walton, Feb. 11th. On Jan. 29, 1688-9, Hannah, who (apparently) married Samuel Crook, gent., of Crook in Whittle. N.B. This last entry has hitherto been mistaken for "Hugh." The word, however, is perfectly distinct. Others occur in later years.

[2] Transcript signed by the Churchwardens only.

Alice, ye D: of Wᵐ Wright, of Alcar ... ... Sept. 24
Andrew, ye S. of Wᵐ Gerrard, of Euxton ... ... Oct. 23
John, ye S. of George Dawson, of Leyland ... ... „ 25
John, ye S. of Richard Nickson, of Leyland ... ... Nov. 3
Jane, ye D. of . . . Woods, of Euxton ... ... „ 5
Richard, ye son of John Sumner, of Lostock[1] ... ... „ 23
William, ye S. of John Hunt, of Keurden ... ... „ 29
Margaret, ye D. of John Cooper, of Leland... ... ... „ 29
Margaret, ye D. of Wᵐ Crosse, of Euxton ... ... „ 29
Alice, ye D. of Lawrance Croft, of Whittle... ... ... „ 29
Anne, ye D. of Roger Sharples, jun., of Leland ... ... Dec. 6
Christopher, ye S. of Tho: Nowell, of Leland ... ... „ 13
Jennet, ye D. of John Johnson, of Heapy ... ... „ 13
Ellen, ye D. of John Brewer, of Leland ... ... Jan. 3
Elizabeth, ye D. of Gilbert Cowling ... ... „ 17
Edward, ye S. of Alexander Brears, of Whittle ... ... „ 21
Robert, ye S. of John Whittle, of Leland ... ... „ 28
Henry, ye S. of Tho. Grier, of Leland ... ... „ 31
Jennet, ye D. of Edw: Whittle, of Leyland ... ... Feb. 7
Alice, ye D. of Richard Hilton, of Whittle... ... ... „ 7
Elizabeth, ye D. of Rich: Farrington, of Farington ... „ 3
Jane, ye D. of William Lever, of Leland ... ... „ 14
Katherine, ye D. of Ellis Hasminough, of Samsbury... „ 21
Alice, ye D. of John Almond, of Leland ... ... „ 25
Elizabeth, ye D. of William Pincocke, of Whittle ... „ 28
Thomas, ye S. of John Woodcocke, of Euxton ... ... March 4
Ellenor, ye D. of Wᵐ Wareing, of Farington ... ... „ 4
Elizabeth, ye D. of Timothy Wardle, of Whittle ... „ 7
Edward, ye son of Rich. Parker, of Farington ... ... „ 21
Elizabeth, ye D. of Andrew Stones, of Leland ... ... „ 22
Ellen, ye D. of Richard Nelson, of Leland Lane ... „ (*sic*)2

[Baptisms] 1686.[2]

Jennet, ye D. of Thomas Garstang, of Whittle ... ... Ap. 2
Elizabeth, ye D. of Ralph Whittle, of Whittle ... ... „ 18

---

[1] The river Lostock rises in the Withnell hills to the extreme east of the parish
of Leyland, flowing northward through Heapey and Whittle as far as Bamber Bridge,
when it turns almost due west but very soon alters its course in a southerly direction
and ultimately joins the Yarrow in Croston parish. The Lostock thus forms the
boundary of Leyland parish (roughly speaking) on the east, north, and west. Thus,
farms said to be "by the Lostock" may be on any side of Leyland but the southern.
In this particular instance it would be difficult to say which is intended out of three
families of the same name dwelling by the Lostock, in Cuerden, in Leyland, or in
Ulneswalton.

[2] Transcript imperfect, the bottom part being destroyed by damp. No signatures.

Elizabeth, ye D. of Rich: Somner, of Leland Lane ... Ap. 25
Ciceley, ye D. of Roger Walton ... ... May 9
Elizabeth, ye D. of Rich. Dobson ... ... „ 9
Alice, ye D. of John Stopford ... ... June 8
Margaret, ye D. of Robt Dickenson, of Clayton... ... „ 27
Bridget, ye D. of James Hall, of Euxton ... ... „ 27
Mary, ye D. of Nich: Whittle, of Leland Mossc-side ... „ 27
Henry, ye S. of John Croston, of Whittle ... ... July 4
Cordelia, ye D. of S^r Ch: Hoghton, Bar^t [at bottom of
    page, entered later—same hand] ... ... „ 23
Thomas, ye S. of Will. Gardner, of Keurden [top of
    page] ... ... „ 19
John, ye S. of Geo: Ward, of Leland ... ... „ 25
Ellen, ye D. of   [blank]   of Whittle... ... „ 25
B. Isabel, ye D. of Isabel Lever, of Clayton ... ... Aug. 1
Matthew, ye S. of Tho: Martin, of Whittle ... ... „ 15
Margaret, ye D. of Law: ffish, of Whittle ... ... „ 15
Lawrence, ye S. of John Sumner, de Hollins[1] ... ... „ 29
Ellen, ye D. of James Gibbons ... ... Sept. 5
Susan, ye D. of Wm Shawe, of Farington ... ... „ 8
Elizabeth, ye D. of John Ryding ... ... „ 9
John, ye S. of John Atherton, of Leland ... ... „ 15
Richard, ye son of Rich: Whittle, of Leland ... ... „ 19
Henry, ye S. of Hugh Waterworth, of Farrington ... „ 19
Ciceley, ye D. of Henry Shaw, of Walton-in-le-Dalc... „ 19
Robert, ye S. of Richard Tootell, of Whittle ... ... „ 26
Ellen, ye D. of John Beardsworth, of Farington... ... Oct. 10
Jennet, ye D. of Tho. Watson, of Whittle ... ... „ 10
Elizabeth, ye D. of Thurstan Sharrock, of Euxton ... „ 25
Hannah, ye D. of Tho. Longton, of Whittle ... ... „ 31
John, ye S. of Adam Blakburn (*sic*).
Jane, ye D. of James Brimeley ... ... Nov. 7
B. Jane, ye D. of ... ... „ 7
Thomas, ye S. of John Smith, of Keurden ... ... „ 21
James, ye S. of James Lowe, of Hollins ... ... „ 28
Robert, ye S. of Ellis Somner, of Leland Lane ... ... Dec. 5
Thomas, ye S. of Tho. Harrison, of Euxton ... ... „ 19
Henry, ye S. of Hen. Eastham, of Leland ... ... Jan. 16
Elizabeth, ye D. of Wm Darwin, of Kureden ... ... „ 23
Robert, ye S. of Thomas Nowell, of Leland ... ... „ 30
Anne, ye D. of John Parker, of Euxton ... ... Feb. 2
Thomas, ye S. of James Hornby ... ... „ 6
William, ye S. of James Hough ... ... „ 6

---

[1] A farm at the south-west corner of Leyland township.

Anne, ye D. of John Sumner, de Nooke[1] ... ... Feb. 8
Katherine, ye D. of Wm Clough, of Farington ... ... „ 13
William, ye S. of John Greene, of Leland ... ... „ 14
Margaret, ye D. of James Bullen ... ... „ 20
Jane, ye D. of Rich: Rose, of Euxton ... ... March 1
Jeoffery, ye S. of Wm Ashton, of Kureden ... ... „ 6
Anne, ye D. of Roger Dewhurst, of Keurden ... ... „ 15

[Baptisms] 1687.[2]

Jennet, ye D. of Rich. Balshaw, of Leland ... ...March 28
Thomas, ye S. of Mr. Robert Bicussteth[3] ... ... „ 31
William, ye S. of John Sharrock, of Walton ... ... Ap. 3
Robt, ye S. of John Harrison, a traveller ... ... „ 3
Anne, ye D. of Tho: Sumner, Taylor ... ... „ 10
Margery, ye D. of Rich: Farington, of Far.... ... ... „ 24
James, ye S. of James Sumner, of Leland ... ... May 1
Anne, ye D. of James Allen, a traveller ... ... „ 1
Margaret, ye D. of John Gooden ... ... „ 5
John, ye S. of John Brewer, of Leland... ... ... „ 8
Jane, ye D. of John Gerard, of Leland... ... ... „ 8
Alice, ye D. of Alex: Breres ... ... „ 15
William, ye S. of Jane Winstandley ... ... „ 15
Evan, ye S. of John Hodson, of Keurden ... ... „ 29
John, ye son of Wm Mackerill, of Farington ... ... June 9
Annas, ye D. of Geo. Dawson, of Leland ... ... „ 9
Richard, ye S. of Thomas Cheetham ... ... „ 26
W^m, ye S. of John Chisnel ... ... „ 26
John, ye S. of Timothy Wardley ... ... „ 26
... , ye ... of Robert Turner, junior ... ... „ 29
John, ye S. of Rich: Sherdley, of Farington ... ... July 1
Alice, ye D. of Rich: Critchlow, of Farington ... ... „ 1
John, ye S. of Wm Burscow, of Leland... ... ... „ 10
James, ye S. of James Low, of Euxton ... ... „ 27
... , ye S. of Tho: Ugnal, of Heapy ... ...Aug. 7
Frances, ye D. of Hen: Garstang, of Heapy ... ... „ 13
William, ye S. of Rich: Holmes, of Leland... ... ... „ 21

[1] A farm near to the Hollins.
[2] There is no transcript for this year or the next, now at Chester.
[3] There is a marriage by licence at Leyland on Feb. 21, 1685-6, between Robert Bickersteth, of Aughton parish (near Ormskirk), and Elizabeth Armetriding, of this parish. Mr. Robert Bickersteth, of Aughton parish, was buried at Leyland on Jan. 2, 1687-8. In Vicar Armetriding's will the sum of £50 is bequeathed to Mr. Thomas Bickersteth, of Aughton, gent. Probably the Elizabeth Armetriding mentioned above was sister to the vicar.

Margaret, ye D. of John Woodcocke ... ... Aug. 28
..., ye S. of John Whittle ... ... „ 28
Margaret, ye D. of Rich: Wiggans, of Whittle ... ... Sept. 4
Katherine, ye D. of Rich: Eaves, of Kureden ... ... „ 5
Charles, ye S. & }
Izabel, ye D. of } John Bradley, of Leland ... ... „ 11
Ann, ye D. of Henry Fell, of Leland ... ... „ 25
Alice, ye D. of Wm Gardner, of Kureden ... ... Oct. 3
William, ye S. of Wm Woodcock, of Leland ... ... „ 6
Skeffington,[1] ye S. of Sr Ch: Hoghton, Bart. ... ... „ 7
Ralph, ye S. of Thurstan Leyland ... ... „ 25
Henry, S. of Henry Chatburn ... ... „ 18
B. John, ye S. of Mary . . . . „ 16

[There appear to be no insertions, but the dates are irregular just as here given.]

John, ye S. of Rich: Cliffe ... ... Nov. 6
William, ye S. of Jo: Cooper ... ... „ 6
Peter, ye S. of Jo. Beardsworth ... ... „ 6
Mary, ye D. of Tho: Garstang ... ... „ 6
John, ye S. of Wm Longton, of Leland ... ... „ 13
Rich: ye S. of Rich: Marsden, of Wheelton... ... ... Dec. 25
B. James, ye S. of Jennet Waterworth, of Walton ... „ 27
Margary, D. of James Morris... ... ... Jan. 1
Henry, ye S. of Rich: Nelson, of Leland ... ... Feb. 7
Edward, ye S. of James Noblet ... ... „ 10
B. Thomas, S. of . . . Hilton ... ... „ 12
John, S. of John Scott, of Whittle [Inserted] ... ... „ 17
Thomas, S. of Edward Clough, of Leyland... ... ... „ 17
..., ye D. of Ralph Pilkington, of Leyland ... ... „ 19
Hannah, ye D. of Thomas Farington, of Farington ... March 4
Anne, ye D. of Richd Sumner, of Leland ... ... „ 11
Jennet, ye D. of John Woodward, of Wheelton ... ... „ 18

[Baptisms] 1688.

Jane, ye D. Tho: Giller, of Leland ... ... March 25
Christopher, ye S. of Tho. Nowell, of Leland ... ... „ 27
William, ye S. of John Somner, of Nooke ... ... „ 29
Katherine, ye D. of Henry Tod, of Leland... ... ... Ap. 4
William, ye S. of John Jackson, of Mosse-side ... ... „ 8
John, ye S. of Rich: Williamson ... ... „ 22
William, ye S. of James Hough ... ... „ 22

[1] Died 8th February, 1768; buried at Walton-le-Dale.

Elizabeth, D. of John Atherton, below lowne[1] ... ... Ap.   29
Isabel, ye D. of Wm Cowling, of Leland ... ... May [blank]
Ellen, ye D. of Wm Wright, of Alcar ... ... May 16
Elizabeth, ye D. of Geo: Porter, of Leland ... ... July   8
Anne, ye D. of Rich: Snape ... ... „   8
Francis, ye S. of John Smith, of Kureden ... ... „   11
Christopher, ye S. of Thurstan Litherland ... ... „   29
John, ye S. of Ralph Whittle, of Whittle ... ... Aug.   5
. . . , ye S. of Wm Wilson, of Leland ... ... „   5
Paul,[2] ye S. of Rich: Fleetwood, Esq. ... ... „   9
James, ye S. of Geo: Dawson, of Leland ... ... „   12
Mary, ye D. of Edward Whittle ... ... „   26
Alice, ye D. of Nich: Whittle ... ... „   26
William, ye S. of Wm Gerard, of Euxton ... ... Sept.   5
Mary, ye D. of Roger Sharples, of Leland ... ... „   7
Grace, ye D. of Mr. Tho: Holme, of Cawbeck[3] ... ... „   23
. . . , ye S. of Wm Pincok, of Whittle ... ... „   23
George, ye S. of Ralph Eaves, of Kureden ... ... „   23
Ellis, ye S. of Robt Sumner ... ... „   17
Myles & Henry, } ye sons of Ellis Sumner, of Leland ... ... „   27
Evan, ye S. of Gilbert Cowling ... ... Oct.   7
James, ye S. of John Taylor, of Chorley ... ... „   7
. . . , ye S. of Robt Dawson, of Leland ... ... „   28
. . . , ye S. of Robt Baron, of Euxton ... ... „   18
Edward, ye S. of Henry Whaley ... ... Nov.   7
Margaret & Jane, } daughters of Rich. Tootell, of Whittle ... „   8
Edward, ye S. of Rich: Farington ... ... [No date]
Jane, ye D. of John Stopford, of Leland [Inserted] ... Dec. 31
Lawrence, ye S. of Alex: Breres ... ... Jan.   1
James, ye S. of Wm Fishwick, of Withnell ... ... „   13
Margery, ye D. of Tho. Critchlow, of Euxton ... ... „   27
Hannah, ye D. of S^r Ch: Hoghton, Bar^t ... ... „   29

---

[1] That is Leyland Lane, which runs nearly north and south through the township, from Farington to Eccleston, and parallel to the River Lostock. There is a farmhouse on the west side of the lane which is still called "Atherton's."

[2] The third son of Richard Fleetwood, Esq. (who was the son of Francis Fleetwood, of Hackinsall, and grandson of Sir Paul Fleetwood, of Rossall), by his wife Margaret (d. and h. of Edward Fleetwood, of Leyland, and granddaughter of Edward Fleetwood, of Penwortham, who died *v.p.* in 1615). The marriage of the parents took place at Leyland, June 16, 1674. Paul Fleetwood, whose baptism is here recorded, lived at Rossall until his father's death in 1709, when he removed to Wharles. He was buried at Kirkham in 1727. For a full account of this family, see Fishwick's *History of Poulton-le-Fylde.*

[3] In Euxton township.

Margery, ye D. of John Woodcock, of Euxton ... ... Feb. 12
Elizabeth, ye D. of Thurstan Sharrock, of Euxton ... „ 17
Margret, ye D. of Tho. Margerison ... ... March 3
Anne, ye D. of Wᵐ Jackson, of Leland ... ... „ 3
Farington, ye S. of Rich: Whittle... ... ... „ 17
Jane, ye D. of Rich: Balshaw, of Leland ... ... „ 22
Ellen, ye D. of Wᵐ Darwin ... ... „ 24

[Baptisms, 1689.[1]]

Hugh, ye S. of Peter Barton, of Kureden ... ... Ap. 4
Susan, ye D. of Timothy Wardley ... ... „ 7
Thomas, ye S. of Tho: Farington, of Far: ... ... „ 8
Robert, ye S. of Tho: Harrison, of Euxton... ... ... „ 9
Margaret, ye D. of Mr. Tho: Crooke,[2] of Leland ... „ 8
Anne, ye D. of Wᵐ Longton ... ... „ 21
B. Katherine, ye D. of Isabel Garstang ... ... „ 21
James, ye S. of Tho: Watson, of Whittle ... ... „ 28
John, ye S. of Tho: Howell, of Leland ... ... May 7
Richard, ye S. of Richard Rose, of Euxton... ... ... „ 19
Elizabeth, ye D. of John Pilkington, of Leyland ... „ 19
Elizabeth, ye D. of Rich: Holmes... ... ... „ 21
James, ye S. of James Hall, of Euxton ... ... June 2
Jane, ye D. of John Garstang ... ... „ 16
Anne, ye D. of Adam Platt ... ... „ 16
Alice, ye D. of Roger Walton ... ... „ 16
Jane, ye D. of Andrew Stones ... ... July 10
Elizabeth, ye D. of Wᵐ Jackson, of Kureden ... ... „ 12
Anne, ye D. of John Atherton, of Leland ... ... „ 15
Lawrence, ye S. of Henry Garstang, of Heapy ... ... „ 20
Nicholas, ye S. of James Hornby ... ... Aug. 4
Elizabeth, ye D. of John Gooden ... ... „ 4
Margaret, ye D. of Richard Cooper ... ... „ 18
Alice, ye D. of Robᵗ Welsh ... ... „ 25
... , ye ... of ... Croft ... ... Sept. 1
Lawrence, ye S. of James Bullon ... ... „ 8
Ralph, ye S. of John Green, of Leland... ... ... „ 23
Thomas, ye S. of John Nightingale, of Whittle ... ... „ 29
Ellen, ye D. of Ralph Cross, of Leland ... ... Oct. 06

---

[1] The transcript is signed by Tho: Armetriding, Vicʳ of Leyland, and the four Churchwardens. It is on parchment, closely written, and in a fair hand.

[2] This Mr. Thomas Crooke was probably of the same family as Mr. Thomas Crooke, of Abram, near Wigan, of whom there is an account in *Local Gleanings*, vol. i., p. 147.

G

Thomas, ye S. of William Whitehead .. .. Oct. 07
Anne, the D. of George Monck, jun^r, of Leland ... ... „ 13
Ellen, ye D. of Robt Turner, jun^r, of Leland ... ... „ 13
Richard, ye S. of Richard Dobson... ... ... Nov. 17
Ellen, ye D. of John Beardsworth, of farington ... ... „ 17
Thomas, the son of Tho: Robinson ... ... Dec. 26
William, the son of Oliver Garstang, in Whittle... ... Jan. 5
John, ye Son of John Smith, in Kuerden ... ... „ 12
Ellen, ye D. of James Blakelidge, in Leyland ... ... „ 16
Alice, ye D. of Ralph Whittle, in Whittle ... ... „ 26
Jane, ye D. of John Gerrard, in ffarington ... ... „ 26
Alice, ye D. of Henry Estham, in Leyland ... ... „ 26
Catherine, the D. of John Calderbank, in Whittle ... ffeb. 9
Alice, the D. of John Riding, in Leyland ... ... „ 16
Elizabeth, ye D. of John Brewer, in Leyland ... ... „ 23
William, the son of William Ugnal, in Wheelton ... March 2
William, the son of James Noblet, in Leyland ... ... „ 23
Ellen, ye Daughter of John Gerrard, in Leyland... ... „ 23
Alice, ye Daughter of Nicholas Whittle, in Leyland ... „ 23

[Here occurs a page filled with entries of collections made in the church, or parish, of Leyland, for various objects, and at different times, from 1653 to 1695-6. These collections were probably made by virtue of a King's Brief. There are thirteen entries, which will be found transposed from this place to the end of the Baptisms.]

Christenings for ye year 1690.[1]

Elizabeth, ye D. of William Taylour, in Heapey ...March 30
Ellen, the D. of Richard Wattmough, in Clayton ... „ 30
Jane, ye D. of Lawrence Croft, in Whittle ... ... Aprill 6
Henry, ye S. of William Cross, in Euxton ... ... „ 9
Jane, the D. of John Jones, Traveller ... ... „ 16
Richard, ye S. of John Low, of Euxton ... ... „ 20
Jane, ye D. of Tho: Cooper, in Euxton ... ... „ 27
Ann, ye D. of James Maurice, of Leyland ... ...June 1
B. Jane, ye D. of Richard Wilson & Cicely Johnson, of
   Whittle ... ... „ 5
William, ye son, & ⎱
Margery, ye Daughter⎰ of James Hough, of Leyland... „ 8
Lawrence, ye son of Lawrence Walmsley, of Whittle.. „ 11

[1] The transcript for this year is signed on the back by Vicar Armetriding and the four Churchwardens.

Margaret, ye D. of Robert Clayton, of Leyland ... ... June 12
James, ye S. of Timothy Wardley, of Whittle ... ... „ 15
Elizabeth, ye D. of Tho: Sumner, of Leyland ... ... „ 15
Agnes, ye D. of Hugh Waterworth, of ffarington-hall[1] July 6
B. Elizabeth, ye D. of John Sharrock & Jennet Baxenden „ 15
Edward, ye S. of Tho: Nowell, of Leyland ... ... „ 30
William, ye son of William Leaver, of Leyland ... ... Aug. 24
Mary, ye Daughter of James Thompson, of Whittle ... „ 31
John & Ellen, twins of Willm Park, of Exton ... ... Sept. 2
Ellen, the D. of John Harrison, of Leyland... ... ... „ 7
Jeophrey, ye S. of John Taylour, in Whittle ... ... „ 14

[1] There are at present two farmhouses of some importance which bear this name. Lower Farington Hall occupies the site of the mansion of Sir Henry ffarington, who was Squire of the Bodyguard to Henry VII., and Knight of the Bodyguard to Henry VIII. During many years Sir Henry was Steward of the King's Manor of Penwortham, and when the dissolution of the monasteries was resolved upon he was chosen as one of the commissioners. Having settled his Farington estates and the lordship of the Manor of Leyland upon the *issue* of his son William, these both descended through females to the Huddlestons, of Sawston, co. Cambridge, and so became alienated from the original proprietors. Sir Henry purchased Werden from the Andertons, and thus provided an estate for the son of his second marriage and his descendants. This son, William ffarington, Esq., who afterwards became Comptroller to Edward, Earl of Derby, was the first of the ffaringtons of Werden, and to him was granted, by Norroy, a change in the family crest and motto. The Huddleston family disposed of the lordship of the Manor of Leyland to the aforesaid William ffarington, Esq., and later on the estates passed from them into the possession of various persons. Several sons of the Huddleston family became notable members of various religious orders. In particular may be mentioned Richard, youngest son of Andrew Huddleston, of Farington Hall. Educated at Rheims, and at Rome he became a Benedictine monk, and was sent to England to win over as many as possible of the Lancashire and Yorkshire gentry to the Roman obedience. He is said to have met with remarkable success, for the Prestons, Andertons, Downes, Traffords, and Sherbournes, of the former county, and the Watertons, Middletons, and Trapps, of the latter, are thought to have been induced by his persuasions to withdraw themselves from the Established Church. When Charles II. was in hiding at Moseley, in Staffordshire, he occupied himself with the perusal of the books left in his chamber. Among them was one by Father Richard Huddleston, upon the Roman Controversy, which the King pronounced to be conclusive, and not to be disproved. This book was the property of another member of the Huddleston family, John (nephew of the aforesaid Richard), who was likewise a Benedictine, and who is well known as the confessor procured by the Duke of York for his brother the King (Charles II.) when death was approaching. (See Lingard, vol. x., p. 109; Macaulay, vol. i., pp. 434-436.) Others of the name became members of the Jesuit order and held important offices therein. A younger branch of the family was settled at Hutton-John, in Cumberland. Lower Farington Hall is now the property of the heirs of the late George Hargreaves, Esq., of Leyland. It retains scarcely anything to testify of its former dignity except a portion of the moat, which is replenished by the River Lostock. The situation of this Hall is within a short distance of the boundary between the parish of Penwortham (which includes Farington township) and the parish of Leyland, and near to the Lostock in its southward course. Higher Farington Hall is less than half a mile to the northward of the Hall just described. Some features of the house and outbuildings denote that it has been in the hands of persons of substance. This may be the Little Farington, where resided a younger branch of the family of that name, which line ended with females in the seventeenth century.

84   *Leyland Registers.*

Alice, ye D. of James Roscow, of Leyland ... ... Sept. 21
Margaret, ye D. of William Burscow, of Leyland ... „ 21
Elizabeth, ye D. of John Pilkington, of Leyland... ... „ 28
Mary, ye D. of Thomas Thornton, in Euxton ... ... Oct. 5
Richard, ye S. of Thurstan Litherland, in Whittle ... „ 8
William, ye S. of Robert Baron, in Euxton... ... ... „ 12
Mary, ye D. of Alexander Briers, in Whittle ... ... „ 16
Thomas, the S. of Richard Almond ... ... „ 19
Henry, ye S. of George Eastham, in Leyland ... ... Nov. 2
Ellen, ye D. of John Jackson, Husbandman, of Leyland „ 2
Jennett, ye D. of John Sumner de Nook, in Leyland... „ 2
Richard, ye S. of William Wright, of Euxton ... ... „ 3
Marjary, ye D. of Edward Sumner, of Leyland ... ... „ 9
James, the S. of William ffarington, of ffarington ... „ 10
Margaret,[1] ye D. of Mr Richard Fletewood, of Leyland. Dec. 4
Catherine, ye D. of Ralph Eves, of Kuerden ... ... „ 7
Sarah, ye D. of George Dawson, of Leyland ... ... „ (?) 28
Alice, the D. of John Parker, of Euxton ... ... Jan. 6
George, ye Son of George Moonk, of Leyland ... ... „ 11
William, ye Son of Richard Crichlow, of Clayton ... „ 11
Margret, ye D. of Oliver Cross, of Euxton ... ... „ (?) 12
John, ye son of Evan Eastham, of ffarington ... ... „ 17
Richard, ye son of Nathaniell Tinklay, of Kuerden ... „ 25
James, ye S. of Sr Charles Hoghton,[2] Bart ... ... „ 6
Margret, ye D. of Tho: Giller, of Leyland ... ... ffeb. 1
Elizabeth, ye D. of Richard Wiggins, of Whittle ... ... „ 1
B. Sarah, ye Daughter of Mary Dawson, of Leyland... „ 1
Henry, ye S. of Robert Dawson, of Leyland ... ... „ 1
Ann, ye D. of John Okenshaw, of Euxton ... ... „ 2
Elizabeth, ye D. of John Blackledge, of Heapey... ... „ 15
William, ye S. of George Charnley, of Leyland ... ... „ 22
Thomas, ye S. of Roger Dewhurst, of Kuerden ... ... „ 22
William, ye S. of Thurstan Leyland, of Leyland... ... „ 24
Elizabeth, ye D. of Richard Williamson, of ffarington... March 15
Henry, son of Hugh Smith, Euxton, Janury (*sic*) ye 23: 1700:

[This last entry is written in a different hand at the bottom of the page, and is also duly entered at its right place.]

---

[1] This lady afterwards married the Rev. T. Robinson, Vicar of S. Michaels-on-Wyre. See earlier entries of this family, pp. 60, 80. Richard Fletewood, gentleman, was one of the trustees named in the conveyance of Leyland Hall to the vicars of the parish, which took place in this year, 1690.

[2] This son of Sir Charles Hoghton is said to have died young. He would probably be buried, with other members of the family, at Walton-le-Dale. See also Baptisms, 1684.

Christenings in ye yeare 1691.[1]

John, the son of John Whittle, of Leyland ... ... March 29
Elizabeth, ye D. of Ralph Cross, of Leyland ... ... „ 29
Lawrence, the son of William Croft, of Whittle ... ... Aprill 5
Thomas, ye son of Lawrence Lucas, of Whittle ... ... „ 19
Ann, ye D. of Thomas Croft, of Whittle ... ... „ 26
Elizabeth, ye D. of Crichlaw, of Euxton ... ... „ 26
Peter, ye son of James Low, of ye Prish of Winwick... May 10
William, son of Thomas Marjory-son, of Kuerden ... „ 10
Jane, the D. of Michael Southworth, of Leyland... ... „ 20
Ann, ye D. of John Walmsley, of Euxton ... ... „ 22
Elizabeth, the wife of Robert Abbot, of Heapey, June ye 10th

[This has been crossed through as a manifestly misplaced
record of burial. Among the burials of 1691 this entry occurs,
but it has been inserted.]

Alice, the D. of Ralph Pilkinton, of Leyland ... ... June 24
[2]Mary, ye D. of Will: Roscow, of Exton ... ... „ 27
Robert, the S. of Thomas ffarington, of ffarington ... July 19
Catherine, ye D. of Joseph Nightingale, of Clayton ... „ 19
[2]James, ye S. of Roger Bromeley, of Clayton [something
  illegible] ... ... „ 17
Ann, ye D. of Timothy Wardley, of Whittle ... ... Aug. 2
William, ye son of James Shakerley, of Euxton... ... „ 2
Jane, ye D. of John Stopforth, of Leyland ... ... „ 12
Henry, ye Son of Henry Chattburne, of Leyland ... „ 29
John, ye son of Andrew Stones, of Leyland ... ... Sept. 8
Ann, ye D. of Henry Todd, of Leyland ... ... „ 20
Mary, ye D. of William ffarington, of Leyland ... ... „ 25
Ann, ye D. of Richard Tootell, of Whittle ... ... „ 27
John, ye S. of Henery Slator, of Euxton ... ... „ 27
Elizabeth, ye D. of John Jackson, of Leyland ... ... „ 27
Martha, the D. of Tho: Nowell, of Leyland ... ... Oct. 18
Margrette, ye D. of Thomas Cooper, of Leyland ... „ 18
Isabell, ye D. of Richard Holmes, of Leyland ... ... Nov. 1
Henry, ye S. of John Atherton, of Leyland ... ... „ 30
Robert, ye S. of John Livesey, of Withnell ... ... Dec. 2
David, ye S. of John ffrierson, of Keurden ... ... „ 6
Margrett, ye D. of John Cooper, of Leyland ... ... „ 13

[1] The transcript is signed by Vicar Armetriding. The names of the Churchwardens are given, but are not signatures. The writing is faint, and in some places
illegible.
[2] This entry is inserted, but is in the same handwriting.

Thomas, ye S. of Thurstan Sharrock, of Euxton ... Jan. 4
Elinor, ye D. of James Hall, of Euxton ... ... „ 21
John, ye S. of John Clough, of Leland... ... ... „ 24
Elizabeth, ye D. of William Gerard, of Leland ... ... „ 24
Thomas, the S. of John Calderbank, of Euxton... ... „ 26
Thomas, the S. of George Porter, of Leland ... ... „ 31
John, ye S. of Alexander Briers, of Whittle ... ... ffeb. 5
Mary, ye D. of John Gooden, of Leland ... ... „ 7
B. Thomas, ye bastard child of Thomas ffletcher &
Mary Lever, of Leland ... ... „ 7
Margaret,[1] ye D. of Sr Charles Hoghton, Baro^nt
[Inserted] ... ... „ 10
Robert, ye S. of Thomas Cooper, of Leland ... ... „ 21
John, ye S. of Michael Taylor, [of] Clayton ... ... „ 21
Martha, ye D. of Tho: Parker, of Wheelton... ... ... „ 28
William, ye S. of Ralph Whittle, of Whittle ... ... „ 28
Alice, ye D. of Richard Cooper, of Euxton ... ... „ 28
Mary, ye D. of William Clough, of ffarington ... ... March 6
Margaret, ye D. of Richard Cooper, of Exton ... ... „ 7
Henery, ye son of James Bullen, of Leyland ... ... „ 13
Catherine, ye D. of Ralph Eves, of Keurden ... ... „ 13
Elizabeth, ye D. of Edward Haworth, of Whittle ... „ 13
Jennet, ye D. of William Wright, of Euxton ... ... „ 24

1692 Ƶstnings.[2]

Ellen, ye D. of Thomas Jackson, of Kuerden ... ... Aprill 3
Thomas, ye S. of Richard Balshaw, of Whittle ... ... „ 10
John, ye S. of Oliver Garstang, of Whittle ... ... „ 10
Alice, ye D. of John Nightingale, of Whittle ... ... „ 10
Henry, ye S. of Matthew Whittle, of Penwortham ... „ 10

[Here occur the two following entries, which have been made later, upon the blank space at the bottom of the page. The last entry has also been inserted in its proper place.]

Isaac & Jacob, sons of John Hilton, of Leyland, Borne twins, ye 5: daye of October, 1696.

grace: D: of Thomas Bromiley, of Withnell, Decemb: 30: 1700.

John, son of John Smith, of Kuerden ... ... Aprill 17
Thomas, son of James Eastham, of Euxton ... ... „ 17

[1] This lady became the wife of Samuel Watson, of Hull, gent. Married at Walton-le-Dale, Aug. 27, 1716.

[2] The transcript is closely written on both sides of the parchment, and is signed by Vicar Armetriding. The names of the Churchwardens are given.

Elizabeth, ye D. of George Dawson, of Leyland... ... Aprill 17
Mary, ye D. of Peter Barton, of Kuerden ... ... ,, 23
Richard, ye S. of Ellis Sompner, of Leyland ... ... May 5
Jennett, ye D. of Richard Whittle, of ffarington... ... ,, 8
Ellen, ye D. of George Woods, of Euxton ... ... ,, 8
Thomas, ye S. of James Noblett, of Leyland ... ... ,, 11
William, ye S. of Henry Eastham, of Leyland ... ... ,, 15
Elizabeth, ye D. of Adam Platt, of Euxton... ... ... ,, 22
James, ye S. of William Crichlaw, of Euxton ... ... ,, 29
John, ye S. of Nicholas Whittle, of Leyland ... ... ,, 29
Alice, ye D. of John Wilkinson, of Leyland ... ... June 5
James, ye S. of James Crichlaw, of Whittle... ... ... ,, 12
James, ye S. of James Hornby, of Clayton ... ... ,, 19
Margery, ye D. of Robert Wareing, of Leland ... ... ,, 26
William, ye S. of Richard Withnell, of Whittle ... ... July 3
Dorothy, ye D. of James Blacklege, of Leyland... ... ,, 3
William, ye S. of Richard Rose, of Euxton ... ... ,, 10
B. Anne, ye Bastard child of John Hodson, of Walton,
and Margret Short, of Kuerden ... ... ,, 21
Jane, ye D. of John Brewer, of Leyland ... ... ,, 24
John, ye S. of John Green, of Leyland... ... ... Aug. 4
Jane, ye D. of William Croft, of Whittle ... ... ,, 14
John, ye S. of Robert Turner, of Leyland ... ... Sept. 4
Jeopherey, the son of William Taylor, of Whittle ... ,, 11
Henery, ye S. of Henry Garstang,[1] of Heapy ... ... ,, 14
Elizabeth, ye D. of Thomas Thornton ... ... ,, 25
Thomas, ye S. of Thomas Nowell, of Leyland ... ... Oct. 2
John, the s. of Michaell Southworth, of Wheelton ... ,, 2
B. Ishmael, ye S. of Ann Taylour, of Kuerden ... ... ,, 6
William, ye S. of Andrew Waterworth, of Euxton ... ,, 9
Ann, ye D. of William Livesay, of Kuerden ... ... ,, 9
John, ye S. of John Martin, of Clayton... ... ... ,, 16
Lawrence, ye s: of William Ugnall, of Wheelton ... ,, 16
John, ye S. of James Cocker, of Clayton ... ... ,, 16
Nicholas, ye S. of Thomas Hey, jun[r], of Heapy ... ... ,, 16
Joseph, ye Son of George Moonk, of Leyland ... ... ,, 30
William, ye S. of Richard Almond, of Leyland... ... Nov. 13
Henery, ye S. of John Gerard, of Leland ... ... ,, 20
Richard, ye Son, & ⎫ twins of George Charnley, of
Elizabeth, ye Daughter,⎭ Leyland ... ... ,, 22
John, ye S. of John Pilkinton, of Leyland ... ... Dec. 18
Thomas, ye S. of Robert Hindley, of Keurden ... ... ,, 18

[1] Henry Garstang, of Heapey, yeoman, was one of the Trustees for the transfer of Leyland Old Hall.

William, ye S. of Thomas Cowper, of Leyland ... ... Dec. 25
John, ye S. of John Harrison, Traveller ... ... Jan. 1
Elizabeth, ye D. of Richard Calderbank, of Hutton[1]... „ 1
John, ye S. of John Gooden, of Leyland ... ... „ 8
Anne, ye D. of Thomas Croft, of Whittle ... ... „ 8
Elizabeth, ye D. of Robt. Baron, of Euxton ... ... „ 22
Ann, ye D. of Joseph Nightingale, of Clayton ... ... „ 29
Catherine, ye D. of Thurstan Litherland, of Whittle ... ffeb. 14
Jennet &⎫Twins of James Bolton & Jennet Martin, of
James, ⎭ Euxton ... ... „ 14
William, ye S. of Thomas Cooper, of Leyland, Shoe-
maker ... ... „ 19
Nathaniel, ye S. of Timothy Wardley, of Whittle ... „ 19
Ellen, ye D. of John Parker, of Leyland ... ... „ 19
John, ye S. Richard Crichlaw, of Clayton ... ... „ 20
Jane, ye D. of John Stephenson, of Leyland ... ... Mar. 5
Thomas, ye S. of John Taylor, of Whittle ... ... „ 12

ɪnings, 1693.[2]

Ellen, ye D. of Robert Waring, of Leyland ... ... Aprill 4
B. John, the S. of Cicely Johnson, of Whittle ... ... „ 6
John, ye S. of Tho: Mackerill, of Leyland ... ... „ 9
William, ye S. of Tho: Watson, of Whittle... ... ... „ 9
James, ye S. of William Man, of Euxton ... ... „ 16
Richard, ye S. of Richard Cooper, of Euxton ... ... „ 23
John, ye S. of John Blackledge, of Heapey... ... ... „ 23
Mary, ye D. of William Stephenson, of Whittle ... ... „ 30
Ellen, ye D. of James Hough, of Leyland ... ... May 7
Ann, ye D. of John Morris, a Traveller ... ... „ 7
Alice, ye D. of John ffreckleton, of Euxton... ... ... „ 14
Elizabeth,[3] ye D. of Sʳ Charles Hoghton, Baronᵗᵗ
[Inserted] ... ... „ 22
Edward, ye S. of Mary Tildesley, of Clayton ... ... „ 25
Thomas, ye S. of John Walmsley, of Euxton ... ... „ 25
Ann, ye D. of John Clough, of Leyland ... ... „ 28
B. James, ye S. of Margret Wright, of Leyland... ... June 15
Lawrence, ye S. of John Harrison, of Leyland ... ... „ 18

[1] A township in Penwortham parish.

[2] The transcript is closely written on both sides of the parchment, and is illegible in places. The signature of Vicar Armetriding is found on the back, but the names of the Churchwardens are not readable.

[3] This lady was afterwards married (Feb. 14, 1715-6) to Thomas Fenton, of Hunslet, Esq. See also Baptisms, 1684.

Thomas, ye S. of Andrew Stones, of Leyland	June	24
Thomas, ye S. of George Woods, of Euxton	July	9
Elizabeth, ye D. of James Roscow, of Leyland	„	9
Jane, ye D. of William Croft, of Whittle	„	23
Henery, ye S. of George Dawson, of Leyland	Aug.	13
Henery, ye S. of William Wright, of Euxton	„	31
James, ye S. of James Noblett, of Leyland...	Sept.	3
Mary, ye D. of Henery Chattburne, of Leyland ...	„	3
Abraham, ye S. of Robert English, Traveller	„	10
B. Peter, ye S. of James Biby & Ann Pierson, of Wheelton [Inserted]	„	17
Margaret, ye d. of William Leaver, of Leyland	„	24
Ann, ye D. of John Sumpner, de Nook[1]	Oct.	8
Margret, ye D. of Edward Crane, of Clayton [Inserted]	„	15
Ellen, ye D. of Gyles Wadington, of Leyland	„	19
James, ye S. of James Tomson, of Whittle	„	22
Margarett, ye D. of John Beardsworth, of Farington...	„	22
Dorothy, ye D. of Mr. William Shurd,[2] of Clayton H[all][3]	„	23
Jane, ye D. of Alexander Briers, of Whittle	„	24
Agnes, ye D. of William Leyland, of Leyland	„	29
Margarett, ye D. of Adam Platt, of Euxton	„	29
William, ye S. of Ralph Pilkington, of Leyland... ...	Nov.	5
Lawrence, ye S. of William Ugnall, of Wheelton ...	„	5
Lawrence, ye S. of Richard Rose, of Euxton	„	8
James, ye S. of Lawrence Lucas, of Whittle	„	12
Margaret, ye D. of William Clough, of ffarington ...	„	19
Edward, ye S. of Thomas Nowell, of Leyland	„	22
Thomas, ye S. of William Cooper, of Leyland	„	26
Mary, ye D. of John Stopford, of Leyland	„	29
Hannah, ye D. of Robert Foster, of Euxton	Dec.	3

[1] See note, page 68.

[2] Mr. William Shurd, of Clayton Hall, was perhaps of the family of Sherd, of Disley, co. Chester, as the name is an uncommon one. There is a pedigree of this family in Mr. Earwaker's *East Cheshire*, and it is possible that the last Mr. William Sherd there mentioned had left Disley and come to Clayton Hall.

[3] Clayton Hall, in the township of Clayton-le-Woods, has still many features of interest to tell of its former importance. The present building is said to be of Elizabethan date, but, if so, it must have replaced an earlier mansion. The ancient family of Clayton, of Clayton, closed (in the direct male line) with John Clayton, Esq., who married Elizabeth, daughter of Sir Richard Langton (of Walton), the Baron of Newton. He died in 1541, leaving two co-heiresses, one of whom married William, the eldest son of Sir Henry ffarrington (the last),' of ffarington. There appears to have been a considerable amount of litigation respecting this estate at the end of the sixteenth century. Finally, a branch of the Anderton family settled here and retained the ownership down to the end of the seventeenth century, when the estate passed into the hands of Lord Molineux. The present proprietor is the Earl of Lathom.

Catherine, ye D. of William Whitehead, of Ulneswalton Dec. 3
John, ye S. of John Jackson, of Leyland, Thatcher ... „ 17
John, ye S. of Henry Croft, of Whittle ... ... „ 17
Jane, ye D. of Thomas Garstang, of Whittle ... ... „ 24
William, ye S. of William ffarington, of Leyland ... „ 31
Isabell, ye D. of Henry Kirkham, of ffarington ... ... „ 31
Jane &
Margarett, } twins of John Woodward, of Wheelton ... Jan. 7
Thomas, ye S. of George Porter, of Leyland ... ... „ 14
Jane, ye D. of John ffreerson, of Keurden ... ... „ 21
Margarett, ye D. of Edward Short, of Kuerden... ... „ 28
Hugh, ye S. of Hugh Waterworth, of ffarington... ... ffeb. 2
Joyce, ye D. of Edward Whittle, of Leyland ... ... „ 10
Margaret, ye D. of Richard Mare, of Whittle ... ... „ 18
Marjory, ye D. of Thomas Cheetham, of ffarington ... „ 18
Marjery, ye D. of Henery Weaver, of Leyland ... ... Mar. 4
Thomas, ye S. of Thomas Marjoryson, of Clayton ... „ 11
Margarett, ye D. of Henry Slaytor, of Euxton ... ... „ 11
William, ye S. of Richard Withnell, of Whittle ... ... „ 11
Margarett, ye D. of Thomas Crichlaw, & ... ... „ 18
Mary, ye D. of George Hilton, of Euxton ... ... „ 18

[Baptisms] 1694.[1]

Ann, ye D. of John Livesay, of Withnell ... ... Mar. 25
William, ye S. of Roger Garstang, of Whittle ... ... Ap. 8
Thomas, ye S. of John Garstang, of Whittle ... ... „ 15
Hamlet, ye S. of Thomas Linford, of Heapey ... ... „ 15
Margarett, ye D. of Robert Low, of Whittle ... ... „ 19
Thomas, ye S: & } twins of Thomas Dawson, of Ley-
Alice, ye D: } land ... ... „ 22
Elizabeth, ye D. of Richard Watmough, of Clayton ... „ 22
Jeopherey, ye S. of Lawrence Taylor, of Heapey ... May 13
Edward, ye S. of Thomas Moulden, of Heapey... ... „ 20
Jane, ye D. of John Smith, of Keurden ... ... „ 20
Margaret, ye D. of John Walmsley, of Euxton ... ... „ 29
Adam, ye S. of John Clayton, of Clayton ... ... June 13
William, ye S. of Thomas Cooper, of ffarington... ... „ 24
Edward, ye S. of Thurstan Sharrock, of Euxton ... „ 25
Mary, ye D. of John Calderbank, of Clayton ... ... July 22
Elizabeth, ye D. of Richard Williamson, of Farington. „ 22
Sarah, ye D. of Roger Walton, Junr, of Leyland ... „ 29
Elizabeth, ye D. of John Martin, of Clayton ... ... Aug. 19

[1] The transcript is signed by the Vicar and Churchwardens. In good condition.

Jennet, ye D. of Ralph Cross, of Leyland ... ... Aug. 19
Ann, ye D. of Edmund Piccop, of Heapey... ... ... Sept. 2
Andrew, ye S. of Andrew Stones, of Leyland ... ... Oct. 9
Ann, ye D. of Ralph Whittle, of Whittle ... ... „ 18
Jane, ye D. of George Moonk, of Leyland ... ... „ 28
Lucia,[1] ye D. of Sr Charles Hoghton, B^{nt} ... ... „ 29
Elizabeth, ye D. of Mr. William Shurd, of Clayton H. Nov. 6
Alice, ye D. of William Jackson ye youngest, of
Cuerden ... ... Dec. 16
Richard, ye S. of Michael Southworth, of Wheelton ... „ 16
George, ye S. of James Eastham, & ... ... „ 19
John, ye S. of Andrew Cooper, both of Euxton ... ... „ 19
Elizabeth, ye D. of John Stopford, of Leyland ... ... „ 19
Henry, ye S. of Oliver Garstang, of Whittle ... ... „ 23
Jennet, ye D. of Thomas Croft, of Whittle ... ... „ 30
James, ye S. of Robert Charnock, of Charnock Richard[2] Jan. 13
John, ye S. of William Hesketh, of Leyland ... ... „ 13
B. William, ye bastard child of Mary Tinsley, of
Euxton ... ... „ 21
John, the S. of Robt. Turner, Junr, of Leyland ... ... ffeb. 10
Margaret, ye D. of Thurstan Litherland, of Whittle ... „ 24
Ellen, ye D. of John Parker, of Leyland ... ... Mar. 3
Charles, ye S. of Thomas Nowel, of Leyland ... ... „ 6
Elizabeth, ye D. of Ralph Eves, of Kuerden ... ... „ 17
William, ye S. of John Hawworth, of Whittle ... ... „ 24
B. Jane, ye D. of Jennet Stephenson, of Whittle ... „ 24

1695 Y'nings.[3]

Richard, ye S. of James Hall, of Euxton ... ... Mar. 31
Edward, ye S. of John Blackledge, of Heapy ... ... „ 31
Alexander, ye S. of Robert Baron, of Euxton ... ... Ap. 7
John, ye S. of John Beardsworth, of ffarington ... ... „ 7
William, ye S. Thomas Ditchfield, of Leyland ... ... „ 28
Elizabeth, ye D. of Andrew Waterworth, of Exton ... „ 28
Margaret, ye D. of Richard Waring, of Leyland ... May 14
Dorothy, ye D. of Richard Lever, of Leyland ... ... „ 14
John, ye S. of William Ugnall, of Wheelton ... ... June 2
Alexander, ye S. of Robert Hindle, of Keurden ... „ 3
Henery, ye S. of Richard Whittle, of ffarington... ... „ 5
Robert, ye S. of Robert Waring, of Leyland ... ... „ 16

[1] She was married Feb. 6, 1721-2, to Thomas Lutwidge, Esq.
[2] In Standish parish.
[3] The transcript is signed by Vicar and Churchwardens.

Richard, ye S. of John Stephenson, of Leyland ...   ... June   30
Margaret, ye D. of Adam Plat, of Euxton ...   .   „   30
Alice, ye D. of John Pilkington, of Leyland   ...   ... July   7
Margery, ye D. of Richard Almond, of Leyland   ...   „   14
B. Dorothy, ye D. of Ellis Sumner & Elizabeth Cook-
  son, of Leyland ...   .   „   14
Elizabeth, ye D. of William Riding, of Leyland...   ...   „   16
Elizabeth, ye D. of John Green, of Leyland   ...   ...   „   21
Jennet, ye D. of William Leyland, of Leyland ...   ... Aug.   4
Jane, ye D. of George Woods, of Leyland ...   .   „   4
Elizabeth, ye D. of George Woods, of Euxton   ...   ...   „   9
Margaret, ye D. of John Leyland, of Leyland   ...   ...   „   11
Frances, ye D. of John Clough, of Leyland...   ...   ...   „   11
Isabel, ye D. of John Clayton, of Clayton ...   .   „   18
Margaret, ye D. of Matthew Walkden, of Heapy   ...   „   18
Elizabeth, ye D. of William Man, of Euxton   ...   ... Sept.   1
William, ye S. of William ffarington, of ffarington   ...   „   1
Christopher, ye S. of Henery Garstang, of Wheelton...   „   12
William, ye S. of James Tomson, of Whittle   ...   ...   „   15
Isabell, ye D. of John Walmsley, of Euxton   ...   ...   „   22
James, ye S. of James Bullaine, of Leyland   ...   ...   „   29
Mary, ye D. of William Gerrard, of Leyland   ...   ... Oct.   6
Ellen, ye D. of James Critchlaw, of Whittle   ...   ...   „   13
Isabell, ye D. of Robert Low, of Whittle ...   .   „   24
Joseph, ye S. of George Moonk, of Leyland   ...   ...   „   27
John, ye S. of George Porter, of Leyland ...   .   „   27
Thomas, ye S. of William Livesay, of Kuerden ...   ...   „   27
B. Jennet, ye D. of Robert Wilkinson & Alice Hey, of
  Heapey...   ...   .   „   27
Hugh, ye S. of Mr. William Shurd, of Clayton Hall ... Nov.   14
Jane, ye D. of Thurstan Leyland, of Leyland   ...   ...   „   17
Thomas, ye S. of John Martin, of Clayton ...   .   „   17
Oliver, ye S. of William Taylor, of Heapey   ...   ...   „   24
Ann, ye D. of Henry Croft, of Whittle   ...   .   „   24
James, ye S. of Richard Carfoot, of Whittle   ...   ... Dec.   1
Mary, ye D. of Thomas Cheetham, of ffarington   ...   „   1
Lawrence, ye S. of William Croft, of Whittle   ...   ...   „   8
Margery, ye D. of Ralph Pilkington, of Leyland   ...   „   22
Thomas, ye S. of Will: Cooper, of Leyland   ...   ...   „   25
Hannah, ye D. of Edward Crane, of Clayton [Inserted]   „   26
Ellen, ye D. of Oliver Garstang, of Whittle...   ...   ...   „   29
Alice, ye D. of Andrew Stones, of Leyland   ...   ... Jan.   7
James, ye S. of Roger Walton, of Leyland...   ...   ...   „   12
Mathew, ye Son of John Moulden, of Heapy ...   ...   „   19
Elizabeth, ye D. of William Roscow, of Wheelton   ...   „   19

Jane, ye D. of John Livesay, of Withnel ... ... Jan. 19
Elizabeth, ye D. of James Noblet, of Leyland ... ... „ 19
William, ye S. of William Hawworth, of Clayton ... „ 19
William, ye S. of John Mackerill, of Leyland ... ... „ 25
Rachel, ye D. of John Taylor, of Keurden ... ... „ 26
John, ye S. of Richard Parker, of Leyland... ... ... ffeb. 2
Elizabeth, ye D. of Thomas Watson, of Whittle... ... „ 16
Henry, ye S. of Ellis Somner, of Leyland ... ... „ 23
Ann, ye D. of Richard Nelson, Junr, of Leyland ... „ 23
Alice, ye D. of John Bury, of Withnell... ... ... Mar. 1
Hugh, ye S. of Edward Sumner, of Leyland ... ... „ 8
Jane, ye D. of John Hey, of Heapey ... ... „ 8
John, ye S. of Henry Eastham, of Leyland ... ... „ 15
John, ye S. of John Wilkinson, of Leyland... ... ... „ 15
Thomas, ye S. of Thomas Cooper, of Leyland ... ... „ 22
Richard, ye S. of John Slater (sd to be born), of Euxton „ (*sic*) 20

[Baptisms] 1696.[1]

Elizabeth, ye D. of Henry Tod, of Leyland ... ... Mar. 29
John, ye S. of Edward Hawworth, of Whittle ... ... Ap. 12
James, ye S. of James Gerrard, of Clayton ... ... „ 26
Margaret, ye D. of John Clayton, of Clayton ... ... May 4
William, ye S. of William Sharrock, of Euxton... ... „ 5
Elizabeth, ye D. of Gilbert Roscow, of Euxton ... ... „ 10
Elizabeth, ye D. of Michael Taylor, of Clayton ... ... „ 24
Thomas, ye S. of Ralph Somner, of Leyland ... ... „ 31
Hannah, ye D. of Thomas Nowel, of Leyland ... ... June 3
Ruth, ye D. of Lawrence Lucas, of Whittle ... ... „ 7
Ann, ye D. of Robert Cocker, of Leyland ... ... „ 14
Alice, ye D. of Ralph Walmsley, of Whittle ... ... „ 14
Margaret, ye D. of George Dawson, of Leyland... ... „ 26
Ellen, ye D. of William Neeld, of Exton ... ... „ 29
Margaret, the D. of Richard Lever, of Leyland... ... Aug. 16
John, ye S. of Henery Weaver, of Leyland ... ... „ 23
Hanna, ye D. of John Piper, of Whittle ... ... „ 23
Margaret, ye D. of Will: Gooden, of Leyland ... ... „ 23
Mary, ye D. of Timothy Wardley, of Whittle ... ... Sept. 6
Thomas, ye S. of William Crook, of Wheelton ... ... „ 13
Lawrence, ye S. of Richard Watmough, of Clayton ... „ 20
Thomas, ye S. of William Burscow, of Euxton ... ... „ 20
Jane, ye D. of John Hawworth, of Whittle ... ... „ 20

[1] The transcript is signed by the Vicar, but the names of the Churchwardens are not signatures.

John, ye S. of Mathew Worthington, of Heapey [Inserted]	Sept.	23
Margery, ye D. of William Mackerill, of ffarington ...	„	27
[¹Isaac and Jacob, sons of John Hilton, of Leyland. Borne twins	Oct.	5]
Thomas, ye S. of John Garstang, of Heapey	„	6
Henry, ye S. of John Atherton, of Leyland...	Nov.	1
John, ye S. of John Gerard, of Leyland [Inserted] ...	„	29
William, ye S. of Richard Rose, of Euxton...	Dec.	2
Ellis, ye S. of Roger Bolton, of Euxton	„	6
Mary, ye D. of John Slaytor, of Euxton	„	6
Marjory, ye D. of Edward Wood, of Worksworth, in Drbyshire	„	6
Thomas, ye S. of William Haydock, of Upper Darwin²	„	14
Lawrence, ye S. of Thomas Croft, of Whittle	„	27
Elizabeth, ye D. of John Wallwork, of Leyland	„	27
Anne, ye D. of Roger Walton, junr, of Leyland	Jan.	3
Alice, ye D. of Michael Southworth, of Wheelton ...	„	4
Mary, ye D. of John Smith, of Cuerden	„	17
Alice, ye D. of Thomas Marjorison, of Clayton	„	17
James, ye S. of Thomas Garstang, of Whittle	„	24
George,³ ye S. of Mr. William Farington, of Shaw-Hall, born [Inserted]	ffeb.	14
Richard, ye S. of John Calderbank, of Clayton	„	14
Edward, ye S. of John Atherton, of Leyland	„	21
Thomas, ye S. of Mr. William Sherd, of Clayton ...	„	23
Jane, ye D. of Henery Slater, of Euxton	Mar.	7
Mary, ye D. of John Stopforth, of Leyland	„	11

¹ See p. 86.

² A township near to Blackburn, now a corporate borough.

³ The eldest son of Mr. William ffarington, of Shawe Hall (who succeeded his cousin, William ffarington, Esq., in the possession of the Worden estates, in 1715), and of his wife, Elizabeth, d. of Dr. James Rufine, of Boulogne, a Huguenot refugee. This George ffarington afterwards married Margaret, daughter and sole heiress of John Bradshaw, of Pennington, Esq., and thus enjoyed both the Worden and the Pennington estates. He died 9th May, 1742, in the forty-sixth year of his age; and his wife on 9th March, 1771, aged 69 years. There are portraits of both at Worden Hall. There is a very handsome marble monument in the ffarington chapel, within Leyland Church, to the memory of Mr. George Farington, which was erected at the expense of Margaret, his widow, "as a testimony of her conjugal love and affection." The names of their ten children are given, of whom two died young. The widow's name was added after her death.

1697 ʒstenings.[1]

B. Mary, ye bastard child of John Beardsworth & Cicely Sumner, of Leyland...	... Ap.	4
John, ye S. of John Clayton, junʳ, of Clayton	„	11
Alice, ye D. of William Hawworth, of Clayton	„	11
Elizabeth, ye D. of John Jackson, of Leyland	„	18
John, ye S. of James Eastham, of Euxton	„	25
William, ye S. Richard Waring, of Leyland... ...	... May	2
Mary, ye D. of Adam Plat, of Euxton	„	9
Marjory, ye D. of William Sharrock, of Euxton ...	„	27
Ann, ye D. of Richard Williamson, of Leyland...	... June	2
Richard, ye S. of Richard Holmes, of Leyland	„	6
Ann, ye D. of William Clayton, of Withnel [Inserted].	July	20
Jane, ye D. of William Hawworth, of Whittle	„	25
Robert, ye S. of John Halliwell, of Whittle... ...	... Aug.	4
John, ye S. of John Pincock, of Euxton	„	8
Margaret, ye D. of Thurstan Sharrock, of Euxton ...	„	11
John, ye S. of John Husband, of Leyland	„	15
Jane, ye D. of John Blackledg, of Heapey	... Sept.	5
William, ye S. of John Riding, of Leyland...	„	7
Michael, ye S. of James Hornby, of Clayton ...	... Oct.	3
William, ye S. of John Cooper, &	„	10
Thomas, ye S. of John Leyland, of Leyland	„	10
James, ye S. of George Porter, of Leyland	„	17
John, ye S. of John Baron, of Euxton	„	24
Robert, ye S. of Robert Foster, of Euxton, &	„	31
Ann, ye D. of Ralph Eves, of Kuerden	„	31
William, ye S. of John Clayton, Snr., of Clayton	... Dec.	12
Martha, ye D. of George Moonk, of Leyland	„	12
Ann, ye D. of Robert Baron, of Euxton	„	25
Thomas, ye S. of Ralph Whittle, of Whittle	„	26
Ann, ye D. of William Marsden, of Whittle ...	... Jan.	16
Mark, ye S. of John Moulden, of Heape	... ffeb.	6
Elizabeth, ye D. of Thomas Harrison, of Euxton ...	„	6
John, ye S. Edward Crane, of Clayton [Inserted] ...	„	13
Lawrence, ye S. of William Ugnall, of Whelton... ...	„	13
Thomas, ye S. of Roger Bolton, of Euxton	„	20
James, ye S. of Richard Wilson, of Whittle	„	24
John, ye S. of William Southworth, of Leyland...	... Mar.	2
John, ye S. of John Clough, of Leyland	„	6
Anne, ye D. of William Croft, of Whittle	„	13

[1] The transcript is signed by the Vicar and Churchwardens. Closely written in a fair hand.

1698 ffstenings.[1]

Mary, ye D. of John Wallwork, of Leyland ... ... Mar. 27
Margaret, ye D. of William Cooper, of Leyland... ... Ap. 3
Hannah, ye D. of Mr. William Shurd, of Clayton Hall „ 9
William, ye S. of John Yate, of Heapey ... ... „ 10
B. John, ye S. of John Talbot & Alice Ainsworth, of
Wheelton ... ... „ 10
Lawrence, ye S. of Richard Almond, & ... ... „ 17
Katherine, ye D. of John Stephenson, both of Leyland „ 17
George, ye S. of John Hilton, of Heapey [Inserted] ... „ 22
Thomas, ye S. of Thomas Abbot, of Heape ... ... May 1
John, ye S. of Richard Crook, of Euxton ... ... „ 15
John, ye S. of Isaac Sharrock, of Leyland ... ... „ 15
Alexander, ye S. of Thomas Nowel, of Leyland... ... „ 18
[Thomas & Martha, twins of Thurstan fficwick, of
Withnell[2] ... ... „ 21]
Thomas & John, ye sons of Andrew Waterworth, of
Euxton ... ... „ 29
Ellen, ye D. of Gilbert Roscow, of Euxton... ... ... June 5
Mary, ye D. of John Pilkington, of Leyland ... ... „ 12
Robert, ye S. of Thomas Parker, of Wheelton ... ... „ 12
John, ye S. of Richard Carefoot, of Whittle ... ... „ 19
James, ye S. of John Beardsworth, of Farington ... „ 26
John, ye S. of William Hawworth, of Whittle ... ... July 10
Elizabeth, ye D. of William Boydall, & ... ... „ 31
Margaret, ye D. of Richard Rose, both of Euxton ... „ 31
B. Richard, ye bastard child of John Somner & Margret
Taylor, of Leyland ... ... Aug. 2
Evan, ye S. of Thomas Withnel, of Heapey ... ... „ 5
Margret, ye D. of William Gooden, of Leyland ... ... „ 21
Alice, ye D. of Edward Whittle, of Leyland ... ... „ 25
Elizabeth, ye D. of William Leyland, of Cuerden ... „ 28
Elizabeth, ye D. of Richard Parker, of Leyland... ... „ 28
James, ye S. of John Livesey, of Withnell [Inserted]... Sept. 10
B. Hugh, ye bastard child of Thomas Moss & Elizabeth
Clayton, of Clayton ... ... „ 13
Richard, ye S. of Mr. Ralph Assheton,[3] of Leyland ... „ 14

---

[1] Transcript signed by Vicar and Churchwardens.   [2] See p. 70.

[3] Among the marriages for the year 1695 is an entry "Mr. Ralph Assheton, of Cuerdale, and Mrs. Sarah Bruen, of the parish of Leyland." The lady there mentioned was the only daughter of Tilson Bruen, of Bruen Stapleford, co. Chester, Esq., by his wife Lucy, d. of Sir Richard Hoghton, Bart. Mr. Ralph Assheton was of Cuerdale, and also of Downham, co. Lanc. He was succeeded in his estates by a son Ralph baptised in 1696, Dec. 28th (? at Walton). The son Richard whose baptism is here recorded died without issue.

Alice, ye D. of John Slaytor, of Euxton ... ... Oct.   2
Elizabeth, ye D. of Thomas Croft, of Whittle ... ...   „   16
Thomas, ye S. of John Green, of Leyland ... ...   „   29
Thomas, ye S. of Michael Tailor, of Clayton ... ... Nov.   6
Cicely, ye D. of Richard Lever, of Clayton ... ...   „   11
Robert & William, ye sons of Ralph Walmsley, of
    Whittle ... ...   „   20
James, ye S. of John Taylor, of Kuerden [Inserted] ...   „   27
Mary, ye D. of Ralph Livesay, of Leyland ... ...   „   28
Ann, ye D. of Richard Waring, of Leyland, & ... ... Dec.   4
B. James, ye S. of James Boys & Ellen Moulden, of
    Whittle ... ...   „   4
Adam, ye S. of Robert Clayton, of ffarington ... ...   „   11
Alexander, ye S. of Lawrence Parsons... ... ...   „   13
William, ye S. of John Sumner, of Leyland... ... ...   „   27
Mary, ye D. of Robert Low, of Whittle ... ...   „   30
Jennet, ye D. of Thomas Bromeley, of Withnell... ... Jan.   1
Jennet, ye D. of William Sharrock, of Euxton [Inserted]   „   3
John, ye S. of Robert Blackburn, of Kuerden ... ...   „   8
Martha, ye D. of John Piper, of Whittle ... ...   „   8
Margaret, ye D. of John Wilkinson, of Leyland ... ...   „   8
Margaret, ye D. of John Mackeril, of Leyland ... ...   „   12
Hugh, ye S. of Lawrence Lucas, of Whittle... ... ...   „   15
John, ye S. of William Cross, of Euxton ... ...   „   22
Thomas, ye S. of Andrew Cooper, of Euxton ... ...   „   29
John, ye S. of John Morris, of Raddlesworth[1] [Inserted] ffeb.   15
Thomas, ye S. of William Calderbank, of Euxton ...   „   19
Robert, ye S. of Robert Cocker, of Leyland... ... ...   „   19
John, ye S. of Edward Sumner, of Leyland... ... ...   „   26
James, ye S. of James Livesay, of Withnel [Inserted].. Mar.   9
John, ye S. of Roger Blackburn, of Keurden ... ...   „   12
Elizabeth, ye D. of Mr. William ffarington,[2] of Ley-
    land ... ...   „   12
Jane, ye D. of Thomas Watson, of Whittle... ... ...   „   19

1699 Ɏstenings.[3]

Miles, ye S. of Henry Weaver, of Leyland ... ... Mar.   26
Thomas, ye S. of Thomas Eastham, of Cuerden... ... Ap.   1
Ann, ye D. of Michael Southworth, of Wheelton ...   „   2
Mary, ye D. of Robert Charnock, of Charnock-Richard   „   2

[1] A township in the Moor quarter of Leyland parish.
[2] See note, ffeb. 14, 1696-7.   This child Elizabeth was buried May 23, 1699.
[3] The transcript is signed (on the back) by the Vicar and Churchwardens.

H

Alexander, ye S. of John Halliwell, of Whittle	Ap.	6
John, ye S. of John Duncalf, of Heapey	"	7
Richard, ye S. of John Bromely, of Leyland	"	9
Dorathy, ye D. of William Haworth, of Whittle... ...	"	9
William, ye S. of Roger Walton, Jun[r], of Leyland ...	"	16
James, ye S. of Thurstan Leyland, of Leyland	"	16
Anthony, ye S. of John Pincock, of Euxton...	"	16
Elizabeth, ye D. of Mr. William Sherd, of Clayton ...	"	19
Isabel, ye D. of Oliver Garstang, of Whittle	"	20
Jennet, ye D. of Robert Baron, of Euxton	"	25
Henery, ye S. of Leonard Cheetham, Traveller	May	15
John, ye S. of William Walmsley, of Hoghton [Inserted]	"	19
Thomas, ye S. of James Hall, of Euxton	"	21
Ann, ye D. of John Atherton, of Leyland	"	21
Ellen, ye D. of William Nield, of Euxton	June	11
Jennet, ye D. of John Calderbank, of Clayton	"	18
William, ye S. of Ralph Somner, of Leyland	July	16
James, ye S. of Thomas Cooper, &⎫	"	23
Thomas, ye S. of Robert Sumner, ⎰of Leyland	"	23
Elizabeth, ye D. of Henry Garstang, of Heapey ...	Aug.	26
Elizabeth, ye D. of Robert Stones, of Euxton	Sept.	3
Elizabeth, ye D. of Hugh Smith, of Euxton	"	3
Jane, ye D. of John Marsden, of Wheelton	"	17
Christopher, ye S. of Thomas Somner, of Euxton ...	"	18
William, ye S. of Thomas Abbott, of Heapey	Oct.	1
James, ye S. of William Marsden, of Whittle	"	1
Ann, ye D. of Lawrence Silcock, of Withnell	"	1
Ann, ye D. of Richard Watmough, of Clayton	"	2
Edward, ye S. of John Clayton, Jun[r], of Clayton ...	"	8
Mary, ye D. of George Bury, of Withnell	"	29
Henery, ye S. of Richard Critchlaw, of Euxton	Nov.	1
Ellen, ye D. of Adam Clayton, of Farington	"	5
William, ye S. of Thomas Garstang, of Whittle	"	7
Jane, ye D. of James Gerrard, of Clayton	"	12
Margret, ye D. of John Stopforth, of Leyland	"	28
Alice, ye D. of William Sharrock, of Euxton	"	29
George, ye S. of George Porter, of Leyland	"	30
Ellis, ye S. of John Somner, of Leyland, Smith... ...	Dec.	3
William, ye S. of William Slater, of Leyland	"	12
John, ye S. of John Clayton, of Clayton, Sen[r]	"	21
John & William, ye sons of John Leyland, of Leyland	Jan.	6
Elizabeth, ye D. of George Moonk, of Leyland	"	7
Ann, ye D. of Charles Rothwell	"	21
John, ye S. of Gilbert Roscow, of Euxton	"	28

Jennet, ye D. of John Hawworth, of Whittle ... ... Feb. 4
John, ye S. of Thomas Low, of Euxton ... ... „ 25
Ann, ye D. of Peter Wethersby, of Leyland ... ... Mar. 1

1700 ʒstenings.[1]

Hugh, ye S. of Richard Nelson, jun^r, of Leyland ... Mar. 25
James, ye S. of Richard Balshaw, of Euxton ... ... Ap. 1
John, ye S. of John Jackson, of Leyland ... ... „ 3
Sarah, ye D. of Henry Seed, of Withnell ... ... „ 5
Henery, ye S. of William Blackledg, of Wheelton ... „ 11
William, ye S. of William Boydal, jun^r, of Euxton ... „ 14
Henery, ye S. of Thomas Eastham, of Leyland ... ... „ 16
Anne, ye D. of John Blackledge, of Wheelton ... ... „ 21
Ellis, ye S. of Roger Bolton, of Euxton ... ... „ 28
Anne, ye D. of John Riding, of Leyland ... ... May 12
Elizabeth, ye D. of William Jackson, jun^r, of Kuerden „ 19
Alice, ye D. of James Asley, of Whittle ... ... „ 21
William, ye S. of John Somner, Junr, of Lostock ... June 9
John, ye S. of William Cooper, of Leyland ... ... „ 9
Ellen, ye D. of Richard Almond, of Leyland ... ... „ 9
Mary, ye D. of Hugh Waterworth, of Leyland ... ... „ 29
John, ye S. of Edward Wood, of Clayton ... ... July 7
George, ye S. of William Hawworth, of Whittle... ... Aug. 11
William, ye S. of Edward Park, of Leyland ... ... „ 18
Mary, ye D. of Ralph Eves, of Keurden ... ... „ 25
William, ye S. of John Surjant, of Leyland... ... ... Sept. 1
Catherine, ye D. of Thomas Tindesly, of Charnock-Ri: „ 8
Elizabeth, ye D. of James Eastham, of Leyland... ... „ 15
Peter, ye S. of Robert Turner, of Leyland, & ... ... „ 29
Michael, ye S. of Michael Taylor, of Whittle ... ... „ 29
Thomas, ye S. of John Tomson, of Leyland ... ... „ 29
Ellen, ye D. of John Freerson, of Cuerden ... ... „ 29
Jane, ye D. of William Hawworth, of Clayton ... ... Oct. 6
Ann, ye D. of George Brown, of Withnell ... ... „ 10
[2]Sarah, ye D. of Edward Crane, of Clayton [Inserted]. Nov. 2
Henery, ye S. of William Croft, of Whittle... ... ... „ 3
John, ye S. of John Slaytor, of Euxton House ... ... „ 10
Sarah, ye D. of Edward Crane, of Clayton ... ... „ 10
Sarah, ye D. of George Dawson, of Leyland ... ... „ 17
Margaret, ye D. of Edmund Piccop, of Heapey... ... „ 24

---

[1] The transcript is signed by Vicar Armetriding and the four Churchwardens.
Writing clear.

[2] Entered twice, in the one case on the 2nd, in the other on the 10th.

James, ye S. of Hugh Crook, of Whittle	... ... Nov.	24
John, ye S. of Thomas Crook, of ffarington...	„	24
Ann, ye D. of Roger Garstang, of Whittle ... ... Dec.	8
Thomas, ye S. of John Shaw, of Whittle	„	15
Jenet, ye D. of Henery Whalley, of Leyland	„	22
William, ye S. of John Smith, of Cuerden	„	25
Margret, ye D. of John Anderton, Traveller	„	30
[1]Grace, ye D. of Thomas Bromeley, of Withnell ...	„	30
Giles, ye S. of Richard Leaver, of Leyland... ... ... Jan.	19
William, ye S. of William Leyland, of Kuerden	„	19
Henry, ye S. of Hugh Smith, of Euxton	„	23
Magdalene, ye D. of Roger ffishwick, of Withnell ... ffeb.	9
Robert, ye S. of Robert Somner, of Leyland	„	16
John Clayton, ye S. of John Abbot, of Clayton ... ... Mar.	2
Alice, ye D. of John Cooper, of Leyland	„	2
Richard, ye S. of William Calderbank, of Euxton ...	„	12
Jane, ye D. of William Slaytor, Sen[r], of Leyland ...	„	15
John, ye S. of John Sumner, Jun[r], of Cuerden	„	16
William, ye S. of John Halliwell, of Whittle	„	16
Henry, ye S. of Henry Moulden, of Leyland	„	16
Edward, ye S. of Peter Clayton, of ffarington	„	16
Elizabeth, ye D. of Roger Walton, Jun[r], of Leyland...	„	16
John, ye S. of John Stephenson, of Leyland	„	23
Ellen, ye D. of John Somner, of Leyland	„	23

1701 Estenings.[2]

Elizabeth, ye D. of John Piper, of Whittle ... ... Ap.	6
James, ye S. of John Harrison, of Kuerden...	„	10
Catherine, ye D. of William Ugnal, of Wheelton ...	„	13
William, ye S. of William Hesketh, of Clayton	„	17
Bridget, ye D. of Thomas Silcock, in Leyland	„	21
James, ye S. of John Willkingson, of Leyland	„	27
William, ye S. of Richard Rose, of Euxton ... ... May	4
Thomas, ye S. of John Bromeley, of Leyland	„	4
Robert, ye S. of Richard Parker, of Leyland	„	4
William, ye S. of George Porter, of Leyland	„	11
John, ye S. of Robert Foster, of Euxton	„	25
Ralph, ye S. of Ralph Whittle, of Whittle	„	25
John, ye S. of John Wallwork, of Leyland... ... ... June	1
Ann, ye D. of Adam Clayton, of ffarington...	„	8

[1] Inserted, but in the same hand.
[2] The transcript is signed as in the previous year. Closely written, but clear.

Jennet, ye D. of Evan Heald, of Euxton, Xstd. at
Chorley [Inserted] ... ... June 8
Ann, ye D. of John Clayton, Junr, of Cuerden ... ... „ 22
Margret, ye D. of John Clough, of Leyland ... ... „ 24
Ralph, ye S. of Robert Low, of Whittle ... ... „ 30
Peter, ye S. of George Wilson, Traveller ... ... July 5
John, ye S. of John Atherton, of Leyland ... ... „ 6
Ellen, ye D. of John Leyland, of Leyland ... ... „ 6
Ruth, ye D. of Lawrence Lucas, of Whittle ... ... „ 20
William, ye S. of Thomas Sumner, of Euxton ... ... „ 24
Hannah, ye D. of William Farington, of Farington ... „ 31
John, ye S. of Thomas Harrison, of Euxton ... ... Aug. 3
Edward, ye S. of William Marsden, of Whittle ... ... „ 3
James, ye S. of Thomas Abbot, of Heapy, Xs^{tnd} at
Chorley... ... ... „ 3
William, ye S. of William Man, of Euxton... ... ... „ 10
Alice, ye D. of Michael Southworth, of Wheelton ... „ 17
Richard, ye S. of Andrew Stones, of Leyland ... ... „ 28
Alice, ye D. of John Slaytor & Catherine Holmes, of
Leyland... ... ... Sept. 1
Henry, ye S. of John Tod, of Leyland... ... ... „ 8
Edward, ye S. of Robert Blackledge, of Heapy... ... „ 21
Ellen, ye D. of William Jackson, of Leyland ... ... „ 21
Hugh, ye S. of Richard Waring, of Leyland [Inserted] „ 29
Jennet, ye D. of William Sharrock, of Euxton ... ... Oct. 3
Richard, ye S. of William Dewhurst, of Withnel ... „ 3
William Edward,¹ ye S. of Mr. William Farington, of
Shaw Hall in Leyland ... ... „ 8
Mary, ye D. of Richard Balshaw, of Euxton ... ... „ 12
Robert, ye S. of Robert Longton & Thomasin Johnson,
of Whittle ... ... „ 12
John, S. to Richard Gooden, in Whittle ... ... „ 16
Jane, ye D. of Hugh Woods, of Withnell ... ... „ 16
Roger, ye S. of James Walton, of Leyland ... ... „ 19
John, Son to William Wiggins, in Leyland... ... ... „ 19
Martha, ye D. of John Sumner, of Leyland ... ... „ 19
Ann, ye D. of George Moonk, of Leyland ... ... „ 26
Ralph, ye S. of Ralph Hey, of Heapey ... ... Nov. 2
Samuel, ye S. of Samuel Duncalf, of Heapey ... ... „ 2
John, ye S. of John Garstang (*alias* Smith), of Whittle „ 21
Lawrence, ye S. of Thomas Croft, of Whittle ... ... „ 23
William, ye S. of John Pincock, of Euxton... ... ... Dec. 14

¹ Buried at Leyland, Sep. 14, 1702. Son of Mr. William Farington and Elizabeth his wife (née Rufine).

Elizabeth, ye D. of Henry Croft, of Cuerden	Dec.	14
Margret, ye D. of Robert Charnock, of Charnock Richar, Standish prsh.	„	21
Agnes, ye D. of Richard Crichlow, of Wheelton ...	„	21
¹Amy, ye D. of Evan Lea, of Leyland, born	Jan.	2
William, ye S. of Thomas Shaw, of Whittle	„	4
John, ye S. of John Marsden, of Wheelton	„	10
James, ye S. of Thomas Watson, of Whittle	Feb.	8
James, ye S. of John Calderbank, in Clayton	„	19
William, ye S. of Edward Sumner, of Leyland	„	22
Ann, ye D. of William Gerrard, &	Mar.	8
Ann, ye D. of Thomas Eastham, of Leyland	„	8
Thomas, ye S. of John Gerrard, of Leyland	„	22

Ystenings in ye year 1702.²

Thomas, ye S. of Elizabeth Waterworth & Thomas Briers, of Euxton...	Ap.	4
John, ye S. of Ralph Somner, of Leyland	„	5
Ann, ye D. of Nicholas Bromeley, of Leyland	„	7
Elisabeth, ye D. of Ralph Longton, of Whittle	„	12
Ellen, ye D. of Roger Bolton, of Euxton	„	19
Margret, ye D. of Francis Serjeant, of Leyland... ...	May	2
Margaret, ye D. of Robert Baron, of Euxton	„	17
Alice, ye D. of William Higginson, of Euxton	„	24
Alice, ye D. of John Scot, of Whittle	June	3
Thomas and James, Sons to Robert Cocker, of Leyland	„	7
Alice, ye D. of Thomas Crook, of Farington	„	14
John, ye S. of John Farnworth, of Wheelton	„	16
Henry, ye S. of Richard Carefoot, of Whittle	„	21
John, ye S. of Ralph Pierson, of Whittle	„	21
Richard, ye S. of Robert Stones, of Euxton	„	28
Richard, ye S. of Thomas Low, of Euxton...	Aug.	2
Evan, ye S. of Richard Haydock, of Whittle	„	2
Mary, ye D. of Oliver Garstang, of Whittle...	„	2
Elizabeth,³ ye D. of Mr. William Farington, of Shaw Hall, Leyland	„	25
Robert, ye S. of Robert Nightingale & Elizabeth Clayton, of Clayton	Sept.	13
Jane, ye D. of John Brady, Traveller	„	27

¹ Inserted, but in the same hand.

² Transcript signed as before. It is closely written. In some places illegible.

³ This lady became the wife of Richard Atherton, of Atherton, Esq., and the great-grandmother of Lord Lilford.

Thomas, ye S. of Thomas Cooper, of Leyland ... ... Oct. 4
John, ye S. of Thomas Clayton, of Farington ... ... „ 4
Elizabeth, ye D. of John Bromeley, of Leyland... ... „ 4
Sarah, ye D. of Thurstan ffishwick, of Radlesworth[1]... „ 5
Ellen, ye D. of William Sharrock, of Euxton ... ... „ 18
Richard, ye S. of John Abbot, of Clayton ... ... „ 25
Elizabeth, ye D. of John Hawworth, of Whittle... ... „ 25
William, ye S. Alexander Gerrard, of Hoghton... ... „ 30
Elizabeth, ye D. of Thomas Bury, of Hoghton ... ... „ 30
Edward, ye S. of Thomas Tildsley, in Charnock Richard Nov. 1
Lawrence, ye S. of Richard Almond, of Leyland ... „ 1
Thomas, ye S. of William Neeld, of Euxton ... ... „ 22
Elizabeth, ye D. of Thomas Sumner, of Euxton ... „ 23
Thomas, ye S. of Henry Smith, of Kuerden ... ... Dec. 1
John, ye S. of Thomas Silcock, of Clayton ... ... „ 6
Mary, ye D. of William Croft, of Whittle ... ... „ 13
Elizabeth, ye D. of Peter Wethersby, of Leyland ... „ 17
John, ye S. of John Wilcock, of Hoghton ... ... „ 24
Ann, ye D. of Thomas Nowel, of Leyland ... ... „ 29
Ellen, ye D. of Gilbert Roscow, of Euxton... ... ... Jan. 1
William, ye S. of William Cooper, of Leyland ... ... „ 1
Margret, ye D. of Edward Park, in Leyland ... ... „ 3
Alice, ye D. of John Sumner, of Leyland, Webster ... „ 6
John, ye S. of John Harrison, of Cuerden ... ... „ 24
John, ye S. of John Clayton, of Clayton ... ... ffeb. 11
Nicholas, ye S. of Thomas Crook, of Leyland ... ... „ 13
Alice, ye D. of John Serjeant, of Leyland ... ... „ 14
Elizabeth, ye D. of John Hawworth, of Euxton... ... „ 14
John, ye S. of John Halliwell, & }of Whittle ... „ 21
Elizabeth, ye D. of William Haworth}
John, ye S. of Hugh Crook, of Whittle ... ... Mar. 1
Elizabeth, ye D. of John Yate, of Heapey ... ... „ 14
Joseph, ye S. of Andrew Wilson, of Whittle ... ... „ 14
Charles, ye S. of Charles Rothwel, of Leyland ... ... „ 14
William, ye S. of Samuel Baxenden, of Euxton... ... „ 14
Hugh, ye S. of Thomas Rigby, of Heapey ... ... „ 17

[1] Radlesworth, otherwise Roddleworth or Rothwelsworth, a township in the Moor quarter of Leyland parish. It anciently formed, with Wythenhull, Ollerton, Stanworth, Whelton, and Euxton, the district called Gunoldsmores, consisting of four carucates and a half of land, part of the inheritance of Richard Bussel, Baron of Penwortham. The name Rothwelsworth is also applied to the stream more generally known as the Moulden Water, which descends on the eastern side of the moors.

¥stenings, 1703.[1]

Elizabeth, ye D. of John Clough, of Leyland	Mar.	25
Ellis, ye S. of Michael Taylor, of Whittle	„	26
B. Alice, ye D. of Will[m] Croston, of Ulneswalton, &		
Ellen Markland, of Leyland	„	26
Robert, ye S. of William ffarington, Jun[r], of ffarington.	„	28
Mary, ye D. of William Gooden, of Euxton	„	28
Ann, ye D. of John Waller, of Whittle [Inserted] ...	Ap.	3
William, ye S. of Thomas Roscow, of Euxton	„	6
Ann, ye D. of Roger Garstang, of Whittle	„	11
Isabel, ye D. of James Eastham, of Leyland	„	11
Samuel, ye S. of Samuel Duncalf, of Heapey	„	18
Jonathan, ye S. of John Sumner, Jun[r], of Lostock[2] in		
Leyland...	„	28
Cicely, ye D. of Roger Walton, Jun[r], of Leyland ...	May	2
Catherin, ye D. of John Brooks, of Heapey	„	2
Thomas, ye S. of John Cooper, of Leyland...	„	17
Mary, ye D. of William Leyland, of Cuerden	„	23
Robert, ye S. of Robert Low, of Whittle	„	24
Elizabeth, ye D. of Henry Whalley, of Leyland ...	„	31
Mary,[3] ye D. of Edward Farnworth, of Runshaw in		
Euxton	„	31
Hugh, ye S. of Roger Crook, of Whittle	June	7
Martha, ye D. of Edward Crane, of Clayton [Inserted]	„	8
Elizabeth, ye D. of Thomas Porter, of Leyland	„	13
Thomas, ye S. of John Woodcock, of Leyland	„	14
Alice, ye D. of Henry Tod, of Leyland	„	27
Jennet, ye D. of John Leyland, of Leyland...	July	4
Mary, ye D. of John Piper, of Whittle	„	18
William, ye S. of John Asley, of Whittle, born	„	20
Richard, ye S. of Richard Wallwork, of Leyland ...	„	25
Roger, ye S. of Thomas Croft, of Whittle	„	25
Mary, ye D. of John Smith, of Cuerden	„	25
Ellen, ye D. of Thomas ffarnworth, of Hoghton[4] ...	„	27
Elizabeth, ye D. of Francis Serjeant, of Leyland ...	Aug.	4
Elizabeth, ye D. of Henry Southworth, of Clayton ...	„	15

---

[1] The transcript is signed by the Vicar and Churchwardens. Closely written and in places illegible.

[2] See note, page 76.

[3] See Baptisms, July 4, 1674, and May 30, 1676. Mrs. Mary Patten was buried at Leyland, Nov. 10, 1784.

[4] A township in Leyland parish, which lies over against Blackburn, now made parochial.

Elizabeth, ye D. of Edward Woodcock, of Euxton ... Aug. 18
Thomas, ye S. of William Cuerden, of Clayton, born... „ 21
Jennet, ye D. of Christopher Marsden, of Withnel, born „ 22
John, the S. of Robert Wilkinson, of Hoghton
[Inserted] ... ... Sept. 6
Ciceley, ye D. of William Tootel, at Swansey house[1] in
Whittle, born, &c. ... ... „ 15
Jane, ye D. of John Bury, of Withnel ... ... „ 25
Benjamin, ye S. of Thomas Withnel, of Heapey ... „ 26
Catherin, ye D. of William Sherd, of Clayton-hall[2] ... Oct. 5
William, ye S. of Isaac Sharrock, in Whittle ... ... „ 7
Thomas, ye S. of William Porter, of Leyland ... ... „ 10
James, ye S. of Evan Heald, of Euxton ... ... „ 24
Alice, ye D. of John Clayton, Jun[r], of Clayton ... ... „ 24
Jennet, ye S. of John Walkden, of Hoghton ... ... „ 30
Thomas, ye S. of Robert Foster, of Euxton ... ... Nov. 14
Jennet, ye D. of Richard Parker, of Leyland ... ... „ 21
Margret, ye D. of Ralph Longton, of Whittle ... ... „ 30
Ellen, ye D. of Lawrence Lucas, of Whittle ... ... Dec. 12
Elizabeth, ye D. of William Jackson, of Leyland ... „ 12
Alice, ye D. of Henry Tomlinson, a Poor Traveller ... „ 19
Richard, ye S. of Richard Briers, of Withnel ... ... „ 23
John, ye S. of John Riding, of Leyland ... ... „ 23
Elizabeth, ye D. of Samuel Baxenden, in Clayton ... „ 26
Thomas, ye S. of Thomas Sumner, of Leyland ... ... „ 27
Francis, ye S. of Richard Nelson, Jun[r], of Leyland ... „ 27
James, ye S. of Richard Lancaster, of Clayton ... ... Jan. 9
Thomas, ye S. of William Croft, of Whittle... ... ... „ 10
Henry, ye S. of Henry Seed, of Withnel ... ... „ 17
Ann, ye D. of James Walton, of Leyland ... ... „ 23
Henry, ye S. of John Kirkham, of Farington ... ... „ 25
John, ye S. of Richard Wilson, of Whittle, sd. to be
Xst[nd] ... ... „ 23
Margaret, ye D. of Ralph Eves, of Cuerden ... ... Feb. 3
William, ye S., & Margaret, ye D. of John Garstang,
of Whittle ... ... „ 5
William, ye S. of Robert Simpson, in Leyland, sd. to
be Xst[nd] ... ... „ 6
Jennet, the D. of John Blackledg, of Wheelton ... ... „ 13
James, ye S. of Nicholas Bromeley, of Leyland... ... „ 27

---

[1] Swansey House is situated just at the point where the boundary between Brindle parish and Whittle-le-Woods township is cut by the Lancaster Canal. It lies only a short distance to the right of the high road from Chorley to Preston. Dr. Kuerden mentions it. *Vide* Baines' *History of Lancashire* (edit. Croston), p. 215.

[2] See note on earlier entry, Oct. 23, 1693.

Thomas, ye S. of Richard Chrichlow, of Wheelton ... Feb. 27
Thomas, ye S. of William Dewhurst, of Withnel ... „ 29
John, ye S. of John Harrison, of Cuerden ... ... Mar. 12

Ᵹstnings, 1704.[1]

Richard, ye S. of William Higgison, of Charnock Rich^rd,
   Stan: P^s [Standish Parish]... ... ... Mar. 26
Margaret, ye D. of Leonard Cheetham, a Traveller ... „ 26
John, ye S., & ⎱of William Wright, of Euxton ... „ 28
Elizabeth, ye D.⎰
A Child of John Slaytor and Mary Sagers, born in
   Euxton ... ... Ap. 2
Mary, ye D. of Richard Baxenden, in Leyland ... ... „ 2
William, ye S., & ⎱of Robert Blackledg, of Heapy ... „ 9
Jane, ye D. ⎰
Alice, ye D. of John Baron, of Euxton ... ... „ 9
Ellen, ye D. of John Slaytor, of Euxton ... ... „ 9
Dorothy, ye D. of Richard Leaver, of Leyland ... ... „ 9
James, ye S. of Thomas Harrison, of Euxton ... ... „ 16
Francis, ye S. of Mr. John Walmsley, of Wigan Lane,
   and Margery Walkden, of Hoghton, sd. to be X^std ... „ 20
William, ye S. of Hugh Woods, of Withnel ... ... „ 30
William, ye S. of William Worden, of Clayton, s^d ... May 4
Henry, ye S. of Richard Crook, of Euxton... ... ... „ 7
John, ye S. of James Walmsley, of Withnel... ... ... „ 14
Thomas, ye S. of Evan Eastham, of Farington ... ... „ 21
Ellen, ye D. of John Tod, of Leyland ... ... „ 21
Ann, ye D. of John Woodcock, Junr, of Kuerden ... „ 29
Margaret, ye D. of William Asley, of Whittle, s^d to be
   X^stnd ... ... „ 29
Elizabeth, ye D. of Samuel Duncalf, of Heapey... ... June 11
P.[2] James, ye S. of William Physakarley, of Whittle,
   s^d to be X^stnd [Inserted] ... ... „ 17
Frances, ye D. of James Noblet, of Leyland ... ... „ 18
Winifrid, ye D. of James Asley, of Whittle, s^d to be
   X^stnd ... ... „ 23

---

[1] Transcript signed by the Vicar and three of the Churchwardens. The writing is clear, but the parchment is torn in places.

[2] The P. here put before the name probably stands for Papist. The expression, "said to be christened," may indicate such a baptism, the entry being made that a public and officially recognised certificate might hereafter be obtainable. In some instances the child may have been privately baptised by some other person than the parish clergyman, and the entry indicates the date of the public reception into the Church.

Agnes, ye D. of William Marsden, of Whittle ... ...June 25
John, ye S. of Ellis Somner, of Leyland ... ... „ 26
Alice, ye D. of Ralph Pierson, of Whittle ... ... July 4
Ralph, ye S. of William Hawworth, of Clayton ... ... „ 16
Margery, ye D. of Robert Waring, of Leyland ... ... „ 16
James, ye S. of Thomas Withington, of Clayton, s[d] ... „ 23
Alice, ye D. of John Hawworth, of Whittle... ... ... „ 30
Mary, ye D. of Thomas Day, of Whittle ... ... Aug. 13
Ann, ye D. of Richard Procter, of Cuerden... ... ... „ 13
Joseph, ye S. of Evan Lea, of Leyland, s[d] to be X[stnd].. „ 15
Henry, ye S. of Matthew Bickursteth, of Farington ... „ 20
Mary, ye D. of John Sumner, of Leyland, Blacksmith . „ 20
Ann, ye D. of Henry Harrison, Jun[r], of Clayton, s[d] to
  be X[stnd]... ... ... „ 25
James, ye S. of William Wiggins, in Leyland ... ... Sept. 7
Richard, ye S. of John Boond, of ye P[rish] of Northmeals[1] „ 10
Elizabeth, ye D. of Ellis Somner, Jun[r], of Euxton, s[d]
  to be X[stnd] ... ... „ 17
Richard, ye S. of Roger Anderton, of Hoghton, s[d] to
  be X[stnd]... ... ... „ 17
Alice, ye D. of John Walmsley, of Heapey... ... ... Oct. 1
Elizabeth, ye D. of Adam Clayton, of Farington ... „ 8
Henry, ye S. of John Yate, of Heapey... ... ... „ 10
Lawrence, ye S. of John Serjant, of Leyland ... ... „ 15
John, ye S. of Richard Tomlinson, of Farington ... Nov. 5
Henry, ye S. of Henry Breckall, of Leyland, & Ann
  Moulden, of Heapey ... ... „ 5
Alice, ye D. of John Abbot, of Clayton ... ... „ 5
John, ye S. of James Brown, of Farington ... ... „ 12
William,[2] ye S. of Mr. William Farington, of Shaw Hall,
  X[stnd] at Preston ... ... „ 13
Elizabeth, ye D. of William Smith, of Leyland ... ... „ 19
Matthew, ye S. of John Talbot, of Wheelton, s[d] to be
  X[stnd] ... ... „ 27
Margaret, ye D. of Christopher Marsden, of Withnel... Dec. 10

---

[1] There has always been a close historical connection between Leyland and North Meols (the northern part of modern Southport). The tithes of both were granted by Warin Bussel, Baron of Penwortham, about 1086, to the Abbey of Evesham, in Worcestershire. This grant was confirmed and added to by his descendants. The ffleetwoods, of Penwortham, became patrons of both livings.

[2] Brother to George ffarington, of Worden, Esq., who married Margaret Bradshaw. This gentleman took holy orders, and in 1734 became Vicar of Leigh (Lanc.); after which he was appointed Rector of Warrington (in 1767), but died in the same year. He married Hester, daughter and coheir of . . . . Gilbody, of Manchester. From this marriage descend the ffaringtons of Wood Vale (Isle of Wight) and the ffaringtons of Wigan.

Alice, ye D. of William Norris, in Leyland	Dec.	10
Isabel, ye D. of John Brooks, of Heapey	„	10
William, ye S. of Francis Serjeant, of Leyland	„	17
Thomas, ye S. of Thomas Clithero, of Euxton	„	17
Ellen, ye D. of Robert Rutter, of Hutton,[1] born in Cuerden & sd. to be Baptized	„	17
Thomas, ye S. of Thomas Garstang, of Whittle	„	24
Jennet, ye D. of Roger Bolton, of Euxton	„	24
Elizabeth, ye D. of Thomas Croft, of Whittle	Jan.	4
James, ye S. of Jonathan Rigby, of Cuerden	„	14
Jane, ye D. of William Jackson, of Leyland	„	14
Seth, ye S. of John Bromeley, in Leyland	„	14
James, ye S. of John Wilcock, of Hoghton	„	16
Christofer, ye S. of John Sumner, of Leyland, Webster	„	21
Thomas, ye S. of Robert Stones, of Euxton	„	21
Henry, ye S. of Henry Cattherall, of Clayton, s^d to be X^{stnd}	„	25
Alice, ye D. of John Hawworth, of Euxton...	„	28
John, ye S. of Andrew Wilson, of Whittle	Feb.	4
Ann, ye D. of Ralph Sumner, of Leyland	„	11
William, ye S. of Thomas Wesby, of Cuerden, s^d to be X^{stnd}	„	11
Edmund, ye S. of Peter Knight, of Euxton...	„	20
Mary, ye D. to James Hodson, in Euxton	„	26
Christofer, S. of John Livesay, of Withnell	Mar.	11
Robert, S. of Evan Trigg,[2] of Wheelton	„	18

Ystenings, 1705.[3]

Elizabeth, ye D. of William Gooden, of Euxton... ...	Mar.	25
Ann, ye D. of Thomas Dewhurst, of Cuerden	„	25
Margret, ye D. of Henry Smith, of Cuerden	„	28
John, ye S. of Roger Crook, of Whittle	Ap.	6
Margret, ye D. of William Shaw, in Leyland	„	15
Elizabeth, ye D. of Robert Cooper, s^d to be X^{stnd} Cuerden	„	16
Richard, ye S. of Richard Almond, of Leyland	„	25
Edward, ye S. of John Farnworth, of Wheelton	„	29
Elizabeth and Jane, Dtrs. of Thomas Silcock, of Clayton	May	6
Henry, ye S. of Hugh Smith, of Euxton	„	13
Alice, ye D. of Thomas Eastham, of Leyland	„	13

[1] A township in Penwortham parish.

[2] A name very uncommon in Leyland parish, but better known in West Derby.

[3] The transcript is very closely written on parchment in a clear hand. It is signed by the Vicar and four Churchwardens.

William, S. of William Porter, of Leyland ... ... May 15
William, ye S. of Richard Bateson, of Withnel ... ... „ 20
Hannah, ye D. of John Piper, of Whittle ... ... „ 27
Richard, ye S. of John Gerrard, of Leyland... ... ... June 3
Edward, ye S. of Thomas Longton, of Whittle ... ... „ 3
Alice, ye D. of Robert Cocker, of Leyland ... ... „ 3
Thomas, ye S. of Roger Walton, Junr, of Leyland ... „ 10
Hannah, ye D. of John Sumner, Junr, of Leyland ... „ 10
William, ye S. of Peter Clayton, & ... ... „ 17
Agnes, ye D. of John Kirkham, of Farington ... ... „ 17
George, ye S. of George Parkinson, of Euxton ... ... „ 24
Alice, ye D. of Alexander Gerrard, of Hoghton ... ... „ 24
Jane, ye D. of William Hawworth, of Whittle ... ... July 1
Roger, ye S. of Richard Anderton, of Hoghton, s^d to
be X^{stnd}... ... ... „ 1
John, ye S. of Thomas Preston, of Withnel ... ... „ 21
James, ye S. of John Dewhurst, of Withnel... ... ... „ 22
Hannah, ye D. of Robert Bury, of Hoghton ... ... „ 22
James, ye S. of Robert Baron, of Euxton ... ... „ 29
Mary, ye D. of William Roscow, of Whittle ... ... Aug. 5
John, ye S. of Roger Blackburn, of Cuerden ... ... „ 26
Alice, ye D. of Thomas Cooper, of Leyland ... ... „ 26
Peter, ye S. of John Halliwell, of Whittle ... ... „ 28
Dorothy, ye D. of Edward Woodcock, of Euxton ... Sept. 4
Ann, ye D. of Samuel Baxenden, of Euxton ... ... „ 9
Ellen, ye D. of John Marsden, of Withnell ... ... „ 9
Henry,[1] ye S. of Mr. William ffarington, of Shaw Hall,
X^{stnd} at Preston ... ... „ 14
Elizabeth, ye D. of William Boydall, Junr, of Euxton... „ 23
Ann, ye D. of Christopher Marsden, of Withnel ... ... „ 23
Ann & Margaret, ye D^{rs} of Richard Clarkson, of
Bretherton,[2] and Elizabeth Waterworth, of Leyland. „ 24
Martin, ye S. of Thomas Pollard, of Cuerden ... ... Oct. 7
Jennet, ye D. of John Pincock, of Euxton ... ... „ 14
Samuel, ye S. of Thomas Smith, of Leyland, s^d to
be X^{stnd}... ... ... Nov. 18
Ellen, ye D. of Richard Bateson, in Leyland ... ... „ 24
William, ye S. of Richard Carefoot, of Whittle ... ... „ 25
Hugh, ye S. of Thomas Sumner, of Leyland ... ... Dec. 5
John, ye S. of John Leyland, of Leyland ... ... „ 9
George, ye S. of Richard Roneson,[3] of Farington ... „ 16

---

[1] This gentleman afterwards married Mary, d. of . . . Peachey, of London.
[2] Bretherton, a township of Croston parish, now made parochial.
[3] The only instance of the name, at all events in this form.

Mary, ye D. of Ralph Walmsley, of Whittle ... ... Dec. 25
Isabel, ye D. of Thomas Walton, of Leyland ... ... „ 28
John, ye S. of Henry Whalley, of Leyland... ... ... Jan. 6
Roger, ye S. of Hugh Crook, of Whittle ... ... „ 20
Mary, ye D. of Richard Biccarsteth, of Whittle ... ... „ 27
Dorothy, ye D. of John Clayton, of Clayton ... ... „ 27
Ann, ye D. of John Bolton, of Hoghton, sd to be Xstnd Feb. 3
Thomas, ye S. of William Morris, of Heapy ... ... „ 3
William, ye S. of James Asley, of Whittle, sd to be Xstnd „ 7
William, ye S. of William Smalshaw, of Holland,[1] &
  Elizabeth Beardwood, of Wheelton ... ... „ 9
Elizabeth, ye D. of Thomas Sumner, of Euxton ... „ 14
William, ye S. of Robert Leaver, of Cuerden ... ... „ 17
Thomas, ye S. of John Nelson, of Leyland... ... ... „ 17
Jennet, ye D. of Henry Kirkham, of Farington... ... Mar. 3
Charles, ye S. of William Worden, of Clayton ... ... „ 5
Richard, ye S. of Thomas Rigby, of Wheelton ... ... „ 7
Elizabeth, ye D. of Thurstan Leyland, of Leyland ... „ 9
Jane, ye D. of Michael Taylor, of Whittle ... ... „ 10
Margret, ye D. of Richard Davies, of Euxton ... ... „ 17
Alice, ye D. of William Hawworth, of Clayton ... ... „ 17
Thomas, ye S. of Ralph Longton, of Whittle ... ... „ 24

[Baptisms] 1706.[2]

Jane, ye D. of William Leyland, of Cuerden ... ... Mar. 31
Agnes, ye D. of Richard Tomlison, of Farington ... „ 31
Ralph, ye S. of Samuel Duncalf, of Heapey ... ... „ 31
Jane, ye D. of John Woodcock, Junr, of Cuerden ... Ap. 1
Joseph, ye S. of Joseph Moonk, of Heapey, & Ann
  Whittle, of Leyland ... ... „ 5
Margret, ye D. of Richard Lancaster, of Leyland, sd
  to be Xstnd ... ... „ 5
Jennet, ye D. of William Porter, of Leyland ... ... „ 11
Amy, ye D. of Richard Eccles, of Hoghton, born ... „ 12
Elizabeth, ye D. of Richard Leaver, of Leyland ... „ 28
Mary, ye D. of Ralph Whittle, of Whittle ... ... „ 28
Thomas, ye S. of Peter Walkden, of Heapey ... ... „ 28
Jane, ye D. of Henry Wadington, Junr, of Hoghton ... „ 28
John, ye S. of John Jackson, of Clayton ... ... May 5

[1] Either Up-holland, in Wigan parish, or Down-holland, in Halsall parish. Probably the former.

[2] The transcript is clearly written, and is signed by Tho: Armetriding, Vicr, and the four churchwardens.

Alice, ye D. of Peter Wethersby, of Leyland ... ... May 5
James, ye S. of James Harrison & Elizabeth Tootel,
of Clayton ... ... „ 5
Alice, ye D. of Richard Armetriding, of Leyland ... „ 10
Alice, ye D. of Lawrence Lucas, of Whittle ... ... „ 12
Mary, ye D. of Richard Briers, of Withnel, s^d to be
X^{stnd} ... ... „ 12
Ann, the D. of James Walmsley, of Withnel [Inserted] „ 26
Richard, ye S. of Peter Unsworth, of Leyland ... ... „ 26
Richard, ye S. of James Higgison, of Euxton ... ... „ 26
James, ye S. of Edward Crane, of Clayton, s^d to be
X^{stnd} ... ... „ 28
Margaret, ye D. of John Sumner, of Leyland, Webster June 9
Mary, ye D. of Evan Lea, of Leyland... ... ... „ 13
Ralph, ye D. of William Higgison, of Whittle ... ... „ 16
James, ye S. of John fforshaw, of Leyland ... ... „ 16
Margaret, ye D. of William Shaw, of Leyland ... ... July 7
Margaret, ye D. of James Hartley, of Ulnswalton ... „ 7
Ann, ye D. of Thomas Marton & Ann Wardley, of
Whittle ... ... „ 7
Thomas,[1] ye S. of Robert Leigh, of Euxton, Gentleman „ 17
Richard, ye S. of Henry Darwin, of Whittle ... ... „ 21
Ann, ye D. of Christofer Marsden, of Withnel ... ... „ 23
Ann, ye D. of Tho: Ainsworth, of Hoghton, s^d to be
X^{stnd} ... ... Aug. 13
Miles, ye S. of Thomas Bury, of Withnel ... ... „ 23
Hugh, ye S. of John Smith, of Walton in Le dale ... „ 25
John, ye S. of Robert Blackledge, of Heapey ... ... „ 25
Ellen, ye D. of Edward Clough, of Leyland ... ... „ 25
Thomas, ye S. of Robert Welch, of Farington ... ... „ 27
Thomas, ye S. of Nicholas Bromeley, of Leyland ... Sept. 8
William, ye S. of William Croft, of Whittle... ... ... „ 15
John, ye S. of William Marsden, of Whittle... ... ... „ 15
James, ye S. of John Tyrer, of Heapey ... ... „ 15
William, ye S. of William Wright, of Euxton ... ... „ 16
Ralph, ye S. of John Walmsley, of Heapey ... ... „ 29
William, ye S. of William Burscow, of Euxton ... ... „ 29
Mary, ye D. of Richard Blackburn, of Withnel ... ... Oct. 6
Ralph, ye S. of Robert Foster, of Euxton ... ... „ 13
Elizabeth, ye D. of Roger Garstang, of Whittle... ... „ 13
Margaret, ye D. of James Walton, of Leyland ... ... Nov. 24

---

[1] There was a family of this name and rank owning property in the adjoining chapelry cf Chorley at this period. Possibly the gentleman named in the text was a connection. See entry on Dec. 16, 1708.

John, ye S. of Robert Low, of Whittle } s^d to be Dec. 9
Hanna, ye D. of Ellis Sumner, Junr, of Euxton } X^{stnd}
Elizabeth, ye D. of Thomas Clithero, of Euxton ... Jan. 6
Elizabeth, ye D. of Hugh Smith, of Cuerden ... ... Feb. 2
Mary, ye D. of Roger Bolton, of Euxton ... ... „ 9
Richard, ye S. of John Tootel, Junr, of Whittle, & ... „ 16
Mary, ye D. of Robert Bury, of Withnel, s^d to be X^{stnd} „ 16
Thomas,[1] ye S. of Mr. Farrond Hodgson, of Leyland,
    S: M: [School Master] ... ... Mar. 3
John, ye S. of Richard Nelson, Junr, of Leyland ... „ 10
Margaret, ye D. of John Wall-Work, of Leyland ... „ 21
William, ye S. of Thomas Cooper, of Leyland ... ... „ 24

Ʒstenings, 1707.[2]

Richard, ye S. of Richard Parker, of Leyland ... ... Mar. 30
Thomas, ye S. of Richard Bateson, of Leyland ... ... Ap. 7
Alice, ye D. of William Rigby, of Leyland ... ... „ 13
Elizabeth, ye D. of John Smith, of Cuerden ... ... „ 13
Richard, ye S. of John Talbot, of Wheelton, s^d to be
    X^{stnd} ... ... „ 13
Alice, ye D. of Thomas Rose, of Euxton ... ... „ 16
Ellen, ye D. of Roger Crook, of Whittle ... ... „ 18
Hugh, the S. of Richard Biccursteth, of Whittle... ... „ 20
Thomas, ye S. of John Slaytor, of Euxton, Taylor ... „ 20
Matthew, ye S. of William Cuerden, of Clayton, s^d to
    be X^{stnd} ... ... „ 21
Alice, ye D. of John Woodcock, Junr, of Cuerden ... „ 29
Margaret, ye D. of Robert Bicursteth, of Euxton ... May 4
Ellen, ye D. of William Cooper, of Leyland ... ... „ 18
Mary, ye D. of Richard Cross, of Leyland ... ... „ 18
Alice, ye D. of John Dixon, of Whittle ... ... „ 18
Hanna, ye D. of James Harrocks, of Euxton ... ... „ 25
Thomas, ye S. of John Abbot, of Clayton ... ... June 1
Thomas, ye S. of Thomas Higham, of Euxton ... ... „ 25
William, ye S. of William Gooden, of Euxton ... ... „ 29
Lawrence, ye S. of Richard Tomlinson, of Farington.. „ 29

[1] See Marriages, March 27, 1705-6. Mr. Farrand Hodgson was licensed as schoolmaster of the Leyland Free Grammar School on Jan. 5, 1703-4, upon the nomination and appointment of the governors and feoffees. Of these latter there were eleven who attached their names to the nomination. The best known of them are Edward ffleetwood, William ffarington, Richard Brooke, George ffarington, and Thomas Armetriding.

[2] The transcript for this year is signed by the Vicar and Churchwardens. Writing very clear.

Ann, ye D. of Henry Smith, of Cuerden	... ...	...July	14
Ann, ye D. of John Hunt, of Cuerden ...	... ...	... „	20
Ann, ye D. of Evan Trigg, of Wheelton	... ...	... „	31
Ann, ye D. of Gilbert Roscoe, of Euxton	... ...	... Aug.	3
Margaret, ye D. of Thomas Longton, of Whittle		... „	10
Thomas, ye S. of Thomas Croft, of Whittle...	...	... „	24
William, ye S. of James Lees, of Heapey	...	... Sept.	6
Thomas, ye S. of Roger Walton, of Leyland	...	... „	7
Henry, ye S. of Ralph Pierson, of Whittle	...	... „	14
Amy, ye D. of Robert Hey, of Heapey	...	... „	21
Margret, ye D. of Hugh Smith, of Euxton	...	... „	21
John, ye S. of John Kirkham, of Farington...	...	... Oct.	2
Ann, ye D. of William Farington, of Leyland	...	... „	4
John, ye S. of Edmund Piccop, of Heapey	...	... „	5
Alice, ye D. of William Smith, of Leyland ...	...	... „	12
Elizabeth, ye D. of Gilbert Cowling, of Leyland...	...	... „	18
Elizabeth, ye D. of John Ditchfield, in Leyland ...	...	... Nov.	1
William, ye S. of John Farnworth, of Wheelton...	...	... „	9
John, ye S. of Thomas Westby, of Cuerden, s[d] to be X[stnd]		„	11
Margaret, ye D. of John Piper	... ...	... ... „	30
Ellen, ye D. of Ralph Longton, of Whittle ...	...	... „	30
John, ye S. of Thomas Parker, of Farington...	...	... Dec.	14
Mary, ye D. of Richard Williamson & Ann Wilson	...	„	28
Richard, ye S. of Robert Hilton, of Euxton	...	... Jan.	1
Ellis, ye S. of Ellis Sumner, of Leyland	... ...	... „	1
Mary, ye D. of George Parkinson, of Euxton	... ...	„	6
Margaret,[1] the D. of William Farington, of Shaw-Hall, Genero[sus]		... „	22
John,[2] ye S. of Richard Armetriding, of Leyland		... ffeb.	16
John, ye S. of Samuel Baxenden, of Euxton	...	... „	29
Ann, ye D. of Robert Wilding, of Leyland ...	...	... „	29
Alice, ye D. of Henry Darwin, of Whittle ...	...	... Mar.	3
James, ye S. of Thomas Sumner, of Leyland	...	... „	7

---

[1] This lady became the wife of William Byssel, of Seabornes, co. Hereford, Esq. She was the sister of George ffarington, Esq., (afterwards) of Worden.

[2] Vicar Armetriding (who died in 1719) bequeathed to this nephew, John, the sum of £150, which was to be increased by the portions of two sisters, Alice and Ann, in case of their early death. John Armetriding received his education at (? Leyland Grammar School, and afterwards at) Kirkham, under Zachary Taylor, M.A., who was head master of the grammar school of that place. On May 1, 1727, John Armetriding was admitted a sizar of Trinity College, Cambridge, and in due course graduated B.A. (1730). His title for ordination seems to have been North Meols, where he was curate for some years. He married at Leyland Church (1736), Jane, d. of Edward Woodcock, of Euxton, yeoman. From 1767 to the date of his death in 1791 he was perpetual curate of Bispham in the Fylde.

‡stnings, 1708.[1]

Thomas, ye S. of John Halliwell, of Whittle	Ap.	2
Thomas, ye S. of William Wiggins, in Leyland	„	6
James, ye S. of John Clayton, of Clayton	„	11
Richard, ye S. of John Cross, of Rixon,[2] & Jennet Gerrard, of Euxton	„	16
William, ye S. of Edward Woodcock, of Euxton ...	„	20
Elizabeth, ye D. of Richard Davis, of Euxton	„	20
Peter, ye S. of Matthew Bickerstaff, of Farington ...	„	22
Mary, ye D. of William Hawworth, of Whittle, Xstnd at Heapey[3] [Inserted]	May	2
James, ye S. of John Knowls, of Euxton	„	4
William, ye S. of John Woodcock, Junr, of Cuerden ...	„	5
Margery, ye D. of John Tomson, of Leyland	„	6
Henry, ye S. of Henry Kirkham, of Farington	„	23
Hanna, ye D. of Thomas Walton, of Leyland	„	30
Elizabeth, ye D. of John Pincock, of Euxton	„	30
Samuel, ye S. of Ralph Sumner, of Leyland	June	14
James, ye S. of John Leyland, of Leyland	„	20
Margaret, ye D. of Edward Clough, in Leyland... ...	„	20
Henry, ye S. of Henry Woods & Mary Walmsley, of Withnel...	„	20
Peter, ye S. of William Boydal, of Euxton	July	4
Elizabeth, ye D. of John Tootel, Junr, of Whittle ...	„	4
Alice, ye D. of John Bromeley, of Leyland	„	4
Susanna, ye D. of William Shaw, of Leyland	„	4
Richard, ye S. of John Gerrard, of Leyland	Aug.	1
John, ye S. of Richard Leaver, of Leyland	„	8
Hugh, ye S. of John Simm, of Euxton...	„	8
Judith, ye D. of Hugh Crook, of Whittle	„	15
Ann, ye D. of John Roocroft & Margaret Sumner ...	„	15
Miles, ye S. of John Berry, of Heapey	„	22
John, ye S. of Thomas Jackson, of Lealand	„	29
Richard, ye S. of Richard Crook, of Euxton	„	29
John, ye S. of Thomas Hall, *alias* Arthrick, of Cuerden	Sept.	2
Henry, ye S. of William Man, of Euxton	„	5

[1] Transcript on parchment. Closely written. Writing fair. Signed as before.

[2] Rixton with Glazebrook, in Warrington parish.

[3] This is the earliest *recorded* instance of the administration of holy baptism in the Chapel-of-Ease at Heapey. There was in existence before 1554 (perhaps only as an oratory) a certain building known as Hepay Chapel, which received notice from the Church Commissioners of Edward VI., and of which they made report. In the Cromwellian Survey of 1650, Hepay was reported as fit to be made parochial. The chapelry became a separate parish under the Blandford Act about 1847.

Ann, ye D. of Robert Cocker, of Leyland ... ... Sept. 19
Mary, ye D. of Richard Sharrock, of Euxton ... ... „ 22
Cicely, ye D. of Thomas Walton ... ... „ 26
Abigall, ye D. of Richard Sumner, of Leyland ... ... „ 26
Eleanor, ye D. of William Farington, of Farington ... Oct. 10
Margaret, ye D. of Thomas Barton, of Leyland ... ... „ 10
B. Trecle,[1] ye D. of Roger Blackstone, of Croston, &
   Elizabeth Smith, of Ulneswalton ... ... „ 13
Ruth, ye D. of Thomas Threlfall & Elizabeth Hough,
   of Euxton ... ... „ 22
Jennet, ye D. of John Walmsley, of Heapey ... ... „ 24
John, ye S. of Richard Loxam, of Cuerden ... ... „ 24
Jennet, ye D. of William Porter, of Leyland ... ... „ 24
Margery, ye D. of John Jackson, Jun[r], of Cuerden ... „ 31
John, ye S. of James Cheetham, of Clayton... ... ... Dec. 5
Lawrence, ye S. of Lawrence Lucas, of Whittle ... ... „ 12
Richard, ye S. of Robert Leigh,[2] Gen: X[stnd] at Chorley „ 16
John, ye S. of Roger Clayton, of Cuerden ... ... „ 19
Jane, ye D. of John Boardman, of Wheelton ... ... „ 19
Mary, ye D. of Robert Eastham, of Leyland ... ... „ 21
Thomas, ye S. of Ellis Waring, of Cuerden... ... ... „ 25
Ann, ye D. of William Leyland, of Cuerden ... ... Jan. 1
Ann, ye D. of Richard Cross, of Leyland ... ... „ 2
Ralph, ye S. of John Hunt, of Cuerden ... ... „ 9
Ruth, ye D. of Daniel Robinson, Traveller ... ... „ 9
Thomas, ye S. of Robert Turner, Jun[r], of Leyland ... „ 10
Alice, ye D. of Roger Bolton, of Euxton ... ... „ 23
Dorothy, ye D. of Michael Taylor, of Whittle ... ... Feb. 6
James, ye S. of Richard Tomlinson, of Farington, in
   P[enwortham] Par[ish] ... ... „ 13
Elizabeth, ye D. of William Rigby, of Leyland ... ... „ 20
Oliver, ye S. of Ralph Pierson, of Whittle ... ... „ 21
Mary, ye D. of Thomas Jackson, of Cuerden ... ... Mar. 6
Margery, ye D. of Ellis Sumner, Jun[r], of Euxton, s[d] to
   be X[stnd]... ... ... „ 9
William, ye S. of Peter Shaw, of Farington... ... ... „ 15

Ystnings for 1709.[3]

Giles, ye S. of John Calderbank, of Clayton... ... ... Mar. 25
Alice, ye D. of John Woodcock, of Leyland ... ... „ 27

[1] Note this peculiar name.
[2] See entry on July 17, 1706. This Mr. Robert Leigh was probably a grandson of the Rev. William Leigh, B.D., rector of Standish, who died 1639.
[3] The transcript is clearly written. Signed by Vicar and Churchwardens.

Ann, ye D. of William Higginson, of Whittle ... ... Mar. 27
Catherine, ye D. of Mr. Farrand Hodgson,[1] of Leyland „ 29
Hannah, ye D. of Joseph Worthington, of Whittle ... Ap. 24
Thomas, ye S. of George Blackledge, of Heapey ... May 29
John, ye S. of James Hartley, of Ulnswalton ... ... „ 29
Alice, ye D. of John Waln, of Cuerden, s^d to be X^{stnd}... „ 29
Thomas, ye S. of Mr. John Woodcock, Junr, of Cuerden June 5
Robert, ye S. of Leonard Cheetham, Traveller ... ... „ 5
John, ye S. of Richard Bateson, of Leyland ... ... „ 13
Elizabeth, ye D. of Richard Biccurstaff, of Whittle ... „ 13
Dorothy, ye D. of John Abbot, of Clayton ... ... „ 19
Elizabeth, ye D. of George Clayton & Jane Crichlow,
both of Leyland ... ... July 10
Thomas, ye S. of Thomas Roscow, of Euxton ... ... Aug. 16
Elizabeth, ye D. of Roger Crook, of Whittle ... ... „ 18
Andrew, ye S. of Henry Stones, of Leyland ... ... „ 20
William, ye S. of Thomas Crook, of Farington ... ... „ 21
Isabel, ye D. of William Shaw, of Lealand ... ... „ 21
Christopher, ye S. of James Higgison, of Euxton ... „ 28
Elizabeth, ye D. of Thomas Silcock, of Clayton... ... „ 28
James, ye S. of William Crichlow & Jane Woods, of
Euxton ... ... Sept. 4
Ellen, ye D. of Thomas Dewhurst, of Cuerden ... ... „ 10
Margery, ye D. of Thomas Thornley, of Leyland ... „ 18
Henry, ye S. of Henry Turner, of Lealand ... ... Oct. 2
Jane, ye D. of Thomas Eastham, of Lealand ... ... „ 2
Ellen, ye D. of Samuel Duncalf, of Whittle... ... ... „ 16
Catherine, ye D. of Richard Leaver, of Lealand... ... „ 18
Mary, ye D. of John Halliwell, of Whittle ... ... „ 20
Mary, ye D. of Peter Wethersby, of Lealand ... ... „ 27
Mary, ye D. of Francis Serjant, of Lealand... ... ... Nov. 5
Ann, ye D. of Richard Armetriding, of Lealand... ... „ 10
John, ye S. of Nicholas Bromeley, of Lealand ... ... „ 13
Margaret, ye D. of Thomas Hey, of Heapey ... ... „ 20
Ann, ye D. of Robert Low, of Whittle... ... ... „ 20
Alice, ye D. of Robert Hilton, of Euxton ... ... „ 27
Hugh, ye S. of Robert Martin, of Heapey ... ... „ 27
Alice, ye D. of Richard Williamson & Ann Wilson, of
Lealand... ... ... Dec. 4
Alice, ye D. of Robert Stones, of Euxton ... ... „ 11
Mary, ye D. of Thomas Croft, of Whittle ... ... „ 15
Elizabeth, ye D. of Thomas Trigg, of Heapey ... ... „ 25
Thomas, ye S. of Thomas Smith, of Leyland ... ... Jan. 6
Hanna, ye D. of Ralph Boardman, of Leyland ... ... „ 8

[1] See the entry in 1706.

John, ye S. of John Almond, of Lealand ... ... Jan. 15
Elizabeth, ye D. of William Cuerden, of Clayton, s^d to
  be X^{stnd} [Inserted] ... ... „ 20
Ann, ye D. of William Ugnall, of Wheelton ... ... Feb. 5
Agnes, ye D. of Richard Sumner, of Leyland ... ... „ 12
Hanna, ye D. of Ralph Longton, of Whittle ... ... Mar. 5
Jane, ye D. of Thomas Rose, of Euxton ... ... „ 5
Margaret, ye D. of John Hawworth, of Euxton ... ... „ 12
Deborah, ye D. of Roger Walton, Junr, of Leyland ... „ 12
John, ye S. of William Jackson, of Leyland ... ... „ 19
Alice, ye D. of Edmund Woodcock, of Leyland... ... „ 19
Ellen, ye D. of Thomas Parker, of Farington ... ... „ 19

Ÿstnings, 1710.[1]

Thomas, ye S. of Henry Darwin, of Whittle ... ... Ap. 2
Richard, ye S. of Richard Carefoot, of Whittle ... ... „ 2
Esther, ye D. of Richard Procter, of Cuerden ... ... „ 9
William, ye S. of Mr. John Woodcock, Junr, of Cuerden „ 20
Margaret, ye D. of James Brown, of Farington ... ... „ 30
Elizabeth, ye D. of John Berry, of Heapey ... ... May 3
Elizabeth, ye D. of Robert Biccurstaff, of Euxton ... „ 7
William, ye S. of William Roscow, of Whittle ... ... „ 7
Alice, ye D. of Thomas Cooper, of Leyland ... ... „ 14
Ralph, ye S. of Ralph Walmsley, of Whittle ... ... „ 14
Robert, ye S. of Robert Wilding, of Leyland ... ... „ 28
Jennet, ye D. of William Man, of Euxton ... ... „ 29
Thomas, ye S. of Roger Bolton, of Euxton... ... ... „ 31
Margaret, ye D. of John Park, of Leyland ... ... June 4
William, ye S. of Robert Hall, of Hoghton, s^d to be X^{stnd} „ 24
James, ye S. of Adam Clayton, of Farington ... ... „ 25
William, ye S. of Roger Blackburn, of Cuerden ... ... July 9
Elizabeth, ye D. of Ralph Pierson, of Whittle ... ... „ 18
Samuel, ye S. of Samuel Baxenden, of Euxton ... ... Sept. 10
Thomas, ye S. of James Fool, of Cuerden ... ... „ 10
William, ye S. of John Clithero, of Euxton... ... ... „ 10
Thomas & Margery, twins of John Ditchfield, of Leyland „ 14
Henry, ye S. of Henry Whaley, of Leyland ... ... „ 17
Susanna, ye D. of William Gooden, of Euxton ... ... Oct. 1
John & James, sons of John Jackson, of Clayton-Hall,[2]
  s^d to be Baptiz'd ... ... „ 3

[1] The transcript for this year is closely written in a fair hand. Is illegible in places. Signed by Vicar and Churchwardens.

[2] The Sherd family (late of Clayton Hall) seems by this time to have left the district, as the name does not appear again.

Thomas, ye S. of Edward Woodcok, of Leyland ...	Oct.	8
Alice, ye D. of Thomas Jackson, of Leyland	„	8
Robert, ye S. of Lawrence Lucas, of Whittle	„	15
Catherin, ye D. of Richard Leaver, of Leyland	„	15
William, ye S. of William Garret, Traveller	„	29
John, ye S. of William Croft, of Whittle	Nov.	12
George, ye S. of Richard Parker, of Leyland	„	12
John, ye S. of Mr. Farrond Hodgson, of Leyland ...	„	14
Margery, ye D. of Thomas Sumner, of Leyland... ...	„	19
Cicely, ye D. of James Walton, of Leyland...	„	19
Elizabeth, ye D. of George Ashton, of Euxton	„	19
Ann, ye D. of Henry Smith, of Cuerden	„	26
Cornelius, ye S. of James Cheetham, of Clayton... ...	„	28
Roger, ye S. of John Piper, of Whittle...	Dec.	3
Mary, ye D. of Thomas Hey, of Heapey	„	17
Peter, ye S. of John Rutter, of Leyland	„	24
Joice, ye D. of Edward Forshaw, of Leyland	„	24
John, ye S. of William Green, of Leyland	Jan.	1
Ann, ye D. of Alexander Gerrard, of Hoghton, born & s^{d} to be X^{stnd}	„	3
Thomas, ye S. of George Clitherow, of Euxton	„	7
Robert, ye S. of Thomas Eastham, of Leyland	„	30
William, ye S. of Hugh Crook, & William, ye S. John Tootle, of Whittle } X^{stnd} at Heapey... ...	„	28
George, ye S. of George Moonk, Junr, of Leyland ...	Feb.	18
Alice, ye D. of John Pincock, of Euxton	„	25
Margaret, ye D. of William Porter, of Leyland	Mar.	11
Hannah, ye D. of John Bromeley, of Leyland	„	11
Margaret, ye D. of John Hunt, of Cuerden	„	18
Ann, ye D. of John Leyland, of Leyland	„	18
Elizabeth, ye D. of William Shaw, of Leyland	„	22
Hanna, ye D. of Henry Wilding, of Leyland	„	23

[*End of Baptisms in earliest extant Register.*]

[COLLECTIONS BY KING'S BRIEFS.

These sixteen entries of Collections made in Leyland Parish fill exactly one page in the original Register. The dates of the entries show that the page, having been selected for the purpose when the book was commenced, was thus used down to the end of the period covered by the baptismal and other entries contained in the volume. There are no other indications of Collections having been made in the parish under similar circumstances, either in the first or any subsequent volume of the Leyland Registers. For the sake of convenience, and to prevent a break in the sequence of baptismal entries these " Collections" have been removed to their present position from the place where they occur in the Register, viz., between the Baptisms for the year 1689 and those for 1690.

KING'S BRIEFS were letters patent granted by the Sovereign, by which permission and authority were given for the solicitation of alms in all parishes and hamlets of the kingdom on behalf of some specified charity. These letters were employed for objects of private, semi-public, or public interest. Calamities arising from fire, flood, or earthquake; the sad effects of war, piracy, or religious persecution; the foundation or sustainment of hospitals; the building, rebuilding, or repair of churches—these were all met by the same method, viz., the issue of a brief or royal letter addressed to the bishops, clergy, and church-wardens of parishes, to the magistrates, mayors, and other civil officers. The special circumstances calling for sympathy and assistance were related in the brief, which was read from the pulpit in the churches. During the reign of Charles I., the issue of these briefs settled into a regular system, which gradually became intolerable because of the abuses which attended it. The Cromwellian Government endeavoured to regulate the business and reform the abuses; but in 1705 an Act of Parliament became necessary to check the "farming" which had become the customary use. In 1828 the Act, to which reference has just been made, was repealed and the system brought to an end. For a time royal letters were issued in recommendation of the objects of the three great church societies, the S.P.C.K., the S.P.G., and the Church Building Society (which had received incorporation in 1828), but this practice was finally allowed to fall into abeyance in the year 1853.]

August 24ᵗʰ, 1653.

Collected in the parish Church of Leyland, for the towne of
Marleborough, in Wiltshire, the sume of sixe shillings & ten-
pence, & paid to John Pincocke, high-constable,

by mee, WILLIAM ROTHWELL.

Collected in Leyland parish the sum of three pounds ⎫   £ s. d.
seuen shillings & sixe pence towards the ran- ⎪
soming of our English subjects frō Turkish slauery, ⎬ 3 – 7 – 6
Septembʳ 8ᵗʰ, 1671 ... ...⎭

WILLIAM ROTHWELL, Vicar.

HUGH MEARE,   ⎱ ROGER DEWHURST,⎱Church-wardens.
JOHN OKENSHAW,⎰ GEORGE CROOKE,   ⎰

1690.

Collected in Leyland Parish, for the towne of New: Alresford,
in Hampshire, the summ of eight shillings & sixpence, and
paid to Isaack Sharp, collector, September 17ᵗʰ, 1690.

May ye 27ᵗʰ, 1690.

Collected in Leyland Parish, for the towne of Bungay, in the
county of Suffolk, the summ of eight shillings & two pence,
and paide to Isaack Sharp, collector, September the 17ᵗʰ, 1690.

June ye 1ˢᵗ, 1690.

Collected for the reliefe of Irish Protestants a 2ᵈ time in the
Parish of Leyland the summ of two pound six shillings (and
paide to Thomas Waite, Registery Deputˢ)

[All within the brackets has been crossed through.]

and paide to Henry Prescot, R. D.,[1] September ye 17ᵗʰ, 1690.

THO. ARMETRIDING, Vicar.

WILLIAM EUXTON,⎱ JOHN EUXTON,⎱Churchwardens.
WILLIAM WRIGHT,⎰ JOHN LIVESAY,⎰

July 29ᵗʰ, 1690.

Collected in the parish of Leyland for the relief of the poor
sufferers in the Parish of Sⁿᵗ George of Southwark, in the

---

[1] He was probably some official at Chester, and not Rural Dean.

County of Surrey, the summ of eight shillings and seven pence, and paide to Isaac Sharp, September ye 17th, 1690.

THO: ARM[ETRIDING] Vicar.

JOHN GREEN, } JOHN EUXTON,} Churchwardens.
OLIVER WILSON,} JOHN LIVESAY,}

Collected in ye Prsh of Leyland for ye reliefe of the poor French Protestants a 2d time ye summ of five pounds.

6th of January, 1694.   THO: ARMETRIDING, Vicar.

JOHN ATHERTON, } JOHN EXTON, } Churchwardens.
THO: FREKLETON,} JOHN PILKINGTON,}

Collected for ye poor sufferers at York ye summ of nineteen shillings and two pnc, May ye 5th, 1695, by ye above named Churchwardens.   THO: ARMETRIDING, Vr.

Collected for the Poor sufferers at Nether-Haven & ffidleton, in Wilts, ye summ of nine shillings & two pence, June ye 23rd, 1695.

WILLIAM MARE, JOHN HODSON,} Churchwardens.
THOM. RIDING, & JOHN WOOD, }

THO: ARMETRIDING, Vicr.

Collected for ye Towne of Gillingham, in Dorsetshire, ye summ of five shillings by ye above named churchwardens, July ye 14th, 1695.   BAGNALL, Collectr for a thrd.

Collected for Warwick ye summ of two pounds eleven shillings and three pence, 1695, by ye above named Churchwardens.

Collected for White Fryar Gate, in Kingstowne upon Hull, ye summ of seven shillings & 5 pence, October ye 27th, 1695.

Collected for Wrockingham, in Salop, ye summ of 5 shillings and 7 pence halfpenny, March ye 1st, 1695/6, by ye above named Churchwardens.

————

(1) Marlborough in Wiltshire.

On the 28th of April, 1653, "a fearful and most violent fire broke out almost at the lower end of the town, which in the space of four hours burnt and destroyed . . . one of the churches, the market house, and 224 [dwelling] houses." Thus does the original Brief describe the calamity which overtook this thriving town, hitherto one of the most important centres of the woollen-cloth manufacture in the Kingdom. Application was speedily made for a Brief to authorize collections throughout the country on behalf of the distressed inhabitants. This being the first occasion of the kind since the accession of the Cromwellian party to power, great efforts were made to reform the whole system of Briefs. A committee was appointed which sat at Salters' Hall, to undertake the management and ordering of this appeal. Regulations were issued to ensure the proper and systematic distribution of the documents, and for their return endorsed with the amounts collected under their authority. From the office of their origin consignments were made to the High Sheriffs, who, in turn, passed on a sufficient supply to the Chief Constables of hundreds, &c., who were required to furnish the ministers (and churchwardens) of parishes with single copies. On the Lord's Day next after the receipt of the document notice was to be given in church of the sad distressed condition [of the town of Marlborough], the better to prepare the people for the collection of the following week. A special requirement which deserves particular attention was that the amount collected should be registered in the books of each parish. *Hence the entry which we are now considering.*

Instead of the customary term "Kings Brief" (which was inapplicable to the changed circumstances of the period) the style and title of the document authorizing these collections was merely "An Order in Council." Those who may be specially interested in this subject will find the "Order in Council" printed at length, together with much additional information, on pp. 21-23 of Mr. C. Walford's little book on "Briefs."

It is said that towards the loss sustained by the town Cromwell subscribed £2,000, but £200 seems more likely to have been the true amount.

In Lewis' *Topographical Dictionary* there is a statement that in the year 1690 an Act of Parliament was passed to prohibit the use of thatch as a covering for houses and other buildings within this unfortunate borough, which had repeatedly suffered by fire prior to that date.

(2) Towards the ransoming of English subjects from Turkish slavery.

The contributions of the charitable had frequently to be asked for on behalf of the many unfortunates who fell into the clutches of the pirates of the Mediterranean. The Sultans of Algiers, Morocco, Tunis, &c., made a very considerable income by the capture and detention of merchants and others for whose release large sums of money were demanded as ransom. Private resources would seldom be able to meet these demands. Hence the appeal for public assistance. Briefs for the aforenamed purpose appear to have been issued in 1670, 1680, 1692, and 1700, in which years contributions were made from the parish of Clent (Salop), where a book for the special entry of the amounts obtained by brief was kept by the Vicar. Possibly the collection in Leyland was made under the authority of the brief of 1670.

The original documents of 1671-2-4 are now among the Records of the City of London.

(3) New Alresford in Hampshire.

This ancient corporate town, which is situated at the head of the river Itchen, lies between Alton and Winchester, at a distance of about six miles from the latter place. On May-day, 1690, it was destroyed by fire, previously to which event the town had been so prosperous that no single individual stood in need of parochial relief. In 1710 a similar calamity occurred.

Mention is made of this and of the following brief in the registers of Brixton, Isle of Wight (*vide Ch. Quarterly Review*, vol. iii., p. 377).

(4) Bungay, in Suffolk.

In the year 1688 a fire broke out in an uninhabited house, and the flames spread with such rapidity that the whole town, with the exception of one small street, was reduced to ashes, destroying property of the estimated value of £30,000, together with the records of the Castle (*vide* Lewis' *Topographical Dictionary*).

In Suckling's *History of Suffolk*, i., p. 27, we are told that "a brief to collect money in church, as well as from door to door, in aid of the sufferers from the fire (of March 1, 1688) was granted on June 7, 1688." The original brief was engrossed on parchment (*vide* Walford " Briefs," Appendix iii., p. 72).

(5) Relief of Irish Protestants (2nd time).

From the "Clent" book (referred to above) we learn that a first collection was made for this object in 1689. This brief of 1690 was also presented in that parish. The original documents connected with this brief and the one for Southwark are preserved among the City of London Records.

(6) Sufferers in the parish of S. George, Southwark.

This appears to have been, like so many others, a "Fire Brief."

(7) Relief of French Protestants.

The very stringent measures adopted by Louis XIV. against the Protestants of his Kingdom, culminating with the revocation of the Edict of Nantes in 1685, caused multitudes of these persecuted people to seek for safety and liberty of conscience in other lands. Great numbers of them succeeded in reaching England by means of the trading vessels which plied to and from the French ports. The destitute and distressed condition of these refugees aroused the sympathies of the English people, and every effort was made to render them assistance. Pressure was brought to bear upon the King (James II.), whose religious sentiment was unfavourable to the refugees, to sanction the issue of a Brief in their behalf. The amount collected by this means (£67,713. 2s. 3d.) is said to be the largest ever produced by a Brief. From the Clent collection book we learn that Briefs were issued with this same object in 1681, 1688, and (on this occasion) in 1694.

(8) This was a "Fire Brief," but no particulars of the damage done or of the part of the City of York affected by the fire are to hand.

(9) Nether-Haven and fidleton. The letters in the Register are quite clear and unmistakeable, but the places which are intended are, most probably, Nether avon and Fittleton, which are two parishes in Wiltshire. These parishes lie in immediate proximity to each other, but on opposite sides of the river Avon, and at a distance of some 13 miles to the north of Salisbury.

(10) Gillingham is a very extensive parish (being about 41 miles in circumference) bordering on the counties of Somerset and Wilts. The town is about 4 miles from Shaftesbury and in the county of Dorset. The manufacture of linen was for a considerable length of time a flourishing industry in the place. The charitable appeal made under cover of a brief seems to have been rendered necessary by a destructive fire which occurred about this time.

(11) Warwick.

In 1695, King William III. visited the town, of which, in the course of the preceding year, more than one half was destroyed by a dreadful conflagration, occasioned by a spark from a lighted piece of wood, in the hands of a boy, communicating with the thatched roof of a dwelling house; a great quantity of goods, probably in a state of ignition, having been removed for safety into the Collegiate Church of S. Mary, set fire to that venerable pile, which (with the exception of the Chancel, the Beauchamp chapel and the Chapter-house) was destroyed. In a few years after the town was rebuilt, in consequence of a national contribution amounting to £110,000 of which £1,000 was bestowed by Q. Anne (*vide* Lewis' *Topographical Dictionary*).

(12) White Fryar Gate in Kingstowne-upon-Hull.

(13) Wrockingham in Salop. The word is thus written in the Register with perfect distinctness. In all probability the place intended is Wrockwardine, which is the only possible identification if the county be correctly given. Moreover, from the "Clent" book (mentioned in note 2) we learn that there was a brief running at this date (1695-6) for the parish of Wrockwardine (or Wreckardine as it is there given), the occasion being (as usual) a fire.

[MARRIAGES AND BANNS OF MARRIAGE,
From 1653—1710.]

Marriage Certificate,[1] 1654.

These are to certifie all whom itt may concerne, that upon due publication of an Intended marriage betwixt Arthur Ingilbie, of Slabdale, in ye countie of Yorke, Esqr,and Margerie ffarrington, Daughter of Wiłłm ffarrington, of Shaw hall, in ye countie of Lanc^r, Esqr, and ye said Arthur Ingilbie and Margerie ffarrington comeing this day before mee and expressed their willingnes to marriage, and contracted to each other according to ye forme and words of ye Acte of parliam^t of the 24th of August, 1653. And yat I, one of the Justices of peace for ye said countie of Lanc^r, have, according to the tennor of ye said Acte, declared them to bee husband and wife together, in ye presence of John ffleetwood, Henry Bannister, and Alexander Nowell, Esq$^{rs.}$ Given under my hand yis second day of Januarie, 1654.[2]

(Signed)   EDWARDE ROBINSONN.

[1] This interesting and valuable certificate occurs on the upper portion of one of the pages subsequently filled with entries of Christenings for the years 1681 and 1682. It has been removed to this place as being here more convenient for reference, and to avoid making a break in the entries of Births and Baptisms. Some one has subsequently crossed through the certificate from corner to corner and from side to side, but these marks do not in any way prevent the words from being legible. Probably Mr. Rothwell would do this on his return to the parish at the restoration. Perhaps this would be considered as a record of an irregular proceeding, and made by a person who had no ecclesiastical status, and so to be obliterated from a volume intended to be a Register of Church Ceremonies duly performed. The handwriting of this Marriage Certificate is the same as that of the certificates at the commencement of the volume (see pp. 22, 23), and the signatures are identical, the resemblance being extended even to the flourishes. Major Robinson must have been a "painful" writer, and not a little proud of his position and acquirements.

[2] The bridegroom was Arthur Ingibie, of Lawkland [or Lakeland], co. York, Esq. He entered as a foreign burgess at the Preston Guilds of 1662 and 1682. The bride was one of the daughters of Wm. ffarrington, Esq. (the younger, the proposed Knight of the Oak) and his wife, Katherine ffleetwood, of Penwortham. Of the witnesses, John ffleetwood, Esq., of Penwortham, was the brother of Mrs. ffarrington and the husband of Anne ffarrington, sister of Wm. ffarrington, Esq., mentioned above. Henry Banister (of Banke) was sister's son to Wm. ffarrington, Esq., and married Dorothy Nowell, sister to the next witness. Alexander Nowell, son of Roger Nowell, Esq., of Read, married Margaret ffarrington, sister to the bride. He was entered on the Preston Guild Roll for 1662 as a foreign burgess.

[The following nine entries are found among the Baptisms for the year 1682. They have evidently been made on the dates given, and overlapped by Baptisms later on.]

publication of Marriages, 1655.

[1]John Darwin, of Leyland parish
Dorathy Cheshire, of Penwortham parish } the 3, the 10, and the 17 daies of } ffebruary.

[1]James Mosse, of Leyland parish
Katharin Cheshire, of Penwortham parish } the 3, the 10, and the 17 daies } of ffebruary.

William Whittle and Elline
Dickonson, both of Leyland pish } the 10, the 17, and 24 dayes } ffebruary.

John Wamsley, of Leyland prish
And Alice Hough, of Leyland parish } the 4th, the 11th, the 18.

George Crooke, of Leyland parish
And Alice Whaleye, of Standish parish } the 4th, the 11th, and the 18, 1656.

John Luckes, of Leyland parish
And Anne Walshe, of Blackborne parish } the 8, the 15, the 22.

Thomas Silcock, of Leyland parish
And Ann Winnell, of oᵣ parish of Leyland } the 13 July, 1656, the 20, the 27.

Thomas Pilkinton, of Leyland parish
And Elisebeth Smith, of Croston parish } the 3 of August, and the 10 of August, and the 17 of August.

John Tornor, of Leyland parish
And Elizabeth Chrichlow, both of ouᵣ } parish,
　　　November 16, and the 23, and the 30, 1656.

[Found between Marriages, 1672, ffeb. 9, and Marriages, 1673, April 27.]

Mariages at the prish Church of Leyland, 1661.

A mariage mad the thirtinth day of October, 1661, betwne William Garston, of Whittell, and Jenet Worsley, of Whelton ... ...[Oct. 13]

A mariage mad betwne William Lowson and Jenet Garston, both of our prish, at the prish Church of Leyland, the owne and twentith day of ffebruary ...[Feb. 21]

---

[1] The first two entries are in Vicar Rothwell's handwriting. Those which follow are written in a straggling and ill-formed style—the same as may be observed in the entries of Baptisms for the corresponding period.

[1662.]

A mariage mad betwne Robert Carffott, of penewortham
prish, and margret Euexton, of our prish, the second
day of ffebruary, 1662... ... ...[Feb. 2]

Henery Garston and Alic Leach, both of our prish,
maried the second day of ffebruary ... ...[„ 2]

A mariage mad betwne Thomas Smith, of our prish,
and Criston Hunt, of Croston prish, the owne and
twentith day of ffebruary, 1662 ... ...[„ 21]

A mariage mad betwne Adam blackeborne, of our
prish, and margret Johnson, of blackeborn prish, the
twentith eight day of ffebruary, 1662 ... ...[„ 28]

A mariage mad betwne John Whitell and Alice Walch,
both of Penwortham prish, the Last day off ffebruary.[„ last]

A mariage mad between George ouserwood and Jane
ward, maried the ffirst day of March, 1662 ... ...[Mar. 1]

A mariage mad betwne Richard boulton, of our prish,
and Alice Heald, of Croston prish, the twentith
second day of March, 1662... ... ...[„ 22]

A mariage mad betwne John ffarington and Ellin
Sumner, both of our prish, the 28 day of March ...[„ 28]

Richard Broxop and Jane W[e]rington,[1] both of [our]
prish, maried the 28 day ... ...[„ 28]

[Squeezed in afterwards—perhaps contemporary.]

A mariage mad betwne Thomas Williamson and
Margret Disley, both of our prish, maried the ffortinth
day of September, 1662 ... ...[Sept. 14]

A mariage mad betwne Thomas Brerley, of this prish,
and Elizabeth bouth [Booth], of Blackeborn prish,
the eightinth day of September, 1662 ... ...[„ 18]

A mariage mad betwne Richard knowles and Janet
horner, both of Penerthnartham[2] prish, maried att
Layland, the towe and twentith of September, 1662.[„ 22]

---

[1] This name *may* be Wrington as written, but the suggested form seems more
likely because familiar in the district. It then represents the local pronunciation of
Warrington.

[2] The scribe seems here to have been in some difficulty as to the spelling of
Penwortham.

A mariage mad between William Walsh, of penworth^m
   prish, and Alice Whittell, of Leyland prish, the Last
   day of Nouember, 1662   ...   .   [Nov. last]
A mariage mad betwne Richard Wright, of Croston
   prish, and katrin muncke, of our prish, the 8 day of
   December   ...   .[Dec.   8]
A mariage mad betwne Robert Blackborn and Elizabeth
   Gabot, both of our prish, maried the twentith eight
   day of December, 1662   ...   .[„   28]

Marriages, 1663.

[Found among Baptisms of the year 1682.]

John Haruy [Harvy] } of Houghton ... ... May 18	
Hannah Aspinall	
William Nicks } ... . June 18	
Margret Waring	
Euan Brindle } ... . „ 24	
Dorathy Dandie	
ffrancis Blackledge } ... . July 25	
Elsabeth Kindsley	
John Jackson } ... . Oct. 17	
Elsabeth Jumpe	
William Sharrok } ... . „ 28	
Alice Leyland	
James ffiswick } ... . Jan. 18	
Margaret Walmersley	
Robert Leekas } ... . ffeb. 23	
Katharin Nelson	

[From this date the Marriages follow on consecutively to the
end of the period contained in the first volume of the original
Register. At the top of the page there has been a heading
(afterwards crossed through), which seems to indicate an intention to continue here the marriage entries for 1655 (or perhaps
1656, for it is difficult to say which, owing to obliterating marks).
The heading runs thus:—" Marriages 1655 (or 6) made according
to the Acte of Parliam^t of the 24 of August 1653." At the top
of the inner margin (at the very edge) occurs a figure 4, as though
connected with something now cut away, and also the letters
"rriages." 1664 is added, but in a different coloured ink. Are
not some sheets missing?]

[Marriages, 1664.]

John Bolton
Elsabeth ffoole } both of this parish ... ... Ap. 12

Thomas Leauer
Ann Werden } both of this parish ... ... May 31

John Wright
Margret Woodcock } both of this parish ... ... „ 31

Robert Dundersdale
Elizabeth Mosse } ... ... June 19

Ralphe Smith, of Leyland parish
Mary Lathom, of Blakburne parish } ... ... „ 25

Thomas Calderbanke
Mary Atherton } both of this parish ... ... Sept. 21

Henry Eastham
Jennet Parker } of Leyland parish ... ... „ 21

Thomas Porter
Elsabeth Tyson } of Leyland parish ... ... Oct. 16

Robert Harrison
Alice Lawson } of Leyland parish ... ... „ 29

John Taylor
Anne Howorth } of Leyland parish ... ... Nov. 5

Henry Smith, of Leyland
Ellin Tomson, of Standish } parish ... ... Dec. 28

William Clayton
Elizabeth Sharples } of Leyland parish... ... ... Jan. 1

William Wielden
ffrances Barrett } of Leyland parish ... ... „ 15

John ffishwick
Margery Clayton } of Leyland parish ... ... „ 17

Edward Tilsley
Katharin ffarington } of Leyland parish ... ... „ 19

[Marriages] 1665.

William Jackson
Elizabeth Hough } of this parish ... ... June 29

John Duddell, of this parish
Elsabeth Allinson, of Chorley } ... ... July 11

Raphe Eccles, of Blackburne parish
Elizabeth Warington, of this parish } ... ... „ 30

J

John Liuesay, of Blackburne pish Anne Wright, of this parish	... ...	Aug. 24
John Urmston Anne Talbot	... ...	Sept. 11
Richard Barnes Margrett Banister }of Whittle	... ...	„ 24
William Johnson Margrett Bigans }of this parish	... ...	... „ 29
Henry Waddington Alice Walkden }of this parish	... ...	... Oct. 19
John Marsden Jennett Winnell}of this parish	... ...	... ... „ 19
John Clayton, of Leyland pish Alice Melling, of Croston pish	... ...	... ... „ 30
Henry Marsh Christian Hodges}of Leyland pish	... ...	... Jan. 22
Roger Bryning Jennett Winstanley}of Leyland parish	... ...	... ffeb. 4
John Eccles Katharin Hartley}of Leyland parish	... ...	... „ 5
[1]Mr Richard Brooke [1]Mris Margrett Charnocke	... ...	... „ 6
John Johnson, of Croston pish Dorathy Darwin, of Leyland pish	... ...	... „ 19

[1] This marriage entry is so written as to attract immediate attention on reference to the page on which it occurs. The titles Mr· and Mris· are placed out of line, and are rather larger than actually necessary. The words are certainly not later additions. The natural conclusion is that the scribe felt himself to be making an important record and (perhaps unconsciously) allowed his penmanship to mark the fact. If this were really the case, to what individuals of social rank in the district could the names belong? The most obvious suggestion is that we have here the marriage by which Astley Hall and the attendant property passed into the Brooke family. Richard, second son of Sir Peter Brooke (afterwards of Mere), certainly did marry Margaret, the heiress of the Charnocks, of Astley, but the date given for that event by Canon Raines (in the notes, vol. ii. of the Stanley papers) is 1673. The Brookes resided at Astley in 1682, and are entered on the Preston Guild roll of that year—the Knight, Sir Peter (who married for his third wife one of the ffarrington family), his son Richard (Armiger) with three grandsons, Peter, Robert, and Richard. From information furnished by T. T. Townely Parker, Esq. (the direct descendant of the Charnock and Brooke families and present owner of Astley Hall), we learn that the heiress, Margaret Charnock, survived her first husband, who died in 1715, and was re-married to John Gillibrand. She survived all her children, and did not die until 1744. If, then, we are to reconcile the latter facts with a marriage taking place in February, 1665-6, then the lady must have lived to the ripe age of 94 years at the least. If this identification be given up, then who were the persons whose marriage is here recorded?

Thomas Leekas
Ruth Howorth } of Leyland pish... ... ... ffeb. 23

Marriages, 1666.

Henry Wignall
Margrett Durram } of Leyland pish ... ... Ap. 16

James Marsden, of Blackburne pish
Alice Lowe, of Leyland pish } ... ... June 22

Raphe Johnson
Elsabeth Garstang } of this parish ... ... July 9

Richard Clough
Elsabeth Leyland } both of Leyland parish ... ... „ 25

Mr William Crosse,[1] of Darwin
Mris Anne Rogers,[1] of Leyland } ... ... Aug. 28

William Leekas
Jennett Lawson } ... ... Sept. 11

Henry Cockar
Mary Winstanley } ... ... „ 29

Henry Blackledge and Anne Pearson were married
October 20, with a licence, 1666. ... ...[Oct. 20]

[This entry was made in the same handwriting as the others of the year, but occurs in the original as the last marriage record for 1666. It is placed here for more convenience of reference.]

Ellis Sumner, of Leyland
Dorathy Rigby, of Standish } pish ... ... Oct. 22

Thomas Woodcock
Elizabeth Sharples } of Leyland pish ... ... Nov. 13

Dauid Jones
Margrett Houlden } of Leyland pish ... ... „ 25

Richard Nelson
Anne Balshaw } of Leyland pish ... ... „ 28

James Haddok
Elsabeth Brindle } of Leyland pish ... ... Dec. 3

William Clayton
Isabell Walmersley } of Leyland pish ... ... Jan. 10

[1] Plaintiffs (also Defendants) in the Old Hall case. Mrs. Rogers was sister of Grace Bold, to whom Mr. Robert Charnock left his estate.

John Slator
Elsabeth Allinson } married ... ... ffeb.   2

[This original entry is found written perpendicularly on the inner margin near to the bottom of the page.   It is in the same handwriting as the other entries.]

John Slater
Elizabeth Allinson } married ... ... ffeb. ye 2

[Repetition of former entry written in a later hand on the broad space at the outside edge of the leaf.   It is doubtful whether these entries belong to ffeb., 1666, or to ffeb., 1667.]

William Clayton, of ffarington
Jane Heskin, of Leyland pish } ... ... ffeb.   4

Lawrance Piccopp
Jane Tilsley } both of this pish ... ... „   17

John Bretherton
Jennett Lawrance } of Croston pish   ... ... „   17

1667,

James Worthington
Mary Ratcliffe } of Chorley ... ... Ap.   8

John Heskett
Elsabeth Tysing } of Leyland ... ... „   13

John Pincock
Jennett ffidler } of Euxton   ... ... May 16

Alexander Breres
Katharin Leyland } of Whittle   ... ... July   4

William Oldham
Jane Gerratt } of Whittle ... ... „   14

Joseph Peacock, of Lerpoole
Ann Whittle, of Leyland } ... ... Aug.   6

Henry Hodskinson
Annice Almond } of Winnell ... ... „   10

Henry Brining
Mary Winnel } of Whittle ... ... Sept. 23

Thomas Metcalf, of Haughton[1]
Anne Atkinson, of Leyland } ... ... Oct.   1

[1] In Leyland parish.

Thomas Leyland }of Leyland Jennett Whitehead	... ... Oct.	14
Thomas Wilson }of great Hoole[1] Alice Carre	... ... „	18
William Wright, of Euxton } Margrett Tilsley, of Charnock[2]	... ... Dec.	2
Matthew ffarror }of Hoole Elizabeth Johnson	... ... „	2
Lawrance Piccop, of lower Darwin[3] } Elizabeth Walkden, of Blackburne	... ... „	11
William Duddell, of Charnock } Elizabeth Harsnipp, of Croston	... ... ffeb.	1

1668.

John Wombwell, of Wheelton } Anne Taylor, of ffarington	... ... May	6
John Woodcocke, of Walton } Anne Woodcocke, of Euxton	... ... „	28
Thomas ffletcher, of Leyland }parish Bridget Rothwell, of Standish	... ... June	24
Andrew Stones, of Euxton } Elizabeth Sharples, of Leyland	... ... „	25
John Parke }of Leyland Elsabeth Banister	... ... July	4
John Baxenden, of Croston } Mary Sumner, of Leyland	... ... „	26
Richard Clough }of Leyland Margrett Jackson	... ... Aug.	10
Raphe Urmstone }of Penwortham Mary Almond	... ... „	11
John Wilson }of Bretherton Anne Eccles	... ... „	22
Thomas Charnley }of Penwortha[m] Elizabeth Tyson	... ... Sept.	20
Thomas Addison }of Bretherton Jennett Dandie	... ... „	27

[1] Anciently in Croston parish. Severed in 1641.   [2] In Standish parish.
[3] A township near to and in the parish of Blackburn.

Thomas Snart ⎱ of Bretherton ... ... Oct. 17
Katharin Wilson ⎰

James Martindale, of Hoole ⎱ ... ... „ 18
Anne Heskett, of Bretherton ⎰

Richard Dewhurst ⎱ of Raddlesworth[1] ... ... Nov. 5
Agnes Ainsworth ⎰

John Lee, of Ulneswalton[2] ⎱ ... ... Dec. 1
Anne Eyues, of Leyland ⎰

Raphe Lowe, of Leyland ⎱ pish ... ... „ 29
Isabell Eastwood, of Burnley ⎰

John Hodskinson ⎱ of More-quart[r] [of Leyland parish]... Jan. 13
Anne Tomson ⎰

Nicholas Woombwell ⎱ of Wheelton ... ... „ 28
Alice Pearson ⎰

Thomas Dawson, of Leyland ⎱ ... ... ffeb. 2
Jane Tyson, of ffarington ⎰

Oliver Martin, of Wheelton ⎱ ... ... „ 9
Elizabeth Cliffe, of ffarington ⎰

[Marriages] 1669.

Thomas Drinkwater ⎱ of Winnell[3] ... ... Ap. 13
Elsabeth Beardsworth ⎰

John Mosse ⎱ of Longton[4] ... ... „ 17
Jane Wielden ⎰

John Daniell, of Euxton ⎱ ... ... „ 18
Anne Winstanley ⎰

Edmund Tasker ⎱ of Cuerden ... ... May 13
Margret Gillar ⎰

Richard Bushell ⎱ of Cuerden ... ... „ 21
Jennett Sharrok ⎰

Robert Cockar ⎱ of Clayton ... ... June 8
Tomasin Cockar ⎰

John Blackburne ⎱ of Cuerden ... ... „ 29
Jennett ffarington ⎰

[1] A township in the Moor quarter of Leyland parish.
[2] A township in Croston parish. It adjoins Leyland.
[3] For Withnell, which is thus pronounced locally.
[4] A township in Penwortham parish.

Richard Woodroofe, of Wheelton Mary Wright, of Leigh[1] parish	... ...	June 29
James Martin, of Heapie Jane Howorth, of Whittle	... ...	July 17
Edmund Tuson, of Longton Elnor Green, of Leigh pish	... ...	„ 25
George Hatch, of Brindle[2] Ellin Marsden, of Winnell	... ...	... Aug. 10
Thomas Hodskinson, of Wheelton Jane Peeres, at Brinscows[3]	... ...	„ 10
William Waterworth Elsabeth Sergeant }of Leyland	... ...	„ 17
Robert Whittle, of Winnell Elsabeth Witton, of Blackburne pish	... ...	„ 24
Edward Hodson Margery Stretford }of Leyland pish	... ...	... Sept. 26
Richard Wigans Isabell Crooke }of Whittle ...	... ...	„ 26
Richard Sharples Isabell Ridd[4]	... ...	... Oct. 25
Thomas Wignall, of Heskett-banke[5] Jennett Sumner, of Leyland	... ...	„ 28
John Crooke Ellin Marton }of Euxton	... ...	„ 30
John Silcock Katharin Ashurst }of Leyland	... ...	... Nov. 10
Richard Walton Jennett Nelson }of Leyland ...	... ...	„ 18
William Duckson, of Brindle Margrett Mather, of Clayton	... ...	„ 30

[1] Leigh, an ancient parish in West Derby hundred.

[2] An ancient parish which adjoins Leyland on the eastern side.

[3] Perhaps for Brinscall, which lies in the Moore quarter, and now forms part of the modern parish of Withnell. Or the woman may have been living with some people named Brinscall or Brinscow.

[4] Ridd, a North Devon name, very uncommon in this district. It may possibly be a contraction for Riding, which is the usual form. This contraction is very common in familiar intercourse at the present day: *e.g.*, Webster is called Web., &c., &c.

[5] For Hesketh-bank, or Hesketh-with-Becconsall, a part of Croston parish (now made parochial) which lies next to the sea, and near to the mouth of the River Douglas. Hesketh is locally pronounced Heskett at the present time. It was frequently spelled "Heskayte" in ancient deeds, &c.

John Lambert, of Ossok[1] pish } Elsabeth Martin, of Leyland }	...	...	...	...	... Dec.	13
Thomas Cowper } Dorathy Sharrok } of Cuerden	...	...	...	...	... Jan.	24
Thomas Gillibrand } Lettice Mutton } of Houghton	...	...	...	...	... ffeb.	2
Christoph[r] Sumner, of Leyland } Margrett Jackson, of Cuerden }	...	...	...	...	... „	7
Thomas Miller } Annice Horrobin } of Wheeleton	...	...	...	...	... „	13

[Marriages] 1670.

George Garstang, of Houghton } Elsabeth Helme, of Preston pish }	...	...	...	...	... Ap.	4
Henry Whaley, of Leyland } Elsabeth Walken, of Heapie }	...	...	...	...	... „	24
Thomas Martin, of Heapie } Ellin Taylor, of Whittle }	...	...	...	...	... „	24
James Ward } Jane Ainsworth } of Blackburne pish	...	...	...	...	... „	25
William Rutter } Margrett Wignall } of Tarleton[2]	...	...	...	...	... May	1
John Okenshaw } Margery Waring } of Euxton	...	...	...	...	... „	19
Christoph[r] Wielden } Elsabeth Whittle } of ffarington	...	...	...	...	... „	24
Richard Almon } Alice Ryley } of Houghton	...	...	...	...	... June	26
M[r] William Anderton,[3] of Euxton } M[ris] Mary Leake, of Worden[4] }	...	...	...	...	... July	6

[1] Ossok, probably Urswick-in-Furness, near Ulverston.

[2] A township in Croston parish, near to the sea. Made parochial 1821.

[3] Mr. William Anderton, whose name occurs in the text, *may have been* the eldest brother of Hugh Anderton who married Katharine Trappes, through whom the present owners of Euxton Hall trace their descent. This William was aged twenty-six years at the Visitation of 1664. No marriage is given in the family pedigree. There is the possibility that a William Anderton of an earlier generation may be the one whose marriage is here recorded. If so, it would be an uncle of the individual just referred to. In that case there might be some connection between the two couples whose names occur together in the Register. Dorothy Anderton, sister to the last named William, married William Rishton, of Pontalgh, who was possibly a relative of Mr. Thomas Rishton, of Preston.

[4] In Leyland parish. Worden Hall was for centuries the home of the ffarrington family.

Mr Thomas Rishton,[1] of Preston M^{ris} Anne ffarneworth, of Euxton	... ... Aug.	2
Thomas Heskett Ellin Wigans } of Bretherton	... ... ,,	5
William Howorth, of Eccleston Mary Bradshaw, of Croston	... ... ,,	8
John Charnock Deborah Woods } of Walton [le Dale]	... ... ,,	15
John Metcalfe Ann Dolphin } of Winnell	... ... ,,	24
Raphe Roscow, of Bolton Ann Haukshead, of Chorley	... ... Sept.	8
Thomas Waring Elsabeth Sumner } of Leyland	... ... ,,	9
Charles Whitehead Dorathy Slator } of Leyland	... ... ,,	22
Roger Horrocks Ellin Threlford } of Euxton ...	... ... Oct.	2
Richard Ainsworth, of Pleasinton[2] Anna Crichlow, of Tocholes[2]	... ... ,,	13
William Ashurst, of Wigan Anne Southworth, of Leyland	... ... Dec.	1
John Smith Mary Nelson } of Croston	... ... ,,	24
Henry Anderton, of Samsbury[3] Ellin Sumner, of Maudesley[4]	... ... Jan.	2
Richard Kertfoot, of Penwortha^m Mary Welsh, of Leyland } pish ...	... ... ,,	10
Hugh Crooke Ellin Pilkinton } of Whittle	... ... ,,	14
William Haslome Mary ffarington } of Leyland	... ... ffeb.	1
Thomas Proctor, of Penwortha^m Alice Loxam, of Hutton[5]	... ... ,,	9

[1] There was a Mr. Thomas Rishton, who was an alderman of the Preston Guild of 1662—would he be the person here named? For notes on the ffarneworth family of Euxton, see pp. 58, 62.

[2] Townships in Blackburn parish.

[3] Samlesbury is in Blackburn parish, but near to the Ribble.

[4] Maudesley, a township of Croston parish, made parochial in 1841.

[5] Hutton, a township of Penwortham parish.

Giles Leauer, of Leyland ⎫
Katharin Hollinhurst, of ffarington ⎰ ... ... ffeb. 11

Peter Leadbeater, of Tarleton[1] ⎫
Mary Crooke, of Leyland ⎰ ... ... „ 21

John Sheardley ⎫ of ffarington ... ... Mar. 9
Jane Cliffe ⎰

[Marriages] 1671.

William Leauer ⎫ of Leyland ... ... Ap. 24
Isabell Robson ⎰

Edward Kerkchin ⎫ of Euxton ... ... „ 24
Alice Wilson ⎰

Henry Blackledge, of ffarington ⎫ ... ... „ 28
Jane Silcock, of Leyland ⎰

Robert Adinson ⎫ of Leyland ... ... May 8
Jennett ffarington ⎰

Robert Charnley, of Penworth[m] ⎫ ... ... June 5
Isabell Croston, of Heskin[2] ⎰

John Clayton, of ffarington ⎫ ... ... „ 6
Joane Cockar, of Cuerden ⎰

Raphe Walkden ⎫ of Leyland parish ... ... „ 25
Elsabeth Almon ⎰

William Morris ⎫ of Leyland parish ... ... „ 25
Jennett Leekas ⎰

Christoph[r] Blakleach ⎫ of Leyland pish ... ... July 1
Anne Garstang ⎰

George Browne, of Copple[3] ⎫ ... ... „ 25
Anne Dalton, of Whittle ⎰

William Jackson, of Leyland ⎫ ... ... Aug. 10
Ellin Garstang, of Whittle ⎰

Thomas Riding, of Otley[4] ⎫ ... ... „ 15
Elsabeth Berkett, of Padiha[m5] ⎰

James ffarington ⎫ of Leyland ... ... „ 17
Jane Hitchin ⎰

---

[1] Tarleton was part of the ancient parish of Croston until severed by Act of Parliament in 1821.

[2] Heskin, a township of Eccleston parish.

[3] Coppul, a chapelry of Standish parish, now made parochial.

[4] Perhaps Otley, near Leeds.

[5] Padiham, a chapelry of Whalley parish, lying between Blackburn and Burnley.

William Roes } of Bretherton	... Aug.	21
Jane Hodges		
William Cowper } of Cuerden	„	26
Katharin Eccles		
William Clayton } of Winnell	„	28
Alice Hornby		
Thomas Sheaphard } of Bury	„	28
Katharin Riding		
Thomas James } of Leyland	„	30
Isabell Haugh		
John Moore } of Eccleston[1] ... ... Sept.		1
Priscilla Dicconson		
Richard Jackson, of Cuerden } ... ... „		16
Jennett Wright, of Leyland		
Lawrance Garstang } of Leyland ... ... „		24
Margrett Crompton		
John Nickson, of Kirkham[2] } ... ... „		24
Margrett Steuenson, of Euxton		
Thomas Sharrok, of Brindle } ... ... Oct.		29
Elsabeth Halliwell, of Leyland		
John Calderbanck, of Leyland } ... ... Nov.		30
Jennett Machon, of Clayton		
William Blakburne, of Cuerden } ... ... Dec.		5
Anne Siddall, of Whittle		
William Garstang, of Whittle } ... ... „		10
Jane Dixon, of Chorley		
Thomas Ugno, of Wheeleton } ... ... Jan.		4
Elsabeth Taylor, of Heapie		
Jeffrey Lassie, of little Harwood[3] } ... ... „		11
Isabell Ainsworth, of Pleasington[3]		
William Wright, of Leyland } ... ... „		20
Anne Sikes, of Baulderston[4]		
William Woodcocke } of Leyland ... ... ffeb.		2
Alice Smith		
Roger Walton } of Leyland ... ... „		2
Anne Smith		

[1] An ancient parish marching with Croston and Standish.
[2] Kirkham, an ancient parish in the Fylde.
[3] Townships in Blackburn parish.   [4] Chapelry of Blackburn parish.

Thomas Jackson, of Leyland }
Jane Mosse, of Hoole[1] } ... ... ffeb. 3

Edward Houghton }
Anne Parkinson } of Houghton ... ... ,, 7

John Bradley }
Anne Short } of Leyland ... ... ,, 19

[Marriages] 1672.

Richard Hunt, of Longton }
Anne Holme, of Croston } ... ... Ap. 8

Thomas Waring }
Margrett Bolton } of Leyland ... ... ,, 9

Thomas Waring, of Eccleston }
Jane Duckworth, of Leyland } ... ... ,, 17

Richard Crooke, of Houghton }
Jennett Entwisle, of Winnell } ... ... ,, 27

John Clayton, of Penwortham[m] }
Mary Threlfall, of Leyland } ... ... July 21

Robert Smith }
Jennett Loxam } of Longton[2] ... ... ,, 30

John Woodcocke, of Cuerden }
Anne Jackson, of Walton } ... ... Sept. 2

Richard Higison }
Alice Howarth } of Whittle ... ... ,, 8

Richard Preston }
Katharin Dewhurst } of More-quarter[3] ... ... ,, 21

Matthew Walkden, of Heapie }
Margrett Woodroofe, of Wheelton } ... ... Oct. 4

Euan Garner, at Werden }
Margrett Hodson, of Euxton } ... ... ,, 14

Robert Hunt }
Margaret Clark } of Cuerden ... ... ,, 25

Thomas Dewhurst }
Alice Walmersley } of Blakburne pish ... ... Nov. 6

Richard ffarington, of ffarington }
Elsabeth Sumner, of Euxton } ... ... ,, 12

[1] Hoole, anciently a chapelry of Croston parish.

[2] Longton, a township in Penwortham parish.

[3] The Moor quarter of Leyland parish consists of the townships of Heapy, Withnell, Wheelton, &c.

Raph Crichlow, of Euxton ⎫
Ellin Latus, of St. Michaells[1] pish ⎭ ... ... Nov. 23

Edward Longton ⎫ of Whittle ... ... „ 24
Alice Leekas ⎭

Edward [Longton, crossed through] Blackledge.
Jane Crooke ... ... Jan. 6

James Marsden ⎫ of Whittle ... ... ffeb. 2
Agnes Marshall ⎭

William ffarnworth ⎫ of Brimecroft[2] ... ... „ 3
Ellen Blakledge ⎭

Arthur Dewhurst ⎫ of Winnell ... ... „ 5
Alice ffishwick ⎭

Thomas Balshaw, of Walton ⎫ ... ... „ 9
Joane Wild, of Clayton ⎭

[Here are found "Marriages at the prish church of Leyland, 1661," which occupy three-quarters of a page. These have been printed in their proper chronological order at page 126.]

Marriages, 1673.

Thomas Pope, of Leyland pish.
Margrett Taylor, of [Blakburn, crossed through] Standish pish ... ... Ap. 27

Richard Jones, of Euxton ⎫ ... ... May 3
Elsabeth ffisher, of Charnock ⎭

Lawrance Oldham, of Leyland ⎫ ... ... „ 12
Ellin Walton, of Whittle ⎭

John Hey, of Blakburne ⎫ ... ... „ 25
Alice Hargreaues, of Haslinden[3] ⎭

John Archer, of Bretherton ⎫ ... ... June 22
Alice Greason, of Leyland ⎭

John Sumner, of Lostock[4] ⎫ ... ... „ 24
Elsabeth Lathom, of Appley[5] ⎭

Robert Harrison ⎫ of Leyland ... ... „ 26
Annice Lithom ⎭

[1] An ancient parish in the Fylde called S. Michael's-on-Wyre.
[2] Brimecroft, a hamlet lying between Hoghton and Withnell, in Leyland parish.
[3] Haslingden, an ancient chapelry of Whalley parish.
[4] Lostock, see page 76.   [5] Appley, near Wigan.

Thomas Taylor⎱ of Heskett Banck[1]   ...   . July   6
Mary Wignall ⎰

Thomas Sumner, of Leyland⎱   ...   .   „   20
Jane Longton, of Preston ⎰

Lawrance Abbott⎱ of Blakburn pish   ...   .   „   29
Katharin Welsh ⎰

Thomas Holden ⎱ of Blakburne pish ...   . Aug.   9
Elsabeth Wensley⎰

John Cheshire, of ffarington ⎱   ...   .   „   24
Elsabeth Wright, of Leyland ⎰

Henry Grimshaw, of Blakburne pish⎱   ...   . Sept. 14
Elsabeth Blakledge, of Brindle pish ⎰

William Tomlinson and Ellizabeth Mellin ...   .   „   22

[Inserted in contemporary hand.]

James Clarkson⎱ of Euxton   ...   .   „   18
Elsabeth Parke⎰

Edward Bordman, of Winnell⎱   ...   .   „   21
Anne Whiteside, of Whittle ⎰

William Dandy, of Walton⎱   ...   .   „   23
Isabell Lowe, of Charnock⎰

Henry Crichlow⎱ of Leyland ...   . Oct.   8
Margrett Catan ⎰

Richard Sumner⎱ of Leyland ...   . Nov.   1
Anne Abbot   ⎰

John Godbar ⎱ of Leyland   ...   .   „   23
Jane Whittle⎰

Thomas Coppok⎱ of Blakburne pish   ...   . Dec. 29
Elsabeth ffoole⎰

William Clough⎱ of Leyland ...   . Jan. 17
Jane Atkinson ⎰

John Pearson ⎱ of Wheelton   ...   .   „   18
Anne Pearson⎰

William Shaw   ⎱   ...   . (*sic*) Jan. 25
Margrett Daniell⎰

William Crosse   ⎱ of Euxton
Margrett ffarington⎰ of Leyland   ...   . ffeb.   1

James Garstang, of Preston⎱   ...   .   „   15
Isabell Whittle, of Leyland⎰

[1] Part of Croston parish, bounded by the sea and the river Douglas.

Robert Gardner, of ffarington⎱
Alice Hodson, of Euxton   ⎰ ... ... ffeb. 26

Henry Eastham⎱of Cuerden ... ... Mar. 1
Mary Mitton ⎰

William Cowper⎱of Cuerden ... ... „   3
Alice Stazaker[1] ⎰

[Marriages] 1674.

William Burscowe, of Leyland⎱
Elsabeth Billing, of Eccleston ⎰ ... ... May 1

Thomas Longton, of Whittle⎱
Margrett Cockar, of Clayton ⎰ ... ... „   3

James Crosse, of Witton⎱in Blakburne pish   ... „ 10
Anne Peeke, of Rishton⎰

M[r] Richard ffleetwood,[2] of Manchester⎱
M[ris] Margrett ffleetwood,[3] of Leyland ⎰ ... ... June 16

John Brindle, of Whittle.
Martha Sauage, of Clayton ... ... Aug. 16

John Richmond⎱of Raddlesworth [in Leyland parish] „ 17
Mary Nihill ⎰

Richard ffiswick⎱ of Winnell ... ... „ 28
Anne Metcalfe ⎰

William Ugno⎱of Winnell ... ... Nov. 1
Anne Winnell⎰

[At this point more than half a page has been previously used for (some) Burials of the years 1658, 1659, 1660, and 1661. These will all be found entered in their proper place.]

Robert Johnson⎱of.Tarleton [in Croston parish]... ... Nov. 22
Anne Norris ⎰

Henry Yates, of Maudsley ⎱
Margrett Yong, of Leyland⎰ ... ... „ 24

Thomas Sumner⎱of Leyland ... ... Dec. 6
Ellin Whittle ⎰

[1] The person making the entry has bungled over the spelling of this name, and after much alteration has written it clearly as here given.

[2] Son of Francis Fleetwood, and grandson of Sir Paul Fleetwood, of Rossall.

[3] Daughter of Mr. Edward ffleetwood, of Leyland, who was brother of John ffleetwood, Esq., of Penwortham, the husband of Ann ffarington, of Worden.

Edward Sergeant, of Charnock⎱ ... ... Jan. 17
Elsabeth Sumner, of Leyland ⎰

William Woodcock, of Euxton⎱ ... ... ffeb. 2
Elsabeth Walton, of Hoole ⎰

John Jones ⎱strangers ... ... „ 8
Jane Chetam⎰

John Sumner, of Leyland ⎱ ... ... „ 16
Margrett Wielden, of Longton⎰

Roger Breres, of Blackburne ⎱ ... ... „ 16
Anne Anderton, of Houghton⎰

[Marriages] 1675.

James ffarneworth, of Wheelton⎱ ... ... Ap. 18
Isabell Horrobin, of Brindle ⎰

Charles Wood ⎱of Pleasington ... ... June 26
Margrett Whaley⎰

Thomas Welsh, of ffarington ⎱ ... ... „ 27
Jane Hodges, of Leyland pish⎰

Hugh Waterworth⎱of Leyland ... ... July 2
Margrett Leyland ⎰

James Garstang⎱of Whittle ... ... Aug. 3
Alice Blakledge ⎰

John Blackburne, of Cuerden⎱ ... ... „ 16
Anne Lancaster, of Copple[1] ⎰

Thomas Pilkinton⎱of Leyland ... ... „ 29
Mary Jackson ⎰

James Martindale⎱of Hoole ... ... „ 31
Elsabeth Hodson ⎰

Raphe Smith, of ffarington ⎱ ... ... Sept. 25
Elizabeth Bushell, of Cuerden⎰

Mathew Bruer, of Preston pish ⎱ ... ... Oct. 10
Anne ffarington, of Leyland pish⎰

John Jackson ⎱of Cuerden ... ... „ 28
Grace Jackson⎰

William Rigby, of Ulneswalton⎱ ... ... Dec. 11
Alice[2] ffarington, of Leyland ⎰

---

[1] Coppul, a chapelry of Standish parish, now made parochial.
[2] Originally written "Anne," but altered by the same hand to "Alice."

William Wilson, of Croston⎫
Anne Sumner, of Leyland ⎬pish ... ... Jan.　9

Richard Cliffe⎫
Mary Sumner⎬of Leyland ... ... „　27

John Miller, at Werden[1]　⎫
Anne Rigby, of Ormeschurch[2]⎬ ... ... ffeb.　7

Marriages, 1676.

Jeffrey Taylor　⎫
Hopestill[3] Munck⎬of Heapie... ... ... Ap.　6

John Jackson⎫
Jane Miller ⎬of Leyland ... ... „　15

William Waterworth⎫
Ellin Yeomanson ⎬of Leyland... ... ... „　15

Richard Sharples⎫
Ellin Rotchett ⎬of Leyland ... ... May　23

Thomas Ainsworth, of Pleasington⎫
Ellin Aspden, of Winnell ⎬ ... ... „　25

John Marsh, of Leyland ⎫
Mary Carre, of Plumton[4]⎬ ... ... June　24

Thomas Clithero⎫
Elsabeth Hilton⎬of Euxton ... ... July　13

James Hough, of Leyland ⎫
Elsabeth Gregson, of Euxton⎬ ... ... Aug.　6

John ffarington, of ffarington⎫
Jane Weake, of Clayton ⎬ ... ... Sept.　9

James Morris ⎫
Ellin Stopford⎬of Leyland ... ... Oct.　9

John Catterall ⎫
Helen Crichlow⎬ ... ... „ ye 26(?)

[This entry has been written perpendicularly along the outer margin of the page, in the later hand which occurs frequently after January 29th.]

[1] The hamlet of Werden is spoken of in the will of Wm. ffarington, 1610, but it has no existence at the present time. It probably, even then, comprised only a few cottages necessary for labourers, &c., employed on the land belonging to Werden Hall.

[2] Now known as Ormskirk.

[3] This unusual Christian name is worth noting.

[4] Plumton, probably Wood-plumpton, near Preston.

K

William Jackson, of Cuerden ⎫
Elsabeth ffarington, of ffarington ⎰ ··· ··· ··· ··· ··· Nov. 30

James Clayton ⎫ of Clayton ··· ··· ··· ··· ··· ··· Dec. 21
Sissaly Harrison ⎰

John Mackrill, of Leyland ⎫
Elsabeth Hoome, of Croston ⎰ ··· ··· ··· ··· ··· Jan. 22

[Different handwriting, which has a more modern appearance, is noticeable from this point.]

Richard Allmon, of this prish ⎫
Jennett Gerrat, of Brindle ⎰ ··· ··· ··· ··· ··· Jan. 29

Richard Slator ⎫ of Leyland ··· ··· ··· ··· ··· ··· ffeb. 6
Jane Godbert ⎰

[Marriages] 1677.

Raphe Walkeden, of Houghton ⎫
Ann Collinson, of Blackborn ⎰ ··· ··· ··· ··· ··· Ap. 16

Thomas ffarington ⎫
Ann Clayton, both of Clayton ⎰ ··· ··· ··· ··· ··· May 12

publication. John Philipps ⎫ both of Leyland ··· „ 27
　　　　　　Elizabeth Wiggans ⎰

pub. Richard Tootell ⎫ both of Whitle ··· ··· ··· ··· „ 27
　　Jane Wignoe ⎰

pub. Thomas Sumner ⎫ both of Leyland ··· ··· ··· July 23
　　Elizabeth Rochett ⎰

Thomas Biby ⎫ ··· ··· ··· ··· ··· ··· ··· Aug. 10
Jennett Waring ⎰

James Hall, of Euxton ⎫ ··· ··· ··· ··· ··· Sept. 3
Helen Heel, of Ormskirk ⎰

Robert Harrison ⎫ of Leyland ··· ··· ··· ··· ··· Oct. 2
Grace Pope ⎰

Nathaniell Allon ⎫ both of Euxton··· ··· ··· ··· ··· „ 12
Margrett Swann ⎰

Robert Walkden, of Brymycroft[1] ⎫ ··· ··· ··· ··· Nov. 12
Margrat Lifesey, of Pleasington ⎰

pub. Thomas Miller ⎫ both of Winnell ··· ··· ··· ··· „ 16
　　Allis Parr ⎰

Roger Sharples ⎫ both of Leyland ··· ··· ··· ··· Dec. 16
Ann Fareclough ⎰

[1] Brimycroft, a hamlet in the Moor quarter of Leyland parish.

John Leekas⎱ of Houghton ... ... Jan. 6
Ann ffeilden⎰

John Liuesey and⎱ both of Winnell ... ... „ 7
Margret Whittle⎰

license. John Clayton, of Midleforth[1]⎱ ... ... „ 16
Allis Chesshire, of ffarington⎰

pub. John Warington⎱ both of Houghton ... ... „ 27
Ellin Whiteside⎰

William Catterall, of Walton-Le-Dale⎱ ... ... „ 28
Jeney Clayton, of Winnell⎰

Henry Hesket, of Croston parrish⎱ ... ... ffeb. 10
Margreat Sargant, of Leyland⎰

[Marriages] 1678.

pub. James Chrichlow⎱ both of Euxton... ... ... Ap. 2
Ann Wright⎰

pub. Thomas Parker⎱ both of this parrish ... ... „ 23
Ellizabeth Withnell⎰

pub. Edward Houlmes⎱ both of this parish... ... ... May 1
Margreat Wareing⎰

lic.[2] Edward Meakinson⎱ of the parish of Bolton ... „ 17
Sarah Willoughby⎰

pub. James Hornby⎱ both of Leyland ... ... July 14
Jennett Charnock⎰

pub. Henry Sydall, of Croston⎱ ... ... Aug. 29
Margaret Stones, of Leyland⎰ [? or 20]

pub. Will: Crook⎱ both of Whitle ... ... Sept. ?
Margaret Brown⎰

pub. John Bridge, of Leyland⎱ ... ... Nov. 21
Mary Birtwisle, of Penwortham⎰

lic.[3] Thurstan Leyland, of Clayton⎱ ... ... Dec. 6
Margaret Nelson,[4] of Ulneswalton⎰

---

[1] Midleforth, or Middleford, *i.e.*, the middle ford over the River Ribble. The main road from Leyland to Preston passes over the bridge erected at that spot. The hamlet lies within Penwortham parish.

[2] By a License from Mr. ffogg, Surrogat.

[3] Licence from Mr. Ry[ley].

[4] Buried at Leyland, July 2, 1686, æt. 27. An overlay to her memory, with letters in bold relief, still remains in the churchyard.

pub. Lawrence ffish ⎱both of this parish ... ... Jan. 27
Izabel Emmatt⎰

pub. Christopher Kenion⎱both of this parish ... ... Feb. 20
And his wife ⎰

pub. Thomas Crichlow⎱ ... ... „ 24
Dorrathy Slator ⎰

[Marriages] 1679.

pub. John Ridging, of this parrish ⎱ ... ... June 12
Margaret Hindle, of Blackborn parish⎰

pub. Thomas Withington ⎱both of Leyland ... ... July 6
Ellin Pooter [? Porter]⎰

pub. James Brimaley ⎱ ... ... „ 6
Ellizabeth Poope⎰

pub. Robert ffoster ⎱ ... Aug. 3
Siscile Ownsworth [for Unsworth] of Euxton⎰

pub. Lawrance Ward, of this parrish ⎱
Jane Ensworth [for Ainsworth], of Blackborn⎬ Sept. 7
parish ⎭

Lawrence Whittle, of this parish⎱ ... ... Dec. 10
Mary Wareing, of Standish pish⎰

pub. James Gibbans ⎱both of this prish leyland ... ffeb. 2
Ellizabeth Willden⎰

lic. John Atherton, of this prish ⎱ ... ... „ 11
Joan Haruey, of Eccleston prish⎰

[This entry written after next heading but apparently contemporary.]

Marriages in 1680.

pub. William Pinckcock, of this prish⎱ ... ... Ap. 13
Ann Howerth, of Standish pish ⎰

pub. John Steward, of Armeschurch[1]⎱ ... ... „ 14
Margrat Holland, of this prish ⎰

lic. John Jackson & Mary knowles, of this prish ... „ 15

pub. Roger Liptrott & Issabell Nellson, both of this
prish ... ... May 4

pub. William Clough & Ann fflecher, both of this parish June 1

---

[1] An old form of the place name Ormskirk.

pub. William Howorth, of this prish }
Sisseley Hach, of ye prish of Brindle } ... ... July 4

lic. Andrew Stones, of this prish }
Margerett Armetriding } [no date given ? same day]

pub. Timmothy Wardle }both of this parish ... ... Aug. 1
Ellizabeth Croft }

pub. Thurstand Chrichlow }both of this parish ... ... „ 1
Ellizabeth Eastham }

pub. John Morras }both of this parish ... ... Nov. 1
Ann Liuesay }

pub. Lawrance Croft }both of this parish ... ... „ 1
Ann Whittle }

pub. William Jackson }both of this parish ... ... Jan. 30
Mary Crichlow } 1681 (*sic*)

[Marriages] 1681.

pub. John Hodskinson and }both of this parrish... ... July 24
Ellizabeth Winnell }

pub. Thomas Liusey, of this parrish }
Ann Garrett, of ye parish of Brindle } ... ... Sept. 25

pub. Gillbert Houghton and }
Ann Euxton, both of this prish } ... ... Nov. 13

pub. William Bury, of this prish }
Isabell Tasker, of Blackburn prish } ... ... Dec. 8

pub. Charles Kerchin & Jony Brethwith ... ... Jan. 9

William ffarington, of Leyland }
Mary Adlinton, at Worden } ... ... „ 24

pub. Thomas Cheetham & Ann Cookson, both of Leyland „ 25

[Marriages] 1682.

John Eastham & Ann Blackborn, of Cuerden, both of
this prish ... ... May 7
Richard Snape & Ellizabeth Entwisle, both of this psh June 5
Richard Pope and Ellizabeth Eaton, both of this prish Sept. 3

lic. John Billings, of Eccleston }
Allis Woodcock, of Leyland } ... ... Nov. 12

pub. William Jackson, of Ceurden }
Katterin Townson, of Walton-in-le-Dale } ... ... „ 19

pub. William Watterworth, of ye parish of Leyland ⎱ ... Dec. 21
Ann Shaw, of ye parish of Croston ⎰

pub. Thomas Poope, of Walton-in-le-dale ⎱ ... ... ffeb. 4
Ann fflecher, of ye prish of Leyland ⎰

[Marriages] 1683.

pub. Thomas Giller and Sicsely Armeriding, both of
this parrish of Leyland ... ... Aprill 10

lic. John Atherton, of ye prish of Leyland ⎱ ... ... May 31
Ann Dawson, of ye prish of pennertham ⎰

pub. William Crook, of Houghton, in ye prish of Leyland ⎱ June 7
Ann Howden, of ye prish of Blackborn ... ... ⎰

pub. Richard Rose and ⎱ both of ye parrish of Leyland Aug. 6
Allis Gregson ⎰

pub. John Thornton, of Croston prish, and ⎱ ... ... Sept. 22
Allis Hodson, of Leyland parish ⎰

Edward Whittle and Ruth (?) Pomfret... ... ... „ 22

lic. Thomas Nowell, of ye prish of Leyland ⎱ ... ... „ 27
Ann Loxam, of pennortham parish ⎰

lic. William Smith & Ellin Liuese [for Livesey] of
Leyland ... ... Dec. 30

lic. Henry Tod, of Eccleston, & Ellizabeth Jackson,
of Leyland ... ... Jan. 17

lic. Mathew Kuerden, of Walton, & Ellin Holme, of
Eccleston ... ... „ 25

lic. John March, of Croston, & Jane Balshaw, of
Layland ... ... „ 27

pub. Georg Hach, of Leyland, & Sicsily Pope, of
Boulton p ... ... „ 28

pub. James Darwin, of this p, and Jane Pemmorton, of
Blackborn p ... ... ffeb. 3

[Marriages] 1684.

pub. Hugh Baxenden and Allis Bannester, both of this
prish ... ... Ap. 24

pub. Thomas Metcalfe and Ellin Beatson, both of this
prish ... ... May 8

Ralph Gorton and Allis Mather ... ... „ 12

pub. Lawrence Allmond & Jenet Walton, of this prish. June 8

lic. Thomas Hicham, of Preston prish, & Ellizabeth
Balshaw, of Leyland ... ... „ 25

pub. Henry Croft & Ellizabeth Worthinton, of this prish. July 7

pub. James Whithead, of ye prish of Maxfield in ⎫
Chishshire ⎬ Aug. 16
Ann Burton, of ye prish of Preston ⎭

pub. Thomas Hey and Ellin Worsley, both of this prish Oct. 6

pub. Georg Dawson and Annas (*sic*) Holms, both of
this prish ... ... Dec. 1

pub. William Garrod & Allis Sharples, both of this
prish ... ... Jan. 11

pub. Edward Clough & Allin Stilson, both of this prish „ 19

pub. John Jackson & Mary Liptrot, both of this prish Feb. 16

pub. John Pilkington, of this prish, & Ann Baron, of
blackborn ... ... „ 17

[Marriages] 1685.

[There is a complete change in the style of handwriting at
this place.]

lic. John Rhodes, of ye Parish of Lancaster ⎫
Ann Higham, of ye Parish of Eccleston ⎬ ... ... May 19

pub. Thomas Garstang & Jennet Watson ⎫
both of this Parish ⎬ ... ... „ 19

lic. Thomas Worsley & Alice Beckansey,[1] both of ye ⎫ June 18
Parish of Eccleston ⎭

pub. Thomas Fowler, *alias* Foole, & Alice Ryley ⎫ ... July 21
Both of this Parish ⎭

pub. John Garstang & ⎫ both of this Parish ... ... Nov. 4
Alice Haworth ⎭

pub. Thomas Woodcocke & ⎫ both of this Parish... ... Jan. 19
Ellen Watmough ⎭

lic. Richard Crossgill & ⎫ both of Penwortham Parish Feb. 15
Ellen Johnson ⎭

lic. John Stopford ⎫ both of this Parish ... ... „ 15
Margaret Sumner ⎭

[1] For Becconsall or Becconshaw.

lic.   Robt Bicursteth,[1] of ye Parish of Aughton ⎫
     Elizabeth Armetriding, of this parish   ⎭ ...   ... Feb.   21

lic.   Thomas Watson & ⎫ both of this parish...   ...   ...   „   21
     Margery Garstang ⎭

[Marriages] 1686.

lic.   John Greene, of this parish ⎫ ...   . May   1
     Anne Greene, of Chorley   ⎭

pub. John Golding ⎫ both of this Parish ...   .   „   11
      Jane Tyler[2] ⎭

pub. Raphe Crosse, of ye Parish of Eccleston ⎫
      Elizabeth Thorneton, of this parish   ⎭ ...   ... June   24

pub. Thomas Preston ⎫ both of this Parish   ...   . July   13
      Ellen Withnell ⎭

pub. Thomas Harrison ⎫ both of this parish ...   . Sept.   9
      Alice Martin   ⎭

James Lowe, of Euxton   ⎫ both of this Parish [(*sic*) no date given]
Mary Sumner, of Euxton ⎭

pub. Richard Williamson ⎫ both of this parish   ...   ... Dec.   15
      Jennet Battersbie   ⎭

lic.   Thurstan Leyland & ⎫ both of this parish   ...   ... June   24
     Jane Armetriding   ⎭

[Marriages] 1687.

pub. James Morris & ⎫ both of this Parish   ...   . Ap.   16
      Jane Baxenden ⎭

lic.[3] Robt Bane   ⎫ both of ye Parish of Eccleston   ... June   20
      Anne Hough ⎭

pub. William Howorth ⎫ both of this Parish ...   . July   25
      Izabel Lever   ⎭

pub. James Livesay ⎫ both of this Parish   ...   . Oct.   24
      Jane Fishwick ⎭

pub. Geo. Porter, of this P: &   ⎫
      Agnes Jackson, of Croston P: ⎭ ...   . Feb.   21

      Christopher Kenion, of Whalley P: & ⎫
      Anne Crooke, of this P: ⎭ ...   ...   „   23

---

[1] See note on page 78.   [2] Blotted and so indistinct. It may be Tylour.
[3] Mr. Haddon, Surrog. [? Vicar of Bolton le Moors.]

[For the year 1688 the Register contains no Marriage entries.]

[Marriages] 1689.

lic. John Charnock & Margaret Sharples } both of this P.... ... ... Ap. 14

pub. Richard [John crossed out] Almond & Margaret Mackeril } both of this Parish ... May 6

pub. John Whittle & Elizabeth Porter } both of this Parish ... ... ,, 9

pub. William Holden, of Blackburn p: & Sarah Lukas, of Leyland p: ... ... Oct. 22

pub. William Croft, of Whitle Ann Benson, of Whitle ... ... Jan. 2

pub. Richard Ryley & Ann Croft } both of y^s Parish ... ... ,, 27

pub. Lawrence Lucas & Sarah Crooke } both of y^s parish ... ,, 30

pub. John Walmsley & Isabel Stackhouse } both of y^s Parish ... ... ffeb. 6

pub. John Clough & Ann Sherborne } both of y^s parish ... ... ,, 6

[Marriages] 1690.

pub. John Slaytour Ellen Woodcock } both of y^s Parish ... ... Ap. 21

pub. George Charnley, of y^s Parish Alice Arthurick, of Penwortham Parish ... ... ,, 22

pub. James Low, of ye Parish of Winwick & Elizabeth Hilton, of this Parish } ... ... June 26

pub. Henry Walton & Mary Sumner } both of y^s Parish ... ... Sept. 29

pub. Thomas Cooper & Sarah Hough } both of y^s Parish ... ... Oct. 13

pub. Robt. Heyes, of this parish, & Margret Taylor, of Croston Parish } ... ... Dec. 29

pub. Henry Slaytour, of this Parish, & Alice Milner, of Croston Parish } ... ... ,, 29

pub. Robert Charnock, of Standish Parish, &⎫ ...   ... Dec. 29
Jane Slaytour, of this Parish   ⎭

pub. William Stephenson &⎫both of yˢ Parish   ... ... Jan. 26
Jennet Raby   ⎭

lic. James Armetriding &⎫both of yˢ Parish   ... ... ffeb. 17
Ellen Sumner   ⎭

pub. John Freerson, of ffarington⎫... ... ... „ 23
Ellen Jackson, of Kuerden ⎭

pub. John Wolfenden, of yˢ Parish, & ⎫ ... ... „ 24
Lettice Asley, of Blackburne Parish⎭

Weddings, 1691.

pub. John Gill, of ye Parish of Bolton, &⎫ ... ... Ap. 14
Elizabeth Gabbot, of this Parish ⎭

pub. James Livesey & Jennet ⎫ ... ... June 29
Gabbot, both of ye Parish⎭

pub. James Chrichlaw & Mary ⎫ ... ... Aug. 3
Walmsley, both of ye Parish⎭

pub. William Croft & Alice ⎫ ... ... ffeb. 9
Brooke, both of ys Parish⎭

[Marriages] 1692.

pub. Thomas Mackerill, of yˢ Prsh ⎫ ... ... Ap. 12
Margaret Robinson, of Penwortham Prsh⎭

These should have been registered before ye other.

pub. William Marton & Alice Parker ⎫all of ye Parish Mar. 29
William Hilton & Mary Tompson⎭

pub. William Leyland &⎫both of yˢ Prish   ... ... Sept. 19
Agnes Bradshaw ⎭

pub. William Roscow &⎫both of ys Prish   ... ... Dec. 24
Alice Pilkington ⎭

lic. John Euxton &⎫both of ys Prish   ... ... ffeb. 5
Ann Wild ⎭

lic. James Cocker, of Penwortham Prish⎫ ... ... „ 23
Martha Piper, of Leyland Prsh ⎭

lic. John Aspinell, of Whaley Prsh ⎫ ... ... „ 26
Eilizabeth Cawsey, of Chorley Prsh⎭

[Marriages] 1693.

pub. Robert Low & Elizabeth Halliwell} both of y^s Prsh ... ... Ap. 18

pub. William Haworth & Alice Johnson} both of y^s Prsh ... ... „ 25

pub. Alexander Hindle, of Blackburn parish, & Civil[1] Euxton, of this parish } ... July 4

pub. Thomas Dawson & Alice Bomber} both of y^s Parish ... ... Aug. 24

pub. Thomas Carthwright & Ellen Crook} both of y^s Parish ... ... Sept. 4

pub. Roger Walton, of y^s Parish Sarah Rose, of Croston Prsh} ... ... „ 19

pub. Andrew Cooper & Alice Walmesley, both of this parish} ... ... „ 21

pub. Richard Mayre, of Penwortham, & Ellen Biggins, of Leyland Parish } ... ... Oct. 11

pub. John Piper & Margaret Croston, both of the parish} ... ... Nov. 30

[Marriages] 1694.

pub. John Clayton & Alice Wigans} both of y^s Prsh ... ... Ap. 12

pub. Charles Rothwell, of y^s Prish Marjory Wilding, of Croston Prsh} ... ... „ 12

pub. Thomas Parkinson & Alice Shaw} both of y^s Prsh ... ... May 3

pub. Ralph Chamberlin & Margaret Fishwick} both of y^s Parish ... ... July 15

pub. Arthur Key & Jane [blank]} both of y^s Parish ... ... Oct. 24

pub. John Scot & Alice Tootell} both of y^s Parish ... ... Dec. 1

lic. Edward Ardern, of Stockport, & Elizabeth Garstang, of Leyland} Parish ... ... Jan. 27

pub. Richard Chephet & Anne Physick} both of ye parish ... ... „ 31

[1] An unusual name, which is worth noting.

[Marriages] 1695.

pub. Richard Calvert & Elizabeth Lawson } both of yˢ Prish ... ... Ap. 9

pub. William Riding & Jane Eccles } both of ye Parish ... ... „ 23

pub. John Mackerill & Agnes Sergeant } both of ye Parish ... ... „ 23

pub. Ralph Somner & Jennet Baxenden } both of yᵉ Parish ... ... May 7

lic. Richard Banister, of Croston Prsh, & Alice Smith, of Leyland Prsh } ... ... Oct. 22

[This entry has been inserted later, but (apparently) by the same hand.]

lic. Mʳ Ralph Asheton,¹ of Cuerdal, in ye Prish of Black-Burne, & Mʳˢ Sarah Bruen, of ye Prish of Leyland } Dec. 19

[Marriages] 1696.

pub. Bryan Chisnhall, of ye Prish of Standish Mary Dobson, of this Parish } ... ... Ap. 16

pub. Roger Bolton, of yˢ Prish, & Elizabeth Yate, of ye Prish of Blackburne ... ... May 26

pub. John Brewer & Ann Nelson } both of yˢ Prish ... ... June 2

pub. Henry Waddington & Ann Turner } both of yˢ Prish ... ... Nov. 9

pub. Charles Hoghton & Alice Smith } both of ye Prish ... ... „ 24

pub. Lawrence Scowcroft & Margaret Webster } both of ye Prsh ... ... Feb. 11

pub. John Baron & Alice Bromeley } both of yᵉ Prsh ... ... „ 15

¹ Mr. Ralph Assheton was the eldest son of Richard Assheton, of Cuerdale, Esq., who, by the settlement of his relative Sir Ralph Assheton, of Whalley, became heir of the estates at Downham and Whalley. Upon the death of Mr. Richard Assheton in 1709 (O.S.), the gentleman whose marriage is here recorded succeeded to the family estates. The lady (Mrs. Sarah Bruen) was the only daughter of Tilston Bruen, of Bruen Stapleford, co. Chester, Esq., by his second wife. Her mother was Lucy, one of the daughters of Sir Richard Hoghton, Bart., and his wife Sarah, daughter of Philip, Earl of Chesterfield. Mr. Ralph Assheton and his wife had two sons, Ralph and Richard, the latter of whom died without issue.

[Marriages] 1697.

pub. John Pincock & Ellen Tootell } both of ye Prish... ... ... Ap. 29

pub. Robert Lockland, of ye Prsh of Brasewell, in Yorkshire
Ann Taylor, of Euxton, in ye Prsh of Leyland } July 30

pub. William Marsden & Ellen Litherland } both of ye Prish ... ... Sept. 21

lic. Thomas Abbot, of Heapy, in ys Prsh, & Ann Brindle, of Andlesark,[1] in ye Prsh of Bolton } Nov. 20

pub. Roger Pilkington, of Croston parish, & Jane Hurst, of Leyland pish } ... ... Jan. 23

pub. Richard Crook & Elizabeth Barton } both of ye Prish ... ... „ 25

pub. Amulet[2] Holm & Ellen Harrocks } both of ye Parish ... ... ffeb. 21

[Marriages] 1698.

pub. Edward Bank & Jennet Armetriding } both of ye Prish ... ... Ap. 25

pub. Samuel Duncalf & Anne Pearson } both of ye parish ... ... June 14

pub. Robert Blackledg & Ann Tootel } both of ye Prish ... ... Sept. 26

pub. John Ainscow, of ye Prsh of Croston Jane Berry, of ye Prsh of Leyland } ... ... Oct. 26

pub. George Woods & Dorothy Tilson } both of ye Prish... ... ... „ 30

pub. Edward Miller, of Stndish parish, & Alice Smith, of ys parish } ... ... Nov. 20

pub. Thomas Eastham & Elizabeth Nelson } both of ye Prish ... ... Dec. 28

Thomas Shaw & Ellen Walmsley
pub. Robert Greenhalgh & Jane Hodskinson } all of ys Prish ... ... Jan. 31

[1] Anglesarch or Anlezargh is the moorland township which lies to the south-east of Heapy. It is included in the district attached to Rivington Church.

[2] Note this peculiar Christian name.

pub. Lawrence Silcock &}
     Alice Stephenson }of y^s P^{rsh} ... ... ffeb. 12

pub. John Somner & }
     Hannah Houghton}both of y^s P^{rish} ... ... „ 20

pub. Henry Croft &}
     Ellen Preston }both of y^s P^{rish} ... ... „ 20

pub. Henry Dawson &}
     Hannah Martin }both of y^s P^{rish} ... ... „ 21

[Marriages] 1699.

pub. Robert Sumner &}
     Ann Ditchfield }both of ye P^{rish} ... ... May 1

pub. Roger Phishwick &}
     Sarah Withnell }both of ye P^{rish} ... ... „ 2

lic. James Cowling, of ye P^{rsh} of Eccleston, &}
     Alice Rigby, of Leyland } ... ... „ 11

pub. John Somner & }
     Margaret Taylor}both of [ye] parish ... ... „ 30

lic. Thomas Somner & }
     Dorothy Woodcock}both of ye P^{rsh} ... ... July 23

pub. Thomas Tinsdley &}
     Elizabeth Martin }both of ye P^{rsh} ... ... Sept. 24

(Robert Cooper, of Curden ... ... Oct. 11)

[Written afterwards in different ink, evidently by mistake; possibly a burial entry.]

pub. Henery Whalley &}
     Elizabeth Loftas }both of ye P^{rish} ... ... Nov. 23

pub. John Tomson &}
     Margret Somner}both of ye P^{rish} ... ... Dec. 28

pub. Richard Goodshaw &}
     Ann Cartmel } ... ... Jan. 7

pub. Hugh Crook, of Whittle, &}
     Mary Lucas, of Chorley } ... ... „ 23

pub. Thomas Crook, of Penworth^m P^{rish}}
     Ann Smith, of ye P^{rish} of Leyland } ... ... ffeb. 2

[Marriages] ffor ye yeare 1700.

pub. Richard Haydock, of Heapey, &
Isabel Walmsley, of Whittle, both of ye P^rish } ... Ap. 2

lic. Mr Henery Dickonson,[1] of Blakeley, in ye parish
of Manchester, & Mrs Elizabeth Greenehalgh, } „ 30
of ye same ... ...

pub. Henry Hartley, of ye P^rish of Rochdale
Mary Pope, of ye P^rish of Leyland } ... ... Aug. 1

pub. John Gabbot &
Ellen Hilton } both of ye P^rish ... ... „ 29

pub. Thomas Silcock &
Margaret ffletcher } both of ye Parish ... ... Oct. 29

pub. Robert Martin &
Ann Walmsley } both of ye P^rish ... ... Nov. 30

pub. William Morrice &
Mary Blakeledg, both of ye P^rish ... ... Jan. 6

pub. William Wigins, of ye parish of Penwortham, &
Margery Clough, of Leyland } „ 12

pub. Ralph Longton &
Margret Stilton } both of ye P^rish ... ... „ 27

pub. William Jackson &
Margaret Bradley } both of ye parish ... ... ffeb. 3

pub. Andrew Wilson &
Catherine Walmsley } both of ye P^rish ... ... Mar. 3

[Marriages] 1701.

pub. Thomas Blackledge, of Penwortham P^rish, &
Ann Cross, of Leyland Parish } ... Ap. 24

pub. Hugh Woods & Jane ffishwick,
both of ye Parish ... ... June 3

pub. John Pincock, of Leyland parish, &
Elizabeth Jackson, of ye Parish of Croston } ... „ 3

---

[1] Mr. Henry Dickanson, of Blackley, was the eldest surviving son of Mr. Samuel Dickanson, of Blackley (who died in 1691), and grandson of Mr. Henry Dickanson, of Manchester, a rich Manchester linen draper, who died in 1682. By this marriage Mr. Henry Dickanson had two sons, Thomas, born 1701, and Samuel, born 1704. His wife died in 1706, and was buried at Blackley on the 26th July in that year. By a second wife he had other issue, and was buried at Blackley on the 24th July, 1718. (Information kindly supplied by Mr. J. P. Earwaker.)

pub. Robert Drinkwater & Ann Preston }both of ye P^rish ... ... July 9

pub. Ralph Pierson & Elizabeth Biggins }both of ye P^rish ... ... „ 31

pub. John Garstang, *alias* Smith, of Whittle, & Ellen Dawson, of Leyland, both of ye P^rish ... ... Aug. 27

pub. Thomas Day, of ye P^rish of Leyland, & Jennet Haydock, of Blacburn P^rish ... ... Nov. 27

lic: Richard Croston,[1] Cleric^s, & Mary Wilson, married at Chorley, both of ye P^rish Dec. 27

lic. Francis Serjeant & Mary Blackledg }both of ye P^rish ... ... Jan. 3

pub. Nicholas Bromcley & Elizabeth Mare, both }of ye Parish ... ... „ 12

pub. William Anderton, of Croston P^rish, & Margret Hodson, of Leyland Parish } ... ... ffeb. 9

[Marriages] 1702.

pub. John Walmsley & Ellen Rigby }both of ye P^rish ... ... Ap. 7

lic. Alexander Gerrard & Ann Bury }both of ye P^rish ... ... „ 19

lic. Tho: Armetriding, Vic^r of Leyland,[2] & Mrs Margret Farington }both of ye P^rish „ 23

pub. John Brooks & Isabel Woods }both of ye P^rish ... ... „ 28

pub. John Farnworth & Ann Farnworth }both of ye P^rish ... ... May 12

pub. John Cooper & Ellen Clough }both of ye P^rish ... ... June 14

pub. Joseph Edg. & Dorothy Riding }both of ye P^rish ... ... „ 28

---

[1] An old table of benefactors to Heapy Chapel has the following: "The Reverend Richard Croston, of Whittle-le-Woods, £20." Among the In-Burgesses of Preston, at the Guild of 1682, we find "Richard Croston, Clericus." There are a few entries in this Register which may refer to members of the same family, *e.g.*: "*vx.* John Croston, buried 25 March, 1637;" "Elizabeth, daughter of John Croston, of Chorley, (born) 1654;" "Alice, d. of Henry Croston, of Whittle, (born) July, 1656." There is a pedigree of the Croston family in Baines' *Hist. of Lanc.* (edit. Croston), p. 123.

[2] See Introduction for an account of this Vicar. See also notes on pp. 32, 33, 42.

pub. Roger Hollinhurst, of ye P^{rish}, & ⎫
Ellen Serjeant, of Blackburn P^{rish} ⎭ ... ... June 30

pub. Tho: ffarnworth &
Ellen Moor, both of ye P^{rish}, marry'd at Brindle... July 8

pub. Bernard Hoghton & ⎫ both of ye P^{rish} ... ... „ 26
Hannah Warbutton ⎭

lic. John Cumberbatch & ⎫ both of ye P^{rish} ... ... Aug. 19
Cicely Hollinhurst ⎭

lic. Roger Crook & ⎫ both of ye P^{rish} ... ... „ 27
Elizabeth Blackledg ⎭

pub. Samuel Baxenden & ⎫ both of ye P^{rish} ... ... Oct. 20
Esther Blackburn ⎭

pub. William Martin, of y^s Parish, & ⎫
Agnes Tomlinson, of Penwortham P^{rish} ⎭ ... ... „ 29

lic. William Wright & ⎫ both of y^s P^{rish} ... ... Nov. 2
Elizabeth Bickursteth ⎭

pub. Thomas Porter & ⎫ both of ye P^{rish}... ... ... Dec. 29
Catherin Woods ⎭

pub. John Hodson (*alias*) Parkinson & ⎫ both of ye P^{rish} Jan. 11
Margaret Forrest ⎭

pub. Christopher Marsden & ⎫ ye Parish ... ... „ 18
Eleanor Crook, both of ⎭

pub. James Bolton, of Croston P^{rish}, & ⎫ ... ... „ 18
Ann Sumner, of ye P^{rish} ⎭

pub. Thomas Somner, of Leyland, &
Susanna Waterworth, of Farrington ... ... „ 31

pub. Thomas Hunt, of Cuerden, Ley[land] P^{rish}
Ellen Parker, of Farington, Pen[wortham] P^{rish} ... ffeb. 2

1703 Marriages.

pub. George Hatch &
Mary Liptrot, both of ye P^{rish} ... ... Ap. 1

pub. William Porter, of Leyland P^{rish} ⎫ ... ... May 7
Elizabeth Cross, of Croston P^{rish} ⎭

pub. Matthew Bickursteth, of Penwortha^m P^{rish} ⎫ ... ... June 2
Ann Knight, of Leyland P^{rish} ⎭

pub. Richard Baxenden, of Croston Parish, & ⎫ ... ... „ 13
Ann Cooper, of Leyland Parish ⎭

L

lic. John Woodcock &⎫ both of ye P^rish
Mary Riding   ⎰s^d to be married   ...   . June 23

pub. Ellis Sumner, of ye P^rish, &⎫
Hannah Chisnall, of Standish P^rish⎰   ...   .   „   30

lic. William Worden &⎱of ye P^rish   ...   . July 13
Jane Aspinal, both ⎰

lic. Thomas ffartclough &⎫ both of ye P^rish
Margret Emmet   ⎰s^d to be married   ...   ...   „   29

pub. Oliver Garstang &⎱both of ye P^rish   ...   . Sept. 21
Cicely Pincock ⎰

pub. Jonathan Rigby &⎱both of ye P^rish, s^d to be married Oct. 17
Ann Proctor ⎰

pub. John ffarnworth &⎱both of ye P^rish   ...   . Nov.   1
Elizabeth Brooks ⎰

pub. James Walmsley & ⎱both of ye P^rish ...   .   „   4
Catherine Ainsworth⎰

pub. Robert Welch, of Farington,[1] of Penwortham⎫
P^rish, &   ⎬   „   9
Ellen Clayton, of Leyland   ⎭

lic. John Boond, of ye P^rish of North Meols,[2] &⎱   ...   „   11
Margaret Leaver, of Leyland P^rish   ⎰

pub. George Dawson &⎱both of ye P^rish   ...   .   „   30
Elizabeth Sirrup ⎰

pub. William Smith &⎱both of ye P^rish   ...   . Dec. 12
Alice Burscow ⎰

pub. Thomas Garstang &⎱both of ye P^rish   ...   . Jan. 10
Margaret Pilkington⎰

pub. Henry Wright, of Leyland P^rish, &⎱   ...   .   „   23
Agnes Carver, of Blackborn P^rish ⎰

lic. James Andlesark, of Duxbury,[3] in Standish P^rish⎱   „   3J
Mary Sharrock, of Euxton, in Leyland Parish ⎰

Richard Lancaster &⎫ both of ye P^rish
Jennet Bank   ⎰s^d to be married   ...   . Feb. 13

pub. Thomas Longton &⎱both of ye P^rish   ...   .   „   17
Alice Taylor ⎰

----

[1] Farington township forms part of the ancient parish of Penwortham. It was made parochial in 1840.

[2] North Meols (or Churchtown), the ancient part of the town of Southport.

[3] Duxbury lies a little to the south of Chorley, and to the east of Coppul. Duxbury Hall was the seat, for many generations, of a younger branch of the Standish family.

pub. Thomas Clitherall &⎱both of ye P^rish ... ... Feb. 19
Ann Longworth ⎰

Henry Catherall &⎫ both of ye P^rish
Elizabeth Brekall ⎰s^d to be married ... ... „ 21

[Marriages] 1704.

pub. John Gregson &⎱both of ye P^rish
Ann Lucas ⎰s^d to be married ... ... Ap. 22

pub. James Marsden, of Withnel, in ye Parish of Ley-⎫
land, & ⎬ May 6
Mary Hooker, of ye Parish of Whaley ⎭

lic. John Whitley & ⎱both of ye P^rish ... ... „ 20
Elizabeth Worsley⎰

pub. Peter Walkden &⎱both of ye P^rish ... ... „ 25
Mary Duncalf ⎰

pub. John Porter, of Hoghton, in ye P^rish of Leyland⎱ July 2
Mary Sharples, of Pleasington in Blacburn P^rish ⎰

pub. Peter Ulnsworth, of Leyland Parish &⎱ ... ... „ 2
Mary Waddington, of Preston P^rish ⎰

lic. John Hindley &⎱of Blackburn P^rish ... ... „ 30
Ann Brown ⎰

Evan Bury, of Withnel, & Elizabeth Oram, of Brindle,
s^d to be married ... ... Aug. 20

[This entry was inserted afterwards by (apparently) the
same hand.]

pub. Christopher Marsden &⎱both of ye P^rish ... ... Aug. 23
Margery Toppin ⎰

lic. John Forshaw, of Leyland P^rish, & ⎱ ... ... „ 31
Elizabeth Tuson, of Penwortham P^rish⎰

Richard Anderton & Jennet Whittle, both of Withnell,
s^d to be married ... ... Oct. 2

pub. Robert Bury &⎱of Withnell, in Leyland P^rish ... „ 18
Mary Bolton ⎰

Richard Wilson, of Clayton, & ⎱s^d to be married ... „ 28
Ellen Haworth, both of ye P^rish⎰

pub. Thomas Dewhurst, of Cuerden, in Leyland P^rish⎱ Nov. 13
Margaret Taylor, of Walton, in Blackburn P^rish ⎰

John Boulton, of Hoghton, & ⎱s^d to be married ... „ 16
Elizabeth Chambers, of Brindle⎰

John Woodcock, of Euxton } both of ye P^rish
Margaret Chesters, of Clayton } s^d to be married ··· ··· Nov. 23

pub. Richard Bateson & } Withnell & ye P^rish ··· ··· Dec. 21
Alice Dale, both of }

lic. Edmund Woodcock & } both of Leyland ··· ··· Jan. 24
Alice Balshaw }

pub. John Jackson, of Cuerden, & }
Elizabeth Cheetham, of Farington } ··· ··· ··· Feb. 12

[Marriages] 1705.

pub. James Lees, of Wheelton, in Leyland P^rish }
Elizabeth Miller, of Ulnswalton, X^ston 1 P^rish } ··· Ap. 9

pub. Henry Kirkham, of Farington, in Penwortham P^rish }
Alice Hesketh, of Leyland } „ 9

pub. George Hey & } both of Leyland ··· ··· ··· ··· „ 10
Cicely Walton }

pub. Richard Davis, of Clifton, in Kirkham P^rish, & }
Ellen Whittle, of Leyland } ··· „ 15

pub. George Clayton & } in Cuerden, s^d to be married... May 3
Margret Dinel }

pub. George Parkinson, of Euxton, & } s^d to be married „ 4
Dorothy Halliwell, of Eccleston }

pub. John Marsden, of Withnell, in Leyland P^rish
Grace ffolds, of Plessington, in Blackburne P^rish ··· „ 31

lic. Richard Armetriding,[2] of Leyland, & }
Ann Wright, of Euxton, both of ye P^rish } ··· ··· June 7

lic. Robert Blackledg, of Whittle, in Leyland P^rish
Margaret Giles, of Blackburn P^rish, married at
Harwood ··· ··· ··· ··· ··· ··· ··· ··· „ 11

pub. John Gillar & } of Farington, in Penwortham P^rish „ 19
Jennet Martin }

John Nelson & } both of Leyland, s^d to be married ··· „ 24
Alice Slaytor }

pub. James Higgison & } both of ye P^rish ··· ··· ··· July 12
Elizabeth ffishwick }

[1] X^ston, *i.e.*, Croston parish.

[2] Brother of Vicar Armetriding, and father of the Rev. John Armetriding, who became perpetual curate of Bispham. Mr. Richard Armetriding and his wife both died within ten years of their marriage, leaving three orphan children. These were provided for by legacies under the will of their uncle, the vicar.

pub. Lawrence Parker, of Wheelton, &} s^d to be married July 21
Catherin Briers, of Brindle

pub. Richard Bateson &} both of Leyland ... ... Aug. 2
Clemence Watmough

pub. Ralph Boardman &} ... ... ,, 26
Alice Hough, both of Leyland

lic. Peter Walkden, of Heapey, in Leyland P^rish
Mary Willoughby, of Heath-Charnock, in Standish
P^rish ... ... Sept. 29

pub. Henry Darwin &} of Whittle, s^d to be married ... Oct. 4
Elizabeth Croston

pub. William Ellison, of Hoghton, &} ... ... Nov. 12
Mary Lees, of Wheelton

pub. Richard Marsden, of Withnell, &} ... ... ,, 12
Mary Walkden, of Tock-Holes[1]

pub. John Bolton, of Blackburn, &} ... ... ,, 13
Jane Roscow, of Leyland P^rish

lic. Thomas Barton, of Leyland, &
Hanna Hodgshon, of Kirkham P^rish ... ... Jan. 6

lic. John Walne &} both of Cuerden, in Leyland P^rish ,, 19
Ann Jackson

pub. William Slaytor, Junr, of Leyland, &} ... ... Feb. 4
Ann Rome, of Walton in Le Dale

[Marriages] 1706.

pub. William Whittle &} Leyland ... ... Mar. 27
Ellen Carter, of

lic. Farrand Hodgson[2] &} of Leyland
Elizabeth Atherton } s^d to be married at Goosner[3] ,, 27

pub. George Crook &} both of Withnell
Elizabeth ffishwick} s^d to be married ... ... ,, 28

pub. Adam Brindle, of Withnel, &} ... ... Ap. 3
Alice Crook, of Wheelton

[1] Tockholes, a township of Blackburn parish which adjoins Withnell. The River
Rothelsworth divides the two townships and the ancient parishes of Leyland and
Blackburn.

[2] See Baptisms, p. 112. Mr. Farrand Hodgson was master of the Leyland
Grammar School. This was probably a second marriage, for Leonora, wife of Mr.
Farrand Hodgson, was buried at Leyland, Feb. 18, 1704-5.

[3] Goosnargh, an ancient chapelry of Kirkham parish, lying to the north-east of
Preston.

pub. Thomas Carthwright, of Farington, in Penwortham Prish
Elizabeth Banks, of Cuerden, in Leyland Parish } May 3

pub. John Almond, of Leyland, &
Frances Slaytor, of Eccleston } married at Eccleston June 12

pub. William Mare &
Ann Jackson } both of Leyland ... ... July 3

pub. John Whittle &
Jennet Gorton } both of Withnell, in Leyland Prish Aug. 26

pub. John Hunt, of Cuerden, &
Ellen Stuart, both of ye Prish } sd to be married ... „ 29

pub. John Walmsley, of Cuerden, &
Ann Ainscow, both of ye Prish } sd to be married... Sept. 10

pub. Richard Dewhurst, of Withnel, in
Leyland Prish
Jane Ward, of Sharples, in Bolton
Parish } at Rivington Oct. 16

pub. John Berry, of Withnel, &
Margery Johnson, of Heapey } both of ye Prish ... „ 24

lic. Robert Eastham, of Leyland, &
Ann Turner, of Harwood, in Blackburn
Prish } married at Harwood Nov. 20

lic. James Fairbrother &
Alice Jackson, of Cuerden } sd to be married ... „ 24

pub. Thomas Jackson, of Clayton, in Leyland Prish, &
Margaret Eves, of Woodplumpton, in Michaels-
Parish [St. Michael's-on-Wyre] } Dec. 1

pub. Lawrence Halliwell, of Hoghton, in Leyland
Prish, &
Jennet Sharples, of Plessington, in Blackburn Prish „ 31

pub. John Gillibrand, of Mellar, in Blackburn Prish, &
Ann Roscow, of Wheelton, in Leyland Parish ... Feb. 25

[Marriages] 1707.

lic. William Walton, of Penwortham Prish, &
Ellen Balshaw, of Leyland } ... ... Ap. 13

pub. Thomas Jackson &
Isabel Kirkham } of Cuerden ... ... May 13

lic. Gilbert Lancaster &
Ann Cowlin, both of } Leyland, sd to (*sic*) ... ... June 24

pub. Richard Sumner & } Leyland... ... ... Sept. 3
Elizabeth Porter, of }

pub. James Watkison, of ye P^rish of Wigan, &
Ann Lawson, of Heapey, of Leyland P^rish ... ... Feb. 5

[Marriages] 1708.

pub. George Blackledge & } Heapey, in Leland P^rish ... May 1
Ann Garstang, both of }

pub. John Crook & } both of Wheelton, in Lealand P^rish „ 25
Mary Blackledg }

pub. Richard Loxam } in Lealand P^rish ... „ 29
Ann Hodskison, of Euxton }

pub. James Leach, of Oswestwistle, in ye P^rish of }
Whalley } June 29
Mary Ainsworth, of Withnel, in Leyland Parish }

pub. Thomas Hey & } both of Heapey, in Lealand P^rish July 20
Ann Taylor }

lic. Henry Okenshaw, of Euxton, & } ... ... Aug. 24
Rose Whittle, of Leyland }

pub. James Jackson & } both of Leyland ... ... Sept. 26
Elizabeth Assheton }

pub. John Lees, of Wheelton, & } in Leyland P^rish ... „ 27
Elizabeth Taylor, of Heapey }

pub. James Low, of Hoghton, & } both of ye P^rish ... Oct. 18
Ann Low, of Leyland }

pub. Richard Greenwood, of Ribchester P^rish, & } ... „ 26
Ann Hesmonall, of ye Parish of Leyland }

pub. William Sharples & } of ye Parish ... ... Nov. 2
Ann Ainsworth, both }

pub. James Bradshaw, of Leyland P^rish, & } ... ... „ 3
Elizabeth Tatersall, of Blackburn P^rish }

pub. Thomas Thornley & } both of ye P^rish ... ... „ 23
Elizabeth Ockenshaw }

pub. Robert Bradshaw & } both of ye P^rish ... ... „ 25
Elizabeth Brining }

lic. William Farington, of Leyland, & } Pen P^rish ... Feb. 2
Elizabeth Bomber, of Farington, in }

pub. Henry Moulden & } both of Leyland ... ... „ 3
Hannah Sumner }

pub. Thomas Ainsworth, of Hoghton, in Leyland Parish \
Mary Ratcliff, of Balderstone, in Blackeburn P^{rish} } Mar.   1

lic. James Worthington, of Ormskirk Parish, & \
Mary Dandy, of Walton in Le dale, in Blackburn \
P^{rish} }   „   5

Marriages for 1709.

pub. John Bonny, of Warbrech,[1] in ye Parish of \
Bispham, & \
Elizabeth Baley, of Whittle, in Leyland Parish } May   24

pub. James Lang, of Hoghton, in Leyland Parish, & \
Hannah Silcock, of Samles-bury, in ye P^{rsh} of \
Blackburn }   „   30

pub. Adam Eastham, of Leyland Parish, & \
Jane Bond, of the Parish of Preston }   ...   ... June   16

pub. John Park & \
Jane Waterworth } of Lealand   ...   . July   26

pub. Richard Preston & \
Mary Southworth } both of Wheelton, in ys Parish Oct.   26

pub. John Rainford, of Rainford, in ye Parish of Prescot \
Elizabeth Welch, of Lealand } Nov.   6

pub. John Clitheroe & \
Elizabeth Morris, both } of Euxton, in Leyland P^{rish} Dec.   18

pub. Peter Waring, of Hoghton, & \
Mary Garstang, of Whittle } both of ye Parish...   „   26

lic. John Rutter, of Ulnswalton, in Croston Parish, & \
Ellen Park, of Leyland } Jan.   10

pub. Richard Jackson & \
Ann Jenkinson, both } of Hoghton, in Leyland P^{rish}   „   25

pub. James Fielding, of Walton, in Blackburn Parish \
Catherin Gill, of Whittle, in Leyland Parish } ffeb.   13

[Marriages] 1710.

pub. John Chadwick & Catherin Preston, both of ye \
Parish ...   . Ap.   10

pub. Thomas Johnson, of Cuerden, & Ellen Audland, \
of Preston   ...   .   „   12

---

[1] Layton-with-Warbreck, a township in which the modern borough of Blackpool has been built.

pub. Thomas Heywood & Ann Cross, both of Leyland Ap. 25

pub. Edward Forshaw & Mary Whittle, both of Leyland „ 30

lic. Mr. John Lomas, of Bispham, & Agnes Threlfall, of Whittle ... ... May 9

pub. Richard Richmond, of Withnel, & Sarah Bleasdale, of Tockholes... ... ... Aug. 10

lic. Robert Eastham, of Samles Bury, &⎫Blackburn
Margaret Robinson, of Mellar, in ⎭ Parish ... Oct. 3

lic. William Rowes, of Bretherton, & Ann Croston, of Croston ... ... „ 24

pub. John Garstang, of Whittle, &⎫
Alice Sumner, of Leyland ⎭ ... ... Dec. 27

pub. William Bilsborrow, of Wheelton, in Leyland P^rish⎫ Jan. 7
Catherin Smalley, of Witton, in Blackburn Parish⎭

pub. Henry Farnworth & Elizabeth Dixon, of Wheelton „ 25

pub. Richard Parker, of Blackburn Parish, & Mary Bury, of Leyland Parish ... ... Feb. 3

pub. William Almond & Alice Walmsley, both of Whittle, in Leyland P^rish ... ... „ 4

pub. William Jackson, of Leyland, & Jane Jackson, of Cuerden ... ... „ 6

[End of Marriages in earliest extant Register.]

[DEATHS AND BURIALS,
From 1653 to 1710.]

The Death[s] of Persons in the yeare 1653.

Margret Sumner, of Leyland, died	Oct.	5
Richard Wilcocke, died	„	29
The wife of Richard Leyland, of Heapie	Nov.	7
Sisley, wife of John Harrison, of Leyland	„	9
Alice, daughter of William Garstang, in Ulneswalton..	„	12
Anne, the wife of John Atherton, of Leyland	Dec.	3
Thomas Watkinson, of Leyland, *alias* ffoulebie	„	19
Margret Mitchin, in Claiton	} „	21
James, son of John Morris, in Charnock		
Thomas Woodcocke, of Exton	„	26
Hugh Parre, in Heapie	„	29
Joane [widow, crossed out] Mearley, in Claiton	„	30
Elizabeth, wife of John Cowper, in Claiton	Jan.	2
Thomas,[1] son of Edward Robinson, Esq., in Exton	„	6
Alice, daughter of Lawrence Croft, in Whittle	„	10
Anne, the wife of James Mayre, of Leyland	„	19
John Walmersley, of ffarington	„	28
William, son of Thomas Harrison	ffeb.	1
Thomas Machon, in Milford [? Middleforth]	„	22
Andrew, son of Thomas Darwin	„	28
Ellin, wife of James Crichlow, of Exton	} March	3
Thomas, son of John Hilton, of Heapy		
Ellin, wife of John Darwin, in Cuerden	„	4
Thomas Day, in Exton	„	6
A child of John Hilton	„	10
George, son of William Hornebies	„	19
John, son of Robert Stones, in Euxton	„	22

[Burials] 1654.

Richard Nickson, of Exton	March	26
A child of John Cowper, of Cuerden	„	28

[1] See the birth of this child on 7th Oct., 1653. Some account of the father will be found on pages 23 and 24 of this volume.

John, son of Richard Cowper, of Exton ... ... April 12
Thomas Cliffe, of Leyland ... ... „ 15
Alice Sharroke, of Exton ... ... „ 28
A child of Thomas Lowe, of Ulneswalton ... ... May 8
Thomas Smith, of Ulneswalton ... ... „ 19
William Stanfield, of Exton ... ... „ 25
Ann, wife of Robert Sergeant ... ... „ 27
Ellin, wife of Richard Martin... ... ... July 12
Mary, wife of John Roscowe ... ... „ 14
Thomas Breers, of Wheelton... ... ... Aug. 2
Robert Lowe, of Leyland ... ... „ 21
Isabell Lowe, of Leyland ... ... „ 25
Richard Winnell, of Whittle ... ... Sept. 8
Christopher Litherland ... ... „ 28
Joane, wife of John Cheshire, of ffarrington... ... ... Oct. 22
Katharin Critchlowe, of Claiton ... ... „ 27
Edmund Smith, of Leyland ... ... „ 29
Elizabeth Claiton, of ffarrington ... ... Dec. 3
Ashton,[1] son of William Maudesley, of Leyland ... „ 5
Jennet Taylor, of Heapie ... ... „ 15
A child of James Benson, of Winnell ... ... „ 22
John Sumner, of Hollins... ... ... „ 25
Margret Burscowe ... ... Jan. 2
Elizabeth, wife of Thomas Parke ... ... „ 4
Margery, wife of Thomas Richardson, of ffarrington ... „ 7
Margret,[2] daughter of Mr Richard Claiton, of Crooke... „ 29
William Adlinton, of Claiton... ... ... ffeb. 2
Robert Walmersley, of Heapie ... ... „ 3
The wife of John Sumner, of Leyland ... ... „ 7
James, son of William Garstang, of Whittle ... ... „ 18
Ellin, wife of John Melling ... ... March 12
Mary, daughter of Robert Paddington ... ... „ 14
The wife of John Peters ... ... „ 22
The wife of Roger Pincocke, of Whittle ... ... „ 24

Burialls, 1655.

Margrett, daughter of William Dewhurst, of Winnell... March 29
The wife of Thurstan Leyland, of Claiton ... ... April 6
Alice, wife of William Blundill, of Leyland... ... ... „ 9

[1] Probably a son of the gentleman whose death is recorded on Dec. 18, 1658, *q.v.*

[2] This infant was the sole issue of Richard Clayton, Esq., of the New Crooke, in Whittle-le-Woods, by his wife Mabel, daughter of William ffarrington, Esq., of Worden. See the note on page 14, where the entry of the marriage occurs.

A child of Raphe Benbrick, of ffarrington ... ... Aprill 10
Thomas Lathom, of Cuerden... ... ... „ 18
John Jackson, of Ulnswalton... ... ... May 22
Margret, wife of William Crooke, of Penwortha^m ... June 8
A child of William Cliffe, of Longton ... ... „ 16
Giles Haidock, of Heapie ... ... „ 25
William, son of Robert Walmersly, of Whittle ... ... July 6
Margret, wife of Richard Hind ... ... „ 13
John Holme, of Leyland... ... ... „ 14
Thomas Sumner, of Leyland ... ... „ 17
Margret Sumner, the daughter of Thomas ... ... „ 21
vx^r Lawrance Dewhurst, of Winnel ... ... Aug. 15
Mr. John Woodcocke,[1] of Cuerden ... ... „ 17
Jennett, daughter of Thomas Sumner ... ... „ 18
John Brindle, in Walton... ... ... Aug. 19
A child of Jennett Longton, of Cuerden ... ... „ 24
The wife of Thomas Leekas, of Whittle ... ... Sept. 2
Thomas Smith, of Leyland ... ... „ 5
Elizabeth Eues, of Leyland ... ... „ 11
A child of Thomas Jackson, of Leyland ... ... „ 14
The wife of William Blundill ... ... „ 21
A child of Thomas Starkies, of Cuerden ... ... „ 30
Hugh, son of Hugh Woodcock ... ... Oct. 7
A child of Lawrance Taylor ... ... „ 21
A child of William Radley ... ... „ 22
A child of William Aspinall, of ffarrington ... ... Nov. 15
The wife of John Smith, of Exton... ... ... „ 19
James, son of Thomas Chrichlowe, of Leyland ... ... „ 22
Margery Blackhurst, of Whittle ... ... „ 29
Thurstan Crichlowe, of Whittle ... ...⎫
Thomas Walker, of Leyland ... ...⎬ Dec. 7
A child of Robert Abbott, of Leyland ... ... „ 8
James, son of John Cowper, of Cuerden ... ...⎫
A child of Robert Dandie, of Cuerden ... ...⎬ „ 10
The wife of Richard Jones, of Exton ... ... „ 12
Annice Kent, of Leyland ⎫
A child of William Slaytor⎭ of Leyland ... ... „ 14
Seth, the son of Edward Claiton, of ffarrington ... ... „ 19
Anne, the wife of Lawrance Taylor, of Leyland... ... „ 20

---

[1] There is a pedigree of the Woodcock family compiled by Thos. Helsby, Esq., which may be found in Croston's edition of Baines' *History of Lancashire*, p. 186-7. For a continuation of that pedigree, see Abram's *History of Blackburn*, page 733. This gentleman was born in 1578, and his name occurs on the Preston Guild Rolls for 1622 and 1642. The family resided at "Crowtrees," or Woodcock Hall as it is now called.

Joshua, the son of John Claiton, of ffarington ... ... Dec. 23
Thurstan, the son of Raphe Leyland, of Claiton... ... „ 24
The wife of Thomas Blakeleach, of Leyland ... ... „ 26
A child of Thomas Crichlowe, of Claiton ... ... „ 29
Anne, daughter of Thomas Smith, in Newton de
Scales[1] ... ... „ 30
Alice, daughter of James Cockar, of Claiton ... ... Jan. 3
Margret, daughter of William Holme, of Leyland ... „ 7
William,[2] son of William ffarington, of Leyland ... „ 12
Margret, daughter of Robert Cowper, of Cuerden ... „ 14
Elizabeth, daughter of John Woodcock, of Leyland ⎫
Jane, wife of ffrancis Woodcock,[3] of Walton le Dale ⎬ „ 17
A child of William Godman, of Leyland ... ... ⎫
William, son of Robert Welsh, of ffarington ... ⎬ „ 22
The daughter of John Cowper, of Cuerden ... ... „ 23
Sisley, daughter of John Nickson, of Leyland ... ... ffeb. 6
Susan Reynes, of Leyland ... ... „ 11
Margret, daughter of John Jolly, of Whittle ... ... „ 13

[1] In the parish of Kirkham in the Fylde.

[2] Canon Raines, in the introduction to the *Stanley Papers* (page xcii), says that the third son of William ffarrington, of Worden, Esquire (the old Comptroller), lived to a great age, and was buried on January 15, 1655-6, and that his tombstone still remains in Leyland churchyard, near the chancel door. If this be so, the entry of January 12th may possibly refer to him, and record for us the date of his death. Probably the title of Esquire was not added to the father's name because of the changed condition of social affairs, and of the length of time which had elapsed since his death. The ninety years of this ancient scion of a Royalist family may have rendered him an object of small consideration in the eyes of the dominant party who at this time had the registers in their charge. Probably, as a younger son and an extravagant man, his worldly wealth was not great—hence the omission of all titles of courtesy. Born in 1566, this William ffarrington was "brought up in the Earl of Derby's household," and in 1597 was living in London. His father had more than once to make arrangements for the payment of his debts, and experienced with this, his youngest son, almost as much anxiety as with Thomas, the son and heir. On his brother's resignation of the office of Steward of the Royal Manors of Lonsdale, in 1599, William ffarrington, the younger, was nominated by the Queen as the successor, and he also succeeded his brother as Castellan of Lancaster Castle. There is a portrait of him in the Worden Collection, taken in 1628, when he was 62 years of age. A companion picture of a lady, taken in the same year and by the same artist, may possibly represent his wife. As there is neither name nor coat of arms on the picture, and no entry in the family pedigree of his marriage, it is impossible to arrive at any conclusion as to whether the lady of the picture was his wife—or whether he ever married at all. Attempts were made to negotiate a marriage suitable to his rank, but these seem to have failed. The incised memorial stone may still be seen in Leyland churchyard, but it is now in an imperfect condition, so that very little information can be obtained from it. All that can be read is as follows: WILLIAM FARRINGTON . YOUNGEST SONNE OF WILLIAM FARRINGTON OF * * * * ESQVIRE BVRIED THE XV D * * * * * * * * *

[3] The name of ffrancis Woodcock, second son of John Woodcock, of Cuerden, gen., occurs in the Preston Guild Roll for 1622 and 1642. ffrancis Woodcock, of Walton (and two sons, John and Thomas), will be found among the Out-Burgesses in the Roll for 1662.

A child of John Philips ... ... ffeb. 16

[From the commencement to this place the handwriting in the original is clear and easy to read, every letter being distinctly formed. The same person who made the baptismal entries for the period (1653—ffeb. 16, 1655-6) has evidently recorded the Burials up to this date. The style and character of the entries from ffeb. 19, 1655-6, onwards, is entirely different, the writing being indifferent and the spelling variable and to a great extent phonetic. On Sept. 21, 1663, the stiff courthand of the early entries commences again, and continues until Sept. 9, 1675. Vicar Rothwell was buried on Sept. 16, 1675. Probably the earlier and later writing was his.]

John, the sonn of M^ris Barett, of Leyland ... ... ffeb. 19
Thomas, the sonne of Richard Cowper, of Exton ... „ 24
Elizab: Cowper, of Leyland, S[pinster] ... ... „ 26
Margrett, the wyffe of Wm Hodson, of Euxton ... ... „ 26
Ellin, the wyffe of Tho: Pilkinton, of Leyland ... ... „ 26
Ellin, the daughter of Tho: Whitle, of Leyland... ... March 9
Elizab: the daughter of Wm. Hodgson, of Clayton ... „ 13
Margrett Bryning, at Whitle ... ... „ 18
Henry Eastham, of Whitle, sonne of Henry ... ... „ 21
Henry, sonne of Tho: Whitle, of Leyland ... ... „ 22
Margarett Taylor, of Whitle ... ... „ 23
Ellin, the daughter of Robert Withington, of Clayton. „ 24

[Burials] 1656.

Jane, the daughter of William Gerrard, of Wheelton...March 27
Ewan, the sonne of Henry Eastham, of Whitle ... ... „ 29
Katherin Hurst, of Leyland, sp[inster] ... ... Aprill 4
Isabell, the daughter of Elline Wynnell, of Whitle ... „ 6
Elizabeth, the daughter of John Shorrock, of Euxton.. „ 20
Elline, the wyffe of Wm Wilding, of Leyland ... ... „ 22
Ann, the daughter of Richard Gardner, of Leyl[and]... „ 28
Marye, the wiffe of John Person, of Whelton, buried ... „ 29
Margret Whaley, of Whitell, Widowe, buried ... ... „ 30
Alice, the daughter of Thomas Boulton, of Winell } „ 30
William, the sonne of Thomas Lowe, of Ulwalton }

[Another change in the writing.]

[After April 30, 1656, I have added the dates at the extreme right of the page, for the sake of uniformity and convenience. They do not so occur in the original.]

Annice, the wyffe of James Matchon, of Layland, May
the thirde ... ... May 3
Ellin, the wyffe of William Whitell, of Leyland, the
twentith of May ... ... „ 20
Ann, the Daughter of Henery Winstanley, of Leyland,
May the ffive and twentith... ... ... „ 25
Ann, the wiff of John Wourden, of ffarrington, May the
ffive and twentith... ... ... „ 25
Margarett, the daughter of William Low, of Ulwalton,
May the six and twentith ... ... „ 26
Doratey, the wiff of Thomas Boulton, of Winnell, May
nine and twentith... ... ... „ 29
John Atherton, of Leyland, the second day of June ... June 2
Cristoper, the sone of John ffiswicke, of Winnell, June
the third ... ... „ 3
Ellin, the daughter of Hennery Nelson, of Leyland,
June the seuenth ... ... „ 7
Ellish, the son of James benson, of Winnell, June the
ninth ... ... „ 9
William Hadocke, of Leyland, June the three and
tweintith ... ... „ 23
Robert, the sonne of William sesley, of Radelsworth,
buired the thirtith day of June ... ... „ 30
Dinnie,[1] the wiffe of George Hough, buried the owne
thirth daye of June (*sic*) ... ... „ 31 [!]
William, the sonne of William Whaley, of Brerthõn,[2]
the eight day of July ... ... July 8
Genet, the wiffe of William Parke, of Leyland, the
eight day of July ... ... „ 8
Alice, the wiffe of George Wadington, of Winnthell,
Buried the eight day of July ... ... „ 8
Edward Pilkinton, of Clayton, buried the towe and
tweintith of July ... ... „ 22
Margery, the daughter of James Charnocke, of Exton,
taylor, Buried the twentith sixt daye of July ... ... „ 26
Isabell, the wiffe of Petter Blackehurst, of Leyland,
yeoman, buried the twentith ninth of July ... ... „ 29
Margret, the wiffe of Ralph Couper, of Clayton, Buried
the sixt daie of August ... ... Aug. 6
James, the sonne of William Howorth, of Whittell,
Buried the eight day of August... ... ... „ 8
Matthew, the sonne of Richard Pincocke, of Whittel,
Buried the twentith ninth day of August... ... ... „ 29

[1] A curious name.   [2] Brerthõn for Bretherton in Croston parish.

Elin, the wiffe of Thomas Clayton, of Extoñ, buried
the thirtith daye of August ... ... Aug. 30
Alice, the wiffe of Adam Busell, of Curden, buried the
ffirst daye of September ... ... Sept. 1
Christopher, the sonne of Robert Pilkinton, of Leyland,
buried the ffifftinth day of September ... ... „ 15
Thomas, the sonne of William Watson, of Whitell,
Buried the eightinth day of September ... ... „ 18
Sisly twokie,[1] of Leyland, Buried the eightinth ... ... „ 18
John, the sonne of Oliver tayler, of heapey, Buried the
nintinth Day of September ... ... „ 19
Ann, the daughter of Thomas (*sic*) [no name], of Ley-
land, Buried the tweintith sixt day of September ... „ 26
John, the sonne of John Hilton, of Whelton, Buried
the eightinth of October ... ... Oct. 18
Henry, the sonne of John Atherton, of Leyland, Buried
the eightinth of October ... ... „ 18
James Horockes, of boulton parish, att ye prish Church,
Buried the twentith day of October ... ... „ 20
Ralph Couper, of Clayton, buried the tweintith day of
October... ... ... „ 20
Alice, the daughter of Henerey Croston, of Whitell,
Buried the ffive and tweintith of November ... ... Nov. 25
Margret, the wiffe of Lambert Court, of Midellfforth,
Buried the second daye of December ... ... Dec. 2
William Wright, of Exton, Buried the Seventh daye (*sic*) „ 7
Marie,[2] the wiffe of Mr Seath Brisell, of Exton, Buried
the tweintith sixt of December... ... ... „ 26
Annis, the wiffe of John Shorroke, of Exton, Buried
the twentith seventh of December ... ... „ 27
William, the sonne of Richard Johnnes, of Exton,
Buried the twentith eight of December ... ... „ 28
Henerey, the sonne of Henery Wright, of Leyland,
Buried the ffourtinth day of January ... ... Jan. 14
John Borscow, of Leyland, Buried the Last day of
January... ... ... „ 31
Margret, the daughter of Richart ffarrington, of Ley-
land, Buried the nintith day of ffeebuaray ... ... ffeb. 9
Richard Charnoucke, of Leyland, Burried the ffiftintith
day of ffeabuarray .. .. „ 15

[1] The letters of this name are quite clear. Is it a nick-name? I cannot under-
stand it.

[2] The daughter of Mr. Wm. Stanfield, of Euxton. Mr. Brisell or Bushell was the
"Minister" of Euxton chapel at this time. He afterwards became Vicar of Preston,
&c. See " Baptisms," page 36, for a short account of him and his family.

James Damforth, of Whittell, Burried the twentith day
of ffeabuararay ... ... ffeb. 20
Marie Balshaw, of Exton, Buried the ffirst day of March March 1
Margery, the wiffe of William Row, of Uleswalton,
buried the sixt day of March ... ... „ 6
Richard Summner, of Leyland, burried the ninth of (*sic*) „ 9
Anne, the daughter of Richard Jackeson, of Curden,
Burried the teintith of March ... ... „ 10
Margret, the daughter of Thomas Smith, of Leyland,
burried the ffowertinth of March ... ... „ 14
Margret, the daughter of Thomas Dewerst, of Leyland,
the sixtinth day of March, burried ... ... „ 16
Hennery Willson, of Leyland, burried the eightinth of
March ... ... „ 18
Tomasin, the wiffe of John Robinson, of Whittell,
burried 23 March... ... ... „ 23
Ann, the wiff of Hugh Doson, of ffarrington, burried
23 of [March] ... ... „ 23
Thomas Starrkey, sonne of Thomas Starrky, of Curden,
buried the ffowre and twentith of March ... ... „ 24

[Burials] 1657.

Anne, the wiffe of Thomas Moody, of Heapey, Buried
the twentith ninth [day] of March ... ... March 29
John, the sonne of Peter M[o]ncke, of Chorley, Buried
the thirtith of March ... ... „ 30
Elin, the daughter of Thomas Dewerst, of Leyland,
Buried the seventh day of Aprill ... ... Ap. 7
Richard of ffarrington (*sic*), of Leyland, Buried the eight
day of Aprill... ... ... „ 8
William, the sonne of Hennery Sclator, of Leyland,
Buried the twelfth day of Aprill... ... ... „ 12
Hugh Doson, off ffarrington, burried the ffiftinth of
Aprill ... ... „ 15
Elin, the daughter of Robert Clayton, of ffarrington,
Buried the eightinth of Aprill ... ... „ 18
Ann, the wiff of Richard Pincoucke, of Whittell, Buried
the nintinth of Aprill ... ... „ 19
John Whittell, of Midellforth,[1] Buried the two: and
tweintith of Aprill ... ... „ 22
Robert, the sonne of Rodger ffarrington, of ffarrington,
Buried the thretweintith of Aprill ... ... „ 23

---

[1] In Penwortham parish. A hamlet near the Ribble.

M

178 *Leyland Registers.*

Elizabeth, the daughter of John Clayton, of ffarrington,
Burried the tweintith therd day of Aprill... ... ... Ap. 23
Em, the wiffe of William Hadocke, of Leyland, Buried
the tweintith ninth of Aprill ... ... „ 29
Katrine, the daughter of Ralph Couper, of Curden,
Burried the sixt daye of May ... ... May 6
Robert Cocker, of Leyland, Burried the 21 day of
May ... ... „ 21
Elin, the wiffe of John Stonanought, of Leyland, burried
the ffirst day of June ... ... June 1
Thomas, the sonne of William Adlington, of Curden,
burried the ninth day of June ... ... „ 9
Jennet, the daughter of Robert Sumner, of Leyland,
burried the tennth day of June ... ... „ 10
Jennet, the daughter of Robert Marton, of Oulerton,[1]
Burried the sixtinth day of June ... ... „ 16
Elizebth Suthworth, of Leyland, burried the seven and
tweintith day of June ... ... „ 27
Ellin, the daughter of John Dewerst, of Curden, burried
the second day of July ... ... July 2
Annice, the daughter of William Aspinaiall, of ffarring-
ton, buried the ffowere and twentith day of July ... „ 24
Alice Dandey, the wiffe of Robert Dandey, of Curden,
burried the thirtith day of July ... ... „ 30
Thomas, the sonne of Robert Couper, of Cuerden,
burried the last daye of July ... ... „ 31
William Wilden, of Leyland, Burried the last daye of
July ... ... „ 31
Thomas, the sonne of William Clayton, burried the
Sixt day of August ... ... Aug. 6
Alice Bentom, of Leyland, burried the eight of August „ 8
Patricke Mouell, of ffarrington, burried the tenth daye
of August ... ... „ 10
John Sumner, of Leyland, burried the seuentinth day
of August ... ... „ 17
Adam Clayton, of Leyland, burried the ffower and
twentith day of August ... ... „ 24
Henney, the sonne of Hennery Heald, of Leyland,
burried the ffower and twentith day of August ... „ 24
William Blackledge, of Whelton, burried the ffower
and twentith day of August ... ... „ 24
William Jacson, sonne of William Jackson, of Curden,
burried the ffower and twentith day of August ... „ 24

[1] Otherwise Ollerton, a township in the Moor quarter of Leyland parish.

Margery Withington, daughter of Thomas Withington,
of Clayton, burried the twentith seuenth day of
August ... ... Aug. 27
Elizabeth Garston, daughter of William Garston, of
Whittell, buried the twentitith (*sic*) day of August... „ (?)
Elizabeth barron, the wiffe of Alixander Barron, of
Exton, Burried the thirtith day of August ... ... „ 30
Elizabeth Parke, the wiffe of George Parke, of Midell-
forth, Burried the tenth day of September ... ... Sept. 10
Elin, the daughter of Robert Barron, of Euxton, Burried
the thirtinth day of September ... ... „ 13
William Parke, of Leyland, burried the ffortinth day of
September ... ... „ 14
James Morres, of Whelton, burried the nintith day of
September ... ... „ 19
Anicee, the wiffe of James Hach, of Brindell, Burried
the twentith ffower day of September ... ... „ 24
Clemmones, the wiffe of Thurstan Crichlowe, of
Whittell, burried the twentith ninth daye of Sep-
tember ... ... „ 29
William Sumner, of Leyland, Burried the twentith
ninth of September ... ... „ 29
Sisly, the wiffe of Hennery Whaley, of Clayton, Burried
the ffirst day of October ... ... Oct. 1
John Clayton, of Leyland, burried the fforth day of
October... ... ... „ 4
Jane, the wiffe of Thomas ffoxe, of Leyland, Buried the
thirtinth daye of October ... ... „ 13
Elizabeth, the daughter of John Woodcocke, of Leyland,
buried the ffiftinth day of October ... ... „ 15
John Robinson,[1] sonne of Richard Robinson, of Euex·
ton, buried the three and twentith day of October ... „ 23
Alice, the wiffe of James Garston, of Ulneswalton,
buried the Last daye of October ... ... „ 31
Robert Marton, of Heapey, burried the second day of
Nouember ... ... Nov. 2
John browne, sonne of John browne, of Anderton,
burried the third day of Nouember ... ... „ 3
Thomas Alonson, of Leyland, burried the seuenth day
of Nouember ... ... „ 7

---

[1] On the strength of this entry the name of John Robinson has been added to
the pedigree furnished by Major Edward Robinson for the Visitation of 1664. See
Introduction (p. xxxii) of the *Discourse of the War* (Chetham Society's volume lxii.).
The relationship assigned to him is that of brother to Major Robinson, and son to Mr.
Richard Robinson, whose burial is recorded a few months later (5 Mar., 1657-8).

Richard Woodcock, of Curden, burried the fortinth
day of Nouember ... ... Nov. 14
Richard Armetriding, of Leyland, burried the nintinth
day of Nouember ... ... „ 19
Ralph Clough, of Leyland, burried the twentith eight
day of Nouember ... ... „ 28
Jennett, the wiffe of James Hadocke, of Whittell,
burried the seuenth daye of December ... ... Dec. 7
Hugh Smith, of Euexton, burried the twentith sixt day
of December... ... ... „ 26
John Sharrock, of Euexton, burried the Last day of
December ... ... „ 31
Thurston Thomson, the sonne of John Thomson, of
Euexton, burried the second day of ffebruary ... ... Feb. 2
John Atherton, of Leyland, burried the seuenth day of
ffeb. ... ... „ 7
Richard Tasker, of Leyland, Burried the eight day of
ffeb. ... ... „ 8
William Wackeffild, of Leyland, Burried the eleuenth
of ffeb. ... ... „ 11
Elinor Latham, daughter of Thomas Latham, of
Curden, Burried the ffourtinth day of ffebruary ... „ 14
Ann Moures, of Heapey, burried the twentith forth
day of ffebruary ... ... „ 24
Jane Couper, the wiffe of Richard Couper, of Exton,
burried the twentith fforth day of ffebruary ... ... „ 24
Mr Richard Robinson,[1] of Euxton, burried the ffifth
day of March, in the yeare of our Lord god one
thousand six hunderd ffifty and seuen ... ... March 5
James Nelson, the sonne of Richard Nelson, of Ley-
land, Burried the eight day of March ... ... „ 8
Richard ffishwicke, the sonn of John ffishwicke, of
Withnell, Burried the eight day of March ... ... „ 8
Robert Barron, of Exton, Burried the sixtinth daye of
March ... ... „ 16
Robert Blackeleidge, of Whittell in Le Woods, Burried
the seuentinth daye of March ... ... „ 17
Doratay Godberd, the daughter of John Godberd,
Burried the towe and twentith day of March ... ... „ 22
Marie Shorrocke, the daughter of Richard Shorrocke,
of Curden, burried the twentith therd day of March. „ 23

[1] This was the father of Mr. Justice Robinson, whose name occurs frequently at the commencement of this Register. See note on pp. 23, 24.

[Burials] 1658.

Elin Dauinall, the wiffe of John Dauinall, of Euexton,
   burricd the twentith ninth day of March... ... ...March 29
Robert Sothwoerth, the sonne of John Southworth, of
   Leyland, burried the thirtith day of March ... ... „ 30
Alice Shorrocke, the wiffe of Richard Shorrock, of
   Curden, Burried the ffirst day of Apriall ... ... April 1
Alice Ugnall, the wiffe of Gilbert Ugnall, of Whelton,
   Burried the eleuenth day of Aprill ... ... „ 11
Henerie Couckerom, of Houll,[1] burried the twelefth day
   of Aprill ... ... „ 12
William Blundell, of Leyland, burried the ffiftinth day
   of Aprill ... ... „ 15
Doratay Parke, the daughter of Alixander Parke, of
   Leyland, Burried the ffiftinth day of Aprill ... ... „ 15
John Leauer, of Leyland, burried the seuentith day of
   Aprill ... ... „ 17
M‍r William ffarrington[2] of Weourden, Esquire, of
   Leyland, Burried the twentith day of Aprill ... ... „ 20

[1] For "Cockerham," of (Great) Hool, in Croston parish.

[2] William ffarrington, Esquire, whose burial is here recorded, was the son of
Thomas ffarrington and Mabel (Benson) his wife, and the grandson of the well-known
William ffarrington, who occupied the honourable position of Comptroller of the
Household to three (at least) of the princely Earls of Derby. The spendthrift habits
of Mr. Thomas ffarrington were of such long standing and so incorrigible that,
although he was the eldest son and heir, his father, the old Comptroller, felt it to be
necessary for the continued permanence and prestige of the family to make a special
settlement of the estates excluding him from the succession. By a deed executed in
1609, about a year before his death, an arrangement was concluded which constituted
William, the eldest son of Thomas, the inheritor of his grandfather's large property.
This younger William was the subject of the present note. Owing to the early death
of his mother and subsequent re-marriage of his father, he was brought up under his
grandfather's care. His after career shows much more plainly the influence and
example of the diligent man of business and worthy landowner than that of the
unmethodical, impulsive, and æsthetic man his father. The death of the Comptroller
happened when William ffarrington was about 17 years of age, so that he was at an
early period in life thrust into a prominent position in the county. He was within
a short time made a magistrate and a deputy-lieutenant, and in 1631 was called upon
to pay the knighthood composition. With the neighbouring gentry he attended the
successive Preston Guilds, and has his name recorded on the Rolls for 1602, 1622,
and 1642. He seems to have been married when a very young man to Margaret,
daughter of Henry Worral, of Wysall, co. Notts, Esq., and subsequently had three
sons and four daughters.

In 1636 William ffarrington was appointed to "undergoe" the office of Sheriff of
Lancashire. Designing to put a check, for the sake of his successors, to the almost
reckless extravagance which was beginning to be displayed in connection with the
official hospitalities expected of the Sheriff, he was unfortunate enough to bring upon
him the ill-will of the Judges of Assize. Various charges of neglect in matters of
etiquette and administration were made the excuse for the infliction of heavy fines.
Although some remission was, with difficulty, obtained, his year of office must have

Ann Garrston, the wiffe of George Garrston, of Whittell,
Burried the ffower and twentith day of Aprill... ... April 24
Edgon Millner, of Leyland, burried the twentith third
day of Aprill (*sic*) ... ... „ 23
John Couper, the sonne of James Couper, of Euexton,
Burried the twentith third day of Aprill (*sic*) ... ... „ 23
John Nixson, of Euexton, burried the twentith ffifth
day of Aprill ... ... „ 25
William Lowe, of Uleswalton, burried burried the
twentith ffifth of Aprill ... ... „ 25
Elizabeth, the wiffe of Antonie Cosne, of Clayton,
Burried the twentith seuenth day of Aprill ... ... „ 27
Elin, the wiffe of Robert Stonnes, of Euexton, Burried
the twentith seuenth day of Aprill ... ... „ 27
William marrton, the sonne of John marton, of Whittell,
Burried the twentith ninth day of Aprill ... ... „ 29
Richard Sumner, the sonne of William Sumner, de
noucke in Leyland, Burried the Ssixt day of
May ... ... May 6
Sisly Heald, the wiff of William Heald, of Leyland,
Burried the seuenth day of May ... ... „ 7

been made a serious drain upon his resources. Like other gentlemen he took a share
in the military organisation of the county, and held the rank of colonel of militia.
When the uneasy condition of public affairs threatened war between Charles I. and
the Parliament, Colonel ffarrington took a very active part as an ardent Royalist.
In 1640 he acted as provost marshal for Lord Strange, when the powder and match
were bought at Warrington to store the magazine at Liverpool. On 11 June, 1642,
he was made a Commissioner of Array, and, when the High Sheriff summoned a
meeting of loyal subjects to hear the reading of the King's two declarations and
answer to the Lancashire petition on Preston Moor, William ffarrington, Esquire,
was there named as a collector and treasurer of the subsidy granted for the King's
use. The importance of this gentleman in the eyes of the Royalist party may be
seen by the special injunction issued by the King himself, which forbad the private
withdrawal from the county of Colonel ffarrington and his son, a proceeding which
seemed not improbable owing to the threats of arrest and removal called forth from
the Parliament by their activity in executing the Commission of Array. On 9 Feb.,
1643, William ffarrington the elder was taken prisoner in the assault on Preston;
and on Sept. 12, 1643, he had all his goods sequestered by Parliament. He was
present at both the sieges of Lathom House, and appears to have laid down his arms
soon after the surrender of the fortress. On his way home he was arrested and
thrown into prison, where he remained from July, 1646, to the following May, when
he was permitted to compound for his estates for the sum of £536, and to return to
his family. In 1649 he appears to have been forced to pay a second composition.
He was then nearing seventy years of age, and would doubtless be thankful to
exchange the turmoil of war for the retirement of his home. It was about this time
that consideration for the poverty and distress of his dependents moved him to found
and erect six almshouses for their benefit, charging certain of his lands for their
maintenance. The care of his successors has preserved and improved his benefaction
down to the present time. See *Stanley Papers*, vol. ii.; *ffarrington Papers; Discourse of the War in Lancashire* (Chetham Society's volumes), for original evidences
relating to the local biography and history of these stirring times.

Thomas Hodson, of Euexton, Burried the ffowertinth
day ... ... May 14
Robert Eastom, of Leyland, Burried Burried the seuen-
tinth day ... ... „ 17
Margret Garret, the daughter of William Garrett, of
Whelton, Burried the nintinth day of May ... ... „ 19
Alice Boutell, the wiffe of Ralph Boutell, of Leyland,
Burried the twentith day of May ... ... „ 20
Alice Garreston,[1] the daughter of Lawrance Garrston,
of Heapey, Burried the six and twentith day of May „ 26
Kattrin Couper, the daughter of William Couper, of
Currden, Burried the seuen and twentith day of May „ 27
M[r] James Anderton,[2] of Clayton, Esquire, Burried the
Laste day of May ... ... „ 31
Ann Mondey, the daughter of Thomas Mondey, of
Heapey, Burried the ssixt day of June ... ... June 6
William Tisin, of Uleswalton, burried the ffortinth day
of Jun ... ... „ 14
Robert barret, the sonne of Mistris barret,[3] of Leyland,
Burried the seuentinth day of June ... ... „ 17
Elin Snart, the wiffe of Thomas Snart, of Leyland,
burried 23 day of June [Inserted in same hand] ... „ 23
Thomas Sumner, of Leyland, burried the eight day of
July ... ... July 8
William Godman, the sonne of William Godman, of
Leyland, Burried the twelfth day of July... ... ... „ 12
Jeannett Tisinge, the wiffe of William tisinge, of
Uleswalton, burried the tow and twentith day of
August ... ... Aug. 22
Thomas ffox, of Leyland, burried the twentith ssixt
day of August ... ... „ 26
Elizabeth Willson, the wiffe of Hennery Willson, of
Leyland, Burried the twentith eight day of August.. „ 28

[1] This name is probably "Garstang," for, in that form, it is very common in the Whittle and Heapy districts.

[2] This appears to be the grandson of that Hugh Anderton who, by his marriage with the heiress of Butler, of Rawcliffe, obtained a moiety of the lordship of Clayton, and, by subsequent purchases, became sole lord. James Anderton, of Clayton, the son of Hugh, appears in the Preston Guild Rolls for 1582, 1602, and 1622, with a son James and four younger sons. On the last occasion the names of five grandsons (children of James, the eldest son) are added. In 1642 the family is represented by James, the grandson of Hugh, who has then become "of Clayton" (arguing his father's death), and his four elder sons.

[3] "Mistris" Barett or Barret was probably a widow lady of some social standing, but she has not yet been identified. She appears to have lost two sons within a short period. See entry on ffeb. 19, 1654.

Jane Tasker, of Euexton, burried the thirtith day of
August ... ... Aug. 30
Elin Wignes, the wiffe of William Wignes, of Whittell,
Burried the first day of September ... ... Sept. 1
Margret ffarrington, of Leyland, burried the thenth
day of September ... ... „ 10
Ann Whitthed, the wiffe of Thomas Whitthed, of
Leyland, Burried the thirtinth day of September ... „ 13
Ann Withnell, the wiffe of Hennery Withnell, of
Whittell, Burried the thirtinth day of September ... „ 13
Elice Lowe, the wiffe of Robert Lowe, of Leyland,
burried the thirtinth day of September ... ... „ 13
Thomas Garrett, of Anellesarke in the prish of
Boulton, Burried the towe and twentith day of
September ... ... „ 22
Richard Johnes, of Euexton, burried the twentith eight
day of September ... ... „ 28
Richard Stones, of Euexton, burried the fforth day of
October... ... ... Oct. 4
Ann, the wiffe of Rodger Dewerst, of Curden, burried
the sixt day of October ... ... „ 6
Margrett Mackerell, the wiffe of John Mackrell, of
Leyland, Burried the eight day of October ... ... „ 8
Elizabeth Garrston, the wiffe of Hennery Garrston, of
Heapey, Burried the ninth day of October ... ... „ 9
John Mackerell, of Leyland, burried the seuentinth day
of October ... ... „ 17
Elizabeth Couper, the daughter of John Couper, of
Clayton, Burried the eighttinth day of October ... „ 18
Jennett Wilkinson, the wiffe of William Wilkinson, of
Curden, Burried the nintinth day of October ... ... „ 19
George Boulton, of Leyland, Burried the twentith day
of October ... ... „ 20
James Couper, of Curden, Burried the twentith ninth
day of October ... ... „ 29
William Hadocke, of Whittell, Burried the eleventh
daye of Nouember ... ... Nov. 11
Margrett Robertes, of Leyland, burried the eighttinth
day of Nouember... ... ... „ 18
Robert Dandey, of Curden, Burried the twentith
ffowerth day of Nouember... ... ... „ 24
Alice Chitom, the wiffe of John Chittom, of Euexton,
Burried the thirtinth day of December ... ... Dec. 13
Thomas Boulton, of Winnell, burried the sixtinth day
of December... ... ... „ 16

M⁏ William Modesley,[1] of Leyland, Burried the
eightinth day of December ... ... Dec. 18
Richard ffillds, of ffarrington, Burried the twentith
seuenth day of December ... ... „ 27
Chrriston Stones, the wiffe of Hennery Stones, of
Euexton, burried the seventh day of January... ... Jan. 7
Richard Hodson, of ffarrington, burried the eleuenth
day... ... ... „ 11
ffrancis Latham, of Euexton, burried the ffirst day of
ffebruary ... ... Feb. 1

[At this point there is some irregularity in the entries. After
the "Marriages" for the early months of 1674 will be found a
number of entries of "Burials," dating from March 10, 1658, to
Oct. 4, 1661. These are apparently in the same handwriting as
the contemporary burials. The entries from the aforesaid extra
list will be here incorporated with the rest, only being distinguished by square brackets.]

Alice Stith, the wiffe [of] Thomas Stith, of Wharles,[2] of
the parish of Cerkom [Cerckom], burried at Leyland,
the tenth day of March ... ... Mar. 10
Ralph Charnley [nely], the sonne [of] Richard Charnley
[Charnely], of Curden, buried the seuentith day of
March ... ... „ 17
[Elizabeth Johnson, daughter of William Johnson, of
Whittell, buried the twentith day of March ... ... „ 20]
[Iasebell Wackeffild, the wiffe of William Wacke-
ffild, of Leyland, buried the twentith third day of
March ... ... „ 23]

[1] Mr. William Modsley (otherwise Mawdesley) was the second son of William
Mawdesley, of Mawdesley, Esq., and, as such, his name is entered in the family
pedigree given by St. George (1613). In the Visitation of 1664 he appears as the
first individual in a short succession under the heading of Mawdesley, of Leyland.
The arms assigned are, Sable, on a chevron between 3 pickaxes, argent, as many
annulets of the first. Crest: An eagle displayed, sable, charged on the breast with
an annulet, or. Mr. Mawdesley married Mary, d. of Edward Bamford, of Bamford,
co. Lancaster, and had (according to the 1664 pedigree) a daughter, Margaret,
married to Ralph, son of Thurstan Leyland, of Clayton, and a son, William, whose
wife was Ellen, daughter of John Lawton, of Budworth, co. Chester. There is an
incised overlay, to the memory of this younger William, now in Leyland churchyard;
but it is unfortunately broken at the corner where the year was given. The initials
E.M. are cut deeply into the stone in the centre. Mrs. Ellen Mawdesley was buried
on March 21, 1696-7. There is a lengthy pedigree of the family of Mawdesley, of
Mawdesley, in Baines' *History of Lancashire* (edit. Croston), on page 182 of the part
which relates to Croston parish. A number of early charters, dating from 1326,
connected with lands now the property of the Rev. H. W. Bretherton, M.A., supply
additional names of the Mawdesley line.

[2] Wharles, a township in the parish of Kirkham.

Elizabeth Pudsay, wiffe of William Pudsay,[1] Late of
   Boulton with [Barford], in the County of Yorke, Esq[r],
   buried at Leyland Church, March the twentith fforth,
   1658 ... ... Mar. 24

[Burials] 1659.

Elizabeth Sargant, daughter of Richard Sargant, of
   Euexton, burried the twellefte day of Aprill ... ... Ap.   12
William Dobson, of Leyland, buried the nintinth day
   of Aprill ... ... „   19
Hennery Nelson, of Leyland, buried the twentith day
   of Aprill ... ... „   20
Marie Loxam, daughter of Richard Loxam, of Ules-
   walton, Buried the twentith sixt day of Aprill ... „   26
Leuas[2] Bushell, of Curden, Buried the twentith sixt
   day of Aprill ... ... „   26
William Bancrofte, of Whelton, buried the eight day of
   May ... ... May   8
Edward Wattson, the sonne of William Wattson, of
   Whittell, Buried the second day of Jun ... ... June   2
M[r] Richard Clayton,[3] of the Crooke, Esqire, in Whittell
   in Le Woodes, buried att Leyland, the seuenth day
   of Jun ... ... „   7
Margret Smith, the wiffe of Richard Smith, of Hindley,
   of the prish of Leayeth [Leigh], buried the eight
   day of Jun ... ... „   8

[1] This is a curious and important entry. The only *William* Pudsey, of Bolton,
Esq., as recorded in the full pedigree in Whittaker's *History of Craven*, last edition,
p. 126, was buried at Bolton on the 7th October, 1629. His first wife, Elizabeth,
died in 1601, but no information is there given as to the death of his second wife,
Katherine. Unless the lady whose burial is here so fully entered is an hitherto unrecorded third wife, it is difficult to conjecture who she can have been, as there is no
other William Pudsey at this period who was the owner of the Bolton estate. Was
she a native of Leyland who had returned there to live and die?

[2] A curious name, perhaps for Lewis or Louis.

[3] Mr. Richard Clayton, of Crook in Whittle, was the last male representative, in
the direct male line, of a younger branch of the family of Clayton of Clayton, which
settled at Crook in the latter part of the sixteenth century. Dr. Kuerden tells us in
his *Itinerary* that Dr. Richard Clayton (who was great uncle to the subject of this
note) built the New Crook, and it was probably the wealth inherited from him which
made the importance of the family at this time. The Dr. Clayton referred to was
Fellow of St. John's College, Cambridge, Master of Magdalene College, and soon
after Master of St. John's College, Dean of Peterborough, and Archdeacon of Lincoln.
In the Inq. *p.m.* (1612) his nearest of kin was declared to be John Clayton, the son
of his brother Ralph (then deceased). This John was the father of Mr. Richard
Clayton, whose burial is here recorded. The widow of this gentleman, who was a
daughter of Wm. ffarrington, Esq. (the Royalist), became the third wife of Sir Peter
Brooke, of Mere.

Katrin Bannister, the wiffe of Richard Bannister, of
  Curden, buried the eight day of Jun ... ... June   8
Richard Whittell, of Whittell, buried the eleuenth day
  of Jun ... ... ,,   11
Ann Barrnes, the daughter of Richard Barrnes, of
  Whittell, buried the owne and twentith day of Jun... ,,   21
Mistris Ann Charnocke,[1] the wiffe of Rodger Char-
  nocke, of Leyland, buried the twentith ffowerth day
  of Jun ... ... ,,   24
Jane Willden, the daughter of Thomas Willden, of
  Leyland, Buried the sixt day of August ... ..., ,,   6
Margret Crichlow, daughter of William Crichlowe, of
  Whittell, buried the twentith eight day of August... ,,   28
John Smith, of Leyland, buried the ffirst day of
  September ... ... Sept.   1
[John Coucker, the sone John Coucker, of Whittell,
  buried buried the fiftinth day of September ... ... ,,   15]
[Kattrin Couper, the wiffe of Thomas Couper, of Curden,
  Buried the nintinth day of September ... ... ,,   19]
[Elizabeth Couper, the wiffe of Robert Couper, of
  Curden, Burried the twentith ffifth day of September ,,   25]
[Alice Garston, the wiffe of Lawrance Garston, of
  Heapey, Buried the thirtinth of October ... ... Oct.   13]
Margret Coucker, the wiffe of James Coucker, of
  Clayton, buried the eight day of Nouember ... ... Nov.   8
Agnes Shoroucke, the wiffe of John Shoroucke, of
  Euexton, buried the tenth day of Nouember ... ... ,,   10
William Winnell, of Whittell, buried the second day of
  December ... ... Dec.   2
Cristopher Litherland, the sonne of Edward Litherland,
  of Whittell, buried the third day of December ... ,,   3
Richard Rosse, of Euexton, buried the ninth day of
  December ... ... ,,   9
Elizabeth Tayler, the wiffe of Lawrance Tayler, of
  Heapey, buried the thirtinth day of December ... ,,   13

[1] Mistris Ann Charnock was the daughter of Robert Manley, of Broughton, co.
Northampton, and widow of Roger Charnock, gentleman, of Leyland, who was
descended from the Charnocks of Charnock and Astley. There is a rudely incised
stone, to the memory of these two persons, now lying within a few feet of the east
wall of Leyland Church. The stone records the death of the husband " Die S. Joseph
sacro A.D. 1632," and of the wife " P. festo S. Johan: Bapt: 1659." In the Subsidy
Roll of 1628, " Roger Charnock, Gent., a Convict Recusant," is mulct to the extent
of 21 shillings and 4 pence. The house where this worthy couple resided (called
Leyland Hall) descended to their son Robert, who was a priest in Roman Orders.
Owing to the disposition which this latter gentleman made of his estate, a considerable amount of litigation arose, which was not concluded until the whole was declared
to be forfeit to the Crown.

Thomas Longton, of Curden, buried the three and
twentith day of December ... ... Dec. 23
William Garston, of Uleswalton, buried the second day
of January ... ... Jan. 2
Mi* Margret ffarrington,[1] Latt wiffe of M\ William
ffarrington of Worden, Esqire, Buried the third day
of January ... ... „ 3
Richard Pare, of Heapey, buried the owne and twentith
day of January ... ... „ 21
Jane Johnson, of Heapey, buried the twentith eight
day of Januaray ... ... „ 28
Kattrin Cartmell, the wiffe of William Cartmell, of
Clayton, buried the twentith ninth of January ... „ 29
Elizabeth Rackley, of Euexton, buried the ffirst day of
ffeburary ... ... Feb. 1
Alice Garston, the daughtr of Lawrance Garston, of
Heapey, Buried the ffirst day of ffeburary ... ... „ 1
Thomas Hadocke, of ffarrington, buried the sixt day
of ffeburary ... ... „ 6
Edward Part, of Leyland, buried the sixt day of ffebuary „ 6
Jane Harison, the wiffe of John Harison, of Leyland,
Bu[r]ied the ninth day of ffebrarry ... ... „ 9
Ann Woodcocke, of Brindell, Buried at Leyland the
thirtinth day of ffeburary ... ... „ 13
Elin Clayton, the wiffe of John Clayton, of Leyland,
buried the seuentinth day of ffeburary ... ... „ 17
Elizabeth Chittom, daughter of Richard Chittom, off
ffarrington, buried the eightinth day of ffeburary ... „ 18
Yeaman Bushell, of Curden, buried the tow and twen-
tith day... ... ... „ 22
Jannett, the wiffe of Richard Loxam, of ffarrington,
buried the tow and twentith of ffeburary ... ... „ 22
Jane Bentonn, of Leyland, buried the tow and twentith
of ffeburary ... ... „ 22
John ffiswicke, off Euexton, buried the twentith eight
day of ffeburary ... ... „ 28
Alice Johnson, the wiffe of Hough Johnson, of Leyland,
buried the third day of March ... ... Mar. 3

[1] This lady was the daughter of Henry Worrall, of Wyssel, co. Notts, Esquire,
and the widow of William ffarrington, Esquire (the Royalist), of whom a notice will
be found on page 181. Her experiences during the Civil War were far from agree-
able, for the Parliamentary sequestrators scarcely left her anything to live upon, and
she could not obtain the "puture" or one-fifth portion officially allowed for her
maintenance. In the *ffarrington Papers* several glimpses of this much harassed lady
may be obtained. Portraits of Mrs. ffarrington and her husband are now in the
Worden collection.

Ann Coucker, the wiffe Richard Coucker, of Euexton,
    buried the seuenth day of March ... ... Mar. 7
Richard Whitthead, the sonne of William Whitthead, of
    Uleswalton, buried the ninth of March ... ... „ 9
Thomas Adlington, of Curden, buried the ffowertinth
    day of March ... ... „ 14
Margret ffoster, the wiffe of William ffoster, of Whittell,
    Buried the nintinth day of March ... ... „ 19
Henery Dewerst, of Curden, buried the ffower and
    twentith of March ... ... „ 24

[Burials] 1660.

Jannett Longton, of Curden, Buried the twentith ninth
    day of March ... ... Mar. 29
William Lathward, of ffarrington, Buried the twentith
    ninth ... ... „. 29
Andrew Hodson, the sonne of John Hodson, of Curden,
    buried the owne and thirtith day of March ... ... „ 31
John Chittom, of Euexton, buried the eleuenth day of
    Aprill ... ... Ap. 11
Martha Asley, the wiffe of William Asley, of Radels-
    worth, buried the eleuenth of Aprill ... ... „ 11
Richard Sshrroke,[1] of Curden, buried the twelfft day of
    Aprill ... ... „ 12
William Wright, of Euexton, Buried the thirtinth day
    of Aprill ... ... „ 13
Ellin Boulton, the wiffe of Elish Boulton, of Leyland,
    Buried the twentith day of Aprill ... ... „ 20
Richard Corby, of the prish of blackeborne, buried att
    Leyland the twentith day of Aprill ... ... „ 20
John Sumnner, the sonne of John Sumnner, of Leyland,
    buried the twentith ninth day of Aprill ... ... „ 29
Margrett Hind, the wiffe of Richard Hind, of Leyland,
    Buried the owne and twentith day of May ... ... May 21
Kattrin Couper, daughter of James Couper, of Curden,
    Buried the owne and twentith day of May ... ... „ 21
Thomas Marton, the sonne of Robert Marton, of Ouler-
    ton, buried the twentith fforth ... ... „ 24
The wiffe of William Occkellshaw, of Euexton, buried
    the twentith seuenth day of May ... ... „ 27
John ffiswicke, the sonne of Christopher ffiswicke, of
    Winnell, buried the fourth day of June ... ... June 4

[1] This is a bungling attempt to spell Sharrock, a family name common in the district.

Thomas Clayton, of Radellworth, buried the owne and
  twentith day of June ... ... June 21
An blackcledge, the wiffe of William blackcledge, of
  Wilton,[1] buried the thirtinth day of July... ... ... July 13
Elizabeth Pearson, daughter of Ralph Pearson, buried
  the ffortinth day of July ... ... „ 14
Roger ffiswicke, of Winnell, buried the thirty own day
  of July ... ... „ 31
William Asbornen, of ffarrington, buried the second
  day of August ... ... Aug. 2
Hugh Taylor, the sonne of Oliuer Taylor, of Heapey,
  buried 3 day of August ... ... „ 3
Edward ffarnworth, of Euexton, buried the third day
  of September ... ... Sept. 3
Janett Asley, daughter of William Asley, of Radelsh-
  worth, buried the twenty fforth day of September ... „ 24
Thomas Pare, of Whelton, buried the fforth day of
  October... ... ... Oct. 4
Alice Winnell, of Winnell, buried the eight day of
  October... ... ... „ 8
Lawrance Garston, of Whittell, buried the thirtinth
  day of October ... ... „ 13
Janett Croston, the wiffe of Thomas Croston, of Whit-
  tell, buried the twentith eight day of October... ... „ 28
James Wattson, of Whittell, buried the ffortinth day of
  Nouember ... ... Nov. 14
Margrey Doson, the wiffe of John Doson, of ffarrington,
  buried the nintinth day of Nouember ... ... „ 19
Elizabeth Hadocke, of Whelton, buried the twentith
  ninth day of Noumber ... ... „ 29
Alice, the wiffe of Richard Whithey, of Leyland, buried
  the twelft day of December ... ... Dec. 12
Ann[2] Anderton, the wiffe of James Anderton, of
  Clayton, buried the ffowere and twentith day of
  December ... ... „ 24
Ellin, the wiffe of Rodger Clayton, of Curden, Buried
  the twentith ninth of December ... ... „ 29
Sisley Arymetrydinge, of Charnocke, buried the ffivft
  day of January ... ... Jan. 5
[Jane, the wiffe of William Lucas, of Whittell, buried
  the ninth day of January ... ... „ 9]

---

[1] Wilton for Wheelton, in Leyland parish.

[2] This may be the Ann, *vxr* James Anderton, Gen. (of Clayton), mentioned with
her husband in the Recusant Roll of 1628.

[William Kelet, of Clayton, buried the tenth day of
January... ... ... Jan. 10]
James Hilton, of Whelton, buried the 13 day of January „ 13
An Whaley, of Whitell, buried the 14 day of January... „ 14
John Hodson, of Euexton, buried the twentith and
third day of January ... ... „ 23
Oliuer Hadocke, the sonne of James Hadocke, of Whit-
tell, buried the twentith third day of January ... ... „ 23
[A child of John Crichlow, of Euexton, buried the
twentith eight day ... ... „ 28]
Margrett Low, of Leyland, burried the sixt day of
ffebr. ... ... Feb. 6
Annes, the daughter of Hennry bickerstafe, of ffarring-
ton, burried the seuenth day ffebruary ... ... „ 7
[Jenet, the wiffe of Richard Hodson, of ffarrington,
buried the tenth day of ffebruary ... ... „ 10]
[Alice, the wiffe of Richard Whittell, of Whittell,
buried the ffortinth day of ffebruary... ... ... „ 14]
John Bickerstaffe, the sonne of Hennery Bickerstaffe,
of ffarrington, burried the ffiftinth day of ffebruary.. „ 15
Adam, the sonne of Hugh Brindell, of Heapey, buried
the ffirst day of March ... ... Mar. 1
Margret, the daughter of John torner, of Euexton,
buried the eight day of March ... ... „ 8
Marie Whittell, of Leyland, buried the ffiftinth day of
March ... ... „ 15
Ann, the daughter of Lawrance Silcicoke,[1] of Whelton
Thomas Brires, of Whelton, buried the three and twen-
tith day of March ... ... „ 23

Burialls, 1661.

Hennery Muncke, the sonne of George Muncke, of
Leyland, buried the third day of Aprill ... ... Ap. 3
Margret ffarrington, the daughter of William ffarring-
ton, of Leyland, buried the seuenth day of Aprill ... „ 7
Ester Penellbery, of Leyland, buried the Last day of
Aprill ... ... „ 30
Ralph Pearson, of Whelton, buried the tenth day of
May ... ... May 10
(Marie, the wiffe of Nicklous Whittell, of Leyland,
buried the ii of May. [Inserted, but by the same
hand] ... ... „ 11)

[1] For Silcock.

Richard Shorrocke, the sonne of Richard Shorrocke, of
  Curden, buried the thirtinth day of Maye ... ... May 13
Gilbert Ugnall, of Whilton, buried the *seuentinth*[1] day
  of May ... ... „ 17
[Gilbert Ugnall, of Whilton, buried the *second*[1] day of
  Jun, 1661 ... ... June 2]
William Waterworth, of Uleswalton, buried the seuenth
  day of June ... ... „ 7
Janett, the wiffe of William Miller, of Leyland, buried
  the twentith fforth day of June ... ... „ 24
William ffarrington, the sonne of Thomas ffarrington,
  of Leyland, buried the twentith ninth day of June... „ 29
John, the sonne of Alice Sumner, of Leyland, bastard,
  buried the third day of July ... ... July 3
[John, the sonne of Alice Sumner, of Leyland, bastard,
  Buried the therd day of July ... ... „ 3]
Richard Ockelshaw, of Eckelston, buried the sixtinth
  day of July ... ... „ 16
[Richard Ockeleyshaw, of Eckelston, Buried the six-
  tinth day of July ... ... „ 16]
[William, the sonne of William Sardgant, of Leyland,
  buried the nintinth day of July... ... ... „ 19]
William Sargant, the sonne of William Sargant, of
  Leyland, buried the nintinth day of July... ... ... „ 19
William Withnell, the sonne of Thomas Withnell, of
  Whittell, buried the twentith third day of July ... „ 23
[William Winnell, the sonne of Thomas Winnell, of
  Whittell, Buried the twentith third day of July ... „ 23]
Margret, the daughter of William Mackerell, of Ley-
  land, buried the eight day of August ... ... Aug. 8
[Margret, the daughter of William Mackerell, of Ley-
  land, Buried the eight day of August ... ... „ 8]
[Jenet, the wiffe of John Brires, of Whelton, buried
  twentith seuenth day of August ... ... „ 27]
Janett, the wiffe of John Brires, of Whilton, buried the
  twentith seuenth day of August ... ... „ 27
William Whaley, of Bretherton, buried the thirtinth
  day of September ... ... Sept. 13
James, the sonne of Robert Charrnocke, of Euexton,
  buried the twentith eight day of September ... ... „ 28
William Dewest, of Withnell, buried the fforth day of
  October... ... ... Oct. 4

---

[1] The word "seuentinth" appears to have been written over a previous word "second." This may help to explain the discrepancy in the two entries, which evidently relate to the same individual.

[James, the sonne of Robert Charrnocke, of Euexton,
buried the twentith eight day of September ... ... Sept. 28]
[William Dewest, of Winnell, buried the fforth day of
October... ... ... Oct. 4]
John, the sonne of John Hilton, of Euexton, buried the
twentith fforth day of October ... ... „ 24
Thomas Dewrst, of Leyland, buried the twentith sixt
day of October ... ... „ 26
John Clayton, of Leyland, buried the twelfth day of
December ... ... Dec. 12
Margret, the daughter of John burscow, of Leyland,
buried the eighttinth day of Desember ... ... „ 18
Elin, the wiffe of William Slator, of Leyland, buried
the ffiftinth day of ffebruary ... ... Feb. 15
Alice Dolton, of Leyland, buried the twentith third day
of ffeb. ... ... „ 23
Mr Richard Orell,[1] of ffarrington, buried the twentith
third day of ffebruary ... ... „ 23
Alice, the daughter of ffrancis grondey, of Uleswalton,
buried the third day of March ... ... Mar. 3
Lawrance Brires, of Whittell, buried the ffifth day of
March ... ... „ 5
Margret Pilkington, of Whittell, buried the ninth day
of March ... ... „ 9
Edward Hodson, of Euexton, buried the tenth day of
March ... ... „ 10
John Slator, of ffarrington, buried the ffortinth day of
March ... ... „ 14

[Burials, 1662.]

Richard, the sonne of Richard Cotherbanke,[2] of Euex-
ton, buried the twentith sixt day of March ... ... March 26
George Muncke, of Leyland, buried the fforth day of
Aprill [Inserted, but contemporary]... ... ... April 4
The wife of Richard tumlison, of ffarrington, buried
the sixt day of Aprill ... ... „ 6

---

[1] A family of this name appears to have been resident in ffarrington since the date
of the third marriage of Isabel, d. of John Clayton, Esquire (the last of Clayton),
with-John Orrell, of Turton, Esquire. This lady's daughter, by her second husband,
also married an Orrell. Isabel Clayton's first husband was William ffarrington, the
son and heir-apparent of Sir Henry ffarrington. Mr. Ric. Orrel compounded for his
estates in 1645.

[2] For Calderbank.

N

Richard Holl, of Euexton, buried the seuenth day of
Aprill ... ... April 7
William Euexton, of Leyland, buried the eight day of
Aprill ... ... „ 8
James, the sonne of James Shorroke, of Clayton, Buried
the ninth day of Jun ... ... June 9
Elizabeth, the wiffe of Richard Wright, of Uleswalton,
buried the twentith therd day of July ... ... July 23
Alice, the wiffe of John Cliffe, of Leyland, buried the
owne & twentith of August ... ... Aug. 21
Richard, the sonne of Thomas Balshaw, of Walton in the
Woodes, buried the twentith seuenth day of August. „ 27
Gilbert Jackeson, of Curden, buried the eightinth day
of October ... ... Oct. 18
Jane, the daughter of Lawrance Worington, of Heapey,
Buried the towe and twentith day of October... ... „ 22
Adam, the sonne of John Cliffe, of Leyland, buried the
second day of December ... ... Dec. 2
Alice Wackeffild, of Leyland, buried the thirtinth day
of December... ... ... „ 13
Elizabeth Wignes, of Leyland, buried 17th day of
December ... ... „ 17
William, the sonn of John Jackeson, of Leyland, buried
the three & twentith day of Desember ... ... „ 23
Richard Boutell, of Leyland, buried the twentith seuenth
day of December ... ... „ 27
(*sic*) the wiffe of Even Eastham, of Whittell, buried
the twentith ninth day of December... ... ... „ 29
Elin, the wiffe of Elish Boulton, of Leyland, the towe
and twentith day of ffebruary ... ... Feb. 22
(*sic*) the wiffe of John Hough, of Whittell, Buried the
three & twentith day of ffebruary ... ... „ 23
William Dewrst, of Radellsworth, buried the twentith
seuenth day of ffebuary ... ... „ 27
Elizabeth, the daughter of Hugh Smith, of Euexton,
Buried the twentith eight day of ffebruary ... ... „ 28
Cristopher ffiswicke, of the Clousehoues, buried the
ninth day of March ... ... Mar. 9
A child of James Coucker, of Clayton, Buried the
ffiftinth day of March ... ... „ 15
Lawarance, the sonne [of] James Howorth, of Heapey,
Buried the ffiftinth day of March ... ... „ 15
A child of Ralph Leyland, of Clayton, Buried the
ffiftinth day of March ... ... „ 15

[Burials, 1663.]

Jane, the wiffe of Thomas Heyes, of Heapey, buried
the six & twentith of March ... ... Mar. 26

Alice, the wiffe of Thomas Houghton, of blackeborn
prish, buried the eight day of Aprill... ... ... Ap. 8

Richard Banister, of Leyland, buried the eightinth day
of Aprill ... ... „ 18

A child of William Miller, of Uleswalton, buried the
towe and twentith of Aprill ... ... „ 22

Adam Mondy, of Leyland, buried the second of May. May 2

Elizabeth, the wiffe of James Adlington, of Curden,
buried the fforth day of May ... ... „ 4

James, the sonne of Edward Woodcocke, of Euexton,
Buried the sixt day of May ... ... „ 6

Margret, the wiffe of William (*sic*), Buried the ninthe
day of May ... ... „ 9

A child of Lewes Banister, of Curden, buried the
eightinth day of May ... ... „ 18

the sister of the wiff of William Wilden, of Leyland,
Buried the ninthtinth day of May ... ... „ 19

A child of Richard Johnes, of Euexton, Buried the
the twentith day of May ... ... „ 20

A child of George Widicker, of Euexton, buried the
twentith therd day of May... ... ... „ 23

A child of John Shorroke, of Whittell, buried the
twentith third day of May ... ... „ 23

Katrin, the daughter of John Wamesley, of Whittell,
Buried the twentith ffifft day of May ... ... „ 25

Anne, the wiffe of Richard Wilson, of Whittell, Buried
the twentith ninth day of May ... ... „ 29

the sonne of Thomas Miller, of Clayton, buried the
ffirst day of June... ... ... June 1

Edward Latham, of Blackeborne prish, buried the
twentith of June ... ... „ 20

Richard Mondey, of Leyland, buried the ffirst of July... July 1

Doraty, the daughter of John blackeledge, of Whittell,
buried the sixt of July... ... ... „ 6

Edmond Melinge, of Charnocke, buried the seventh
day of July ... ... „ 7

the daughter of William Asley, of Radellsworth, buried
the eleventh day of July ... ... „ 11

Thomas, the sonne of Thomas Miller, of Clayton,
Buried the sixtinth day of July ... ... „ 16

A child of Cristopher Wilden, of ffarrington, Buried
  the nintinth day of July ... ... July 19
William Southworth, of Leyland, buried the nintinth
  day of July ... ... „ 19
the daughter of Cristopher Willden, of ffarrington,
  buried the twentith fforth day of July ... ... „ 24

[Here there is a change in the handwriting—a return to the
style (? the same hand) used from 1653 to ffeb. 16, 1655. The
same change is noticeable in the entries of Baptisms at exactly
the same dates.]

Mᵣⁱˢ Alice Anderton[1] ... ... Sept. 21
vxʳ George Bolton, of Leyland ... ... „ 26
John Sharrok, of Whittle ... ... Oct. 7
Mᵣⁱˢ Anne Currer,[2] of Worden ... ... „ 13
A child of John Hodson, of Curden ... ... „ 16
Margret, daughtʳ of francis Eastham, of Walton... ... Dec. 7
A child of Edward Latham, of Cuerdale[3] ... ... „ 14
A child of Mʳ Bradshaw,[4] at Exton-hall ... ... Jan. 4
The wife of John Brearly, of Raddlesworth... ... ... „ 13
A child of Edward Woodcock, of Exton ... ... „ 15
Hugh ffarnworth, of Wheelton ... ... ⎫
John Sharrok, of Exton ... ... ⎬ „ 16
Rosamund, the wife of William ffarington, of ffarington „ 23
Simon Walmersly, of Heapie... ... ... ⎫
The wife of William Crichlowe, of Whittle ... ... ⎬ „ 28
Richard Sharples, of Cuerden ... ... „ 30
A child of Mʳ Bushell,[5] of Exton ... ... „ 31
William Gerrat, of Wheeleton ... ... Feb. 12
James Asley, of Whittle ... ... „ 19
John Cliffe, of Leyland ... ... „ 20
Robert Wigans, of Heapy ... ... „ 24
Richard Pincocke, a̅s Norbanke, of Whittle ... ... „ 28

[1] Possibly one of the unmarried daughters of Hugh Anderton, of Euxton, Esquire, and his wife Margaret, d. of Roger Kirkby.

[2] Née ffarington, third daughter of William ffarington, of Worden, Esquire, and Katherine (ffleetwood) his wife, and married to Mr. William Currer, citizen of London.

[3] A township in Blackburn parish, but lying very near to Preston.

[4] Dorothy, one of the daughters of Hugh Anderton, of Euxton, Esquire, married John Bradshaw, of Laniog. Perhaps her husband was the Mr. Bradshaw mentioned in the text.

[5] Probably the Seth Bushell who was "Incumbent" of Euxton in 1650, and afterwards Vicar of Preston, and then of Lancaster. He married the daughter of William Stanfield, of Euxton. See page 36.

A child of Edward Clayton, of ffarington ... ... Mar. 1
A child of Thomas Rowes, of Exton ... ... „ 9
The wife of Robert Harrison, of Leyland ... ... „ 10
A child of Henry Whittle, of Clayton ... ... „ 11
Henry Heald, of Leyland ... ... „ 14
The wife of Robert Heskett, of Bretherton ... ... „ 16
The wiffe of William Bordman, of Winnell ... ... „ 18
Ellin Rigby, of Clayton, widow ... ... „ 23

[Burials] 1664.

vxor. William Pilkinton, of Leyland ... ... Aprill 1
vxor. Raphe Sherdley, of ffarington ... ... ⎫
William, son of Mr Currer[1] ... ... ⎬ „ 5
A child of Thurstan Sharrok, of Whittle ... ... „ 10
A child of William Crooke, of Exton ... ... ⎫
A daught^r of Edward Clayton, of ffarington ... ⎬ May 8
vx^r Henry Beardsworth, of Leyland ... ... „ 24
Richard Whittle, of Wheelton ... ... June 22
William Crichlow, of Exton ... ... „ 27
A child of James Holmes, of Leyland ... ... July 3
James Wright, of Euxton ... ... „ 7
Thomas Whitehead, of Leyland ... ... „ 10
vxor. James Crichlow, of Euxton ... ... „ 25
Edward Whittle, of Clayton ... ... Aug. 8
Robert Lowe, of Whittle ... ... „ 18
Widow Pincock, of Whittle ... ... „ 28
vx^r William Oldha^m, of Whittle ... ... Sept. 8
Widow Cowper, of Euxton ... ... „ 12
Thomas Wielden, of Leyland ... ... „ 25
vx^r Thomas Howorth, *vid:* of Whittle ... ... Oct. 7
John Darwin, of Cuerden ... ... „ 20
Thomas, son of Richard Hodson, of Euxton ... ... „ 21
William Wild, of Euxton ... ... Nov. 9
A bastard child of Alice Whittle, of Leyland ... ... „ 13
A child of William Garstang, of Whittle ... ... „ 16
Margret Waterworth, of Ulnswalton ... ... „ 25
vx^r John Burscow, of Leyland ... ... „ 27
Elizabeth Tasker, of Leyland ... ... Dec. 13
Elizabeth Haulgh, of Leyland ... ... „ 18
A child of Christopher Wielden, of ffarington ... ... „ 20

---

[1] See note on entry of October 13, 1663. This was a grandson of William
ffarrington, Esq., of Worden, and his wife Katherine (ffleetwood). Mrs. Ann Currer
died in October, 1663.

The wife of Richard Walmersley, of Whittle ... ... Dec. 25
Widow Sumner, of Ulnswalton ... ... „ 28
Widow Cowper, of Leyland ... ... „ 29
The wife of William West, of Whittle ... ... „ 30
James Werden, of Clayton ... ... Jan. 1
A daughter of William Wielden, thatcher, of Leyland... „ 20
Robert Dewhurst, of Raddlesworth ... ... „ 31
Alexander Lauett, of Clayton ... ... ffeb. 5
A child of James Gorton, of Clayton ... ... „ 7
Robert ffarington, of Leyland ... ... „ 9
James Woodworth, of Leyland ... ... ⎫
Anne, wife of Thomas Holland, of Bretherton ... ⎭ „ 12
John Bigans, of Whittle ... ... „ 17
Widow Cowper, of Cuerden ... ... „ 25
Euan Cocker, of Clayton ... ... Mar. 4
Henry, son of Henry Jackson, of Leyland ... ... „ 10
The wife of John Eastham, of Walton ... ... „ 11
Robert Walmersley, of Whittle ... ... „ 12
Ellin Nickson, of Euxton ... ... „ 21

Burialls, 1665.

vxor. William ffernsall, of Euxton... ... ... Aprill 8
Robert ffiswick, of Winnell ... ... „ 10
vxor. Henry Whittle, of Clayton ... ... „ 12
Anne Mawuet, of ffarington ... ... „ 16
William Heald, of Leyland ... ... May 9
A child of Thomas Winnell, of Whittle ... ... „ 10
William West, of Whittle ... ... „ 15
A child of Edward Wielden, of Charnok ... ... „ 19
Margery Okenshaw, of Euxton ... ... „ 26
A child of John Dewhurst, of Cuerden ... ... „ 27
Thomas, son of John Leyland, of Whittle ... ... June 4
m. William Garstang, of Whittle ... ... „ 5
vxr John Martin, of Whittle, widow ... ... July 5
James, son of William Hollinhurst, of ffarington ... „ 7
Richard Hodson, of Cawbek[1] in Euxton ... ... „ 12
A child of Thomas Machon, of Kuerden ... ... ⎫
A daughter of Richard Sharples, of Cuerden ... ⎬ Aug. 3
m. Widow Euxton, of Clayton ... ... „ 4

[1] Cawbeck is the name of a stream which runs into the River Yarrow. The local explanation of the name is, that a certain Prince (generally stated to have been Charles II., when seeking refuge at Euxton hall) exclaimed, after drinking a draught from it, ''What a refreshing *cool-beck*.'' The Cawbek or Culbeck of the text is farm house. See p. 64.

William Philips, of Leyland ... ... Oct. 13
Alice, wife of Edward Slator, of ffarington ... ... „ 14
m. Thomas Snart, of Leyland ... ... „ 16
William, son of William Sumner, of Lostock ... ... „ 27
Roger Pincock, of Whittle ... ... Nov. 4
The wife of Henry Bickerstaffe, of ffarington ... ... „ 17
Widow ffarnworth, of Wheelton ... ... „ 27
m. William Hartly, of Cuerden ... ... ⎫
vx^r John Clayton, of ffarington ... ... ⎬ Dec. 1
Margret, daughter of Thomas Clough, of Leyland ... „ 10
John Harrison, of Leyland ... ... „ 23
Henry Jackson, of Leyland ... ... „ 24
The wife of Richard Rowes, of Euxton ... ... „ 28
Katharin, daught^r of George Moncke, of Leyland ... „ 29
A son of William Asley, of Raddlesworth ... ... Jan. 14
George, son of George Moncke, of Leyland... ... ... „ 15
The wife of James Asley, of Whittle ... ... „ 21
John Blakburne, of Cuerden ... ... „ 30
Widow Gerratt, of Anicearke[1] ... ... ffeb. 8
William, son of John Hodson, of Cawbeck[2] ... ... „ 13
The wife of Robert Blackeledge, of Whittle... ... ... „ 19
Robert Wright, of Leyland ... ... March 1
John Ward, of Leyland ... ... „ 2

[Burials] 1666.

Richard, son of John Beardsworth, of Leyland ... ...March 31
Henry Slator, of Euxton ... ... ⎫
Anne, daught^r of Richard Leekas, of Winnell ... ⎬ Aprill 8
Hugh Brindle, of Wheeleton ... ... ⎫
James, son of Thomas Whitehead, of Leyland ... ⎬ „ 20
John, son of Thomas Porter, of Ulneswalton ... ... May 11
Roger, son of Robert ffarington, of ffarington ... ... „ 18
m. Alice ffarington, widow, of Leyland ... ... „ 21
A child of William Wilson, of Leyland ... ... June 3
Margrett Cockar, of ffarington ... ... „ 6
William Leekas, of Whittle ... ... „ 17
Margery Bennett, of Euxton ... ... „ 23
Lawrance Breres, son of Lawrance, of Whittle ... ... July 8
vx^r Henry Brining, of Whittle ... ... „ 14
Elizabeth Cowper, of Cuerden ... ... „ 22

[1] Anicearke, a various spelling for Anlezarch, the hill district lying to the south-east of Heapey.

[2] See note on previous page.

A child of Ellis Sumner, of Leyland ... ... July 26
A child of John Jackson, of Cuerden ... ... Aug. 5
Robert, son of Peter Charnock, of Ulneswalton ... ... Sept. 6
William, son of Richard Cheshire, of ffarington ... ⎱
Widow Hodson, of Euxton ... ... ⎰ „ 8
Mary, wife of John Browne, of ffarington ... ... „ 9
A child of William Watson, of Whittle... ... ... „ 14
m. The wife of Thomas Allinson, of Leyland ... ... Oct. 18
Alice, ⎫
Ann, ⎬ children of John Clayton, of Clayton ... ... „ 25
Jennett, ⎭
vxʳ William Woodcocke, of Euxton ... ... „ 30
Raphe Bootle, of Leyland ... ... Nov. 6
John Dawson, of Leyland ... ... ⎱
Elizabeth Baron, of Euxton ... ... ⎰ „ 11
Elizabeth, daughtʳ of Richard Loxam, of Ulnswalton... „ 12
A child of William Blakburne, of Cuerden ... ... „ 18
Richard Loxam,[1] of Ulneswalton... ... ... „ 26
A son of Henry Garstang, of Heapy ... ... „ 26
m. The wife of Ellis Hough, of Whittle ... ... Dec. 3
John, son of Richard Charnly, of Cuerden ... ... „ 14
James Pilkinton, of Whittle ... ... „ 27
m. William Jackson, of Cuerden ... ... „ 31
m. William Hough, of Whittle ... ... Jan. 5
m. John Cockar, of Whittle ... ... „ 13
William Dickonson, of ffarington ... ... „ 17
A child of Richard Clough, of Leyland ... ... „ 21
Henry Beardsworth, of Leyland ... ... „ 28
Elizabeth Cockar, widow, of Mosse-side[2] ... ... ffeb. 7
James Martin, of Walton ... ... „ 9
vxʳ John Withington, of Clayton ... ... „ 18
A child of Thomas Withington, of Clayton... ... ... „ 26
Richard Cockar, of Euxton ... ... March 13
vxʳ Henry Watson, widow, of Whittle ... ... „ 17

[Burials] 1667.

A child of James Holmes, of Leyland ... ... March 27
Ann, the wife of John Liuesay, of Darwin ... ... Aprill 1
Edward, son of John ffarnworth, of Wheelton ... ... „ 3

---

[1] There is a flat stone now lying within Leyland churchyard, near to the north-west door of the church, having an incised inscription running round the edge of it, which records the burial of Richard Loxam, of Ulneswalton, on November 2[6], 1666.

[2] The extreme western side of Leyland township.

m. William Whittle, of Whittle	Aprill	6
A child of Thomas Cartwright, of Euxton	May	24
m. Robert Pilkinton, of Whittle	„	27
Alice, daught^r of Henry Whittle, of Leyland	„	28
Elsabeth Parker, of Charnock, widow	June	7
Roger, son of Roger ffarington, of ffarington	} „	8
Ellin Cockar, of Whittle, widow		
Ellin, daughter of James Sharrok, of Clayton	„	9
m. Richard Sharrok, of Clayton	„	11
m. Thomas Starkey, of Leyland	} „	22
A child of William Clayton, of Cuerden		
A child of Hugh Winnell, of Whittle	„	27
Thomas Woods, of ffarington	„	28
Mr Edward ffleetwood,[1] of Leyland	July	22
John Withington, of Clayton	„	24
Elsabeth, wife of Richard Clough, of Leyland	Aug.	1
Robert Wigans, of Cuerden	„	7
Jane, the wife of William Oldham, of Whittle	„	11
William Morris, of Heapie	„	19
Ellen Cockar, of Leyland, widow	„	26
Roger Leyland, of Heapie	„	28
Grace Whittle, widow, of Leyland	„	29
Elsabeth Chisnall, of Leyland, widow	Sept.	4
William Howorth, of Whittle	„	8
John Oldhouse, of Leyland	„	9
vx^r John Blakburne, de Cuerden	„	12
John Walmersley, of Whittle	„	15
vx^r Thomas Martin, of Heapie	„	17
vx^r Robert Cockar, of Clayton	„	18
Euan Pearson, of Heapie	„	21
vx^r William Cowper & her child, of Cuerden	„	25
James Beardsworth, of Walton in le dale	„	30
Alice, daughter of William Leekas, of Whittle	Oct.	5
Alice Euxton, of Leyland, widow	} „	10
Ellin Bushell, of Cuerden, widow		
Ellin, wife of John Hodson, of Cuerden		
Alice, wife of William Blakburne, of Cuerden	„	17
——, son of Thomas Withington, of Clayton	„	30
Jane, the wife of John Morris, of Heapie	Nov.	9

[1] Third son of Edward ffleetwood, of Penwortham, Esq., and his wife Margaret, d. of Sir Thos. Norreys, of Speke. He and his eldest brother, John ffleetwood, of Penwortham, Esq., married two sisters, the daughters of Wm. ffarington, Esq., of Worden (the Royalist). By his wife Margaret he had a daughter of the same name, who was married at Leyland in 1674. Hence the Fleetwood Hesketh family. Mr. Edw. ffleetwood was a guild burgess at Preston in 1622 and 1642.

Robert Wilcock, of Leyland ... ... Nov. 16
John Wilcock, of Leyland ... ... „ 22
vx^r Robert Sumner, of Leyland ... ... Dec. 9
Nicholas Parke, of Euxton ... ... „ 13
Anne Welsh, widow, of Leyland ... ... „ 20
vx^r Thomas Winnell, of Winnell ... ... „ 27
William, son of William Oldham, of Whittle ... ... „ 28
Margrett Welsh, of ffarington ... ... „ 29
Jennett, daught^r of George Munck, of Leyland ... ... Jan. 1
Elsabeth, daughter of John Taylor, of Whittle ... ... „ 15
A child of William Clayton, of Cuerden ... ... „ 26
Richard Loxam, of ffarington ... ...
Thomas Starkie, of Cuerden ... ... } ffeb. 9
Raphe Hollinhurst, of Ulneswalton, &... ... ...
Alice, his wife, buried together ... ... } „ 12
Elsabeth, wife of Roger Pilkinton, of Leyland ...
Elsabeth Riuington, of Clayton ... ... } „ 18
A child of Henry Unsworth, of Euxton ... ...
Alice, wife of William Dandie, of Cuerden ... ... „ 29
Isaac, son of William Sharrok, of Euxton ... ... March 12
Thomas Woodcock, of Cuerden ... ... „ 17
Alice, wife of James ffarington, of Leyland... ...
A child of William Asley, of Whittle ... ... } „ 23

[𝔅urials] 1668.

Randle, son of William Crooke, of Leyland... ... ... March 28
m. Roger Lockwood, of Owlerton[1] ... ... Aprill 4
m. Sisley Jackson, of Cuerden, widow... ... ...
Alice Atkinson, of Leyland, widow ... ... } „ 8
vx^r James Armetriding, of Whittle ... ...
Ellin, daught^r of Thomas ffarington ... ... } „ 11
William Crichlow, of Wheelton ... ... „ 14
A child of William Balshaw, of Euxton ... ... „ 25
Henry Gillar, of Walton in le dale ... ... May 7
Raphe, son of John Pearson, of Wheelton ... ...
vx^r Roger Crooke, of Whittle... ... ... } „ 8
m. Thomas Crichlowe, of Leyland ... ... „ 9
Jennett Crichlowe, of Leyland ... ... „ 11
Ellin Thonton, of ffarington ... ... „ 18
Widow Unsworth, of Euxton... ... ... „ 22
Robert Withington, of Clayton ... ... „ 24
vx^r William Bolton, of Heapie ... ... „ 25

[1] Ollerton, a hamlet lying on the eastern side of Leyland parish.

ux Richard Jones, of Euxton	... May	26
Mary, wife of Raphe Smith, of Lostock-hall ...	... June	2
Elsabeth, wife of Michael Taylor, of Euxton	„	12
Widow Pearson, of Wheelton...	„	15
James Martin, of Leyland ... ... ⎫		
John ffarnworth, of Wheeton ... ... ⎬	„	16
ux John Hilton, of Whittle ... ... ⎭		
A child of Nicholas Bromily, of Leyland	July	2
m. Richard Charnley, of Cuerden	„	13
A child of Jeffrey Taylor, of Heapie	„	15
Richard Sharrok, of Leyland...	June	17
m. Margrett Jackson, widow, of Leyland	„	23
Elsabeth, daught*r* of Thomas Crichlow, of Leyland ...	„	27
m. James Sharrok, of Clayton	„	29
Ellin, wife of John Phillips, of Leyland	„	30
Thomas Leaver, of Leyland	... Aug.	3
Mary, wife of William ffarington, of Snubsnape[1] ...	„	4
Jane, wife of Arthur Dawson, of ffarington	„	12
Elsabeth, daught*r* of Thomas Watson, of Raddlesworth	„	13
Arthur Dawson, of ffarington	„	15
Ellin Waring, of Lidyate[2] in Eccleston	„	22
Tomasin Snart, of Leyland	„	27
m. Margrett Sumner, of Hollins,[3] widow ... ... ⎫		
Dorothy Eastham, of Walton in le Dale ... ... ⎬	„	31
Sisley Clayton, of Cuerden	Sept.	4
Anne Hough, of Whittle	„	10
Margrett Dawson (*sic*)	„	13
James Cockar, of Mosse-side	„	24
m. Henry Cockar, of Mosse-side	„	26
Ellin Oldhouse, of Mosse-side, widow ... ... ⎫		
ux John Pope, of Winnell ... ... ⎬	„	27
Henry, son of Henry Croston, of Whittle	„	28
ux Lawrance Worthington, of Heapie...	Oct.	14
John, son of Robert Martin, of Wheelton	„	15
ux John Marsh, of Mosse-side	„	20
John Crooke, died at Walton-hall, & buried	„	30
Raphe ffidler, of Clayton...	... Nov.	6
A child of Roger ffiswick, of Winnell ... ... ⎫		
Margrett, wife of Thomas Rowes, of Euxton ... ⎬	„	13

[1] Snubsnape is a farm which is situated on the south-west of Leyland township and near to the boundary of Euxton.

[2] There are several places in the surrounding districts which are known by the name of Lidyate. This in the text is a farm near to Eccleston Rectory.

[3] A farm on the south-east of Leyland township, by the Hollins brook.

Robert Glaseborow, of Leyland ... ... Dec.   2
Thomas Wignall, of ffarington ... ... „ 12
m. Isabell Ward, widow, of Leyland ... ... „ 15
Dorathy Marshhouse, of Leyland, widow ... ... „ 25
The wife of John Leyland, of Whittle ... ... Jan.   2
A child of John Slator, of Euxton ... ... „   4
vx^r Henry Cockar, of Moss-side ... ... „   5
Thurstan Sharrok, of Euxton... ... ... „   7
A child of John Smith, of Walton... ... ... „   8
m. Edward Whittle, of Clayton ... ... „ 11
vx^r William Clayton, of Winnell ... ... „ 20
m. John Gerratt, of Clayton ... ... „ 29
A child of Lawrance Whittle, of ffarington ... ... ffeb. 16
Margret ffarington, widow, of Ulneswalton ... ... „ 27
Widow [Moodie crossed out] Haddok, of Heapie   ... March 7

Burialls, 1669.

Richard Gregson, of Euxton ... ... March 28
Thomas [Richard crossed out] Morris, of Garstang pish Aprill 1
John Nickson, of Leyland   ... ... ⎫
John Blakburne, of Leyland ... ... ⎬ „   2
Margrett, wife of William Sergeant, of Leyland ... ... „ 15
Anne, wife of Thomas Parke, of Euxton ... ... „ 19
Christian Clayton, of Raddlesworth ... ... „ 23
Nicholas Whittle, of Mosse-side ... ... „ 26
Elizabeth Chetam, of ffarington ... ... „ 27
Margrett Werden, of Ulneswalton... ... ... May   8
Thomas Parke, of Euxton ... ... „ 15
John Adlinton, of Cuerden ... ... „ 17
M^{ris} ffrancis,[1] daughter of Mr Edward Tilsley ... ... „ 19

[1] M^{ris} ffrances Tyldesley was probably only a child or a very young person at the date of her death. To account for her burial at Leyland we may suppose that she was living with her grandmother, Lady Frances Tyldesley, who at this time resided at Leyland Hall. Lady Tyldesley was the daughter of Ralph Standish, of Standish, Esquire, and the widow of the gallant major-general who fell at Wigan Lane in 1651. We learn from the evidence given by her before the Commissioners appointed to interrogate witnesses for the Exchequer Court in the case (Attorney-General *v.* Gaynor Jones and William Crosse) that Lady Tyldesley farmed the estate called Leyland Hall for seven years after the death of Robert Charnock's mother in 1659, and that she continued to reside there, for the most part, until the death of Mr. Charnock himself in 1670. She also stated that her eldest son, Edward Tyldesley, Esq. (mentioned in the text), who was deceased in 1687, the date of the depositions, had assisted Robert Charnock in various ways, and in particular by the gift and allowance of the tythes of Fulwood (amounting to some £25 per annum). We may conjecture that this gift would be employed by Mr. Charnock in the propaganda which he was actively carrying on in the neighbouring districts in his capacity as Vicar Apostolic. See the note on p. 210.

—— Winnell, of Whittle, widow	May	22
John Pearson, of Wheelton	„	29
John, son of John Clayton, of ffarington	June	1
A child of John Pearson, of Wheelton	„	16
Raphe Wood, servant at Werden	„	28
Lawrance Taylor, of Heapie	July	20
Anne Godman, of Mosse-side, widow ... ... ⎫		
Anne Pilkinton, of Whittle ... ... ⎭	„	23
vxr John Silcock, of Leyland...	„	24
A child of Richard Sheardly, of Leyland	„	25
Anne, the wife of Richard Sheardly, of ffarington ...	Aug.	6
Thomas Garstang, of Whittle... ... ... ⎫		
vxr John Scot, of Whittle ... ... ⎭	„	7
The wife of William Howorth, of Whittle	„	8
Mr Thomas Clayton,[1] of ffulwood...	„	13
John Hodson, of Euxton ... ... ⎫		
James, son of Thomas Garstang, of Whittle ... ⎭	„	14
The wife of Edgeon[2] Miller, of Leyland	„	18
Alice Blakburne, of Ulneswalton	„	20
John, son of William ffiswick, of Winnell	„	21
The wife of Christophr Wielden, of ffarington	„	22
The wife of Thomas Walker, of Leyland ... ... ⎫		
The wife of William Sumner, of ffarington ... ... ⎭	„	24
Alice, daughtr of John Garner, of ffarington	„	27
m. Jane Slator, of Euxton, widow	Sept.	9
A child of James Holme, of Leyland	„	11
Jennett Stamfield,[3] of Euxton	„	16
Jane, daughtr of James Walker, of Whittle	„	17
vxr Hugh Meare, of Leyland... ... ... ⎫		
John Wild, of Clayton ... ... ⎭	„	20

[1] Mr. Thomas Clayton, of Fulwood, near Preston, mentioned in the text, was apparently the eldest son of William Clayton, of Leyland, gent., by his wife Elizabeth, daughter of Nicholas Rigbye, of Harrock, Esquire. His name occurs with those of his father and four brothers in the Preston Guild Rolls for 1602 and 1622. In 1642 and 1662 he is entered as "Thomas Clayton de Fulwood, gen:" with sons, brothers, and brothers' sons. William Clayton, his father, is said to have died in 1631, and these entries help to that conclusion. In the Heralds' Visitation of 1664 he is entered as of Old Croke (in Whittle-le-Woods) and Fulwood, and his age is given as 78 years. In the *Discourse of the War* (Chetham Soc., vol. 62) we read that Colonel (Alex.) Rigbye in 1643, among the captains whom he appointed within the Hundred of Amounderness, selected "Mr. Claton an Ancient Gentleman dwelling about ffulwood More." As the age of the gentleman noted above would be about 57 years, this reference may possibly apply to him. See also note on Jan. 16, 1670-1.

[2] Notice this unusual name; the letters are quite distinct.

[3] The letter *m* is written, but *n* is probably correct. Mr. Wm. Stanfield was the father-in-law of Seth Bushell, the Puritan minister of Euxton. There is a well-known farm in Euxton which is still called Stanfield House.

m. Thomas Moore, of Euxton ... ... Sept.		24
vxʳ John Gerratt, of Clayton ... ... Oct.		2
vxʳ Roger ffarington, of ffarington... ... ... }	"	3
A child of Thomas Pilkinton, of Whittle		
m. William Miller, of Leyland	"	13
m. Mary Wright, of Euxton, widow	"	14
Nicholas, son of George Crooke, of Heapie, a priest[1]...	"	15
m. Roger Clayton, of Cuerden ... ... }	"	17
Widow Mayre, of Euxton		
Margrett Mayre, of Euxton	"	19
Thomas Pope, of Whittle	"	20
William Sumner, of ffarington	"	22
Jane, wife of ffidler, of ffarington	"	29
John ffidler, of ffarington ... ... }	"	30
James Browne, of ffarington		
Anne, wife of John Daniell, of Euxton...	"	31
The wife of James Browne, of ffarington ... ... }	Nov.	2
m. Widow Haughton, of Euxton		
Annice Clayton, of ffarington, widow	"	6
Jennet, wife of Edward Sherdley, of ffarington	"	11
Mary Asley, of Heapie ... ... }	"	13
A child of Thomas Hall, of Euxton		
m. William Bolton, of Heapie	"	17
m. Anne Sumner, of Leyland, widow	"	19
m. Roger Southworth, of Leyland	"	23
m. Jennett Muncke, of Leyland, widow ... ... }	"	24
m. William Dalton, of Whittle		
Margrett Chetam, of ffarington, widow	"	25
m. Henry Wright of Leyland, of Leyland ... ... Dec.		1
Jennett, wife of Richard Cheshire, of ffarington	"	6
Mʳⁱˢ Anne, wife of William Rothwell,[2] vicar	"	12
A child of John Clayton, of Clayton	"	22
James Waring, of Charnock	"	24
Hugh Johnson, of Leyland	"	26
m. William Wilson, of Leyland	"	27
Thomas Silcock, of Wheelton ... ... }	"	29
John Orrell, of ffarington		
A child of Edward Clough, of Leyland		
m. Margrett Cowper, of Leyland	"	31
Widow Holme, of Leyland ... ... Jan.		1

---

[1] Not to be found in Foley's *Jesuits.* May perhaps have been a secular priest.

[2] The Rev. Wm. Rothwell, vicar from 1650–1675, survived his wife. At the commencement of the Register are entries of the baptism of two sons, Nathaniel and James. There appears to have been another son, Charles, to whom letters of administration were granted at his father's death.

The wife of John Calderbanke, of Leyland ... ... Jan. 5
m. John Morris, of Heapie ... ... „ 7
A child of Roger ffiswick, of Winnell ... ... „ 13
Joane Melling, of Euxton ... ... „ 20
Richard Whitehead, of Leyland ... ... ⎫
vxᵣ Ellis Sumner, of Euxton ... ... ⎬ „ 26
m. James Walton, of Mosse-side ... ... „ 27
Elsabeth, wife of Robert Welsh, of ffarington ... ... „ 29
Ellin Slator, of Euxton, widow ... ... „ 30
William Breres, of Euxton ... ... ffeb. 9
Margrett, *vxᵣ* Robert Cowper, of Euxton ... ... ⎫
m. Elsabeth Cowper, of Euxton ... ... ⎬ „ 14
m. Thurstan Pincock, of Whittle ... ... ⎭
A child of Adam Blackburne, of Cuerden ... ... „ 15
m. John Leyland, of Whittle... ... ... „ 17
m. Richard Morris, of Heapie ... ... „ 19
Adam, son of John Eastham, of ffarington ... ... „ 23
Mary Smith, of Leyland, widow ... ... „ 27
Alice, wife of Thomas Parre, of Brindle ... ... March 3
Ann, wife of John Godbar, of Leyland... ... ... ⎫
Thomas Latham, of Lostock-hall[1] ... ... ⎬ „ 5
Anne Cockar, of Clayton, widow ... ... „ 16
Katharin, wife of John Silcock, of Leyland ... ... „ 17
A child of Oliuer Martin, of Wheelton... ... ... ⎫
Annice Jackson, of Ulneswalton, widow ... ... ⎬ „ 19

Buriallis, 1670.

John Mackerill, of Walton ... ...March 27
Dorathy, wife of John Blakburne, of Cuerden ... ...Aprill 11
The wife of William Dewhurst, of Raddlesworth[2] ... „ 12
The wife of Dauid Jones, of Euxton ... ... „ 18
m. Thurstan Leyland, of Clayton... ... ... „ 27
Dorathy, wife of Thomas Cowper, of Cuerden ... ...May 4
The wife of William Leauer, of Leyland ... ... „ 7
Thomas Clayton, of Midford [Middleford in Penwortham] „ 21
William Parke, of ffarington ... ...June 2
Jane Sumner, of Almeshouse[3] ... ... „ 7

[1] In Cuerden township, a part of Leyland parish.
[2] Part of the Moor quarter of Leyland parish.
[3] Apparently an inmate of the almshouse founded by William ffarrington, Esq., in 1649, and reconstituted temp. James II. There is a large charter, with the King's broad seal still attached to it, now in the care of the Vicar of Leyland, which relates to this second settlement. Unfortunately it is so much injured by damp as to be legible only in the central portion.

m. Robert Charnock, of Euxton	June	20
Thomas Garstang, of Whittle ... ... ⎫	"	21
m. John Cockar, of Cuerden ... ... ⎭		
Katharin, wife of William Sharrock, of Clayton	"	23
Robert Adlinton, of Cuerden...	"	30
Ellin ffoster, of Charnock, widow	July	6
Isabel Wielden, of Leyland, widow	"	16
John Park, of Middleford	Aug.	12
Jane Loxam, of ffarington	"	15
Katharin Longton, of Whittle, widow	"	16
A child of Ellis Bolton, of Leyland ... ... ⎫	"	19
A child of Richard Godman, of Mosse-side[1] ... ⎭		
m. George Crichlowe, of Euxton	"	20
m. Hugh Woodcock, of Euxton	"	21
Sisley Tootel, of Whittle	"	24
William, son of William Godman, of Leyland	"	28
Margery, wife of John Pearson, of Heapie ... ... ⎫	Sept.	2
John Knowles, of Whittle ... ... ⎭		
m. James Adlinton, of Cuerden	"	5
m. William Blakledge & his wife, of Whittle ... ⎫		
m. William Walmersley, of Whittle ... ... ⎬	"	6
m. Thomas Leekas, of Whittle ... ... ⎭		
m. James Crichlowe, of Whittle	"	8
Thurstan Sharrock, of Whittle	"	14
Thomas Rowes, of Euxton	"	16
John Clayton, of Clayton ... ... ⎫	"	20
James Haddok, of Whittle ... ... ⎭		
John Lambert, of Leyland	"	22
John Leekas, of Leyland	"	23
m. James Wilson, of Whittle...	"	24
A child of Richard Walton, of Leyland	"	25
A child of Thomas Lowe, of Euxton	"	26
William Bonkin, of Leyland	"	27
A child of Thomas Caulderbank, of Leyland	"	29
Robert Cockar, of Mosse-side	Oct.	1
m. Elsabeth Starkie, of Leyland, widow	"	2
vx Samuell Baxenden, of Euxton ... ... ⎫	"	6
Bridget Bane, of Ulneswalton ... ... ⎭		
Alice Nixon, of Euxton, Widow	"	8
m. William Machon, of Clayton	"	12
m. John Bury, of Winnell ... ... ⎫		
Edward Sheardley, of ffarington ... ... ⎬	"	20
Jane Werden, of Clayton ... ... ⎭		

[1] The western portion of Leyland township, beyond the River Lostock.

Alice, Wife of Thomas Rydings, of Leyland ...	} Oct.	21
Anne, wife of Thomas Croston, of Ulneswalton ...		
Mary, daughter of John Crichlow, of Clayton	„	25
m. Thomas Whittle, of Leyland	„	27
vxr William Hollinhurst, of ffarington	„	28
Henry Knowles, of ffarington	„	29
William, son of Witt: Pilkinton, of Leyland ... ... Nov.		4
Margrett Walmersley, of Whittle, widow	„	5
vxr. William Jackson, of Whittle	„	6
m. John Eckles, of Cuerden	„	7
William Pilkinton, of Leyland	„	11
Elsabeth, wife of Thomas Eyues, of Leyland ...	} „	12
A child of John Calderbanck, of Leyland		
A child of William Jackson, of Whittle	„	13
James Sheardley, of ffarington	„	14
Ellin Withington, of Clayton, widow	„	16
John Garstang, of Whittle	„	21
John Cliffe, of Longton	„	22
Ellen,[1] wife of Edward Robinson, Esq\', of Euxton ...	„	23
John Welsh, of Leyland	„	25
William Hollinhurst, of ffarington...	„	26
Robert, son of Robert Charnock, of Euxton	„	28
Annice Marsden, of Whittle	„	30
A child of Richard Godman, of Mosse-side... ... ... Dec.		1
Elsabeth, wife of William Taylor, of Whittle	„	2
Margrett, wife of Henry Blakledge, of ffarington ...	„	6
m. Roger Crooke, of Whittle...	„	10
Annice, wife of Henry Tyson, of Ulneswalton	„	12
Alice Balshaw, of Leyland	„	20
Thurstan Adlington, of Cuerden	„	21
Widow Lathom, of Samsbury[2]	„	23
Ellin, wife of Thomas Cowper, of Leyland	„	24
Elsabeth Woodcocke, of Cuerden, widow	„	27
A child of Richard Hilton, of Euxton	„	29
Margrett, wife of William Cowper, of Leyland	„	31
A child of Arthur Dawson, of ffarington	} Jan.	1
Katharin, wife of Alexander Breres, of Whittle ...		
Raphe Cowper, of Cuerden	„	5
Ellis Smith, of Leyland	} „	6
William Breres, of Wheelton		

[1] Mrs. Robinson, of Buckshaw, in Euxton, was the daughter of John Brown, of Scale Yate, in the parish of Kirkham. By her husband Major Edward Robinson, she had two sons, John and Edward, also five daughters, Margaret, married to Edward Parr, of Wood, in Eccleston, Bridget, Lucy, Anne, and Jennet. See note pp. 23, 24.

[2] Samsbury, for Samlesbury, in Blackburn parish.

m. John Silcock, of Leyland ... ... Jan.	13
M^{ris} Clayton,[1] of ffulwood, widow... ... ... ,,	16
Thomas Garner, of ffarington ... ... ,,	18

m. John Silcock, of Leyland ... ... Jan. 13
M^{ris} Clayton,[1] of ffulwood, widow... ... ... ,, 16
Thomas Garner, of ffarington ... ... ,, 18
Thomas, son of Edward Litherland, of Whittle ... ⎫
A child of Dauid Jones, of Euxton ... ... ⎬ ,, 19
Dorathy, wife of Thomas Jackson, of Leyland ... ⎫
Anne, wife of William Shaw, of Leyland ... ... ⎬ ,, 21
vx^r John Hilton, of Euxton ... ... ,, 23
Henry Proctor, of Euxton ... ... ,, 26
Ellin, daught^r of Thomas Cowper, of Leyland ... ... ,, 28
Elsabeth Stratbarrell, of Cuerden ... ... ffeb. 1
m. Euan Eastham, of Whittle ... ... ,, 3
m. Mr Robert Charnock,[2] of Leyland ... ... ,, 4

[1] M^{ris} Clayton was doubtless the widow of the Mr. Thomas Clayton, of Fulwood, buried on August 13, 1669. If so, her name was Anna, and her father was Robert Blundell, of Ince Blundell, Esq. She had two sons and one daughter. Robert, the elder, seems to have made himself a name and a fortune in Liverpool. Gregson, *Fragments*, p. 175, says that he was buried at S. Nicholas' Church in that town. He succeeded to the Fulwood and other property of his father. Thomas, the younger son, became a successful and wealthy merchant (? first in Liverpool), and in 1664 is entered in the pedigree as a "citizen of London." He purchased the manors of Worthington and Adlington, and became the head of the family of Clayton, of Adlington. He lived to a great age, and did not die until 1721. The two brothers married two sisters, Helen and Ann, daughters of John Atherton, of Atherton, Esquire. Their own sister, Ann Clayton, married Mr. Robert Livesey, of Livesey, in Blackburn parish. Robert Clayton, de Fulwood, gen: was entered on the Preston Guild Roll of 1682 with four sons, Thomas, William, John, and Richard. To the name of the eldest son Thomas is added "Armiger," which is not easy of explanation seeing that he became a clergyman, and in 1664 was Rector of Bolton in Bolland. From the third son John, who appears to have been an M.D. in Dublin, descended Bishop Robert Clayton, of Killala, then of Cork, and finally of Clogher, who, at the death of his father John Clayton (Dean of Kildare), entered upon the possession of the Fulwood property as the eldest male representative of the direct line. The Bishop, having at his death (25 Feb., 1758) neither brother nor son, bequeathed his Lancashire estates to Chief Justice Richard Clayton, of the Adlington branch, a grandson of the subject of this note. Among the Foreign Burgesses at Preston Guild in 1682 we find "Thomas Clayton de Leverpool, Mercator," together with sons Richard, Thomas, and Robert. If this be the Thomas who married Ann Atherton, we have two names not usually found in the published pedigrees. Richard, the eldest son, succeeded to the manor of Adlington, and died in 1728. Robert is conjectured to have become a courtier, and finally the first Viscount Sundon and the husband of Charlotte Dyves, Mistress of the Robes to Caroline, Queen of George II. There were seven daughters, of whom three only were married. Eleanor became the wife of Nicholas Rigbye, of Harrock, Esquire. I am much indebted to W. Browne Clayton, Esq., for kind assistance with the Clayton pedigree.

[2] Mr. Robert Charnock was the second but eldest surviving son of Roger Charnock, gentleman, of Leyland, and his wife Ann, daughter of Robert Manley, of Broughton, co. Northampton. From the 1664 pedigree of his family, which was a younger branch of that of Charnock, of Charnock and Astley, he appears to have been the youngest child. His parents, in common with many others of their name, were resolute in their unwillingness to conform to the public ministrations of religion. Mr. Robert Charnock, the subject of this note, was early destined for the priesthood, and was sent to Lisbon for training. His name does not appear among the Jesuits who came to England, and there is reason to believe that he was a secular priest.

Edward Parker, of Leyland ... ... ffeb. 6
James Watson, of Whittle ... ... „ 7

He was known "in religion" as Father Manley, taking, according to a common custom, the name of his maternal grandparent. His activity in the work to which he was appointed is sufficiently attested by the various references to his visits in the secret diaries which are here and there in existence (*e.g.*, at Scarisbrick), and by his future eminence among his brethren. Apparently he was known to most of his neighbours and fellow-countrymen as a gentleman possessed of landed estate which he farmed for his own benefit. As a matter of fact he did devote some of his attention to these matters, even while carrying on his mission duties. He exercised considerable influence in Lancashire and the neighbouring counties among those who shared his convictions, for he held the office of Vicar Apostolic for the North, which gave him the Pope's authority to fulfil all the duties of a bishop which are possible to one not of that order. Only the power to confirm and to ordain deacons or priests was withheld. Being the last of his family he desired to settle his estate in such a manner as to benefit his co-religionists. Allusion has already been made in a previous note (page 204) to the residence of Lady Frances Tyldesley at Mr. Charnock's house during eleven years. Also that M^ris Grace Bold acted as housekeeper for Mr. Charnock for the last four of these. This latter person had been the personal attendant of Lady Tyldesley, to whom she came when in distressed circumstances. In after years Grace Bold used to assert that her father turned her out of his home owing to her forsaking the Church of England for the Romish religion. That fact is more than doubtful, but at all events she did yield to the arguments and persuasions of Mr. Charnock, and in 1644 was by him received into the Roman communion. In course of time Mr. Charnock came to place great confidence in her, and conducted much pecuniary business in her name. Hence when making a settlement of his affairs in January, 1660, he conveyed his estate to Willoughby Manley and Robert Charnock, and at their death to Grace Bold. At the death of Mr. Charnock, Grace Bold held possession of his estates, asserting that Leyland Hall had been purchased by her from the late owner. No objection was raised at the time, because Mr. Charnock's friends understood that a fictitious transfer had been made, in order to render the fulfilment of Mr. Charnock's wishes a possibility. At Grace Bold's death the estate was passed to Mr. William Crosse, of Darwin, and Mrs. Gaynor Jones, widow. The former of these had married a sister of Grace Bold, and the latter was another sister. In the opinion of Mr. Charnock's co-religionists who were privy to the trust the lands were misapplied, and they "discovered the matter."

In 1686 the Attorney-General brought an Information against the Appellants, and witnesses were examined. The case submitted to the jury at the Summer Assizes held at Lancaster was "Whether the conveyance of Leyland Hall, &c., to Grace Bold was made, declared, or intended upon any Trust, and upon what Trust." The verdict on this occasion was given in the following terms:—"That Leyland Hall was conveyed to Grace Bold in Trust, for the support and maintenance of Priests of the Romish Religion, viz., In Trust for the Support of the Priests of the Secular Clergy of the Romish Religion in the County of Lancaster." Upon this verdict the Court of Exchequer in 1688 decreed these lands and the trust thereof to the King as forfeited. A petition from the vicar of Leyland, with certain knights of the shire and burgesses, was presented to the Crown praying that the estate might be conveyed to trustees for the benefit of the present and future orthodox ministers holding the vicarage of Leyland, which was then of very small value. After directions were given for this grant, and as the same was passing, the Defendants Crosse and Jones brought in a Bill of Review of this decree of the Exchequer Court. The result was that the Court affirmed the decree, with the explanation or addition that "the Premises should be disposed of to such charitable and pious uses as their majesties [William and Mary] should appoint and think fit." Again directions were given for passing the grant in trust for the vicar of Leyland, but again Crosse and Gaynor Jones appealed; but they were not successful in averting the final transfer of the lands to the vicar of Leyland. The original papers connected with every stage of

m. Robert Cowper, of Euxton ... ... ffeb. 11
Henry, son of Henry Whittle, of Leyland ... ... „   14

this interesting case are deposited at Leyland vicarage, as well as the trust deed
engrossed on parchment and having a very fine specimen of the broad seal of
William and Mary appended to it. The depositions of witnesses taken at Leyland
in 1687 contain a considerable amount of interesting local information, and enable
one to become *en rapport* with the people and the times. The following may
perhaps prove worth recording. The examination was held at the house of Henry
Breckhill, of Leyland, innkeeper, on April 3rd, before John ffarnworth, Thomas
Hodgkinson, Robert Pigott, and John Roberts, gentlemen. Lady Tyldesley, of
Morleys, gave her age as 71 years or thereabouts. She stated that Mr. Charnock at
one time expressed his intention of so leaving Leyland Hall that "in case the
Catholique religion came again to be established in England the same should go to
Jesus Chappel in Leyland Church." [This must have meant the founding of a *new*
chantry, for there is no mention of any such dedication in pre-Reformation days.]
Another witness asserted that Mr. Charnock had declared his resolution "that if itt
please God to send them a Bishopp he intended the same house for him until a
better should be provided."
    The evidence of Mr. William Gradell (Gradwell), of Berbers Moor in Ulnes-
walton, gent., is interesting and important. He gave his age as 68 years and
upwards, and stated that he was intimately acquainted with Mr. Charnock and his
affairs. There was indeed a tie of relationship between them, although not a very
close one. From a pedigree published by W. A. Abram, Esq., in the *Preston
Guardian* of 1884, we learn that this gentleman had married Elizabeth, daughter of
John Butler, of Kirkland, Esq., and that he succeeded as a minor to his father's
property in 1630. The date of his death is thought to have been near the end of the
seventeenth century. From this present evidence it may be concluded that he was
born in 1619, and was still living in 1687. After repeating at length similar testimony
to that contributed by Lady Tildesley and others, Mr. Gradwell stated that shortly
after Mr. Charnock's death one Mr. Gerard, a Romish priest (deceased in 1687),
visited Grace Bold, and urged her to convey and settle the estate according to the
trust reposed in her. This she agreed to do, and a conveyance was drawn by a Mr.
George Pigot, of Preston, leaving blanks for the names, which were afterwards filled
in, with Grace Bold as grantor and Richard Sherbourne, Esq., and Thomas Walton,
late (in 1687) of Walton, gent., as grantees. This deed was deposited in the care of
Mr. Gradwell; but in a short time Grace Bold demanded it back, and threatened an
action in Chancery for that purpose. Mr. Gradwell thereupon "repaired to" Mr.
Gerard (mentioned above) and one Mr. Moore, another Romish priest (then a
Superior), who agreed that "the times were not for them nor had they a purse
wherewith to controvert the matter," and so the conveyance had better be given up.
[It is difficult to identify these two priests, as no names given in Foley's *Jesuits* seem
to correspond.] Mr. Gradwell further stated that Grace Bold died "within two
years last past" (*i.e.*, in 1685). He acknowledged the genuineness of various writings
signed by Robert Charnock and others, thus incidentally giving information, *e.g.*,
Susan Charnock, of Leyland, signs as a spinster on 13 Feb., 1659-60; the purchase
of Starkie's tenement [still known in Leyland] from Henry Wright took place on
Dec. 14, 1664; Mrs. Westbie lived at Leyland Hall "about five or six years agoe"
[1681-2] when M^ris Bold was reported as willing to sell the estate owing to her then
residence with her relations in Wales.
    Several other gentlemen and yeomen gave evidence, and among them we may
mention Mr. Christopher Anderton, of Clayton, gent., of the age of 60 years and
upwards; Mr. Alex. Butler, of Goderstaffe, co. Lanc., gent., of the age of 38 years
or thereabouts; Richard Sherdley, of Leyland, yeoman, &c., &c. Mrs. Susan
Orrell, of Leyland, widow, of the age of 80 years, was one of the sisters of Mr.
Charnock and probably the relict of Mr. Richard Orrell, whose name appears on
some of the writings certified to by Mr. Gradwell. The Letters Patent for the conveyance of the disputed lands, which was issued in 1690 under the Great Seal,
contains an enumeration of the fields included within the demesne mentioning them

A child of John Martinscroft, of Leyland ... ... } ffeb. 15
Margery, wife of Thomas Williamson, of Leyland }
William Taylor, of Whittle ... ... „ 22
Elsabeth Primott, of Leyland ... ... March 1
Richard Chetam, of ffarington ... ... „ 2
Edward, son of William Wielden, of Leyland ... ... „ 4
William Godman, of Mosse-side ... ... „ 5
William Sharples, of Leyland ... ... „ 7
m. Alexander Parke, of Leyland ... ... „ 10
The wife of William Cowper, of Cuerden ... ... „ 15
m. Peter Walkden, of Heapie ... ... „ 16
m. Oliuer Crosse, of Euxton ... ... „ 19
m. Katharin Clayton, of Leyland, widow ... ... „ 20
M^ris Taylor, of Euxton, widow ... ... } „ 21
m. Roger Worsley, of Wheelton ... ... }
George Lockar, at ffarington-hall[1] ... ... „ 22

[Burials] 1671.

Margrett, daughter of Thomas Starky, of Cuerden ... March 30
Edmund, son of James Garstang, of Whittle ... ... Aprill 1
Thomas, son of Richard Whittle, of Leyland ... ... „ 4
A child of Richard Dewhurst, of Raddlesworth[2] ... „ 8
Jane Stretbarrell, of ffarington ... ... „ 8
Ellin Dewhurst, of Winnell ... ... „ 12
A child of Thomas Porter, of Leyland ... ... „ 13
Mr Thomas Woodcock,[3] of Cuerden ... ... „ 14
John, son of John Jackson, of Cuerden... ... ... „ 21
Mary Euxton, of Leyland ... ... „ 24
John Tootell, of Whittle... ... ... „ 26
A child of Thomas Winnell, of Whittle ... ... „ 27
Ellin Tootle, of Whittle ... ... May 3

by name. The trustees named are as follows:—Sir Richard Standish, of Duxbury, Bart.; Sir Edw. Chisenhall, of Chisenhall, Knight; Henry ffarrington, of Werden, Esq.; George ffarrington, of Shaw Hall, Richard ffleetwood, of Leyland, John Woodcock, of Cuerden, gentlemen; Henry Garstang, of Heapey, Alexander Breres, of Whittle-le-Woods, and Hugh Armetriding, of Euxton, yeomen.

Mr. Charnock was buried in the family vault in the churchyard near to the east end of the parish church of Leyland, and the inscribed slab with a lengthy epitaph placed over him may still be seen. It will be found described in the Introduction.

[1] See note on p. 83.
[2] See page 103.
[3] Eldest son of Mr. John Woodcock, whose death is recorded on Aug. 17, 1655. He was an Out-Burgess of Preston at the Guilds of 1622, 1642, and 1662. His brothers, Francis and William, were also entered at the Guild of 1622. See notes on pages 15, 57.

Philip Bootle, of Leyland ... ... May		4
vx^r James Bromiley, of Clayton	} "	8
Widow Nelson, of Leyland		
Thomas Wielden, of Leyland...	} "	17
William Gerratt, of Tootell-Milne...		
Margrett Garstang, of Whittle, widow ... ... "		18
Ellin Breres, of Wheelton ... ... "		19
Edward Hodson, of Leyland...	} "	24
William Tootell, of Gleydhill[1]		
Jane Cliffe, of Clayton ... ... June		5
Thomas Munck, of Leyland ... ... "		9
Alice, daughter of Thomas Smith, of Leyland ... ... "		12
A child of John Bigans, of Whittle ... ... "		16
William, son of Adam Blakburne, of Cuerden ... ... "		18
Sarah, daught^r of John Beardsworth, of Leyland ... "		19
James, son of John Clough, of Leyland	} "	21
B. Henry, son of Richard Aspin, of Tockholes ...		
John Martin, of Clayton ... ... "		22
John Cowper, of Clayton	} "	30
Katharin Pope, of Clayton		
Richard, son of William Watson, of Whittle ... ... July		2
Jane, wife of John Sheardley, of ffarington ... ... "		3
John, son of John Cowper, of Clayton ... ... "		10
Sarah, daught^r of Richard Sheardley, of Leyland ... "		11
Mary, daught^r of Raphe Leyland, of Clayton ... ... "		12
A child of John Wright, of Leyland ... ... "		25
Thomas Haulgh, of Leyland ... ... Aug.		1
Raphe Pincock, of Whittle ... ... "		2
The wife of Richard Cowper, of Whittle ... ... "		4
Alice, wife of William Blakledge, of Whittle ... ... "		7
Anne ffisher, of Euxton, widow ... ... "		11
Peter Tootell,[2] Clarke of Leyland ... ... "		14
Mr Oliver Crichlow,[3] of Clayton, pr. [priest] ... ... "		29

[1] The name of a farm in Euxton, otherwise spelled Gleadhill. It lies near to the River Yarrow, and not far from the point at which the road from Preston to Wigan crosses it.

[2] See a memorandum respecting the ringing of the bells on page 22.

[3] In Foley's *Jesuits*, vol. vi., pp. 314, 317, 320, will be found a short account of three sons of Ralph Crichlow, senior, and Catherine Tootel, his wife, of the parish of Leyland. There were four sons and two daughters in the family, of whom three sons, William, Oliver, and Richard, were admitted and took the oath at Douay in successive years, 1627, 1628, and 1629. Condensing the information given we may say that the parents belonged to the middle class of society and were in moderate circumstances. "All their relations except one were Catholics." William, the eldest (born about 1600), after beginning his education took to mercantile pursuits until 23 years of age, when he again returned to his studies. On June 17, 1626, he left England. He was known "in religion" as William Foster. His ordination as

Alice, wife of William Watson, of Whittle	Sept.	2
William Slator, *als.* Cockar, of Mosse-side	„	8
Robert Cowper, of Cuerden	} „	16
Richard Howorth, of Whittle		
vx^r Thomas Waring, of Norbrooke[1]	„	19
A daughter of Oliuer Tootell, of Clayton	„	27
William Holmes, of Whittle	Oct.	9
A daughter of Oliuer Tootell, of Clayton	„	10
Ellin, daughter of Thomas Sharrok, of Euxton	„	21
Theophilus, son of Michaell Taylor, of Euxton	„	22
John, son of John Taylor, of Whittle	„	24
Katharin Smith, of ffarington	„	27
Anne, wife of Robert Hunt, of Hoole	„	29
Abraham, son of Raphe Johnson, of Cuerden	Nov.	3
Isabell, daught^r of William Cowper, of Cuerden... ...	„	4
A child of Thomas Thomas Cowper, of Cuerden	} „	6
A child of William Johnson, of Leyland		
Roger Crooke, of Leyland	} „	8
M^ris Margrett Rigby, of Euxton		
Margrett Werden, of Leyland	„	16
Alice, daught^r of John Jackson	„	19
Raphe Sharrok, of Clayton	„	20
Anne, daught^r of Henry Unsworth, of Euxton	„	24
The wife of Oliuer Tootell, of Clayton	„	26
Ellin, wife of William Jackson, of Whittle	„	28
Elsabeth Sharrok, of Clayton	„	30
Esther Sumner, of Ulneswalton	} Dec.	2
A child of John ffidler, of ffarington		

sub-deacon, deacon, and priest took place in September and October, 1631. After a few years he was sent to England, and left the College on April 2, 1634. He is spoken of as "a pious man and an example of all good." Oliver, the second brother [known as John Foster], his brother William, and others were arrested between London and Dover on their way to Douay about the year 1624, and were thrown into the Tower, from which a bribe of £20 effected their escape. Oliver was admitted to the College in 1628, when about 21 years of age, and received ordination as priest in 1634. On April 12, 1635, he was despatched to England as a missioner. He is described as "a man of remarkable virtue, distinguished for humility." Richard, the youngest son [known as Christopher Foster], was admitted to Douay in 1629, being then about 19 years old. He was ordained priest on April 15, 1634, and sent on the English mission in March, 1636. In the students' replies he states that he "studied at home until fourteen years of age; then, when on his way in company with others to prosecute his studies in Lower Germany, he was captured on the River Thames and taken back to London, and was detained there in gaol by the Archbishop of Canterbury, who examined him. Some months after, having obtained his liberty, he was compelled to return home. In the following year he went to London, seeing an opportunity of embarking; but the plague raged there, and he was compelled a second time to return home. He made his humanities at St. Omer's College for three years."

[1] A farm to the N.W. of Leyland township.

Ellin Sharrok, of Clayton ... ... Dec.		6
A bastard child of John Bradley, of Cuerden ... ... „		15
Robert ffarington, of ffarington ... ... „		18
Hugh Tootell, of Whittle ... ... „		26
Margrett Clough, of Leyland, widow ... ... „		27
Thomas, son of John Beardsworth, sen^r, of Leyland ... „		29
Dorathy, the wife of Thomas Sumner, of Mosse-side... Jan.		1
Jane, the wife of William Hornby, of Leyland ... ⎫		
A child of Thomas Leyland, of Leyland ... ... ⎬ „		3
Anne, the daught^r of James Martin, of Leyland... ... „		7
Elsabeth Taylor, of Clayton, widow ... ... ⎫		
Richard, son of Edward Tilsley, of Euxton... ... ⎬ „		12
A child of Thomas Waring, at Norbrooke[1]... ... ... „		14
Anne, daught^r of Robert ffarington, of Leyland... ... „		[2]15
Robert Almon, of Walton in le dale ... ... „		[2]16
Jennett, wife of Robert Adinson, of Leyland ... ⎫		
Jane Charnock, of Leyland ... ... ⎬ „		17
Robert Adinson, of Leyland ... ... ⎫		
The wife of William Godman, of Mosse-side ... ⎬ „		20
A child of William Miller, of Ulneswalton ... ... „		22
The wife of George Dawson, of Mosse-side... ... ... „		29
The wife of Richard Parke, of Middleford ... ... ffeb.		1
The wife of William ffarnworth, of Wheelton ... ⎫		
A child of William Blackburne, of Cuerden ... ⎬ „		5
A child of Euan Winnell, of Heapie ... ... „		7
John ffarington, of Cowood, in Yorkshire ... ... „		12
Will: son of John Okenshaw, of Euxton ... ... „		12
ffrances Grundy, of Ulneswalton ... ... ⎫		
Elsabeth Cowper, at Crooke ... ... ⎬ „		21
Roger, son of Roger Crooke, of Whittle ... ... „		25
The wife of Peter Walkden, of Heapie... ... ... „		26
William Wigans, of Cuerden ... ... „		29
A child of John Cockar, Junr, of Mosse-side ... ... March		3
A child of William Tootell, of Whittle... ... ... „		6
Thomas Johnson, of Heapie ... ... „		14
John Eastha^m, of Leyland ... ... „		18
Anne, daught^r of ffrances Grundy, of Ulneswalton ... „		20
Thomas Sharples, of Leyland ... ... „		22
vx^r William Garstang, of Whittle, Smith ... ... „		23

[1] See page 54, note (²).

[2] These two dates have been altered from 16 and 17, respectively, to 15 and 16, but probably by the original hand.

[Burials] 1672.

William, son of Will: Sergeant, of Leyland... ...	...March	26
A child of Thomas Hilton, of Wheeton	„	31
A child of James ffarington, of Leyland	...Aprill	1
The wife of John Martin, of Clayton	} „	8
The wife of Thomas Cliffe, of ffarington		
Robert Sumner, of Mosse-side	} „	11
Jennett Sergeant, of Leyland		
A daughter of John Rotchet, of Leyland	} „	12
A daughter of John Garstang, of Heapie		
Ellin, wife of Robert Cockar, of Mosse-side...	„	15
William Blakburne, of Cuerden	„	17
Elsabeth, wife of William Waterworth, of Leyland	} „	25
A child of Richard Broxop, of Euxton		
Elsabeth Hilton, of Wheelton, widow	„	27
James, son of James Sumner, of Euxton	„	29
William Dandy, of Cuerden	...May	1
A child of Thomas Martin, of Whittle...	„	11
A child of William Woodcock, of Leyland	„	12
A child of John Hodson, of Euxton	„	15
Richard, son of John Marsh, of Mosse-side	„	16
Elsabeth, daughter of James Cockar, of Clayton ...	„	20
m. William Watson, of Whittle	} „	21
William, son of William Hornby, of Leyland ...		
A child of Richard Parke, of Leyland		
A child of William Moncke, of Leyland	„	23
Dorathy, the wife of Ellis Sumner, of Leyland	...June	2
m. Lawrance Garstang, of Whittle	} „	5
m. William Chorley, of Leyland		
A child of John Cliffe, of Bretherton	„	9
The wife of John Blakburne, of Cuerden	„	18
Mr. Raphe ffarnworth,[1] of Euxton	...July	2
The wife of William ffishwick, of Winnell	„	7
A child of John ffidler, of ffarington	„	29
Elsabeth, daughtr of Richard Chetam, of ffarington ...	Aug.	6
A child of Richard Sheardley, of ffarington	„	13
Anne, wife of Thomas Butler, of Clayton	„	20
Elsabeth Anderton, at Werden	...Sept.	6
A child of John Eastham, of ffarington	„	9
The wife of Thomas Starkie, of Cuerden	„	24

[1] Probably identical with a gentleman of this name entered as an In-Burgess of Preston at the Guild of 1662. Others of the family appear at later Guilds. See notes on pp. 58, 62.

m. Hugh Armettriding, of Euxton ... ... Sept. 28
The wife of William Crooke, of Maudsley ... ... Oct. 5
Peter Charnock, of Ulneswalton ... ... „ 8
m. William ffarington, of Leyland, webster... ... ... „ 11
Thomas Jackson, of Leyland... ... ... „ 18
Alice, wife of William Chetam, of ffarington ... ... „ 19
m. Henry Brining, of Whittle ... ... Nov. 13
John ffidler, of ffarington ... ... „ 15
William Waring, of Ulneswalton ... ... „ 26
Ruth Leekas, of Whittle, widow ... ... Dec. 12
A child of Roger Brining, of Whittle ... ... „ 13
George Crooke, of Heapie ... ... „ 27
Agnes Tomlinson, of ffarington, widow ... ... Jan. 3
vxr Johannis Bootle, de Leyland ... ... „ 4
Marke Couper, a stranger, died in Euxton ... ... „ 6
Alice, wife of John Powell, a passenger in Euxton ... „ 10
m. William Sumner, of Lostocke... ... ... „ 27
vxr Edwardi Clayton, de ffarington ... ... „ 28
Margrett Brereley, of Raddlesworth ... ... „ 30
William Crichlowe, of Whittle ... ... ffeb. 1
Henry Allinson, of Euxton ... ... „ 10
m. William Cowper, of Leyland ... ... } „ 17
Christopher, son of Robert Sumner, of Leyland... }
m. William ffarington, of Leyland, taylor ... ... „ 23
William ffarington,[1] of Werden, Esq. ... ... „ 27
William Chetam, of ffarington ... ...March 11
Alice, wife of Robert Harrison, of Leyland... ... ... „ 17
Thomas, son of Charles Whitehead, of Leyland... ... „ 24

[Burials] 1673.

m. Elsabeth Mearley, of Cuerden, widow ... ...March 26
Robert, son of John Wielden, of ffarington ... ... „ 28

---

[1] William ffarrington, of Worden, Esq., was the eldest son of the High Sheriff of 1636 and his wife Margaret (Worral), and succeeded to the family estates in 1658. He and his father were very actively engaged during the Civil War on the King's behalf. It is often difficult to distinguish these gentlemen in the accounts, owing to the identity of name; but William ffarington the younger is meant when we read of the doings of Captain ffarrington. Both assisted in the defence of Lathom House. The elder is usually called "the Royalist," or "Colonel ffarrington." At the restoration the honour of admission among the proposed Knights of the Oak was intended for Captain ffarrington had not the scheme been abandoned. His name is found among the Foreign Burgesses on the Preston Guild Rolls for 1622, 1642, 1662. By his wife Katherine (ffleetwood) he had two sons (perhaps three) and four daughters. He was one of the parties to the deed of settlement, &c., respecting the Almshouses mentioned on page 207. His will (dated Feb. 20, 1672) was proved at Chester in 1673.

Ellin Charnley, of Cuerden	...March	29
A child of William Southworth, of Leyland	„	30
m. Richard Slator, of Euxton	Aprill	4
Jennett Wigans, of Cuerden, widow	„	5
A child of Richard Slator, of Euxton	„	10
Margrett, wife of William Jackson, of Leyland	„	19
A child of John Wielden, of ffarington...	„	20
John Starkie, of Cuerden	„	25
Margrett Withnell, of Euxton	„	26
ffrancis Eastham, of Walton	} May	6
Agnes Hough, of Whittle, widow		
Anne ffishwick, of Winnell, widow	} „	8
Alexand^r, son of John Baron, of Euxton		
Mary ffarington, of Leyland	...June	2
A child of John Neuitts, of Heapie	„	25
Abraham, son of Richard Clough, of Leyland	...July	3
A child of Thomas Hilton, of Wheelton	„	18
M^{ris} Alice Rigby, of Euxton	„	20
Margrett, daught^r of Ellis Sumner, of Euxton	„	21
A child of John Crooke, of Euxton	Aug.	7
The wife of Thomas Walmersley, of Euxton	Sept.	11
A child of Thomas Blundell, of ffarington	„	12
m. John Rotchet, of Mosse-side	„	22
Elsabeth, daught^r of William Wielden, of Leyland ...	„	23
The wife of Roger Cliffe, of Whittle	„	30
Eleanor Waring, of Leyland	Oct.	1
A child of Thomas Walmersley, *als.* ffranks, of Euxton	„	23
Elsabeth, wife of Richard Eastham, of Chorley	„	29
William Atherton, of Leyland	Nov.	vi.
A child of John Eastham, of ffarington	„	23
Richard, son of Richard Chetam, of ffarington	Dec.	5
m. George Abbot, of Heapie...	„	18
A child of Richard ffarington, of ffarington...	„	19
The wife of James Brindle, of Wheelton	„	20
A child of James Ugno, of Wheelton	Jan.	17
Roger Starkie, of Cuerden	„	24
A child of Mathew Walkden, of Heapie	„	28
James, son of Robert Whittle, of ffarington...	ffeb.	7
m. William Leekas, of Whittle	} „	16
A child of Thomas Calderbank, of Leyland ...		
The wife of William Silcock, of Withnell	„	17
The son of William Garstang, of Whittle	„	23
A child of Lawrance Piccop, of Heapie	March	7
William Garstang, of Euxton, a servant	„	12
William, son of William Atherton, of Leyland	„	14

Roger Cliffe, of Whittle ... ...March 15
John Blacburne, of Cuerden ... ... „   19
A daught^r of John Jackson, of Ulneswalton   ... ... „   21

[Burials] 1674.

Anne, daughter of William Atherton, of Leyland   ...March 28
John Gerratt, of Tootel-milne   ... ... ⎫
Thomas, son of John Wielden, of Leyland ... ... ⎬ Aprill 4
Henry, son of Ellis Bolton, of Leyland   ... ... „   11
William, son of William Woodcock, of Euxton ... ... May   2
Ellin, daughter of William Tasker, of ffarington... ... „   18
m. Richard Cowper, of Crooke in Whittle ... ... „   20
A child of John Cheshire, of ffarington   ... ...June 20
Thomas, son of Arthur Dawson, of ffarington ... ...July   4
Dorathy, wife of Charles Whitehead, of Leyland ... „   13
Hugh, son of Mr Hugh Bonkin,[1] of Leyland   ... ... „   20
m. Thomas Butler, of Clayton   ... ... „   28
A child of William Cowper, of Cuerden   ... ...Aug.   5
Jane, daught^r of Henry Heald, of Leyland ... ... „   8
William Pincock, Junr, of Whittle... ... ... „   13
William ffarnworth, of Wheelton ... ...Sept. 12
Elsabeth Walton, of Howick,[2] died at Ellis Sumners... Oct.   6
Richard, son of Tho: Withington, of Clayton   ... ...Nov.   9
John Beardsworth, of Leyland, sen^r ... ... ⎫
Dorathy Rothwell, of Whittle, widow ... ... ⎬ „   10
Ellin, wife of Will: ffoster, of Charnock[3]   ... ...Dec.   7
Anne, wife of Ellis Bolton, of Leyland... ... ... „   15
m. George Carter, of Leyland   ... ... „   22
Elsabeth, wife of Arthur Dewhurst, in Wheelton   ... „   27
Elsabeth, wife of Thomas Pilkinton, of Leyland... ...Jan. 11
Alice ——, wife of Richard Hodson, of Euxton... ... „   19
Elsabeth, wife of Raphe Pincock, of Whittle   ... ⎫
Anne ——, wife of James Haugh, of Leyland   ... ⎬ „   22
Jane, wife of Thomas Winnell, of Whittle ... ... „   28
m. Elizabeth Hilton, of Leyland, widow   ... ...ffeb. 24
Robert Whittle, of ffarington... ... ... „   27
Thomas Watson, of Raddlesworth   ... ...March 2
Jennett, daught^r of Richard Calderbank, of Euxton ... „   23

---

[1] Mr. Hugh Bonkin was probably the master of the Leyland Grammar School at this date.   See Introduction; also entries on Sept. 27, 1670, and March 28, 1681.

[2] Howick is a township in Penwortham parish.

[3] Charnock Richard, in Standish parish.

Burialls, 1675.

Elsabeth Garstang, of Ulneswalton	...March	31
Anne Miller, of Ulneswalton, widow	...Aprill	1
m. Anne Sumner, of Lostock, widow	„	3
Jane, wife of William Wigans, of Cuerden	„	17
m. Euan Whittle, of Leyland	„	22
William Walmersley, of Leyland	...May	8
Anne Greyson, of Leyland	„	11
Nicholas,[1] son of M[r] Rishton, of Euxton	„	29
m. ——, wife of George Crooke, of Heapie...	June	10
Raphe, son of John Lowe, of Euxton	„	12
m. Thomas Winnell, of Winnell	„	19
Jane Pendlebury, of Whittle, widow	„	21
Jennett, daught[r] of Thomas Blundell, of ffarington ...	„	26
m. Raphe Partington, of Clayton	...July	3
A child of Richard Jackson, of Cuerden	„	3
William, son of Thomas ffarnworth, of ffiswick[2]... ...	„	10
John, son of John Martinscroft, of Leyland... ...	...Aug.	10
——, son of Richard Slator, of Euxton	„	13
Elsabeth Chetam, of ffarington	„	23
vx[r] John Whittle, of Whittle	„	24
m. Richard Calderbank, of Euxton	Sept.	10
The wife of Thomas Silcock, of Winnell[3]	„	15
Ellin Whittle, of ffarington, widow	„	19
Lawrance Piccopp, of Heapie	„	20
Elizabeth, wife of Richard Sheardley, of ffarington ...	„	22
Henry, son of Thomas Croston, of Ulneswalton... ...	„	23
m. Agnes ffarington, of Leyland, widow	Oct.	26
Jennett, daught[r] of James Haughton, of Charnock ...	„	31
Ellin, wife of Thomas Jackson, of Leyland	Nov.	3
Henry Parke, of ffarington	„	7
Elsabeth, daught[r] of John Wright, of Leyland	„	11
Thomas Miller, of Clayton ... ... }	„	13
John Worsley, of Heapie		
Margrett, wife of Robert Hodson, of Euxton	„	16
vx[r] Euan Winnell, of Whittle	„	23
m. James Howorth, of Heapie	„	24

[1] This child was baptised in April, 1674. The father is then described as "Mr. John Rishton, Curate of Eccleston, now living in Leyland." Mr. Rishton was related to the Andertons, of Euxton Hall. He became Vicar of Leyland in 1677.

[2] ffishwick, a township in the parish of Preston, now included in the parliamentary borough.

[3] Winnell for Withnell.

Jennett More, of Euxton, widow ... ... Dec.		3
Robert Sergeant, of Mosse-side ... ... „		7
Thomas Eyues, of Leyland ... ... „		11
A daught^r of Richard Sheardley, of ffarington ... .. „		15
m. Richard Stopford, of Leyland ... ... „		21
Mary, wife of Richard Whittle, of ffarington ... ... „		29
Elsabeth, daught^r of Thomas Winnell, of Whittle ... „		30
A child of Thomas Winnell, of Whittle ... ... Jan.		3
m. Edward Woodcocke, of Euxton ... ... „		4
Richard Wigans, of Leyland ... ... „		6
Hugh Tootell, of Gleadhill, in Euxton ... ... „		13
A child of George Garstang, of Whittle ... ... „		22
Ellin, daught^r of Richard Parker, of ffarington ... ... „		26
John, son of John Garstang, *als.* Smith... ... ... „		27
Margrett, daught^r of Richard Loxam, of Ulneswalton.. ffeb.		1
A child of Thomas Sumner, of Mosse-side ... ... „		2
William Jackson, died at Werden ... ... „		3
Thomas Cowper, of Leyland ... ... „		11
A child of Thomas Winnell, of Whittle ... ... „		12
m. Mr John Robinson,[1] of Euxton ... ... „		15
Alice, wife of Henry Garstang, of Whittle ... ... „		19
Margrett, wife of William Whitehead, of Leyland ... „		22
John Nelson, of Leyland ... ... „		26
A child of John Breres, of Wheelton ... ... „		27
Ellis, son of William Jackson, of Whittle ... ... March		1
James, son of John Roscow, of Euxton ... ... „		2
John Roscow, of Euxton... ... ... „		13
William Hornby, of Leyland ... ... „		14
Jane, wife of Thomas Sumner, of Leyland ... ... „		18
Thomas Waring, of Leyland ... ... „		20
Anne, wife of Henry Garstang, of Heapy ... ... } „		22
William Dandy, at Cuerden-hall ... ... }		
m. Ellin Balshaw, of Leyland, widow ... ... „		23
Euan Eastham, of ffarington ... ... „		24

[Burials] 1676.

James, son of Richard Sheardley, of Leyland ... ... March 25		
Mary Leyland, of Leyland ... ... } „ 31		
——, son of Hugh Crooke, of Whittle ... ... }		
Thomas, son of Edward Sergeant, of Leyland ... ... Aprill 18		

[1] The eldest son of Major Edward Robinson, cf Buckshaw in Euxton. He was entered as a Foreign Burgess at the Preston Guild of 1662 with his brother Edward. His wife was Alice, daughter of Thomas Birch, of Birch, Esquire. See pp. 23, 26.

Dorathy Rigby, of Wrightington,[1] widow ... ... Aprill 23
Ellin, wife of William Hilton, of Wheelton ... ... ,, 29
John Bootle, of Leyland ... ... May 1
Ellin, wife of William Hodson, of Leyland ... ... ,, 5
William Dandy,[2] of Lostock ... ... ,, 6
Alice Garstang, of Leyland ... ... ,, 10
Jane Grimsditch, of Almes-house[3] ... ... ,, 11
m. John Whittle, of Raddlesworth ... ... ,, 20
John, son of M[r] James Murrey ... ... ,, 22
Thomas, son of Raph Leyland, of Clayton ... ... June 8
A son of John Cockar, Jun[r], of Mosse-side ... ... ,, 15
Christoph[r] Litherland, of Whittle ... ... ,, 16
Anne, wife of Thomas Watson, of Raddlesworth ... ... ,, 17
Anne Hodson, of Leyland, widow... ... ... July vi
John Clough, of Leyland ... ... ⎫
Margrett, daught[r] of Thomas Ugno, of Wheelton ⎬ ,, 15
Isabell Winnell, of Whittle, widow ... ... ,, 16
Elsabeth, daught[r] of George Dawson, of Mosse-side ... ,, 22
Margrett Thornley, of Heapie, widow ... ... Aug. 7
Jennett, wife of Robert Martin, of Winnell ... ... ,, 19
m. Robert Cockar, of Clayton ... ... ,, 25
Thomas Woodcock, of Walton in le dale ... ... ,, 26
John Marsden, of Raddlesworth ... ... ,, 28
Anne, wife of James Armettriding, of Whittle ... ... Sept. 9
Robert, son of Robert Pilkinton, of Leyland ... ... ,, 12
M[r] William Rothwell,[4] Vicar of Leyland ... ... ,, 16

[The handwriting changes at this point.]

Thomas Jackson, of Ulneswalton ... ... ,, 16
Thomas Martin, of Wheelton... ... ... ,, 18
George, son of Will: Boydell, of Euxton ... ... ,, 22
Robert, son of Thomas Cooper, of Walton in le dale... ,, 25
John Hilton, of Wheelton ... ... ,, 27
Jane, daughter of John Browne, of farrington ... ... Oct. 11
m. John, son of Mr. James Morres, of farrington ... ,, 26
George Waddington, of oullerton [Ollerton] ... ... ,, 28
——, the wife of George Abbott, of Heapy... ... ... ,, 28

[1] A township in Eccleston parish. Now a separate parish under the Blandford Act.

[2] There is a large slab lying in Leyland churchyard, near to the Grammar School, with an inscription running round the edge in Longobardic characters, which records the decease of William Dandy, of Lostock, on May 3, 1676, aged 27 years.

[3] See pp. 182, 207.

[4] Mr. Rothwell was vicar from 1650–1676. His predecessor was the Rev. James Langley, and his successor the Rev. John Rishton. See Introduction, under List of Vicars.

Robert Dawson, of Leyland ... ... Oct. 29
Henry Woodcock, of Ulnswalton ... ... „ 29
Thomas, son of Edmond Balshaw, of Leyland ... ... „ 31
Elsabeth, widow Beery,[1] oth height in moore quarter... Nov. 8
James Houghton, of Charnock ... ... „ 9
Ellin Brineing, of Whittell ... ... „ 9
Elsabeth Whittle, of Leyland... ... ... „ 27
Mr. Roger Pearson, of ffarrington hall[2] ... ... „ 27
James Crichlow, of Wheelton... ... ... „ 29
Hugh, son of Edward Woodcock, of Euxton ... ... Dec. 2
Thomas ffild, of ffarrington, and ... ... ⎫
m. Robert Hodson, of Euxton ... ... ⎭ „ 8
Ellisabeth Asley, of Whittle ... ... „ 26
Richard Wright, of Euxton ... ... „ 27
Elsabeth, daughter of John ffarrington, of ffarrington... Jan. 5
Alice Dewherst, of Cuerden ... ... „ 8
m. John Melling, of Whittell... ... ... „ 14
Edward Raineford, of Clayton ... ... „ 19
Ann, wife of William ffarnworth, of Weelton ... ... „ 20
Robert Willden, of ffarington... ... ... „ 27
Robert, son of John Cliffe, of Longton ... ... „ 27
Elsabeth, the wife of John Melling, of Whittell ... ... „ 28
m. William Duckson, of Leyland ... ... „ 29
m. Mary Woodcock, of Euxton ... ... ⎫
Ann Nelson, of Leyland... ... ... ⎭ „ 31
James, sone of Olliuer Martin, of Welton ... ... ffeb. 2
James, son of Roger Dewhurst, of Cuerden... ... ... „ 3
Jane, the wife of Thomas Hoome, of Exton ... ... „ 6
Margrett, the wife of William Duckson, of Leyland ... „ 19
Thomas Martine, of Heapey, Buried ye ... ... „ 20
Richard Kennion, of Heapey... ... ... „ 22
Mary Eastham, of Whittlell ... ... „ 23
m. Sisley, the wife of James Soñar [Somner], of
Euxton ... ...March 14
m. William Sharrocke, of Euxton... ... ... „ 25

[Burials] 1677.

Jennett Whaley, of Leyland ... ...March 31
Thomas, sone of Raph Lowe, of Wittle ... ... April 9
m. Hugh Poope, of Clayton ... ... „ 15

---

[1] For Berry, or Bury, which is a common name in the hill districts lying on the eastern side of Leyland parish.

[2] See note on page 83.

Olliuer, son of Jeffery Taylor, of Heapey ... ... April 25
John Wiggans, of Cuerden ... ... „ 28
Thomas, son of William Assley, of Whittle... ... ... „ 30

[The thirteen entries which now succeed are in a different and more modern hand. On Sept. 8 the former scribe resumes.]

m: pap: [papist] William Woodcock, of Euxton... ⎫
Robert Martin, of Wheelton ... ... ⎬ May 4
Alice, wife of Will: {Slater[1] / Cockar} of Moss side... ... ⎭

m. William Mellin, of Euxton ... ... „ 5
Alice, wife of Robert Harrison, of Leyland... ... ... „ 15
Will: Maudsley, son of John Maudsley,[2] of Leyland... „ 19
Elizabeth Kenion, of Heapay ... ... „ 20
Jane, wife of William Leyland, of Leyland... ... ... „ 24
Thomas, son of Ralph Ellison, of heapay ... ... „ 25
Helen, daughter of Ralph Smith, of ffarrington ... ... „ 26
Helen Pilkington, of Whitle, widdow ... ... „ 27

[No entries in June.]

Thomas Bolton, of Cureden ... ... July 8
William ffarrington, of ffarrington... ... ... Aug. 3
Richard Armerydinge, of Euxton... ... ... Sept. 8
Anne, the wife of Richard Kenion, of Heapey ... ... Oct. 13
William Cartmell, of Clayton ... ... „ 17
m. William Ockenshaw, of Euxton ... ... „ 19
m. William Willden, of Leyland ... ... „ 23
Anne, the wife of Richard Sharrocke, of Euxton ... Nov. 1
Joshua Waireing, of Leyland... ... ... „ 2
James Low, of Wellton [Wheelton] ... ... „ 10
Anne, the wife of Georg Woodcock, of Euxton ... ... „ 12
William, son of William Clough, of Leyland ... ... „ 21
William, son of Richard Richmond, of More quarter... „ 22
William ffarneworth, of Wheeleton ... ... „ 24
Widdow Brandwood, of Winnell ... ... Jan. 7
Annes Pope, of Whittle ... ... „ 13
William Pincock, of Euxton ... ... „ 14
Robert, son of Thomas Cooper, of Leyland... ... ... „ 19
Ann, the wife of John Woomell, of Wheelton ... ... Feb. 1

[1] This may indicate that the man was known by either of these names, as is now commonly the case with an eldest son born before his parents' marriage.

[2] Possibly the son of Mr. Wm. Mawdsley and his wife Ellen. If so, was aged 16 years at the herald's visitation in 1664. See note on page 185.

P

m. James Cooper, of Cuerden ... ... } Feb. 4
Margrett, wife of Robert Cooper, of Cuerden ... }
Roger, son of Lawrance Whittle, of ffarrington ... ... „ 9
William Banckcroft, of Wheelton ... ... „ 18
John Cheshire, of ffarrington... ... ... „ 19
Mary, wife of Thomas Pilkinton, of Leyland ... }
Annes, wife of James Chrichlow, of Winnell ... } „ 26

[Inserted at the bottom of the page in different handwriting.]

Mary, daughter of John Harrison, of Clayton, Bu: 12
decemb., 83. [Entered also in its right place.]
Robert, yᵉ son of Richard Wiggans, [of] Whittel,
January 6, 84. [Entered also in its right place.]

Ellin Sharrock, of Clayton ... ... March 2
Jennett, yᵉ wife of Richard Caulderbanck, of Euxton.. „ 9
Mary, daughter of Thomas Winnell, of Whittle ... ... „ 21
Ellizabeth, yᵉ wife of Richard Haworth, of Whittle ... „ 26
a child of Matthew Walkdens, of Heapey ... ... „ 27

1678.

James Garstang, of Whittle ... ... Aprill 8
Jane, the wife of William Clough, of Leyland ... ... „ 17
Ellizabeth, daughter of Richard Tootell, of Whittle ... „ 20
Joney, the wife of Peter Tootell: Late Clark of Leyland „ 21
Ann, the wife of Thomas Woodcock, of Walton in Lae
Dalle ... ... „ 23
Ellsabeth Southworth, of Whittle ... ... „ 25
Elizabeth Biggans, of Whitle, wid: ... ... May 3
John Beardsworth, of Leyland ... ... „ 6
Thomas, son of Thomas ffild, of ffarrington... ... ... „ 13
John ffiswick, of Withnell ... ... }
Robert Taylour, of Euxton ... ... } „ 14
Thomas, son of Will: Whitehead, of Ulneswalton ... „ 20
m. William Wild, of Clayton... ... ... June 4
William, son of Ralph Leyland, of Clayton... ... ... „ 12
m. Nathaniel Woodworth, of Leyland... ... ... „ 14
m. George Bury, of Euxton ... ... „ 17
Jane Chrichlow, of Euxton ... ... „ 23
Elizabeth Armetriding ... ... „ 29
John, son of William Assley, of Whittle ... ... July 2
Margret Parke, of Leyland Mosse Side ... ... „ 12
Margarett Longton, of Keurden, wid: ... ... „ 14

Henry,[1] eldest son of Henry ffarington, of Werden,
Died ye 13, Buried ye 17 of July ... ... July 17
Helen Clayton ... ... „ 20
Margery, ye wife, &c.: More Quart^r ... ... „ 25
Isabel Abbott, of Leyland ... ... ⎫
Christoph^r, son of Robert Woodroof, of Whitle ... ⎬ Aug. 11
Elizabeth Nelson, of Leyland ... ... ⎭
Richard, son of Thomas Clough, of Leyland ... ... „ 28
m. Arthur Dewhurst, of Withnell ... ... „ 30
Alice Calderbank ... ... Sept. 6
Margarett, wife of Thomas Whitle, of ffarington ... „ 20
Thomas, son of Thomas Morris, of Heapey ... ... Oct. 5
Will: ffiswick, of Withnell ... ... „ 17
——, son of Oliver Martin, of Wheelton ... ... „ 23
Helen, Daught^r of James Gorton, of Clayton ... ... „ 26
Alice, Daught^r of Thomas Biby, of Withnell .. ... Nov. 2
M^r ffrancis Woodcock,[2] of Keurden ... ... „ 12
Izabel Loxom, of ffarrington ... ... „ 15
ELizabeth, Daugh^r of Will: Stevenson ... ... „ 23
Mis Elizabeth Anderton,[3] of Clayton ... ... Dec. 18
Will: Chrichlow, of Leyland ... ... Jan. 9
Ellen fforshaw ... ... „ 14
Margery Martin ... ... „ 21
Elizabeth Richmond, of Withnell ... ... Feb. 3
Jeffcory, son of John Taylor, of Whittle ... ... „ 6
Elizabeth, daughter of Ralfe Johnson, of Whittle ... „ 20
Elizabeth, daughter of Robert Torner, of Leyland ... „ 26
Thomas, son of Samuell Halle, of ffarrington ... ... March 12

[1] The Henry ffarington whose burial is here recorded was baptised at Leyland on July 17, 1655. He married Anne, daughter of Henry Dicconson, of Wrightington (in Eccleston parish), and died without issue and before his parents. His mother was Susan, daughter of Degory Weare, D.D., Professor of History at Oxford. His father was the son and heir of William ffarington, Esq. (the proposed Knight of the Oak), and his wife Katharine (ffleetwood).

[2] Mr. ffrancis Woodcock was the second son of John Woodcock, gent., of Cuerden (Crowtrees). He was entered with his father and brothers, Thomas and William, at the Preston Guild of 1622. In 1642 the youngest brother was not entered with them. John Woodcock, the father, was dead in 1662 (? buried at Leyland, Aug. 17, 1655), but the eldest son, Thomas (brother of ffrancis), was entered at that Guild as "of Cuerden Green, Gent." There is an entry of a "ffrancis Woodcock de Walton," with sons John and Thomas, at that same Guild. Possibly this person may be identical with the gentleman whose burial is here recorded.

[3] Probably an unmarried daughter of James Anderton, of Clayton, Esq. Her name is mentioned in a deed of conveyance (made in July, 1655) whereby her father sold to Robert Low, of Whittle, sundry property of which the latter had been tenant. Four brothers and four sisters are named in the deed.

[Burials] 1679.

James Somner, of Leyland de Nocke[1]... ... ...March 26
m. William Croock, of Leyland ... ...Aprill 1

Lawrance Boulton, of Ceuerdon ... ... ⎫
Ralph, son of Richard Tootell, of Whittle ... ... ⎬ „ 7
William, son of William Wright, of Euxton ... ⎭

John Cliff, of Longton ... ... ⎫ „ 12
Elnor: daughter of Robert Cooper, of Ceuerden... ⎭

John Person, of Heapey...	„	13
m. James Marsden, of Winnell	„	14
Elizabeth Coopper, of Ceurden, widow...	„	15
James Dickenson, of Leyland	„	22
Mis Eleanor Ande[r]ton,[2] of Clayton	„	22
m. James Bury, of Withnel	„	25
Ralph, son of John Hilton, of Leyland	„	28

Allis, daughter of John Richmond, of Winnell ... ⎫ May 13
Ann, the wife of John Beardsworth, of Leyland... ⎭

William, son of William Tootell, of Whitlee (*sic*) ...	„	16
[(Crossed out) Thomas, son of Thomas Martin, of Heapey...	„	18]
Hugh Brindle, of Heapey	„	28
Jane, wife of William Clayton, of ffarington ... ...June		1
Sissaly Garstang, of Chorley	„	2
Ellin Rigby [Crichlow crossed out], of Leyland, widow	„	4
Allis, wife of John Miller, of Clayton	„	7
Mr Thomas Singleton,[3] died at Clayton halle	„	9
John ffarrington, of ffarrington	„	12
Allis, the wife of John Garnor, of ffarrington	„	19
Jenatt Woodcock, of Ulneswalton...	„	25
Aggnus Entwisley, of Winnell ... ...July		7
James,[4] son of Mr William Rothwell, who died ye 5 and was Buried ye 7 day of July	„	7
Margery, Daughter of Thomas Somner, of Leyland ...	„	9
Margrett, the wife of William Poope, of Whittle... ...	„	21
Katterin, daughter of Henry Watterworth, of Ulneswalton	„	26

[1] A farm. See page 68, note (²).

[2] Another daughter of James Anderton, Esq., of Clayton, mentioned in the deed of 1655. See note, Dec. 18, 1678.

[3] Mr. Thos. Singleton, of Staining-in-the-Fylde, married Dorothy, daughter of James Anderton, of Clayton, Esq.

[4] Son of Vicar Rothwell. Was baptised by his father on May 8, 1653. See the entry on page 25.

Hugh Parker, of Charnock, in ye pish of Standish ... July 27
Dorathy, the wife of Thomas Blundell, of ffarrington... „ 30
Ann, daughter of William Crooke, of Whittle ... ... Aug. 26
William Houlmes, of Leyland Moss-side ... ... „ 28
John Smith, a traueler, died in Ceurden ... ... „ 29
Richard, son of James Morris, of Heapey ... ... „ 31
Ann, the daughter of Richard Clough, of Leyland ... Sept. 3
Allis Somner, of Leyland, widdow ... ... „ 8
Edward, son of William Woodcock, of Ulneswalton ... „ 26
Jennat, the wife of John Werden, of Leyland ... ... „ 29
Jane, the wife of William Tasker, of ffarington ... ... Oct. 14
Magery, the daughter of William Willden, of ffarington „ 29
John, son of Thomas Somner, of Leyland leane... ... Nov. 14
Ann, daughter of Adam Eastham, of Walton in le dale „ 15
Ann, the wife of Adam Eastham, of Walton in le dale. „ 21
Lawrance Tomlinson, of ffarington ... ... „ 23
Allis, daughter of William Stephenson, of Whittle ... „ 27
Robert Walsh, of ffarington ... ... Dec. 2
John Godbeard, of Leyland ... ... „ 14
John Slaytor, senior, of Leyland Moss-side... ... ... „ 16
Jane, ye wife of Richard Armatryding, of Euxton ... „ 17
Elizabeth, ye wife of Andrew Stones, of Leyland ... „ 19
Ann, ye wife of Hugh Martin, of Leyland ... ... „ 20
Jennatt, the daughter of John Chesshire, of ffarington.. „ 27
James Dutton, of Scharsbrick, died in ffarington ... „ 29
Susan Watterworth, widow, of Ulneswalton ... ... Jan. 4
Jane Hodson, of Calbeck, of Euxton ... ... „ 4
Mary, daughter of John Biggans, of Leyland ... ... „ 12
William, son of John Modsley, of Leyland ... ... Feb. 4
Allis, daughter of James Holmes, of Ulneswalton ... „ 13
Allis, daughter of Robert Garnor, of Longton ... ... „ 19
Jennett, ye daughter of William Woodcock, of Euxton „ 20
Edmond Balshaw, of Leyland ... ... March 8
Arthur Dewhurst, of Winnell, senior ... ... „ 11
William Leyland, of ffarington ... ... „ 25

[Crowded in at the bottom of a page in the original.]

Charles Caddock [Rothwell[1] crossed out], a traueler,
    Bureyed ye 6: ffebruary, 1683.
Thomain Wright, of Ulneswoton: ffebruary ye 9: 1684.

---

[1] Charles Rothwell (? the eldest son of Vicar Rothwell) was the parish clerk at this time. Probably he made some of the entries of this year, and so inadvertently wrote his own name. There are two different handwritings—one a modified court hand, and the other an easy running hand.

𝕭urialls, 1680.

Henry, son of Henry Barshall, of Euxton	Aprill	5
Jency, yᵉ wife of Edward Longton, of ffarington ...	„	4
John, yᵉ son of Richard Sherdley, of ffarington	„	10
Mary, yᵉ wife of Thomas Clough, of Leyland	„	11
Jane, yᵉ wife of William Howorth, of Whittell	„	17
m. William Houghton, of Leyland	„	24
William, son of Thomas Martin, of Whittle...	„	26
Kattering,[1] daughter of Mʳ Henry ffarington, Esq. ...	„	29
Margreat, yᵉ wife of Mathew Walckden, of Hepey ...	May	3
James Houlmes, of Ulneswalton	„	7
Sara, the wife of James Houlmes, of Ulneswalton ...	„	26
James, yᵉ Son of John Jackson, of Ceuerden	June	3
William Burscow, of Leyland	„	8
m. Richard Winnell, of Euxton	„	12
m. William Garstang, of Norbanck fould in Wittell ...	„	16
James & ⎫ twins of Roger ffishwick, of Winnell ... ... Thurstan,⎭	„	27
Kattering ffild, of ffarrington...	July	3
Kattering Greene, of Leyland, spinster	„	10
Mary & ⎫ daughters of William Wrigh[t], of Alker in Euxton Ellen, ⎭	„	12
William Tasker, of ffarrington	„	13
Georg, son of William Shaw, of Leyland	„	18
m. Thomas Cooper, of Leyland, smith...	„	19
Thomas Cliffe, of ffarrington	„	24
Ellis Leuer, of Leyland	„	28
Ellin, daughter of John Garrett, ffarington	Aug.	1
Margret, daughter of William Burscow, of Leyland ...	„	11
A child of Richard Hillton, of Euxton	„	22
Christopher Cennion [Kenyon], of Hepey	„	29
Ann Breeres, of Wheelton	„	31
Margeret, daughter of Mʳ Georg ffarington[2]	Sept.	9
Ellis, son of Robert Somner, of Ulneswalton	„	11
m. John Hillton, of Wheelton	„	23
A child of Thomas Cheetham, of ffarington...	„	24
Mary, yᵉ daughter of Georg Woodcock, of Euxton ...	Oct.	1

---

[1] Daughter of Henry ffarington, Esq., and his wife Susanna (Weare). See note on entry, 17 July, 1678.

[2] Mr. George ffarington, of Shawe Hall, here mentioned, was the second son of William ffarington, Esq., and Katherine (ffleetwood) his wife. Mr. George ffarington married Elizabeth, daughter of Valentine Whitmore, of Thurstaston, co. Chester. Their daughter Margaret, whose burial is here recorded, died unmarried and (apparently) an infant.

James, son of Richard Walton, of ffarrington ... ... Oct. ii
Richard Sharrock, of Euxton ... ... ,, 16
John Jackson, of Cuerden ... ... ,, 22
m. Thomas Blackledg, of Leyland ... ... Nov. 3
Margret, ye wife of Roger Sharples, of Leyland... ... ,, 14
Ann Parke, of Midleforth ... ... ,, 23
John, son of John fforshaw, of Leyland ... ... ⎫
——, daughter of Roger Cliffe, of ffarington ... ⎬ Dec. 5
Hugh, son of Will: Tasker, of ffarington ... ... ⎭
Allis, ye wife of John Jackson, of Leyland ... ... ,, 8
Thomas Somner and Ellin his wife, of Leyland Moss-
side ... ... ,, 10
Richard Wright, of Ulneswalton ... ... ,, ii
John Philips, of Leyland ... ... ,, 13
James Walker, of Whittle ... ... ,, 13
Annes Chetham, of ffarington ... ... ,, 19
Ellizabeth, ye daughter of Nicolas Woomell, of
Whelton ... ... ,, 20
Ellin Cocker, of Euxton... ... ... ,, 23
William Clough, of Leyland ... ... ⎫
Margret, ye wife of Ralph Leyland, of Clayton ... ⎬ ,, 25
Thomas, son of Richard Dewhurst, of Radlsworth ... ,, 27
William Whithead, of Leyland ... ... ,, 30
Charistopher Somner, of Leyland ... ... Jan. 3
m. Richard Dewhurst, of Radlesworth ... ... ,, 6
m. Mr Edward Robinson,[1] of Euxton ... ... ,, 7
Mary Brining, of Whittell ... ... ,, 8
Ellizabeth, ye wife of James Sharrocke ... ... ,, 13
m. Richard Balshaw, of Euxton ... ... ,, 14
Richard Walton, of ffarington ... ... ,, 14
Lawrance Worthington, of Heape ... ... ,, 18

[1] Of Buckshaw in Euxton; formerly major in the Parliamentary army for the Kirkham district. Some account of this gentleman will be found on pages 23 and 24, also see pp. 26, 179, 180. From the *ffarington papers* we may add the following local touches to the story of the Civil War, *e.g.* as given by the author (? Major Robinson himself) in the *Discourse of the War*. "In August, 1643, certain soldiers under com̃and of Major Robinson did take out of the demayne grounds [of W^m ffarington, Esqre], at Littlewood, one and twentie steers, valued by Alex^r Brears and Henry Wiggans at £90." "In the same year, Troopers, under command of Major Robinson, did take out of the demayne grounds at Penwortham one and twenty stears all 3 yr old, valued att £73: 10." Abram's *Memorials of Preston Guilds* informs us that "In April, 1643, Preston was occupied by a detachment of Col: Ashton's Parliamentarian force under Captain Edward Robinson, of Westby Hall, and of Buckshawe, in Euxton . . ." In the Council Book of Preston I find this entry: "Edward Robinson, gent, admitted [a Burgess by copy of Court Roll] 23 daie December, 1644, pro seipso tantum [for himself alone] gratis." Mr. Robinson was not entered at any succeeding Guild, but his sons, John and Edward, appear in 1662 and again in 1682.

John, son of John Garnor, of ffarrington   ...   ...   } Jan. 19
Roger Wareing, of Ulneswalton   ... ...
Ellin Whittel, of Leyland   ... ...   „   21
James Cooper, of Brindle   ... ...   „   24
Ellizabeth Madsley, of goulden-Hill,[1] widdow   ... ...   „   25
Margerett, y[e] wife of Richard Balshaw, of Euxton ...   „   27
Ann, y[e] wife of James Liuesey, of Winnell ... ...   „   29
Katterin Nelson, of Leyland lane... ... ...   „   30
M[rs] Mary Crook, of Leyland... ... ... Feb.   3
William Balshaw, of Leyland   ... ...   „   5
Mary, daughter of John Somner, of Lostock   ... ...   „   9
Robert, son of Thomas ffarington, of ffarington ... ...   „   14
Ellizabeth, y[e] wife of John Cocker, of Leyland ... }
William, son of Lawrance Whittle, of ffarington...   } „   17
Ellizabeth, daught of Nicolas Woomell, of Whelton ...   „   24
M[rs] Margret Crooke,[2] of Lealand, widdow ... ...   „   25
Ann Park, of Leyland, widdow   ... ... March 3
Ellizabeth, y[e] wife of Thomas Boulton, of Clayton ...   „   12
Annas Whittle, of Clayton   ... ...   „   15
m. Thomas Pilkinton, of Whittle ... ...   „   19
M[rs] Margret Crooke, of Leyland, Spinster ... ...   „   24

[Burials] 1681.

m. M[r] Hugh Bonkin,[3] of Leyland   ... ...   } March 28
Elizabeth, daughter of John Giller   ... ...   }
Ellizabeth, daughter of Robert Eccles, of Euxton ...   „   31
Edward, son of Thomas Boulton, of Clayton   ... ... Aprill 1
Thomas Walmersley, of Heapey ... ...   „   3
Hugh Crook, of Whittle... ... ...   „   9
Mary, daughter of Thomas Whittell, of ffarington   ...   „   15
Ann, daughter of William Cocker, of Leyland ... ...   „   17
Ellizabeth, daughter of William Boydell, of Euxton }
Ellizabeth, daughter of M[r] John Hillton, of Leyland } „   18
Henry, son of William Atherton, of Leyland   ... ...   „   20
Jane, daughter of William Leauer, of Leyland ...   }
John Leyland, of Heapy... ... ...   } „   22

---

[1] Known by the same name at the present time. It is applied to an ill-defined district lying to the north of Leyland township, and parallel to the boundary between Leyland and Farington.

[2] Probably the daughter of Peter Anderton, of Anderton, Esq., and Grace (Rishton) his wife. Married to Mr. Roger Crooke, of Leyland. See Anderton pedigree given in Baines' *Hist. of Lanc.*, under *Standish* parish.

[3] Furnished report concerning Leyland Grammar School, with list of names of masters, &c. See Introduction.

Mrs Mary Maltby, of Leyland ... ... Aprill 28
John, son of Wiłł Tasker, of ffarington ... ... „ 30
Edward Sargent, of Leyland ... ... ⎱ May 2
Mary Cooper, of Brindle ... ... ⎰
Ellizabeth, daughter of Thomas Stilson, of Whittle ... „ 8
Izabell Couert, of Wheelton ... ... „ 12
Roger, son of John Madsley [Mawdesley], of Leyland. „ 13
m. Thomas Thornley, of Leyland ... ... „ 15
Ellizabeth Cooper, of Euxton ... ... ⎱ „ 18
Hugh, son of John Browne, of ffarington ... ... ⎰
Allis Parke, of Euxton ... ... „ 20
William Cliff, of Longton ... ... „ 21
a child of Robert Coopers, of Brindle ... ... ⎱ „ 24
Rober, son of Richard Hillton, of Whittle ... ... ⎰
Margret, daughter of Georg Bury, of Winnell ... ... „ 25
Thomas, son of Thomas Cooper, blacksmith in Leyland June 8
——, daughter of John Yeat, of Whittle ... ... „ 10
Richard, son Adam Blackborn, of Cuerden ... ... „ 17
James Partinton, of Clayton ... ... „ 18
Robert, son of Thomas ffarington, of ffarington ... ... „ 19
Henry, son of Henry Vickerstaf,[1] of ffarington ... ... „ 21
Euan Winnell, of Heapey ... ... „ 21
Ann, the wife of Henry Croston, of Whittell ... ... „ 25
Janett, the wife of Ellis Somner, of Leyland ... ... „ 30
Ellizabeth, ye wife of Thomas ffarington, of ffarington July 9
John Hall, a traueller, died in Euxton ... ... „ 12
John, son of John Woodcock, of Kuerden ... ... ⎱ „ 14
James, son of William Cowper, of Cuerden ... ... ⎰
William, son of Ralph Walmersley, of Winnell ... ... „ 18
William Leyland, of Heapy ... ... „ 19
Ellin Cowper, of Leyland ... ... „ 21
James, son of Thomas Pilkinton, of Whittle ... ... „ 26
Iszabell, ye daughter of Thomas Withington ... ... Aug. 13
Richard, son of Evan Winnell, of Heapey ... ... „ 16

[Thrust in at the bottom of the page.]

Roger Parke, of Croston Prish, December ye 28.

Margret, daughter of John Biggans, of Leyland ... ... Aug. 22
Katterin, daughter of Mrs Garner, of ffarington ... ... „ 23
Christopher, son of Roger ffishwick, of Winnell ... ... „ 25
Jennet, ye daughter of Richard Walton, of ffarington ... „ 29
Richard, son of John Park, of Leyland ... ... Sept. 1

---

[1] Probably meant for Bickerstaff or Bickersteth.

Robert, son of John Somner, of Ceuerden	} Sept. 3
John, son of John Charnock, of Ceuerden	
William, son of Thomas Porter, of Leyland... ... ... „ 5	
Ann, daughter of Edward Tinsley, of Euxton ...	}
Dorathy, daughter of John Chissher [Cheshire], of	„ 7
ffarington	

m. Jane, yᵉ daughter of John Bradley, of Leyland ... „ 8
Mary Whittle, of Leyland, widdow ... ... „ 9
Jennet, daughter of Euan Winnell, of Heapey ... ... „ 10
William Asley, of Clayton ... ... „ 11
mortuary Due
m. Jane, widdow fidler, of Clayton ... ... „ 20
Olliver Taylor, of Heapey ... ... } Oct. 11
John Worthington, of Heapey ... ...
Ellizabeth Cocker, of Clayton ... ... „ 14
Margery, daughter of Wiłł: Sharrock, of Euxton ... „ 27
Ann, the wife of Richard Somner, of Leyland ... ... Nov. 8
Edward, son (a child) of Thomas Woodcock, of Whittle „ 9
Jane [Ann crossed through], the wife of William Park,
of Euxton ... ... „ 13
Ellizabeth, yᵉ daughter of Robert Harrison, of Leyland „ 14
Thomas Dewhurst, of Radlesworth ... ... „ 16
Allis Parkinson, of Colne, a traveler ... ... „ 17
Mary, yᵉ wife of Henry Blackledg, farington ... ... „ 20
John Burscow, of Eccleston ... ... „ 24
Jane, yᵉ wife of William Whithead, of Ulneswalton ... „ 28
Thomas Low, of Ulneswalton ... ... Dec. 1
Ellizabeth, yᵉ wife of Lawrance Armerid [Armetriding],[1]
of Borderston [Balderstone] ... ... „ 15
Ellizabeth, yᵉ wife of Robert Pilkinton, Leyland ... „ 19
John Crooke, of Euxton... ... ... } „ 31
Allis, yᵉ wife of William Harieson, of Clayton ...
Robert, yᵉ son of William Cooper, of Leyland ... ... Jan. 2
William, yᵉ son of John Wright, of Leyland ... ... „ 10
Ellizabeth, wife of Robert Barron, of Clayton ... ... „ 18
Thomas Roscow, of Euxton ... ... } „ 25
Allis, yᵉ Daughter of James Somner, of Leyland
Margret, yᵉ Daughter of John Jackson, of Leyland ... „ 27
Allis Somner, of Hollins[2] in Leyland ... ... „ 28
Allis, yᵉ Daughter of Edward ffowler, of Whittel ... Feb. 3
James ffarington, of Leyland... ... ... „ 7

[1] Lawrance Armetriding, son of John, was entered with his father and brothers at the Preston Guild of 1622.

[2] Hollins, a farm off Leyland Lane, on the south-west of Leyland township.

Robert Blackledg, of Heapy ... ... Feb. 9
Thomas Liptrot, of Leyland ... ... „ 17
Jane, yᵉ wife of James Cocker, of Clayton ... ... „ 18
Ann Holmes, of Leyland ... ... „ 19
m. widdow Dewhurst, of Darley side in winnell... ... „ 20
[Ellizabeth crossed through], Jane Garstang, of Euxton „ 22
John Jackson, of Cuerden ... ... „ 26
Ellin Browne, of Clayton ... ... ⎱
Allis Yeate, of Leyland, Spinster ... ... ⎰ March 3
James, yᵉ son of Hugh Crooke, of Whittell... ... ... „ 10
Ellin, yᵉ wife of William Waterworth, of Leyland ... „ 11
Nicolas Bromiley, of Leyland ... ... ⎱
m. James Mosse, of Clayton ... ... ⎰ „ 18

[Burials, 1682.]

Jennet, yᵉ wife of John Calderbank, of Leyland ... ... March 30
m. Thomas Dobson, of Leyland ... ... ⎱
Ellizabeth, daughter of Richard ffarington, of farington ⎰ April 1

[By a mistake in the original, the entries for 1682 begin here.]

Samuel Baxenden, of Euxton ... ... April ii
Jony Cocker, of Cuerden ... ... ⎱
Ann Woodcock, of Cuerden ... ... ⎰ „ 15
Kattering Sharrock, of Whittell ... .:. ... ... „ 16
Mary Cowlin, of Leyland ... ... „ 19
John Cheetham, of ffarington... ... ... „ *(sic)* 17
Isabell, yᵉ wife of William Clayton ... ... „ 25
John Southworth, of Leyland ... ... May 2
William ffarington, of Snubsnape, younger, of Leyland „ 5
Thomas, son of Richard Goodman, of Leyland... ... „ 6
Ellin, yᵉ wife of Hugh Mare, of Leyland ... ... „ 15
John Woodcock, of Leyland ... ... ⎱
Grace, yᵉ wife of John Jackson, of Cuerden... ... ⎰ „ 20
[1]James Smith, of Warley, in yᵉ Prish of Hallifax, in
    Yorkshire ... ... „ 21
[1]John Taylor, of Leyland ... ... „ 22
Richard Broxup, of Euxton ... ... „ 30
Jane, yᵉ daughter of Lawrance Wattmough, Leyland ⎱
John Worden, of Hutton[2] ... ... ⎰ „ 31
Ellin Woodcock, of Cuerden ... ... June 8

[1] The position of these entries is altered to bring them into chronological order.
They occur in the original after the two succeeding ones.

[2] Hutton, a township in Penwortham parish.

Margret, yᵉ daughter of Edward Litherland, of Whittle June 9
William Miller, of Ulneswalton ... ... „ 17
——, yᵉ wife of Thomas Cooper, of Cuerden ... ... „ 27
Adam Balshaw, of Euxton ... ...July ii
James Broune, of Leyland ... ... „ 27
Ann, yᵉ daughter of William Westby, of Cuerden ... „ 30
Jane, yᵉ daughter of James Somner, of Leyland ...Aug. 9
Ellizabeth, yᵉ daughter of Henry Sudell, of Croston... „ 2i
Sissile, yᵉ daughter of William Tootel, of Whittell ... „ 29
Ellin Wareing, widow, of Ulneswalton... ... ...Sept. 15
[¹Edward Longton, of ffarington, Buried yᵉ 16th September.]
Margret Johnson, of Heapey, widdow ... ... „ 22
Allis ffairclugh... ... ...Oct. 2
Ellizabeth, yᵉ wife of Richard Sherdly, of ffarington ... „ 5
Richard, yᵉ son of John Parke, of Leyland ... ... „ 24
Richard Martin, of Heapey ... ...Nov. 2
Allis, yᵉ daughter of Johne Allmon, of Leyland... ... „ 10
Ellin, yᵉ daughter of Thomas Warring, of Leyland ...Dec. 6
William Woodcock, of Euxton ... ... „ ii
Richard, son of Robert Woodrofe, of Heapy ... ⎫
Ralph Norbanck, of Whittle ... ... ⎭ „ 14
Roger ffarington, of ffarington ... ... „ 16
Ellizabeth, yᵉ daughter of John Hodson, of Eccleston Jan. 12
Ellin, yᵉ daughter of William Tootell, of Whittle ... „ 20
Ellizabeth Wood, a servant at John Millers, in Clayton „ 30
George,² yᵉ son of Mʳ John Robbinson, of Euxton ... „ 31
John Dannell, a child of Richard Parkers, of ffarington. ffeb. 2
Henry Blecledg, of ffarington... ... ... „ 8
John Coupper, of ffishwick, in preston prish ... ... „ 12
John ffarnworth, of Wheelton... ... ... „ 18
Hugh, yᵉ Son of Thomas Morres, of Heapy ... ... „ 19
Adam Cliff, son of Richard Cliff, of Leyland ... ⎫
——, a child of James Marsden, of Whittell ... ⎭ „ 27
Martha, yᵉ daughter of Nathanell Woodworth, of Ley-
land ... ...March 8
Margaret, yᵉ wife of Adam Clayton, of Clayton ... ... „ 10
Margaret ffishwick, of Winnell, widow ... ... „ 11
Jane Martin, of Heapy ... ... „ 12
Edward Longton, of ffarington, Buried yᵉ 16 September.

---

¹ Occurs at the end of the year's entries.

² A grandson of Major Edward Robinson (see p. 23), and son of Mr. John Robinson, of Preston, and afterwards of Buckshaw. This George was entered on the Guild Roll of 1682 with brothers, Edward, Thomas, and John. Their mother was Alice, daughter of Thomas Birch, of Birch Hall, Esquire. Mr. John Robinson (senr.) was buried ffeb. 15, 1675.

[Burials] 1683.

Abigall, ye wife of Thomas Garstang, of Heapy... ... Aprill 9
Janett Partinton, of Clayton, widow ... ... „ 20
John, ye son of Mary Smith, by John Whittle, Leyland,
a Bastard ... ... „ 30
Ann Martin, of Heapy, widdow ... ... May 1
Ellizabeth Garstang, of Wheeleton, widdow ... ... „ 2
Thurstan, ye Son of Roger fficwick [fishwick],of Withnell „ 3
Ralph Gorton, of Withnell ... ... „ ii
Ellizabeth, ye wife of Edward ffarnworth, of Wheelton „ 12
Jenet, ye daughter of William Woodcock, of Euxton... „ 26
Tabatha, ye daughter of Alexander Breers, of Whittle „ 29
William Cowper, of Cuerden ... ... June 2
Ann, ye daughter of James Gorton, of Clayton ... ... „ 5
Mrs Ann Carter, of Leyland, widow ... ... „ 9
Thomas Stillton, of Leyland ... ... „ 16
——, ye wife of Thomas ffell, of Whittle in le Woods July 4
Ann Smith, of Leyland, widdow ... ... „ 9
Margaret, ye wife of Edward Clough, of Leyland ... „ 14
Cristopher, ye son of Thomas Woodcock, of Whittle... „ 20
——, ye daughter of Thomas Biby, of Winnell ... ... „ 26
William, ye son of John Wright, of Leyland ... ... Aug. 4
Bridget Halle, of Euxton, widdow... ... ... „ 28
Mr Thurston Anderton,[1] of Clayton ... ... „ 29
Ann Simson, widdow, of Wheeleton ... ... Sept. 6
Ann, ye daughter of John Browne, of ffarington ... ... „ 22
James, ye son of William Roscow, of Euxton ... ... Oct. 20
Ann, ye daughter of Cester [?] Willden, ffarington ... „ 25
Margret Cowper, of Cuerden, spinster ... ... „ 30
Ellizabeth, ye wife of Thomas Adlinton, of Claiton ... Nov. ii

[Crowded in at the bottom of a page.]
Ann, ye wife of ffrancis Dandy, of Ulneswalton, 28 July, 84.

[1] Mr. Thurstan Anderton was the second son of James Anderton, of Clayton, Esq., and brother of Elizabeth and Eleanor Anderton, buried Dec. 18, 1678, and Ap. 22, 1679. The lordship of Clayton, which had been mortgaged by James Anderton, Esq., to — Dicconson, of Wrightington, Esq., was after several years redeemed by Caryl, Lord Molyneux, Viscount Maryborough, in the name of Thurstan, Christopher, and William Anderton (about 1672). After the death of Thurstan, the two latter sold their right in the lordship to Viscount Maryborough, and retired to Bardsey. See Baines' *History of Lancashire*, under *Clayton* township. Bardsey-in-Furness became their inheritance through the marriage of Elizabeth, the elder heiress of Nicholas Bardsea, who died in 1642. This Elizabeth married James Anderton, Esq., of Clayton. William and Christopher Anderton occupied the mansion in 1672. In 1726 that estate also passed into the hands of the Molineux family.

John Tomlinson, of ffarington, 30 July, 84.
John Hesketh, of Leyland, Noumber 8, 84.

[¹Mary, daughter of John Harrison, of Clayton, Bu: 12
   decemb. 1683.]
Margret Wareing, widdow of Standish parrish, Buried yᵉ Dec.   15
Ann ffarington, of Leyland, widdow   ...   .   „   17
Thomas Southworth, of Leyland ...   .   „   29
Ellin Worden, of Clayton   ...   .   „   30
Thomas Withington, of Clayton ...   .   „   31
William Cowper, of Euxton ...   . Jan.   2
Ellizabeth, yᵉ wife of William Willden, of Leyland   ...   „   16
Ellizabeth Adlinton, of Kuerden, widdow ...   .   „   25
Thomas James, of Leyland   ...   .   „   26
Elizabeth Machon, of Leyland   ...   .   „   28
John, yᵉ son of Andrew Stones, of Leyland...   ...   ... Feb.   2
[²Charles [Rothwell crossed through] Caddock, a
   traueller, Buried yᵉ 6: ffebruary, 1685.]
Ann Dawson, of Leyland   ...   .   „   2i
William, son of Henry ffell, of Leyland   ...   .   „   26
Jane, yᵉ wife of Edward Tinsley, of Euxton   ...   ... March 1
Ellin Slattor, of Leyland moss-side   ...   .   „   18
Ellin Eastham, of ffarington, widdow ...   .   ⎫
Ellizabeth, yᵉ daugh: of John Garrard, of ffarington ⎬ „   24

[Burials] 1684.

William Clayton, of Kuerden...   ...   . Aprill 13
Thomas Jackson, of Leyland ...   .   „   14
Ann, yᵉ wife of Thomas Jackson, of Leyland   ...   ...   „   19
Ellin, yᵉ daughter of John Cocker, of Leyland moss-side   „   19
——, a child of John fforshaw, of Leyland ...   . May 24
Mʳˢ Ellizabeth Anderton,³ of Euxton-Hall...   ...   ... June 6
Ellizabeth, yᵉ wife of Henry Whaly, of Leyland...   ...   „   16
James Chetham, of ffarington...   ...   .   „   25
Jane Somner, of Leyland, widow ...   . July 7
Ellizabeth, yᵉ daughter of Ralph Bowth, of pish of
   Preston ...   .   „   14
Margret, yᵉ wife of Roger Dawson, of Clayton ...   ...   „   17

---

¹ Occurs among Burial entries of 1677, at the bottom of the page.

² Found among the entries for 1679, at the bottom of a page.

³ No Elizabeth Anderton appears in the pedigree of the Euxton family. Perhaps this entry refers to a daughter of Hugh Anderton, Esq., and his wife Catherine (Trapps).

Thomas Cowper, oth noock,[1] in Leyland lane ... ... July 18
[[2]Ann, y[e] wife of ffrancis Dandy, of Ulneswalton ... „ 28]
[[2]John Tomlinson, of ffarington ... ... „ 30]
Allis, y[c] wife of Nicolas Woomell, of Wheelton ... ... „ 30
William Madsley, of Leyland... ... ... Aug. 1
Ann, y[e] wife of Will: Dalton, of Dalton, of Whittle ... „ 2
Milles, y[e] son of John Scot, of Whittle... ... ... „ 9
John Armetryding,[3] of Euxton ... ... „ 13
William Wadsworth, of Euxton ... ... „ 16
Allis Stopford, spinster, Leyland ... ... „ 20
Ellin Chrichlow, widdow, of Whittle ... ... „ 24
Mary, y[e] wife of Ralph Crosse, of Leyland ... ... „ 27
Allis, y[c] wife of John Smith, of Leyland ... ... „ 28
Richard Balshaw, carpenter, of Leyland ... ... Sept. ii
Allis, y[e] wife of William Abbot, of Chorley pish... ... „ 17
Richard Withnell, of Withnell ... ... „ 27
Jane, y[e] daughter of Richard Somner, of Leyland ... Oct. 5
Jane, y[e] daughter of John Cliffe, of Longton ... ... „ 6
Margret, freland [? Ireland], of Leyland ... ... „ 15
William Exton, of Claton ... ... „ 25
Jane, y[e] wife of Robert Woodrofe, of Hepey ... ... „ 26
Jane Watson, of Whittle, widow ... ... „ 27
Thomas Abbot, of Adlinton ... ... „ 29
Thomas Cocker, of Clayton ... ... Nov. 1
Thomas, son of Lawrance Whittel, of ffarington... ... „ 2
[[2]John Hesketh, of Leyland ... ... „ 8]
John, y[e] son of John Godberd, of Oweswalton[4] ... ... „ ii
——, y[e] daughter of Henry Blackledg, of Wheeton (*sic*) Dec. 5
Thomas, y[e] son of Hugh Browne, of Heapey ... ... „ 25
[[5]Robert, y[e] son of Richard Wiggans [of] Whittel,
    January 6, 84.]

[1] A farm. See page 68, note ([2]).

[2] Found among entries for 1683.

[3] There is a rather roughly cut slab (of Wheelton stone) close to the outer wall on the S.E. side of Leyland Church which records the names and dates of burial of several members of the Armetriding family, of which this John Armetriding is the first. He is described as "of the Armetryding in Euxton, Maltster." According to the stone, he died on Aug. 13, 1684, aged 63 years. He was the father of the Reverend Thomas Armetriding, M.A., Vicar of Leyland from 1689 to 1719. He was probably the son of Richard, and grandson of John Armetriding, who was admitted at the Preston Guild of 1602, as a stallenger, on payment of liiijs iiid., and entered at the successive Guilds of 1622 and 1642. Richard Armetriding seems to have lived through four Guilds, being entered in 1602, 1622, 1642, and 1662. At the two last his son John (supposed to be the subject of this note) is entered with him.

[4] For Ulneswalton.

[5] Occurs among entries for 1677, at the bottom of the page.

Lawrance Watmough, of Leyland... ... ... Jan.		7
Ann, yᵉ wife of Thomas Johnson, of Heapy ... ⎫		
Daniell, yᵉ son of Nicolas Woomell, of Wheelton ⎬ „		13
Ellizabeth, yᵉ wife of William Clayton, of Cuerden ... „		18
Clamence Stanfield, of Euxton, widdow ... ... „		21
John Slaytor, of Euxton... ... ... „		22
Mary, yᵉ daughter of Robert Whittel, of Leyland ... „		24

[¹Thoma[s]in Wright, of Ulneswoton [Ulneswalton], ffebruary yᵉ 9: 1684.]

John, yᵉ son of William Watterworth, of Leyland ... Feb.		12
Jane Anderton, of Clayton, & Henry ffarnworth, of		
Wheelton ... ... „		13
John Pincock, of Euxton ... ... „		18
Robert Coope, of Whelton ... ... „		19
Margret Nixson, of Leyland moss-side ... ... March		2
Allis, yᵉ daughter of Andrew Stones, of Leyland ... „		7
Allis, yᵉ wife of Henry Eastham, Senior, of Leyland... „		9
Thomas Adlinton, of Clayton Towne,² & John Bennett,		
a traueller ... ... „		15
Ellin, yᶜ daughter of Ellizabeth Martin, of Leyland ... „		17

[Burials] 1685.

William Wareing, of Ulneswalton, Croston pish... ... March		30
Ellizabeth, yᵉ wife of John Clayton, of Clayton ... ... „		31
James, yᵉ son of Timythy Wardle, of Whittle ... ... Aprill		5
Hugh Mare, of Leyland, & Allis, yᵉ wife of John Dobson,		
of ffarington ... ... „		8
Mary, yᵉ daughter of Thomas Chitham, of ffarington... „		14
Jane, yᵉ daughter of Robert Walsh, of Leyland ... ... „ *(sic)*		9
Allis, yᵉ daughter of John Jackson, of Kuerden ... ... „		20
Grace, yᵉ wife of Thomas Woodcocke, of Whittle ⎫		
Ellizabeth, yᵉ daughter of John Jones, a traueller ⎬ „		28
Mary, yᵉ wife of Henry Waring, of Ulneswalton... ... „		30

[The handwriting changes at this place. The same person continues to make the entries from May 5th down to July 23rd, 1689. Vicar Walmesley was buried on Sept. 10th, 1689.]

Thomas Porter, of Leland Mosse-side ... ... May		5
James Butler, of Ulneswalton ... ... ⎫		
Hannah, yᵉ w: of Wᵐ Farington, of Farington ... ⎬ „		7

¹ Found among the entries for 1679, at the bottom of a page.

² Notice this use of the word town. It is here applied to the "township" of Clayton.

Frances Wilding, of Leland ... ... May	9
Katherine, yᵉ daughter of Rich: Nelson ... ... „	12
Lawrence, yᵉ son of Law[rence] Croft ... ... „	29
Jane Cowper, widdow, de Nooke[1] in Leland ... ... June	4
Dorothy, yᵉ w: of Roger Cliffe, of Farington ... ... „	9
James, yᵉ S. of James Lever, of Oldham Parish ... ... „	14
Thomas, yᵉ s: of John Bradley ... ... „	15
John, yᵉ s. of Wᵐ Burscow, of Leland Lane... ... ... „	17
Martin, yᵉ Son of Roger ffiswick, of Withnell ... ... July	3
Ellen, yᵉ wife of Ralph Cooper, of Kureden ... ... „	24
George, yᵉ S. of Wiłt: Baxenden, of Euxton ... ⎫	
Anne, yᵉ D: of Rich: Slater, of Leland ... ... ⎭ „	27
Thomas Sumner, of Leyland... ... ... Aug	4
Margaret, yᵉ w: of John Brown, of Farrington ... ... „	5
Eliz: Low, of Leyland, wid: ... ... „	9
John, yᵉ S: of Evan Withnell, of Heapy ... ... „	12
Margaret Sharrock, wid:... ... ... „	20
Mary, yᵉ w: of Rich: Moore, of Euxton ... ... „	24
Lawrence Ainsworth, of Heapy ... ... Sept.	29
Margaret, yᵉ D: of Adam Clayton ... ... Oct.	3
Alice Jackson, of Keverden ... ... „	16
Anne, yᵉ w: of Wᵐ Ugnall, of Wheelton ... ... „	26
Ciceley Cliffe, vid. of Longton ... ... „	30
Margaret, yᵉ D: of Richard Balshaw ... ... „	31
Thomas, yᵉ S. of Tho: Jackson, of Keurden ... ... Nov.	9
Katherine, yᵉ W. of Wᵐ Hilton, of Wheelton ... ... „	13
Alice, yᵉ w: of Robᵗ Dewhurst, of Wheelton ... ... „	17
Richard, yᵉ S. of Wᵐ Tasker, of Farrington ... ... „	25
Alice Marsden, of Raddlesworth, wid: ... ... Dec.	12
John, yᵉ S. of Rich: Clarkson, of Euxton ... ... „	22
Grace, yᵉ D: of Wᵐ Roscow, of Euxton ... ... „	28
Amery[2] Hey, of Withnell ... ... „	31
Jane Cooper, of Clayton, *vid:* ... ... Jan.	9
Thomas Cooper, of Clayton, her son ... ... „	11
Frances, yᵉ W: of John Critchlow, of Clayton ... ... „	16
Ellis Bolton, of Leyland... ... ... „	19
Jane, yᵉ D. of Matthew Walkden, of Heapy ... ... „	20
Thomas [John crossed out], yᵉ son of Richard	
Bromeley, of Leland ... ... Feb.	1
Elizabeth, yᵉ Daughter of James Lowe, of Leland ... „	11

[1] Nooke is a farm which lies within an angle formed by the parish boundary at the south-west of Leyland township.

[2] This is an uncommon name. There is a piece of land off Leyland Lane which is known as the Amery Meadow.

Q

Margaret, yᵉ D: of Thomas Lowe, of Euxton ... ... Feb. 19
John Cheshire, of Farington, & ... ... ⎫
Alice, yᵉ wife of Robᵗ Garner, of Longton ... ... ⎬ „ 22
Ellen, yᵉ wife of Thomas Withington, of Clayton ... Mar. 9
James Charnley, of Kuerden ... ... „ 11
Bridget, yᵉ wife of Tho: ffletcher, of Leland ... ... „ 20

Burials in yᵉ yeare 1686.

Alice Robinson, of Farington ... ... ⎫
Elizabeth, yᵉ daughter of James Cheetham, of Faring- ⎬ March 27
ton ... ... ⎭
Anne, yᵉ wife of Thomas Lever, of Leland ... ... „ 29
Wᵐ Walton, of Leland, Mosse Side ... ... Aprill 1
m. Wᵐ Wright, of Euxton ... ... „ 2
Annas [Lowe crossed out] Woodcock, of Ulneswalton
[Leland crossed out] ... ... „ 7
Tho: Standley,¹ Esqʳ. Buried from Dʳ Keurdens ... „ 17
Anne, yᵉ wife of Mʳ John Hulton² ... ... „ 23
Widow Barton, a traveller ... ... „ 28
Peter Marsden, of Raddlesworth ... ... ⎫ May 8
Alexander Walmsley, of Whittle ... ... ⎭
Elizabeth, D: of Rich: Dobson ... ... „ 20
Alice Cheetham, of Farington, widdow ... ... „ 21
Jane, yᵉ D: of William Whitehead, of Mosse Side ... „ 29
Margaret Harrison, of Clayton, wid. ... ... June 5
Samuel,³ yᵉ Son of Mʳ Richard Fleetwood ... ... „ 15
Robᵗ Baron, of Clayton ... ... July 10

¹ Although unable to identify with certainty the individual here named, it may be useful to note the following:—Mr. Thomas Stanley, son of Edward Stanley, of Moor Hall, Esq., was a legatee under the will of his brother-in-law, Mr. Thomas Walmesley, of Banister Hall (in Walton-le-Dale), who died in 1637. As Mr. Walmesley was only a little over thirty when he died, the dates do not altogether forbid an identification. Banister Hall is not far from Cuerden Old Hall, the home of Dr. Kuerden. Thomas Stanley, gen., was entered as present at the Preston Guild of 1642. In the succeeding Guilds of 1662 and 1682 we find Thomas Stanley, Esq., of Eccleston, and his son Richard, among the Foreign Burgesses.

² There is a family of the name Hilton or Hulton, of Brindle, enrolled among the Burgesses of the Preston Guilds of 1642–1682. The first member is a "tanner," another is a "farmer," while a third has the title "generosus." Possibly the Mr. Hulton of the text was one of them.

³ This was the second son of Mr. Richard Fleetwood and his wife Margaret (see page 60, also page 143, note). There is a memorial stone to his memory now lying outside the vestry door of Leyland Church, where it was placed on its removal (with several others) from the floor of the chancel in 1875. It is from the Wheelton quarries, of a dark red colour, and has the letters in relief. This child only lived two years, having been born on May 7, 1684.

Margaret, yᵉ D. of Ralph Walmsley, of Withnell ... July 15
Jane, yᵉ D. of Tho: Woodcocke, Stoneman... ... ... „ 17
Margaret, yᵉ W. of Michael Southworth, of Leland ⎫
——, yᵉ S. of Richard Critchlaw, of Farington ... ⎭ „ 19
An Infant of Adam Platts ... ... „ 20
Ellen [Elizabeth crossed out], yᵉ D. of John Forshaw... „ 22
Anne, yᵉ D. of Thomas Langtree, of Euxton ... ... „ 24
Margaret,¹ yᵉ W: of Thurstan Leland, of Clayton ⎫
Thomas, S. of William Gardner, of Kureden ... ⎭ „ 29
Elizabeth, yᵉ D. of Richard Somner, of Leland Lane... Aug. 2
——, yᵉ D. of Thomas Cheetham, of Farington ... ... „ 11
Alice Atherton, of Leland, widow ... ... ⎫
William, yᵉ S. of Widow Crooke, of Euxton ... ⎭ „ 12
Jennet Wareing [Sumner crossed out], of Hoole, widow „ 14
Thomas, yᵉ S. of John Woodcocke, of Euxton ... ... „ 15
Ann, yᵉ D. of Roger Sharples, Junior, of Leland ... Sept. 20
Margaret Wigans, stepD: of Ch: Whitehead, of Leland „ 28
Alice, yᵉ w: of John Walmsley, of Whittle ... ... Oct. 14
m. Tho: Lowe, of Euxton ... ... „ 23
Matthew, yᵉ S. of Tho: Martin, of Whittle ... ... „ 31
Wᵐ Farington, of Snub-snape² ... ... Nov. 2
Ellen, yᵉ D. of John Beardsworth, of Farington ... ... „ 16
Margaret, yᵉ D. of Tho: Farington de Brooke, & ⎫
Hannah, yᵉ D. of Hen: Brookes, a traveller ... ⎭ „ 31
Matthias,³ yᵉ S. of Alex: Breres, of Whittle ... ... Dec. 18
m. Margaret Tootell, of Glead-hill,⁴ widd: ... ... „ 20
Lawrence,³ yᵉ S. of Alex: Breres, of Whittle ... ... „ 23
Izabel Holmes, widd, of Leland mosse-side ... ... „ 25
Eliz: Hesketh, widd: ... ... „ 26
Susan, yᵉ D. of Richard Parker, of Farington ... ... „ 29
Edmond,³ yᵉ S. of Alex: Breres, of Whittle... ... ... „ 30
Ellenor & Ellen [Susan & Anne crossed out], yᵉ Dˢ of
Rich: Nelson ... ... „ 31
Ellen Withington, of Clayton, widow ... ... Jan. 3
Robᵗ, yᵉ S: of John Brindle, of Clayton ... ... „ 6

---

¹ There is a stone lying to the south-west of the tower of Leyland Church recording the death of Margaret, wife of Thurstan Leyland. It is in an excellent state of preservation, as is generally the case with memorials which have the letters standing up in relief. The marriage of Margaret Nelson, of Ulneswalton, with Thurstan Leyland, of Clayton, took place at Leyland Church on Dec. 6, 1678. She was 27 years old at her death.

² See page 7 (note).

³ These three sons of Alexander Breres, yeoman, were entered with him at the Preston Guild of 1682. See the entry of their baptisms on page 70.

⁴ Gleadhill, a farm in Euxton.

m. p^d. Wᵐ Lever, of Leyland	... Jan.	8
Elizabeth, yᵉ D. of Thurstan Sharrock, of Euxton	... „	11
Annas, yᵉ D. of John Tomlinson, of Farington ...	... „	14
Wᵐ, yᵉ S. of Tho: Whittle, of Farington	... „	15
Clemence Critchlaw, of Whittle [Inserted]	... „	19
Wᵐ, S: of Wᵐ Tootell, senʳ, of Whittle	... „	21
Wᵐ, yᵉ S of Wᵐ Clayton, of Farington	... „	23
Thomas Whittle, of Farington	... „	24

Elizabeth, yᵉ wife of John Parke, of Leland ... }
Hannah, yᵉ D. of Tho: Farington, of Farington ... } „ 26

Alice, yᵉ w: of Robᵗ Hoskar, of Kureden. ... ... }
Hannah, yᵉ D. of Rich: Whittle, of Leland ... ... } „ 27

Lawrence Croft, of Whittle ... ... }
Robᵗ, S. of Wᵐ Dawson, of Clayton ... ... } „ 29
Jane, d. of Thomas Longton, of Whittle ... ... }

John, s. of Tho: Giller, of Leland	... „	30
William, s. of James Clayton, of Clayton	... „	31
Margaret, D. of John Cooper, of Leland	... Feb.	1
Deborah, yᵉ wife of John Charnock, of Kureden...	... „	10
Elizabeth, yᵉ D. of Evan Gardner, of Farington ...	... „	11
John, yᵉ S. of Hugh Baxenden, of Clayton	... „	14

Henry, yᵉ S. of Roger Cliffe, of Farington, & ... }
Elizabeth, yᵉ D. of Hugh Baxenden, of Clayton... } „ 17

Thomas, yᵉ S. of James Darwin, of Walton... ...	... „	18
John Clayton, of Farington	... „	21
Elizabeth, yᵉ D. of Tho: Roscow, of Wheelton ...	... „	25
Ellen, yᵉ D. of Tho: Pilkington, of Whittle	... Mar.	2
Christopher, yᵉ S. of Tho: Nowell, of Leland ...	... „	3
Anne, yᵉ D. of John Sumner, de Nooke[1]	... „	6
James Lowe, of Euxton	... „	7
William, yᵉ S. of James Hough, of Leland	... „	8

Margaret, yᵉ w: of John Lowe, of Euxton, & ... }
George [Robᵗ crossed out], yᵉ S. of Ralph Morris, of } „ 9
  Euxton ... ... }

Ellen, yᵉ w: of James Morris	... „	10
m. Tho: Taylor, of Euxton Burgh[2]	... „	15
John Daniel, of Euxton	... „	17
m. p^d. James Bromeley, of Clayton	... „	18
Anne, yᵉ W: of John Daniel, of Euxton	... „	19

[1] A farm. See on June 4, 1685.

[2] A portion of the village of Euxton is still called by this name. A stranger to the district would scarcely recognise the local pronunciation "Exton-Böth" as representing it.

[Burials] 1687.

Anne, yᵉ D. of Roger Dewhurst, of Keurden ... ... March 31
John Loxam, of Ulnes-Walton ... ... Aprill 8
John, yᵉ S. of John Tumlinson, of Farington ... ... „ 10
Thomas Standley, from Worden[1] ... ... ⎫
Alice Worstley, of Heapy ... ... ⎬ „ 14
m. pᵈ· William Cocker, of Keurden ... ... ⎭
Jennet Kellet, of Leland... ... ... „ 16
Robert, yᵉ S. of Rich: Tootell, of Whittle ... ... „ 25
Elizabeth, yᵉ D. of John Dobson, of Farington ... ... „ (?) 28
Alice, yᵉ Daughter of Alex: Breres ... ... May 4
Susan, yᵉ D. of Henry Wareing, of Euxton... ... ... „ 8
James, yᵉ S. of wid: Porter, of Leland. [Inserted] ... „ 10
Wᵐ Jackson, of Whittle ... ... ⎫
Anne, yᵉ D. of Wᵐ Hilton, of Wheelton ... ... ⎬ „ 11
Wᵐ Bomber: *Felo de Se:* ... ... ⎭
Rich: Brimiley, of Leland Lane ... ... „ 23
m. p. John Smith, of Leland ... ... „ 27
Wᵐ Clayton, of Penwortham ... ... June 4
Annas, yᵉ D. of Geo: Dawson ... ... „ (*sic*) 9
——, yᵉ wife of Henry Unsworth, of Euxton ... ... „ 6
John, yᵉ S. of Wᵐ Mackerill, of Farington ... ... „ 10
Edw: Tildesley, of Euxton ... ... „ 22
Wᵐ Entwisle, of Withnell ... ... „ 26
Edw: yᵉ S. of Rich: Simpson, of Wheelton ... ... „ 28
Margaret, yᵉ D. of Hugh Woodcocke ... ... ⎫ July 3
——, An Infant of, or Chrysom,[2] of Wᵐ Burscows ⎭

[1] Probably some retainer or servant in the household of Henry ffarington, Esq. Worden, the family home of the ffaringtons, lies at the south-eastern corner of the township of Leyland, where the boundary touches Whittle-le-Woods and Euxton. The estate was purchased from the Andertons by Sir Henry ffarington in 1534 for his male heir, who was the fourth but only surviving son, and the only child of Sir Henry's second wife. The ancient family domain of ffarington was settled on the *heirs* of Sir Henry's eldest son, so that it passed away through the female line to the possession of strangers. The Worden mansion was reconstructed by Sir Henry's son, afterwards known as the old Comptroller. It remained as the chief seat of the family until about 1736, when George ffarington, Esq., made Shawe Hall to be the more important residence. Sir William ffarington, who succeeded to the estates in 1742, completed the migration by transferring all of the furnishing, pictures, panelling, &c., which were thought to be interesting and valuable to the more modern mansion. The old hall at Worden was much reduced in size, and degraded to the position of a farm house for the demesne. Notwithstanding all this the building is a noticeable one, and presents many features of interest. Can anyone suggest how it came by its name? Did the estate at any time belong to a family of the name of Worden before it came into the possession of the Andertons? There has been a family of the rank of yeomen or lesser gentry of that name resident in Clayton, or thereabouts, from remote times.

[2] A chrysom was a white linen vesture given to the newly baptised to signify the

James, yᵉ S. of Wᵐ Bancroft ... ...July 4
Jennet Clayton, of Clayton, widow ... ... „ 7
m. Thomas Woodcock, of Whittle ... ... „ 23
Ellen, yᵉ D. of John Browne, of Farington ... ... „ 25
Anne Garstang, of Whittle ... ...Aug. 6
Jane Litherland, of Whittle ... ... „ 11
Mary, yᵉ D. of Wᵐ Farington, of Farington... ... ... „ 18
Jeffery, yᵉ S. of Wᵐ Asheton, of Kureden ... ... „ 21
Katherine, yᵉ D. of Rich: Eaves, of Kureden ... ...Sept. 6
——, ye D. of Wᵐ Harrison, of Walton ... ... „ 19
m. pᵈ· Ellis Somner, of Euxton ... ... „ 26
Alice, yᵉ wife of William Woodcock, of Leland ... ...Oct. 6
Wᵐ, S: of Wᵐ Woodcocke, of Leland ... ... „ 7
James, yᵉ S. of Wᵐ Fishwicke ... ... „ 16
John, yᵉ S. of Edward Wilding, of Charnock ... ... „ 17
Margaret Banister, of Leyland ... ... „ 28
Richard, s: of Wᵐ Hilton, of Wheelton ... ...Nov. 1
Ellen, yᵉ w: of John Hodgson, of Euxton ... ... „ 4
Alice, yᵉ w: of William Gardner, of Kureden ... ... „ 14
Agnes, yᵉ D. of Rich: Snape, of Withnell ... ... „ 20
John, S: of Henry Wareing, of Euxton ... ...[no date]
Henry, S: of Henry Chatburn, of Leland ... ...Dec. 8
m. pᵈ· Ralph Cooper, of Kureden ... ... ⎫
—— Jackson, of Kureden ... ... ⎬ „ 9
Samuel, S: of Wᵐ Gardner, of Kureden ... ... „ 11
Mary Whitehead, Spinster, Euxton ... ... „ 24
John Garstang, of Heapy ... ... „ 26
Elizabeth Gorton, of Withnell ... ... „ 28
Mʳ Robert Bickursteth,[1] of Aughton parish ... ...Jan. 2
Cicely Worthington, of Euxton, widow ... ,.. ... „ 3
Margret Somner, of Leland, widow ... ... „ 7
Richard Sherdley, of Farington ... ... „ 12
B. Ellen, yᵉ D. of Ellen Whalley ... ... „ 16
Anne, yᵉ D. of H. Waddington, of Tockholes[2] ... ... „ 22
Lawrence, yᵉ S: of Hen: Garstang, of Heapy ... ... „ 26
Mary, yᵉ wife of Henry Eastham, of Kureden ... ...Feb. 6
John —— Eastham, of Kureden ... ... „ 24

---

necessity for holiness. It was worn until the mother went to be churched. A chrysom-child was one which died in the interval. The final rubric of the Churching Service in the Prayer Book of 1549 ordered the woman to "offer her chrism and other accustomed offerings," when she made her thanksgiving. The use of the chrysom was abandoned in 1552, and not resumed at any subsequent revision.

¹ Married on February 21st, 1685-6, to Elizabeth Armetriding, probably a sister of Vicar Armetriding. See p. 78 (note).

² Tockholes, a township in Blackburn parish.

——, yᵉ D. of Ralph Pilkington, of Leland ... ... Mar.   1
Ellen Morris, of Heapy, widow   ... ... „   5
Ellen, yᵉ D. of William Pincocke, of Whittle   ... ... „ 10
Ellen, yᵉ w: of Richard Robinson, of Charnocke... ... „ 14
Hannah, yᵉ D. of Thomas Farington ... ... „ 18
Thomas Leaver, of Leland   ... ... „ 23

[Burials] 1688.

Ann, yᵉ w: of Henry Blackledge, of Wheelton ... ... March 26
Mary, ye D. of Rich: Robinson, of Charnock   ... ... April 4
Jennet Ainsworth, of Heapy, widow   ... ... „   5
William Fidler, of Farington... ... ... „ 22
Ralph, S: of Ralph Gorton   ... ... „ 23
Elizabeth Blackburn, of Kureden ... ... „ 24
James, yᵉ S: of Wᵐ Haworth, of Whittle   ... ... May   2
Henry Wareing, of Euxton ... ... „ 20
Tho: Marshall, of Heapy   ... ... „ 30
Margaret Taylor, of Heapy ... ... „ 11
Ralph Johnson, of Keurden ... ... June 17
Effam [? Ephraim] Forshaw, of Leland   ... ... „ 19
Wᵐ, yᵉ S. of —— Hough, of Leland   ... ... „ 12
Edward Beardsworth, of Leland ... ... „ 18
Margaret, yᵉ D. of Edw: Kilshaw, of Euxton   ... ... „ 19
Jane, yᵉ w: of John Godbert, of Eccleston ... ... „ 27
Alice [Mary crossed out], yᵉ w: of Thomas Dickenson,⎫
   of Heapy ... ...⎬ „ 31
Mary, yᵉ w: of Thomas Fletcher, of Leland... ...⎭
John Bowman, of Leland   ... ... Aug.   2
Alice Haddock, of Wheelton... ... ... „   4
John Blackledge,[1] of Copthurst   ... ... Sept. 9
Jane, yᵉ D. of Lawrence Croft, of Whittle ... ... Oct. 10
Alice, yᵉ D. of Tho: Withington, of Clayton   ... ... „ 14
Richard, yᵉ S: of John Ellison, of Chorley ... ... „ 15
Sarah, yᵉ D. of Rich: Woodcocke, of Clayton   ... ... „ 20
Grace, yᵉ D. of Mʳ Tho: Hulm, of Cawbeck[2]   ... ... Nov. 18
Alice Johnson, of Leland   ... ... „ 21
Ellin Farnworth, of Wheelton   ... ... „ 19
Henry, yᵉ S. of Ellis Somner, of Leland   ... ... „ —
Thomas, S. of Ellis Somner, Senʳ, of Leland   ... ... Dec.   4

[1] There is a stone in the churchyard to the memory of John Blackledge, of Copthurst in Whittle, yeoman, interred Sept. 9, 1688, aged 70 years. A number of later members of the Blackledge family are also named on the stone.

[2] A farm in Euxton, more commonly called Culbeck. See note on p. 64.

Ciceley, yᵉ wife of Robert Foster, of Euxton ... ... Jan. 24

Wᵐ Wareing, of Eccleston ... ... ⎫
Martha [Margery crossed out], yᵉ wife of John Sharples, ⎬ „ 26
of Heapy ... ... ⎭

Margaret, yᵉ wife of Wᵐ Pincock, *alias* Norbank ... „ 30

Anne Martin, of Leland ... ... „ 31

Jennet, yᵉ wife of Tho: Garstang, of Whittle ... ... Feb. 8

Ellen Wilson, of Leland, widow ... ... „ 15

Jane Withnell, of Euxton-burgh ... ... „ 20

Roger Sharples, Junʳ, of Leland ... ... ⎫
Thomas, yᵉ S: of John Richmond, of Withnell ... ⎬ „ 25
Elizabeth, yᵉ D. of Robert Cooper, of Blainscow... ⎭

Jane, yᵉ D. of Edm: Lees, of Wheelton ... ... March 2

John, yᵉ S: of Richard Cliffe ... ... „ 11

Jane, yᵉ D. of Rich: Rose ... ... „ 4

Anne, yᵉ D. of Wᵐ Jackson, of Leland ... ... „ 15

Elizabeth Fishwick, of Withnell, widow ... ... „ 17

Alice Whittle, of Withnell ... ... „ 22

Richard Hoghton, of Charnock ... ... (*sic*) „ —

[Burials] 1689.

m. Mary[1] Croston, of Whittle ... ... April 9

m. Anne Low, of Whittle ... ... „ 15

Anne Sharples, of Leland, widow ... ... May 11

Wᵐ Haworth, of Whittle ... ... „ 22

Chrofʳ Blackledge ... ... June 1

James Wilson, of Whittle ... ... „ 3

James Crichlaw, of Euxton ... ... „ 5

Rich: Walmsley, of Whittle ... ... „ 12

Mary Garstang, of Whittle ... ... July 23

——, yᵉ —— of Tho: Watson, of Whittle ... ... [no date]

Jane, yᵉ w: of Tho: Jackson, of Keurden ... ... Aug. 26

John Law, of Euxton ... ... Sept. 1

Mʳ George Walmesley, Vicar of Leland[2] ... ... „ 10

Anne Litherland, of Whittle ... ... „ 29

---

[1] There is just a possibility that this name may be Henry.

[2] Instituted February 17th, 1684-5, on the death of the late Vicar, the Rev. John Rishton. At the Preston Guild of 1682 the name of George Walmesley, "Clericus," appears among the In-burgesses. Until the restoration of Leyland Church, in 1875, a flat stone with an inscription to the memory of Vicar Walmesley used to lie under the Communion Table. For some years it lay near the exterior of the vestry, but has now been fixed in an upright position on the south side of the chancel. It may there perhaps escape the destruction which was inevitable while it lay exposed to daily traffic. The Rev. George Walmesley is described on his memorial as "hujus parochiæ vicarius, vir prope divinus." He was 34 years old at his death.

James Entwisle, of Radlesworth ... ... Oct. 5
Henery Eastham, Senr, of Leland... ... ... „(*sic*) 4
Anne, the daughter of Geo: Monk, Junr, of Leland ... „ 28
Jane, ye wife of James Livesey, of Hoghton ... ... Nov. 10
William Harrison, of Clayton ... ... „ 13
Cicely, ye D. of William Tootell, of Euxton ... ... „ 14
Elizabeth, ye wife of George Berry, in Withnell ... ... „ 22
ffrances, ye D. of John Clough, of Leland ... ... „ 22
Alice Cocker, of Whittle ... ... „ 27
Katherine Somner, of Leyland ... ... „ 29
Ann Worthington, of Leyland ... ... Dec. 1
John Wilding, of Leyland ... ... „ 23
Eliza, ye wife of Tho: Ugnall, of Wheeton ... ... „ 24
Johannah Slaytour, of Heapy, widow ... ... „ 26
Ellen Leyland, of Heapy ... ... Jan. 1
Margrett Woodcock, of Leyland ... ... „ 1
Eliza, ye Daughter of Thurstan Phiswick,[1] in Radles-
worth ... ... „ 6
Eliza, ye D. of William Jackson, of Kuerden ... ... „ 7
James, ye S: of Willia^m Darwin, of Leyland ... ... „ 29
Eliza, ye D. of Edward Farnworth, in Wheelton ... „ 30
Agnes, ye D. of Tho: Cheetham, of ffarington ... ... ffeb. 7
John fforshaw, of Leyland ... ... „ 20
Lawrence Walmsley, of Whittle ... ... „ 24
Alice, ye W. of John Gerrard, in ffarington ... ... „ 24
Hannah, ye daughter of George Bury, in Withnell ... „ 25
Margrett Woodcock, widowe, in Leyland ... ... „ 27
William Darwin, in Leyland ... ... March 3
Farington, ye S. of Richard Whittle, in ffarington ... „ 7
Richard, ye S: of James Hall, in Euxton ... ... „ 11
Mary, ye D. of John Whittle, in Leyland ... ... „ 21
Henry, the S: of Edmund Hawworth, in Whittle ... „ 21
Robert, the S: of Ralph Pilkinton, in Eccleston ... ... „ 23

Burialls, 1690.

Richard Haydock, of Whittle ... ... March 26
William, ye S: of Tho: Hey, in Heapey ... ... Aprill 4
Helen Martin, widow, in Clayton ... ... „ 7
Thomas, ye S. of Thomas Robinson ... ... „ 9
Edward, ye S. of John Park ... ... „ 16
Margery, ye D. of Tho: Critchlaw, of Euxton ... ... „ 19

[1] For Fishwick, which is derived from a township now embraced within the parliamentary borough of Preston.

Nicholas, yᵉ S. of Tho: Hey, Senʳ, in Heapey	May	2
Lawrence, yᵉ Son of Tho: Thornley, in Leyland ...	„	2
William, yᵉ S. of Ralph Johnson, of Kuerden	„	11
Richard, yᵉ So: of Richard Dobson, in Leyland	„	12
Jane, yᵉ D. of Lawrence Croft, in Whittle	„	14
John Wright, of Leyland	„	24
William, yᵉ S. of James Noblet, of Leyland...	„	31
Ann, yᵉ D. of Williaᵐ Tilson, of Euxton	June	7
Margret Wright, of Leyland	„	16
Margaret, yᵉ D. of Mʳ Thomas Crook, of Leyland ...	„	25
Jeyne, yᵉ wife of Edward Whittle, of Leyland	„	26
Margaret, yᵉ D. of James Garstang, of Andlesark¹ ...	„	27
Ann Martin, of Keurden...	„	28
Robert ffarington, of ffarington	July	3
Richard Somner, of Leland	„	7
Jane, the D: of John Smith, of Leland...	„	10
Margret, the D of Thomas Parker, in Wheelton... ...	„	28
James, yᵉ S. of Timothy Wardley, in Whittle	Aug.	15
Thomas, yᵉ S. of Evan Garner, in ffarington	„	17
Elizabeth, the D. of Gilbert Jackson, in Kuerden ...	„	31
William, the Son of Edward Kelsall, in Euxton... ...	Sept.	13
Alice Heming, of Leyland	„	16
Ellen, ye D. of William Park, in Euxton	„	17
Edward Bradshaw [Collier crossed out], of Adlington..	Oct.	6
Roger Dawson, of Clayton	„	17
Robert Cooper, of Cophall [? Coppull]...	„	22
Catherine Cooper, of Kuerden	„	22
John, yᵉ S. of John Smith, of Kuerden...	„	26
William, the son of Tho: Smith, of Preston	„	30
Jane Litherland, of Whittle	Nov.	2
m. Oliver Cross, of Euxton	„	3
Roger, the S. of William Howorth, of Whittle	„	4
James, yᵉ son of William ffarington, of ffarington ...	„	12
Thomas Martin, of Whittle	„	16
Roger Worthington, of Kuerden	„	25
Katherine, yᵉ D. of Ralph Eves, of Kuerden	Dec.	8
Ann, yᵉ wife of Lawrence Croft, of Whittle...	Jan.	7
Elizabeth, yᵉ wife of John Blackburne, of Euxton ...	„	8
John, yᵉ S: of Evan Eastham, of ffarington...	„	18
Ellen Wright, of ffarington	„	23
Cicely, the wife of John Riding, of Leyland	„	26
m. pᵈ· William Woods, of Withnell	ffeb.	1
Hugh Martin, of Leyland	„	1

¹ A township of Bolton parish, lying to the S.E. of Heapy.

Richard, yᵉ son of Nathaniel Tinklay, of Kuerden ... ffeb. 2
m. pᵈ· William Blackledge, of Leyland ... ... „ 3
Margret, yᵉ wife of William Burscow, of Leyland ... „ 7
Jane Hough, of Whittle ... ... „ 12
Elizabeth, yᵉ D. of John Martin, of Clayton ... ... „ 14
John, yᵉ S. of John Armetriding, of Euxton ... ... „ 19
Alice, yᵉ D. of John Riding, of Leyland ... ... „ 22
John, yᵉ S. of Henry Eastham, of Kuerden ... ... „ 24
John Hilton, of Whittle ... ... „ 26
John, the son of Henry Harrison, of Clayton ... ... „ 28
m. p. James Livesey, of Withnell ... ... March 4
Mary Fidler, of ffarington ... ... „(*sic*) 2
Thomas Somner, of Leyland ... ... „ 11
Jane, yᵉ D. of John Armetriding, of Euxton ... ... „ 14
Ann, yᵉ W: of Robert Blackburne, of Kuerden ... ... „ 14
James Lucas, of Heapey... ... ... „ 17
Roger Sharples, of Leyland ... ... „ 23

1691, Burialls.

Margrett, yᵉ wife of John Johnson, of Hools-Walton[1].. Aprill 2
m. pᵈ· Richard Bushell, of Kuerden ... ... „ 5
Jennet, the wife of William Croft, of Whittle ... ... „ 6
Thomas, the Son of John Park, of Leyland... ... ... „ 17
Nathaniell Tinklay, of Kuerden ... ... „ 21
Mary, the daughter of John Clough, of Leyland... ... „ 25
Sarah, yᵉ D: of George Dawson, of Leyland ... ... May 7
Grace, yᵉ wife of Robert Harrison, of Leyland ... ... „ 13
Lawrence, yᵉ S: of Henry Garstang, of Heapey ... ... „ 16
Ann, yᵉ D. of John Breares, of Euxton... ... ... „ 16
Ann, yᵉ wife of Thomas Wilson, of Wheelton ... ... „ 31
[2]Elizabeth, yᵉ wife of Robert Abbott, of Heapey ... June 10
Christian Dewhurst, of Wheelton ... ... „ 21
John Bradley, of Leyland ... ... „ 26
Robert Serjeant, of Leyland ... ... July 20
James, yᵉ S. of Tho: Cooper, of Leyland ... ... „ 31
Alice Worseley, of Wheelton, widow ... ... Aug. 4
Jennett Greenhalgh, of Wheelton ... ... „ 4
Marjary Nixon, of Euxton ... ... „ 11
Elizabeth, yᵉ wife of James Holmes, of Kuerden ... „ 13
m. pᵈ· John Woodcock, of Euxton ... ... „ 13

---

[1] For Ulneswalton, a township of Croston parish. The local pronunciation is here represented.

[2] This entry is inserted, but in the same hand as the rest.

Ann, y⁰ wife of John Catterall, of Clayton ... ... Aug.		15
Ann, y⁰ wife of Robᵗ Turner, of Leland ... ... Sept.		o1
m. John Withnell, of Euxton... ... ... „		o5
John, y⁰ S of Robert Somner, of Hool-Walton ... ... „		23
Henry, y⁰ S. of Henry Chattborne, of Leyland ... ... „		23
Ann, y⁰ D. of Timothy Wardley, of Whittle ... ... „		29
Margret, y⁰ W: of William Hilton, of Wheelton... ... Oct.		3
James Gibbons, of Leyland ... ... „		7
Richard & John, twins of John Armetriding, of Euxton „		21
Abraham, y⁰ S. of Ralph Johnson, of Kuerden ... ... „		25
Ann, y⁰ D. of Robert Turner, of Leyland ... ... „		29
Grace Mason, of Euxton... ... ... Nov.		6
John ffarnworth, of Euxton, Gen:[1] ... ... „		16
Margrett, y⁰ D. of Thomas Cooper, of Leyland ... ... „		19
Andrew, y⁰ S. of Richard Clough, of Leyland ... ... „		30
William, y⁰ S. of Will Stephenson, of Whittle ... ... Dec.		2
James Allanson, of Leland ... ... „		19
Elizabeth, y⁰ D of Giles Wadington, of Chorley ... ... „		14
Margrett, y⁰ W: of Thomas Cartwright, of Euxton ... „		16
William Tomson, of Leland ... ... „		30
Hannah, y⁰ W: of John Waller, of Wheelton ... ... Jan.		7
Ann, y⁰ wife of John Garstang, of Heape ... ... „		10
Richard Hodson, of Euxton ... ... „		19
Elizabeth, y⁰ wife of John Abbot, of Withnel ... ... „		26
Roger Cliffe, of ffarington ... ... „		27
John, y⁰ S. of John Clough, of Leyland ... ... ffeb.		1
Alice, y⁰ wife of Thomas Croston, of Ulneswalton ... „		2
Ellen Lever, of Heath Charnock ... ... „		4
Thomas, y⁰ S. of George Porter, of Leyland... ... ... „		8
Elizabeth, y⁰ D. of Richard Williamson, of ffarington „		8
Mary, y⁰ D. of John Gooden, of Leland ... ... „		12
Thomas Stephenson, of Leyland ... ... „		18
Edward Clayton, of ffarington ... ... „		18
Mary, y⁰ D. of Alexander Briers, of Whittle ... ... „		19
Thomas Riding, of Leyland ... ... „		22
Alice, y⁰ Wife of John Euxton, of Clayton ... ... „		24
Robert, y⁰ S. of Thomas Cooper, of Leyland ... ... March		7
Henery ffarington,[2] of Worden, Esqʳ ... ... „		14
Robert Dobson, Traveller ... ... „		20

[1] See pages 58, 62, 67.

[2] Henry ffarington, Esq., entered upon the family estates in 1672, at the death of his father, William ffarington, Esq. (the younger), who was so actively engaged in the Civil War, and in particular at the siege of Lathom House. The eldest son and namesake of Henry ffarington, Esq., having died before this date (in 1678), he was succeeded by his next son, William, whose baptism at Leyland will be found on page 40. The widow, Susanna (daughter of Dr. Degory Weare), was buried on Nov. 6, 1699.

1692, Burials.

Thomas Wilson, of Wheelton	...March	28
Edward Horscer [? for Oscar], of Kuerden	„	31
Ellen Hoghton, of Charnock, widow	„	31
Robert Abbott, of Heapey	...April	2
Ellen, yᵉ D. of Richard Dewhurst, of Radlesworth ...	„	5
Jane Roscow, of Charnock Richard, &... ... ... }	„	11
Dorothy, yᵉ wife of Henry Chattburne, of Leyland }		
Jane, yᵉ D. of Robert Gregson, of Farington	„	14
John, yᵉ S. of James Cocker, of Clayton	„	18
Elizabeth Tomlinson, of Clayton	„	19
Charles Stanfield, of Carrhouse Lane	„	21
Mary, yᵉ D of William Wright, of Euxton	„	23
John, S: of Gilbert Jackson, of Kuerden, Priest	„	23
Peter Barton, of Kuerden	„	25
Elizabeth Cross, of Euxton, widow	„	26
Jennet Blackledge, of Heapey ... ...May		2
Margrett, yᵉ D. of James Cocker, of Clayton	„	3
Ann, yᵉ w: of Thomas Dewhurst, of Raddlesworth ...	„	13
Thomas Croston, of Ulneswalton, & ... ... } June		11
Jennet Worthington, of Kuerden ... ... }		
Mary, yᵉ D. of William Clough, of ffarington	„	14
Grace, yᵉ Wife of James Shackley, of Euxton	„	17
Margarett, yᵉ wife of Thomas Clark, of Kuerden ...	„	23
Thomas, yᵉ S. of Richard Nelson, of Leland ... } July		6
William Rigby, of Ulneswallton ... ... }		
Grace, yᵉ wife of George Woods, of Euxton	„	7
Oliver Tootell, of Whittle	„	10
Ann, yᵉ w: of John Atherton, of Leyland ... ...Aug.		5
Elizabeth, yᵉ D. of George Dawson, of Leyland	„	6
Marjery, yᵉ D. of Robert Waring, of Leyland	„	11
Jane, yᵉ D. of William Croft, of Whittle	„	15
Elizabeth,¹ yᵉ D. of Mʳ George ffarington, of Shawe		
Hall	„	25
Martha, yᵉ D: of John Brindle, of Whittle, & ... }	„	25
Christopher Wilding, of ffarington ... ... }		
Mary, yᵉ wife of Robert Whittle, of ffarington ... ...Sept.		25
Mary, yᵉ D. of James Gorton, of Clayton	„	26
Margaret Blackledge, of Whittle	„	29
Robert Stones, of Euxton ... ...Oct.		11

¹ Baptised at Leyland, Sept. 5, 1672. She was therefore about twenty years old at her death. Her mother was Elizabeth, daughter of Valentine Whitmore, Esq., of Thurstaston, co. Chester.

B. Joseph, yᵉ Bastard Child of Peter Clayton and Jennet Marsh, of ffarington ... ... Oct. 15
B. Ishmael, yᵉ S: of Ann Taylor, of Kuerden ... ... „ 17
Ann, yᵉ W: of James Lucas, of Heapey ... ... Nov. 7
Margaret Walmsley, of Whittle ... ... „ 12
Anne, the D: of Thomas Croft, of Whittle ... ... „ 24
Lawrence, yᵉ S: of William Ugnall, of Wheelton ... „ 28
Alice, yᵉ w: of William Asley, of Whittle ... ... Dec. 2
John, ye S: of Robert Turner, of Leyland ... ... „ 4
Ralph Leyland, of Clayton ... ... „ 21
Alice Holme, of Whittle ... ... „ 22
Richard, the Son of George Charnley, of Leland ... Jan. 4
William, yᵉ S: of Richard Withnell, of Whittle ... ... „ 21
Margery Leland, of Heape ... ... „ 23
Susannah Dewhurst, of Wheelton ... ... „ 28
Ellen, yᵉ D. of William Hilton, of Wheelton ... ... ffeb. 8
Ellen, yᵉ D. of James Gibbons, of Leyland ... ... „ 11
Alice Clayton, of Raddlesworth, widdow ... ... „ 17
James, yᵉ S. of James Bolton & Jennet Martin, of Euxton ... ... „ 28
Robert Pilkington, of Leyland ... ... March 2
Jennet, yᵉ D. of James Bolton & Jennet Martin, of Euxton ... ... „ 5
Robert Harrison, of Leyland, & ... ... ⎫
James Phishwick, of Whittle ... ... ⎬ „ 18
William Hilton, of Wheelton ... ... „ 22
William, yᵉ S. of Tho: Cooper, of Leyland, Shoomaker „ 25

1693, 𝔅urᵺals.

Jane, yᵉ D: of John Stephenson, of Leyland ... ... April 1
Henry Eastham, of Whittle ... ... „ 2
Thomas, yᵉ S. of James Noblett, of Leyland ... ... „ 9
Elizabeth, yᵉ D. of Tho: Thornton, of Exton ... ... „ 23
Tho: yᵉ S. of Thomas ffletcher and Mary Leaver, of Leyland ... ... „ 28
Ellen, yᵉ D. of John Parker, of Leyland ... ... May 4
Christian, yᵉ wife of Tho: Smith, of Leyland ... ... „ 5
Henry, yᵉ S: of John Pearson, of Wheelton ... ... „ 9
Jane Barelow, of Heape ... ... „ 16
Thomas, yᵉ S. of Edward Wilding, of Charnock-Richard „ 19
Ellen, yᵉ D: of Robert Waring, of Leyland... ... ... „ 23
Alice Riding, of Leyland, widow ... ... „ 26
John Johnson, of Heapey ... ... June 6
John, yᵉ S. of James Cocker, of Clayton ... ... „ 9

Ann, yᵉ D. of Richard Somner, of Leyland	June	16
James, yᵉ S. of William Man, of Euxton	„	17
Lawrence, yᵉ S. of William Croft, of Whittle	„	28
Thomas, yᵉ S. of William Milner, of Ulneswalton ...	„	29
Mary, yᵉ D. of David Williams, of Ulneswalton	July	7
Robert Dawson, of Leyland	„	8
Elizabeth, yᵉ W: of James Gibbons	„	20
Richard Higinson, of Whittle	Aug.	25
Alice, yᵉ D: of Lawrence Croft, of Whittle	Sept.	4
Richard, yᵉ S: of Richard Cooper, of Euxton ... ⎫ Ellen, yᵉ D. of William ffarington, of Leyland ... ⎬	„	5
William, yᵉ S. of Willᵐ Gerard, of Leyland...	„	12
Henry,⎱yᵉ S. Ann, ⎰yᵉ D. of John Atherton, of Leyland	„	19
William, yᵉ S. of Hugh Browne, of Heapey	„	20
William Stephenson, of Whittle	„	24
Ellen, yᵉ w: of Ralph Duncalf, of Heapey ... ... ⎫ Ann Asley, of Heapey ... ... ⎬ Oct.		2
Edward, yᵉ S. of Thomas Nowell, of Leyland	„	4
James, yᵉ bastard child of Margret Wright, of Leyland	„	6
Henery, yᵉ S. of Robert Dawson, of Leyland	„	7
Ellen, yᵉ D. of James Hough, of Leyland	„	8
Michaell Taylor, of Euxton	„	17
Alice, yᵉ D. of John Almond, of Leyland	„	20
Jane Margeryson, of Clayton...	„	22
Jane, yᵉ D. of Richard Balshaw, of Leyland ... ⎫ Mary, yᵉ D. of Thomas Dickenson, of Heapey ... ⎬ „ Sarah Baite, of Euxton ... ... ⎭		23
Jennet, yᵉ D. of Thomas Croft, of Whittle	Nov.	10
John Armetriding, of Shaw-Green¹ in Euxton	„	16
Margaret Charnock, of Ulneswalton	„	27
William, yᵉ S. of Richard Liptrot, of Euxton	„	28
Henery Worden, of Clayton	„	29
James Sharrock, of Euxton ... ... ⎫ Mrs Susan Orrell,² of Leyland ... ... ⎬ „		30

¹ See page 54, note (¹).

² The eldest sister of Mr. Robert Charnock, of Leyland Old Hall. (See pp. 210-213.) Her name appears in the pedigree entered by the Heralds in 1616. She was called as a witness before the Commissioners in 1687, and there stated that she was a widow, and of the age of eighty years or thereabouts. If born in 1607 she must have been the eldest child of the family, and, apparently, was the last survivor. If the signature referred to in Mr. Grawell's evidence was her's, then she was unmarried as late as February 13, 1659-60. Mr. Richard Orrell was also a party to some of Mr. Charnock's pecuniary transactions, and there is reason to believe that he became the husband of Susan Charnock, the sister. If so, their married life was very brief, as Mr. Orrell died February 23, 1661-2, and was buried at Leyland.

Ann Southworth, of Leyland...	} Dec.	4
John, yᵉ S. of Thomas Harrison, of Clayton ...		
Elizabeth, yᵉ D. of Richard Liptrot, of Euxton	„	5
William ffarington, of Leyland	„	7
Mary, yᵉ D. of John Stopforth, of Leyland	„	8
Richard, yᵉ S. of Thomas Calderbank, of Euxton ...	„	9
Peter, yᵉ S. of James Biby & Ann Pearson, of Wheelton	„	11
Ann, yᵉ w: of John Blackborn, of Kuerden	„	15
Alice, yᵉ D. of William Taylor, of Whittle ... ,... ...	„	16
Ellen Melling, of Euxton	„	17
Margarett, yᵉ D of Adam Platt, of Euxton...	„	23
Roger Brining, of Whittle	„	28
Mary, yᵉ W. of William ffarington, of Leyland	Jan.	1
Jane, yᵉ D. of Michael Southworth, of Heapey	„	1
Marjary, yᵉ w. of William Mackerell, of Leyland ...	„	6
Mʳ Ralph Rushton,¹ of Leyland	„	9
Jane, the D. of Thomas Clitherall, of Euxton	„	17
William, the S. of Robᵗ Whittle, of Withnell	„	21
Jane, the D of John ffreerson, of Keurden	„	23
Ralph Chriclaw, of Euxton ... ... ,...	„	28
Margarett, yᵉ wife of Edward Short, of Kuerden ...	„	29
Margarett, yᵉ D. of Edward Short, of Kuerden	„	30
Robert, yᵉ S. of John Cliff, of Longton ... ... '...	„	30
Joseph, yᵉ S. of George Moonk, of Leyland...	ffeb.	1
Ellen, yᵉ D. of Thomas Jackson, of Keurden	„	5
Jennet, the wife of Robᵗ Eccles, of Samlsbury	„	9
Anne Woodburn, of Leyland...	„	9
Bridget, the D. of Henery Waterworth, of Leyland ...	„	10
John Eastham, of ffarington, & ... ... }	„	14
William Slaytor, of Leyland		
Ellen, the D. of George Woods, of Euxton...	„	20
William, yᵉ S. of John Sumner, de Nook in Leyland...	Mar.	5
Anne, yᵉ D. of Thomas Croft, of Whittle	„	7
Elizabeth, yᵉ w: of Thomas Harrison, of Clayton ...	„	10
Marjory Hilton, of Whittle	„	14
——, yᵉ D. of Edward Whittle, of Leyland...	„	16
Marjory, yᵉ D & } Henery Croft, of Whittle	„	17
John, yᵉ S. of }		

¹ Mr. Ralph Rushton (or Rishton) may perhaps be identified with the person of that name, who was elected as a member of the Council of Preston on March 4, 1678-9, and acted as an Alderman of the Guild of 1682. Among the In-Burgesses at the Guild of 1662 we find Geoffrey Rishton, Esq., with sons, Edward and Ralph. The last of these took the oath on August 6, 1674. The Rev. John Rishton, Vicar of Leyland (from 1677-1684), had an elder brother named Ralph. Their mother was a daughter of William Anderton, of Euxton, Esq. These last were of the "Ponthalgh" family.

Margaret, y⁰ D. of John Beardsworth, of ffarington ... Mar. 18
Hannah, y⁰ D. of William Bolton, of Withnell ... ... „ 24

[Burials] 1694.

Evan Haydock, of Heapey	...March	26
James Darwen, of Kuerden	...Aprill	1
Henry Bicursteth, of ffarington	„	3
Henry Low, of Hutton [in Penwortham parish]	„	11
Elizabeth Hawworth, of Whittle	„	16
William Garstang, of Whittle	„	19
James ffairhurst, off ffarington	„	20
Alice, y⁰ D. of Thomas Dawson, of Leyland	„	24
William, y⁰ S. of Henery Harrison, Junʳ, of Clayton ...	„	26
Thomas, y⁰ S. of Thomas Dawson, of Leyland	„	30
Elizabeth, the wife of John Mackerill, of Leyland ... May		2
John Hilton, of Euxton	„	10
(?) Tinklay, of Kuerden	„	11
John Pincock, of Euxton	„	12
Hannah, y⁰ D. of Robert ffoster, of Leyland	„	22
Margarett, y⁰ W. of Robert Whittle, of Leyland ... „		24
Elleanor, y⁰ D. of Richard Nelson, of Leyland ... ... June		1
Thomas Machen, of Leyland	„	5
Ann, y⁰ W. of James Cocker, of Clayton [Inserted] ...	„	8
William, y⁰ S. of Richard Rose, of Euxton, & ... }		
Christopher, y⁰ S. of Richard Marsden, of Withnell }	„	9
William Hodson, of Leyland	„	18
Alice Rigby, of Leyland ... ... July		3
Lawrence, y⁰ S. of William Ugnall, of Wheelton ...	„	4
Margery, y⁰ D: of Thomas Cheetham, of ffarington ...	„	8
Anne Livesey, of Withnell	„	23
William Moonk, of Leyland ... ... Aug.		1
Edward, y⁰ S. of Thomas Moulden, of Heapey	„	12
Ellen, y⁰ D. of William Milner, of Ulneswalton	„	24
Richard Sherdley, of Leyland	„	31
Mary Clayton, of Middleford [in Penwortham] ... ... Sept.		1
Elizabeth, y⁰ wife of John Scott, of Whittle	„	8
John Gooden, Junʳ, & } both of Leyland ... ... Oct.		13
John Jackson, Thatcher }		
Simon Hesketh, of Kuerden	„	14
Elizabeth Green, widow, & } both of Leyland ... „		23
Elizabeth, y⁰ w: of John Whittle }		
Margaret, y⁰ w: of John Piper, of Whittle ... ... Nov.		6
Margaret Clayton, of Kuerden	„	20
Elizabeth, y⁰ w: of Roger Garstang, of Clayton	„	29

R

Alice Parkinson, of Leyland, widow ... ... Dec.	3
Margaret Somner, of Euxton, widow ... ... ,,	5
Jane, yᵉ D. of George Moonk, of Leyland ... ... ,,	7
Thomas, yᵉ S. of Henery Chapburn, of Leyland... ... ,,	26
Richard, yᵉ S. of William Crook, of Euxton ... ... ,,	27
B. John, yᵉ S. of Cicely Johnson, of Whittle ... ... Jan.	1
Henry, yᵉ S. of Oliver Garstang, of Whittle ... ... ,,	5
Richard Marsden, of the Close-Houses,¹ in Withnell... ,,	9
Thomasin Critchlow, of Euxton ... ... ,,	10

Mary, yᵉ D. of Nicholas Whittle, of Leyland, & ...	
Evan, yᵉ S. of Thomas Withnell, of Heapey ...	,, 14
Alice, yᵉ w: of Robert Parker, of Leyland	
Mary, yᵉ D. of John Browne, of ffarington	,, 16

Elizabeth, yᵉ D. of Mʳ William Shurd,² of Clayton-Hall	,,	23
Martha, yᵉ W: of Mʳ Christopher Nowell,³ of Leyland.	,,	31
Katherine Mosse, of Clayton, widow ... ... ffeb.	10
Thomas, yᵉ S. of William Cooper, of Leyland ... ... ,,	26
Mary, yᵉ D. of William Stephenson, of Whittle ... ... March 7
Robert, yᵉ S. of Edmund Balshaw, of Leyland ... ... ,,	11
Elizabeth ffarnworth, wid: of Wheelton ... ... ,,	13
Thomas Whitehead, of Leyland ... ... ,,	17

¹ See entry on March 9, 1662, also on Dec. 2, 1696. There are two tenements, Close House and Lower Close House, situated to the south-east of the township, and near to Stanworth.

² See note on page 89. Clayton Hall had at this time passed from the Andertons into the possession of Caryll, 3rd Viscount Molineux. Mr. Sherd was probably a lessee or tenant. Six of his children were baptised at Leyland, three of which were also buried there as infants. A son Hugh, probably born earlier than any of these, was buried in 1695. No entries connected with this family occur after 1705.

³ In *Abram's Memorials of Preston Guilds*, page 71, we find the following extract from the Council Book: "11 July, 1701. Mʳ Christopher Nowell, having now some considerable time been an inhabitant of Leyland, was at his own request discharged from the Council, &c." "13 May, 1685. Ordered that Cristopher Nowell bee desired to procure a box for putting in of ye new Charter and that he also take care to send ye same to Mʳ Mallory at London with direc'cons to deliver ye same to Mʳ Will'm Patten, when he shall call for ye same in order to passe it under ye Dutchy Seale." Mr. Christopher Nowell was one of the seventeen Capital Burgesses or Councilmen named in the second Charter of Charles II. (dated 1684-5) granted to the town of Preston. Mr. Christopher Nowell was an Alderman of the Guild of 1682, and his name, together with sons Thomas and John, is recorded on the Roll. Among those who paid a fine and so were admitted at the Guild of 1662 we find a certain Christopher Nowell, and a similar means procured the admission of an apprentice of Christopher Nowell in 1682. Apparently there were two individuals of the same name citizens of Preston about this time. There was a family connection between the Nowells, of Reed, and the ffaringtons, of Worden, Alexander Nowell, Esq., having married Margaret, daughter of William and Katharine ffarington, of Worden. The Guild Rolls from 1622 to 1682 contain entries of the heads of the Nowell family, but no Christopher appears among them. He may have been a younger son of a younger son.

[Burials] 1695.

Mary, yᵉ W: of Thurstan Whittle, of Withnell ... ... March 29
Roger Dewhurst, of Cuerden ... ... April 1
Alice, the W: of Richard Goodman, of Leyland... ... „ 4
Jennet, yᵉ W: of John Pincock, of Euxton ... ... „ 12
Mathew, yᵉ S. of Tho: Worthington, of Heapey... ... „ 21
Robert Whittle, of Leyland ... ... „ 22
William, yᵉ S. of Henry Tising, of Ulneswalton ... ... May 1
Edmund Hawworth, of Whittle ... ... „ 6
Thomas, yᵉ S. of John Okenshaw, of Euxton ... ... „ 7
Isabel: Dickonson, of Charnock-Richard ... ... „ 8
Margaret, yᵉ W. of Thomas Mackerill, of Leyland ... „ 11
Jennet, yᵉ D. of William Wright, of Euxton ... ... „ 18
Ann, yᵉ W: of John Jackson, of Leyland, Wheelwright June 6
William, yᵉ S. of John Hawworth, of Whittle ... ⎫
Dorothy, yᵉ D. of Richard Leaver, of Leyland ... ⎬ July 12
Ellen, yᵉ D. of William Burscow, of Euxton ... ... „ 25
Mʳ Ralph Pudsay,[1] from Blainscow, in yᵉ Parish of
   Standish ... ... „ 31
Jane, yᵉ D. of Jennet Stephenson, of Whittle ... ... Aug. 1
Mary, yᵉ W: of George Woods, of Euxton ... ... „ 10
Ellen, yᵉ W: of Thomas Hey, Junʳ, of Heapey ... ... „ 12
Anne, yᵉ D. of John Taylor, of Whittle ... ... „ 13
Ellis Somner, of Leyland-Lane ... ... „ 17
Margrett Sherdley, of Leyland ... ... Sept. 8
Elizabeth, yᵉ W: of William Southworth, of Leyland... „ 17
William Tilson, of Euxton ... ... Oct. 12
Ralph Gregson, of Euxton ... ... Nov. 6
Richard, yᵉ S. of James Cooper, of Chorley... ... ... „ 14
William, yᵉ S. of John Cooper, of Leyland ... ... „ 22
Margaret, yᵉ D. of Lawrence Whittle, of ffarington ... Dec. 8
William, yᵉ S. of Roger Southworth, of Leyland ... „ 11
Elizabeth Pincock, of Whittle ... ... „ 20
Robert, yᵉ S. of James Cooper, of Chorley ... ... „ 24
Anne Renison, traveller ... ... „ 25
Roger, yᵉ S. of John Garstang, of Whittle ... ... „ 28
Hugh, yᵉ S. of Mʳ William Shurd,[2] of Clayton-hall ... Jan. 1
William, yᵉ S. of Ralph Pilkington, of Leyland ... ... „ 2
Thomas Smith, of Leyland, senʳ ... ... „ 6
John Biggins, of Brindle... ... ... „ 9

---

[1] Probably some connection of the person buried on March 24, 1658-9. Ambrose Pudsay, Esq., was entered as a Foreign Burgess at the Preston Guild of 1702.

[2] See note, p. 89.

Anne, yᵉ D. of Lawrence Bibby, of Heape ... ... Jan. 17
James Hewitt, of Clayton ... ... ,, 18
William, yᵉ S. of William Barker, of Warington... ... ffeb. 19
James, yᵉ S. of Roger Walton, Junʳ, of Leyland... ... ,, 25
Anne, yᵉ D. of Ralph Pincock, of Whitle ... ...March 14
James Marsden, of Whittle ... ... ,, 17

Buryalls, 1696.

Margret, yᵉ D. of Law: Taylor, of Whittle ... ...March 29
Thomas, yᵉ S. of Thomas Woodcock, of Whittle ... April 10
John, yᵉ S. of Richard Lancaster, of Keurden ... ... ,, 23
Anne Taylor, of Keurden ... ... ,, 24
Robert Dewhurst, of Wheelton ... ... ,, 27
Roger Garstang, of Clayton ... ... ,, 29

[No entries in May.]

Bridget, yᵉ wife of John Baron, of Euxton ... ... June 18
John Person, of yᵉ Windy Arbor[1]... ... ... ,, 19
Elizabeth, yᵉ D. of John Livesey, of Withnell ... ... ,, 25
B. Thomas, yᵉ S. of Margaret Bate, of Cuerden ... ... July 5
John Whittle, senʳ, of Leyland, &... ... ... ⎫
Henry, yᵉ S. of Richard Whittle, of ffarington ... ⎬ ,, 8
Alice, yᵉ D. of Ralph Walmsley, of Whittle ... ... ,, 15
Thomas Dawson, of Leyland... ... ... ,, 21
Thomas Preston, of Whittle ... ... Aug. 7
Thomas, yᵉ S. of John Taylor, of Whittle ... ... ,, 29
Margaret Cross, of Euxton ... ... Sept. 16
Catherine Cliff, of Longton ... ... ⎫
Catherine, yᵉ D: of William Hilton, of Wheelton ⎬ ,, 18
James Martin, of Heapey ... ... ,, 19
Isabel Bradshaw, of Heapey ... ... ,, 29
Margaret, yᵉ D. of John Clayton, of Clayton ... ... Oct. 7
William Charnock, of Whittle ... ... ,, 8
George Woods, of Leyland ... ... ,, 11
Ralph Johnson, of Whittle ... ... ,, 27
Alice, yᵉ W: of Ri: Marsden, of yᵉ Close-Houses[2] in
　　Withnel... ... ... Dec. 2
Ralph Ellison, of Heape... ... ... ⎫
William, yᵉ S: of Richard Rose, of Euxton... ... ⎬ ,, 5
Alice, yᵉ D: of Richard Wilson, of Whittle ... ... ,, 11

[1] In Wheelton. See entry on June 1, 1700.
[2] See note on entry Jan. 9, 1694 (Burials).

Andrew, yᵉ S. of Ralph Cooper, of . . . (*sic*) ... ... Dec. 12
Thomas, yᵉ S: of William Haydock, of uper Darwin¹.. „ 16
Ann, yᵉ W: of William Baxenden, of Euxton [In-
serted] ... ... „ 23
Alice Bisbrown, of Wheelton... ... ... „ 28
Alice Lucas, of Whittle ... ... „ 30
Elizabeth, yᵉ W: of Henry Croft, of Whittle ... ... Jan. 4
Margaret Jackson (*vidua*), of Leyland... ... ... „ 5
Elizabeth, yᵉ D. of Mʳ John Mayre, of Leyland ... ... „ 28
William, yᵉ S. of Roger Walton, senʳ, of Leyland ⎫
B. William, yᵉ S. of Mary Tildesley, of Euxton, & ⎬ „ 30
Ellen, yᵉ W: of Thurstan Litherland ... ... ⎭
Thomas, yᵉ S. of John Garstang, of Heape ... ... ffeb. 2
John, yᵉ S. of John Cliff, of Longton ... ... „ 4
William, yᵉ S. of John Yates, of Heape [Inserted] ... „ 9
William Garstang, of Whittle ... ... „ 18
William Balshaw, of Euxton ... ... „ 22
Margaret, yᵉ D. of Mathew Walkden, of Heape ... ... „ 26
Ralph Longton, of Whittle ... ...March 15
Thomas, yᵉ brother of Andrew Stones, of Leyland ... „ 18
Mʳˢ Ellen Mawdesley,² of Leyland ... ... „ 21

1697, Burials.

Grace Johnson, of Heapey ... ... April 10
Alice, yᵉ D of Thomas Hey, of Heape... ... ... „ 23
Lawrence, yᵉ S. of Mathew Worthington, of Heapey ... May 3
Mary, yᵉ D. of John Smith, of Cuerden ... ... „ 9
Elizabeth, yᵉ D: of William Bank, of Leyland ... ... „ 26
Anne, yᵉ wife of Henery Whaley, of Clayton ... ... June 12
John, yᵉ S. of Richard Nixon, of Leyland ... ... „ 15
William Mackeril, of Leyland ... ... „ 20
James, yᵉ S. of Richard Lancaster, of Keurden ... ... „ 27
Ralph Low, of Whittle ... ... July 3
Ann, yᵉ W: of William Wright, of Euxton ... ... „ 7
Jennet, yᵉ D. of William Leyland, of Keurden ... ... „ 15
William Ellison, of Withnel ... ... Aug. 3
William, yᵉ S. of Richard Waring, of Leyland ... ... „ 5
Thomas, yᵉ S. of John Gooden, of Leyland ... ... „ 21
Ann, yᵉ D. of Margaret Sharples, Traveller... ... ... Sept. 1

¹ In Blackburn parish. Otherwise Over Darwen, now a corporate town.

² The daughter of John Lawton, of Budworth, co. Chester, and widow of Mr.
William Mawdesley, of Leyland, a grandson of William Mawdesley, of Mawdesley,
Esq. Her name appears in the Visitation of 1664. See note on page 185.

Elizabeth, yᵉ W: of John Husband, of Leyland ... ... Sept. 2
Ellen Martin, of Whittle, widow ... ... „ 4
Elizabeth, yᵉ D. of John Gerrard, of ffarington ... ... „ 5
Thomas Leaver, of Leyland ... ... „ 22
Hugh, yᵉ S. of Richard Nelson, of Leyland... ... ... Oct. 15
Margaret Clough, of Leyland, *vid:* ... ... „ 18
Dorothy, yᵉ W: of Lawrence Taylor, of Whittle... ... „ 20
Alice, yᵉ W: of Ellis Waring, of Walton-Le-dale ... „ 26
Isabel, yᵉ D. of Edward Rosthorn, of Kuerden ... ... „ 27
William Tootell, of Whittle ... ... Nov. 9
Elizabeth Mackerill, of Walton Le dale ... ... „ 10
Elizabeth, yᵉ D. of William Lee, of Euxton ... ... „ 17
Ellen, yᵉ D. of John Nightingale, of Whittle ... ... „ 29
Thomas Calderbank, of Euxton ... ... ⎫
John Slaytor, of Leyland ... ... ⎬ Dec. 4
Richard Bolton, of Heapey, & ... ... ⎪
Margret, yᵉ D. of Lawrence Fish, of Whittle ... ⎭
Alice, yᵉ D. of William Hawworth, of Clayton ... ... „ 7
Robert, yᵉ S. of Thomas Cooper, de Nook[1] in Kuerden. „ 8
Ruth, yᵉ D. of Lawrence Lucas, &⎫of Whittle ... ... „ 9
Lawrence, ye S. of Thomas Croft⎭
Thomas Withington, of Clayton, & ... ... ⎫ „ 16
Margaret Wadsworth, of Euxton ... ... ⎭
Ann, yᵉ W: of Robert Blacklidge, of Whittle ... ... „ 21
Ann, yᵉ W: of Ralph Pope, of Whittle... ... ... „ 25
John Walmsley, of Euxton ... ... „ 31
James, yᵉ S. of Robert Lucas, of Heapey ... ... Jan. 3
John Blackburn, of Cuerden ... ... „ 8
Robert, yᵉ S. of John Brindle, of Whittle ... ... ⎫ „ 14
Anne, yᵉ D. of Robt: Baron, of Euxton ... ... ⎭
Alice Bromeley, *vid:* of Leyland ... ... „ 20
Elizabeth, yᵉ D. of John Slater, of Euxton ... ... ffeb. 2
Roger, yᵉ S. of Richard Southworth, of Holland[2] ... „ 7
Mark, yᵉ S. of John Moulden, of Heape ... ... „ 10
Thomas &⎫ss. of Thomas Cooper, of Keurden ... ... „ 17
Oliver,⎭
William Whitehead, of Ulneswalton ... ... „ 20
John Brears, of Euxton ... ... „ 21
John, yᵉ S. of John Gerrard, of Leyland ... ... „ 28
James, yᵉ S. of James Bullon, of Leyland ... ... March 9
John Wilden, of ffarington ... ... „ 10
William Whitehead, Junʳ, of Ulneswalton ... ... „ 11

---

[1] Off the Higher Green, in Cuerden.
[2] Either Up-Holland or Down-Holland. See p. 110 (note).

Margaret, yᵉ D. of Adam Platt, of Euxton ... ...March 15
Margaret, yᵉ D. of James Gerard, of Euxton ... ... „ 16
John Wilcockson, of Euxton... ... ... „ 19

1698, Burials.

Mary, yᵉ D. of William Garstang, of Charnock-Ri ...March 29
Richard Holmes, of Leyland... ... ...April 5
Ann Charnock, of Charnock-Ri[chard], *vid.* ... ... „ 9
Mary Humphreys, of Leyland ... ... „ 11
Robert Hindle, of Keurden ... ... „ 14
Ann Eastham, of Keurden, widow ... ... „ 17
William Crook, of Whittle ... ... „ 20
Jane, yᵉ Wife of John Welch, of Euxton ... ... „ 21
Margaret, yᵉ D. of William Rawlinson, of ffarington ... „ 23
Ann, yᵉ W: of John Gerrard, of Leyland ... ... „ 28
Alice, yᵉ W: of William Blake, of Euxton ... ... „ 29
Elizabeth, yᵉ D. of Andrew Stones, of Leyland ... ... „ 30
Mary, yᵉ W: of William Balshaw, of Euxton ... ...May 1
Cicely Wild, of Clayton ... ... „ 7
Elizabeth, yᵉ W: of Henry Brining, of Whittle, & ⎫
Jacob, yᵉ S. of John Hilton, of Leyland ... ... ⎬ „ 8
Elizabeth, yᵉ D. of Leonard Cheetham, Traveller ... „ 13
John Whittle, of Leyland ... ... „ 14
Ellen, yᵉ W: of Tho: Farington, of Farington ... ... „ 16
Richard Sudall, of Charnock-Richard ... ... „ 24
Jsabel, yᵉ D. of John Walmsley, of Euxton... ... ... „ 29
John, yᵉ S. of David Williams, of Ulneswalton ... ...June 12
Ellen, yᵉ D. of John Cliff, of Longton ... ... „ 15
Hannah Taylor, of Leyland, *vid.* ... ... „ 17
Mary Beardsworth, of Leyland, *vid.* ... ... ⎫
John, yᵉ S. of Thomas Hilton, of Wheelton... ... ⎬ „ 20
John Crichlow, of Wheelton ... ... „ 21
Thomas, yᵉ S. of Roger Bolton, of Euxton... ... ... „ 21
Ann Nelson, of Leyland ... ... „ 22
Jeofferey, yᵉ S. of Lawrence Taylor, of Whittle ... ...July 3
Margret, yᵉ D. of William Golden, of Leyland ... ... „ 13
Ellen, yᵉ D. of Gilbert Roscow, of Euxton ... ... „ 17
William Euxton, of Leyland... ... ... „ 24
Jsabel, yᵉ W. of George Moonk, of Leyland ... ...Aug. 5
William Crook, of Euxton ... ... ⎫
Thomas, yᵉ S. of Thomas Cooper, of Leyland ... ⎬ „ 7
William, yᵉ S. of William Roscow, of Charnock-
Richard... ... ... „ 27

Elizabeth Atherton, of Leyland, *vid.*, &	} Aug.	28
Jennet, yᵉ D. of John Almond, of Leyland ...		
Dorothy, yᵉ Wife Tho: Critchley, of Euxton ...	„	30
Lawrence, yᵉ S. of Richard Almond, of Leyland	Sept.	1
Mary, yᵉ D. of Ralph Low, of Whittle ...	„	7
John Baron, of Euxton ...	„	8
Thomas, yᵉ S. of Andrew Waterworth, of Euxton	„	26
Mary Low, of Euxton, *vid:* ...	Oct.	21
B. Hugh, yᵉ S. of Thomas Mosse &	} Nov.	13
Elizabeth Clayton, of Clayton		
Isabel Makinson, of Euxton ...	„	20
Ellen, yᵉ D. of William Neeld, of Euxton ...	Dec.	20
Margaret Cooper, of Euxton...	„	30
Richard Cliff, of Leyland	Jan.	1
Thomas Cooper, Senʳ, of Cuerden...	„	19
Ellen, yᵉ D. of James Blackledge, of Leyland	„	26
A D[aughter] of Peter Wethersbyˢ, of Leyland, born		
27 Janʸ, buried the	„	28
Alice Burscow, of Leyland	„	31
Robert Welch, of Leyland	ffeb.	6
Ann, yᵉ W: of Ralph Walmsley, of Whittle	„	8
B. Thomas, yᵉ S. of Jane Parkinson, of Clayton		
[Inserted]	„	19
Hannah, yᵉ D. of Roger Harrocks, of Euxton ...	„	21
Robert, yᵉ S. of Robert Cocker, of Leyland	„	23
Ellen Critchlow, of Euxton ...	„	26
Ellis, yᵉ S. of Roger Bolton, of Euxton	„	27
Jane, yᵉ wife of Richard Entwisle, of Withnell ...	March	2
Margaret Thornton, of Euxton	„	8
Ellis Somner, of Leyland	„	9
Thomas Clitherall, of Euxton	„	19
Robert Hunt, of Keurden	„	22
James, yᵉ S. of John Taylor, of Kuerden	„	24

1699, Burials.

Mary Grundy, of Leyland	March	25
William Bank, of Leyland	„	29
Jannett Crook, of Withnell	„	31
Katherine Garstang, of Whittle	April	2
Anne, yᵉ wife of Richard Eastham, of Heape	„	3
Ellis, yᵉ S. of Robert Sumner, of Ulneswalton ...	„	11
Ellen Woodcock, of Euxton, *vid:*...	„	12
William, yᵉ S. of John Gerard, of ffarington	„	17

Jane, yᵉ D. of James Cocker, of Clayton ... ... April 25
William Boardman, of Withnel ... ... May 8
Margaret, yᵉ D: of Mʳ Edward ffarnworth,[1] of Runshaw
in Euxton ... ... ,, 12
Mary, yᵉ D: of Ralph Livesey, of Leyland ... ... ,, 15
Ralph Livesey, of Leyland ... ... ,, 17
John, yᵉ S: of Roger Blackburn, of Kuerden ... ... ,, 22
Elizabeth,[2] yᵉ D. of Mʳ William ffarington, in Ley-
land ... ... ,, 23
John, yᵉ S. of William Cross, of Euxton ... ... ,, 26
Jane, yᵉ W: of Richard Tootel, of Whittle ... ... ,, 27
Edward Clough, of Leyland ... ... June 3
Henry Smith, of Euxton, & ... ... ⎫
Ann, yᵉ W: of John Taylor, of Whittle ... ... ⎬ ,, 5
Elizabeth Woodcock, of Euxton ... ... ,, 10
James, yᵉ S. of William Burscow, of Euxton ... ... ,, 11
Andrew Waterworth, of Euxton ... ... ,, 27
Hannah, yᵉ D. of Mʳ William Sherd, of Clayton ... ... July 16
John Riding, of Clayton, Junʳ ... ... ,, 26
Jane Haydock, of Heapey, *vid:* ... ... Aug. 7
Richard Martin, of Wheelton ... ... ,, 19
Edward Farnworth, of Wheelton ... ... Sept. 1
George Sharples, of Leyland ... ... ,, 3
Lawrence, yᵉ S. of Jo: Singleton, of Euxton ... ... ,, 4
John Kenion, of Heapey ... ... ,, 12
Ellen, yᵉ W: of John Pincock, of Euxton ... ... Oct. 5
William ffishwick, of Withnell ... ... Nov. 3
Mrs. Susanna Farington,[3] of Worden, *vid:* ... ... ,, 6
Elizabeth Tootell, of Whittle, *vid:* ... ... ,, 9
Jennet Lucas, of Whittle ... ... ,, 21
Katherine, yᵉ W: of James Noblet, of Leyland ... ... ,, 23
Margaret, yᵉ W: of Thomas Longton, of Whittle ... ,, 24
Margaret, yᵉ W: of John Martin, of Heapey ... ... ,, 28

[1] See notes on pp. 58, 62, 67.

[2] The infant child of Mr. William ffarington and his wife Elizabeth (Rufine), and grandchild of Mr. George ffarington, of Shawe Hall. Her father afterwards suc-ceeded to the Worden estates, owing to the death of William ffarington, Esq. (a first cousin) without issue.

[3] Mrs. Susannah Farington was the widow of Henry ffarington, Esq., of Worden, the entry of whose burial will be found on March 14, 1691-2. Her father was Dr. Digory Weare, Professor of History at Oxford, and Principal of Gloucester Hall. The marriage seems to have taken place in 1658—probably in Oxford. There were two sons and four daughters as the issue of the marriage. Henry, the eldest son, died in the lifetime of his parents, and without children, so that his brother William succeeded to the family honours. The wife of Vicar Armetriding was the eldest daughter of Mrs. Susanna Farington.

Jane, ye D. of James Gerrard, of Clayton	... Dec.	11
William, ye S. of William Slater, of Leyland	„	14
John, ye S: of Richard Loxam, of Ulneswalton	„	16
William, ye S. of Thomas Thornley, of Leyland... ...	„	25
John Clayton de Bank-head, in Clayton	... Jan.	2
Margaret Allen, of Euxton	„	6
John & William, S^{ns} of John Leyland, of Leyland ...	„	7
Margaret, ye D. of Thomas Crichlow, of Euxton ...	„	9
Thomas, ye S. of Thomas ffarington, of ffarington ...	„	13
Ann, ye D. of Richard Waring, of Leyland	„	14
Thomas, ye S. of John Nightingale, of Whittle	„	16
Mary, ye W: of John Pilkington, of Leyland	„	26
Robert, ye S. of John Low, of Euxton	„	29
Roger ffishwick, of Withnell ... ... ffeb.		4
Henery Garstang, of Wheelton	„	7
Jane, ye D: of William Hawworth, of Whittle	„	14
Charles Whitehead, of Leyland, &	} „	17
Edward, ye S. of John Low, of Euxton		
Mary Bradbury, of Clayton	„	23
Catherin Hilton, of Wheelton		
Jane, ye D: of John Blackledg, of Wheelton, & ...	} „	24
Ann, ye D. of Charles Rothwel, of Leyland ...		
Ellen, ye W: of Henery Croft, of Whittle	„	28
Thomas, ye S. of William ffassacherly,[1] of Clayton ... March		4
Ellen Ashborner, of ffarington, *vid:*	„	4
George, ye S: of George Porter, of Leyland...	„	12
John Man, of Leyland, &	} „	19
Alice Johnson, of Heapey		
John Pincock, of Euxton	„	22
Ellen Wilding, of ffarington	„	23

1700, Burials.

John ffishwick, of Withnel	... March	26
Elizabeth Eastham, of ffarington, *vid:*...	„	27
Jennet, ye D: of Richard Whittle, of Cuerden	„	31
Margret Wadsworth, of Euxton	... April	3
John, ye S. of Edward Rawsthorn, of Cuerden	„	4
Alice Jackson, of Cuerden, *vid:*	„	13
Elizabeth Longton, of Whittle, *vid:*	„	14
William Southworth & } both of Leyland ...	„	20
Martha, ye W: of John Jackson		

---

[1] The more common spelling of this name is **Fazackerley.**

Hugh Armetriding,[1] of yᵉ Armetriding, in Euxton ... April 23
Mary Woods, of Leyland, *vid:* ... ... „ 29
Thomas Walmsley, of Leyland ... ... May 16
Jennet, yᵉ W: of Robert Somner, of Ulnes: Walton ... „ 25
John, yᵉ S. of John Clayton, of Clayton, senʳ ... ... „ 29
Ellen, yᵉ D: of Ralph Pearson, of yᵉ Windy Harbor, in
    Wheelton ... ... June 1
Margaret, yᵉ D: of John Wright, of Leyland ... ... „ 2
Elizabeth Pincock, of Whittle ... ... ⎫
Dorothy Sherburn, of Great Eccleston... ... ... ⎭ „ 12
Anne, yᵉ W: of Richard Whittle, of Clayton ... ... „ 22
James, yᵉ S: of John Clough, of Leyland ... ... „ 23
John Scott, of Whittle ... ... July 2
Agnes Dickonson, of Withnel ... ... „ 11
Alice, yᵉ W: of Henry Wilson, of Bretherton ... ... „ 13
Anne, yᵉ D: of Henery Mouldin, of Leyland ... ... „ 28
John, yᵉ S: of John Mann, of Whittle ... ... „ 31
Elizabeth, yᵉ D: of Margery Cliff, of Whittle ... ... Aug. 2
Agnes Walmesley, of Whittle ... ... „ 4
Henery Eastham, of Keurden ... ... „ 7
Richard, yᵉ S. of John Singleton, of Euxton, & ... ⎫
Mary, yᵉ D. of John Pilkington, of Leyland ... ⎭ „ 10
Elizabeth, yᵉ D: of Gilbert Cowling, of Leyland ... „ 16
James Hornby, of Clayton ... ... Sept. 11
Elizabeth, yᵉ D. of Edward Farnworth, of Euxton ... „ 18
John Farington, of Leyland ... ... „ 21
Jennet, yᵉ D: of William Sharrock, of Euxton ... ... „ 26
Adam Clayton, of Clayton ... ... Oct. 10
Ellen, yᵉ D. of Robert Baron, of Clayton ... ... „ 22
Ralph, yᵉ S. of John Hunt, of Cuerden ... ... „ 25
Jenet, yᵉ W: of Roger Brining, of Whittle ... ... Nov. 5
William Marsh, of ffarington ... ... Dec. 17
Elizabeth Trueman, of Leyland ... ... „ 20
Elizabeth Roscow, of Euxton ... ... „ 28
Roger Bromeley, of Whittle ... ... „ 30
Ann, yᵉ W: of John Smith, *alias* Garstang, of Whittle Jan. 1
Alice, yᵉ D: of John Nightingale, of Whittle ... ... „ 2
Elizabeth, yᵉ D: of William Boydal, Junʳ, of Euxton... „ 11

[1] Hugh Armetriding was baptised on January 10, 1657, at Leyland. He was the eldest brother of Vicar Armetriding, and son of John Armetriding, maltster, of Euxton, who was buried on August 13, 1684 (see note thereon). The inscription on the family tomb states that at death he was in his 42nd year. His name is given in the Letters Patent, issued under the Great Seal in 1690, as one of the Trustees to whom Leyland Hall was conveyed for the benefit of future Vicars of Leyland. (See note on ffeb. 4, 1670, when Mr. Robert Charnock was buried.) See entry of Baptism, Jan. 10, 1657.

John Singleton, of Euxton, & ... ...   } Jan. 14
Ellen, yᵉ D: of Richard Jackson, of Wheelton ...
John Martin, of Heapey ... ...   ,, 15
John Marsden, of Withnell ... ...   ,, 21
Elizabeth Serjant, of Leyland, *vid.* ... ...   ,, 28
John, yᵉ S: of Evan Gardiner, of ffarington ... ... ffeb. 9
John Hollinhurst, of Tarleton ... ...   ,, 12
Nicholas Norris, of Leyland ... ...   ,, 15
William Hollinhurst, of Cuerden ... ...   ,, 18
⟋Elizabeth Bromeley, of Whittle, *vid:* ... ...   ,, 19
Margaret, yᵉ W: of Richard Dobson, Traveller ... ... March 3
William Farnworth, of Brimicroft, in Withnel ...   }
Mary, yᵉ W: of John Rigby, of Euxton ... ...   } ,, 19
Richard, yᵉ S. of Richard Hodson, of yᵉ Dawbers-
Lane,[1] in Euxton ... ...   ,, 24

Burials, 1701.

Thomas Hall, of Euxton ... ... March 29
Jane Walker, of Whittle, *vid:* ... ... April 7
George Bancroft, of Leyland, & ... ...   }
Agnes, yᵉ Wife of George Dawson, of Leyland ...   } ,, 14
Anne Croft, of Whittle, *vid:* ... ...   ,, 19
Alice, yᵉ D: Michael Southworth, of Wheelton ... ...   ,, 30
John, yᵉ S: of James Cocker, of Clayton ... ... May 3
[2]Henry Ounsworth, of Euxton ... ...   ,, 8
[2]James Wiggans, of Kuerden ... ...   ,, 10
John, yᵉ S. of Thomas Roscow, in Euxton ... ...   ,, 11
Thomas, yᵉ S. of Thomas Nowel ... ...   ,, 17
Henry, yᵉ S. of William Blackledge, of Wheelton ...   ,, 18
William, yᵉ S. of William Willson, of Leyland ... ...   ,, 21
Jane, yᵉ W: of George Hough, in Bolton Parish ... ...   ,, 22
Ann Piccop, of Heapey, *vid:*... ... ...   ,, 23
Thomas, yᵉ S: of Thomas Hilton, of Wheelton ... ...   ,, 29
Jane, yᵉ D. of George Woods, of Leyland ... ...   ,, 31
Ellen Dewhurst, of Cuerden, *vid:*... ... ... June 10
John Nutter, of Leyland ... ...   ,, 15
Jennet, yᵉ W: of Thomas Biby, of Heapy ... ...   ,, 24
Thomas Longton, of Whittle ... ... July 4
Elizabeth Hilton, of Whittle ... ...   ,, 9

---

[1] Starting from the main road, a short distance south of Euxton Hall, it runs almost parallel to the River Yarrow, but rises as it gets west, and passes through Shaw Green.

[2] There has been some scratching out here, but the handwriting appears to be the same.

George, yᵉ S. of George Bancroft, of Leyland ... ... July 16
Elizabeth, yᵉ D: of William Taylor, of Heapey, & ⎫
Thomas, yᵉ S: John Bromeley, of Leyland ... ... ⎭ „ 24
Ellen, yᵉ D: of Thomas Morris, of Heapey, & ... ... Aug. 16
Jennet, yᵉ W: of Henry Armetriding, of Charnock-Ri.,
Stan[dish] Pa[rish] ... ... „ 16
John, yᵉ S. of John Jackson, of Leyland ... ... Sept. 8
Alice, yᵉ W: of Richard Lancaster, of Clayton ... ... „ 15
Elizabeth, yᵉ D: of Richard Farington, of Farington ... „ 22
Ann Garstang, of Ulnes-Walton ... ... „ 27
Benjamin, yᵉ S. of Thomas Withnel, of Heapey ... ... Nov. 6
Ralph Hilton, of Sowrby,[1] in yᵉ Pʳⁱˢʰ of Michaels ... „ 7
Ralph Duncalf, of Heapey ... ... „ 11
Samuel, yᵉ S. of Samuel Duncalf, of Heapey ... ... „ 19
Elisabeth Dickonson, of Cuerden ... ... „ 30
Elizabeth Mayo, Traveller ... ... Dec. 1
William Serjeant, of Leyland ... ... „ 12
Elizabeth Brownlow, *vid:* of Whittle ... ... „ 15
Margret Ellison, of Andlesark, in Bolton Pʳⁱˢʰ ... ... „ 18
Ann, yᵉ W: of James Roscow, in Leyland ... ... „ 22
Thurstan Litherland, of Whittle ... ... Jan. 1
Alice, yᵉ W: of Thomas Worthington, of Heapey ... „ 4
Margret Johnson, of Leyland ... ... „ 5
Ellen, yᵉ D. of Roger Liptrot, of Leyland ... ... „ 7
William Cross, of Leyland ... ... „ 13
Thomas Latham, of Clayton ... ... „ 19
James, yᵉ S. of William Critchlow, of Euxton ... ... „ 21
Ellen Hindle, of Cuerden, *vid:* ... ... „ 25
Richard Robinson, of Charnock Richard, in Standish
Pʳⁱˢʰ ... ... ffeb. 12
Ann Martin, of Eccleston ... ... „ 23
Isabel, yᵉ D. of John Withnel, of Withnel ... ... „ 25
Isabel, yᵉ W: of Roger Liptrot, of Leyland... ... ...March 17
Joseph, yᵉ S. of Thomas Withnel, of Heapey, &... ⎫
Margret, yᵉ D: of James Hornby, of Clayton ... ⎭ „ 18

1702, Burials.

Ann, yᵉ W: of Thomas Farington, of Leyland, & ⎫
Alice, yᵉ D. of Richard Whittle, of Withnel ... ⎭ March 25
Thomas, yᵉ S. of Andrew Stones, of Leyland, & ⎫
Sarah, yᵉ W: of William Hawworth, of Whittle ... ⎭ „ 28

---

[1] A township which goes with Inskip. Both are within the parish of S. Michael's-on-Wyre, which lies between Preston and Lancaster.

Alice, yᵉ D. of James Livesay, in Withnel ... ... April 10
Ann, yᵉ D. of John Tootel, of Whittle ... ... „ 15
Elizabeth, yᵉ W: of John Gooden, of Leyland ... ... „ 16
Gilbert, yᵉ S. of William Ugnal, of Wheelton ... ... „ 21
Alice, yᵉ W: of John Tootel, of Whittle ... ... „ 25
Elizabeth, yᵉ W: of Roger Hollinhurst, of Leyland ... May 9
William, yᵉ S. of William Roscow, of Charnock⎫
Richard, & ... ... ⎬ „ 14
Isabel, yᵉ W. of Henry Kirkham, of Farington ... ⎭
James, yᵉ S. of Thomas Cooper, of Leyland ... ... „ 18
Edward Whittle, of Leyland ... ... ⎫ „ 28
Elizabeth, yᵉ W: of Thomas Garstang, of Whittle ⎭
Dorothy, yᵉ D: of Richard More, of Euxton ... ... „ 29
Lawrence, yᵉ S: of Thomas Croft, of Whittle ... ... „ 31
Cicely Clayton, of Clayton, *vid:* ... ... June 3
Thomas, yᵉ S: of Thurstan Sharrock, of Euxton ... „ 10
Dorothy, yᵉ D: of William Hawworth, of Whittle ... „ 20
William, yᵉ S. of Robert Somner, of Ulneswalton ... „ 24
William, yᵉ S. of Thomas Cooper, of Leyland ... ... July 4
John, yᵉ S. of John ffishwick, of Withnel ... ... „ 11
Jane Longton, of Whittle ... ... „ 12
John Atherton, of Leyland below yᵉ Town[1] ... ... Aug. 11
Elizabeth Riding, of Leyland, *vid:* ... ... „ 18
William Hesket, of Clayton ... ... „ 22
Thomas, yᵉ S. of Roger Harrocks, of Euxton ... ... „ 25
William, yᵉ S. of Andrew Waterworth, of Leyland ... „ 27
Elizabeth Woodruff, of Wheelton, *vid:*... ... ... „ 28
Alice, yᵉ D. of John Scot, of Whittle ... ... Sept. 4
William Edward,[2] yᵉ Son of Mr. William Farington, of
Leyland S[hawe] Hall ... ... „ 14
Ralph, yᵉ S. of Henry Smith, of Euxton ... ... „ 17
Elizabeth, yᵉ W: of William Blackledg: of Wheelton... Oct. 8
William Pincock, of Whittle ... ... „ 14
Jane Woods, of Leyland, *vid:* ... ... „ 23
Alexander, yᵉ S. of Hugh Brown, of Heapey ... ... Nov. 4
Margaret, yᵉ W: of Richard ffishwick, of Wheelton ... „ 17
Jane Hawet,[3] of Parbold, in Eccleston Parish ... ... „ 18
Roger Hollinhurst, of Leyland ... ... „ 25

---

[1] Part of Leyland is still known as Lower Side. It is applied to the portion of the township which lies west of Leyland Lane or of the River Lostock. There is a farm on the left of Leyland Lane called "Atherton's."

[2] This infant, baptised on Oct. 8, 1701, was the son of Mr. Wm. Farington and his wife Elizabeth (Rufine), and grandchild of Mr. George Farington, of Shawe Hall.

[3] This gives almost exactly the local pronunciation of the more common name "Heywood."

Hugh Southworth, of Clayton ... ... Dec. 4
Bernard Hoghton, of Leyland ... ... „ 13
Richard Farington, of Farington, & ... ... ⎱
Jennet Bushel, of Cuerden, *vid:* ... ... ⎰ „ 16
John Jackson, of Leyland, Wheelwright ... ... „ 23
Margery, yᵉ W: of John ffishwick, of Withnel ... ... „ 24
Jane Gregson, of Euxton, *vid:* ... ... „ 31
Thomas, yᵉ S: of George Longworth, of Euxton ... Jan. 1
John Parker, of Charnock Ri: in Standish Parish ... „ 4
Jonathan, yᵉ S. of Evan Eastham, of Farington ... ... „ 10
Mary, yᵉ D: of William Croft, of Whittle ... ... „ 16
Henry Brining, of Leyland ... ... „ 20
Jennet Bickursteth, of Farington ... ... „ 23
Elizabeth, yᵉ W: of Oliver Garstang, of Whittle ... „ 24
Mary, yᵉ D: of Oliver Garstang, of Whittle ... ... „ 25
Catherin Farrington, of Farrington, *vid:* ... ... „ 27
William Walmsley, of Euxton 28
Ann, yᵉ D: of William Gerrard, of Leyland ... ... ffeb. 2
Elizabeth, yᵉ Wife of Henry Tising, of Ulneswalton ... „ 5
Thomas, yᵉ S. of Roger Cocker, of Leyland ... ... „ 10
Gilbert Cowling, of Leyland ... ... „ 24
John Yate, of Whittle ... ... „ 27
Mary,[1] yᵉ Wife of Mʳ William Anderton, of Euxton ... March 1
Alice, yᵉ W: of Richard Rose, of Euxton ... ... „ 4
Elizabeth, yᵉ W: of William Jackson, of Cuerden ... „ 8

1703, Burials.

John Euxton, of Clayton ... ... April 28
Richard Waring, of Leyland ... ... May 20
Christian, yᵉ W: of Hugh Brown, of Heapey, & ... ⎱
Alice, yᵉ D: of Richard Richmond, of Withnel ... ⎰ June 6
William Clough, of Hool ... ... „ 28
John Richmond, of Withnel ... ... „ 29
Elizabeth, yᵉ D: of Thomas Porter, of Leyland [In-
serted] ... ... „ 30
Richard, yᵉ S: of John Okenshaw, of Euxton ... ... July 2
Cicely Loxam, of Ulnswalton ... ... „ 17
John Marsh, of Leyland ... ... „ 23

[1] Mrs. Mary Anderton was a daughter of William ffarington, Esq., and his wife Katharine (ffleetwood). Can she be identified with the Mary (Mʳⁱˢ Mary Leake), of Worden, married at Leyland on July 6, 1670, to Mr. William Anderton, of Euxton? If so, there must have been a previous marriage. The family pedigrees give no assistance. See note on page 136.

Alice Fishwick, of Livesay, in Blackburn Prish	July	25
William ffarnworth, of Wheelton, & Frances, ye D. of James Richmond, of Withnel	Aug.	2
Margery Bomber, in Leyland	"	7
Mary Richmond, of Withnel, *vid:*	"	16
William, ye S. of William Hesketh, of Leyland	"	23
Jennet, ye D. of John Johnson, of Heapey	"	30
Elizabeth Wilding, of Farington, *vid:*	"	31
Mary, ye D: of Matthew Walkden, of Heapey	Sept.	8
Henry Litherland, of Whittle	"	17
Ann Bowling, of Euxton, *vid:*	"	28
Ann Euxton, of Clayton, *vid:*	Oct.	16
Ann Lucas, of Higher Charnock,[1] in Standish Parish	Nov.	3
Grace Wilson, of Whittle, *vid:*	"	4
Ellen, ye D. of Richard Hodson, of Euxton	"	13
Thomas, ye S. of Richard Johnson, of Cuerden	"	19
John Garstang, of Leyland	"	23
William Milner, of Ulnswalton	"	24
William Sharrock, of Euxton	"	26
Ellen Farington, of Ulnswalton, *vid:*	Dec.	10
Alice, ye W: of Geffrey Taylor, of Heapy	"	11
William, ye Peter Clayton, of Farington, & Elizabeth, ye D: of William Jackson, of Leyland	"	18
Hugh Withnel, of Whittle	"	23
Alice, ye w: of George Moonk, of Leyland	Jan.	1
John, ye S: of William Milner, of Ulnswalton	"	7
Agnes Walmsley, of Euxton, *vid:*	"	12
Ellen, ye D: William Cooper, of Leyland	"	14
Ann Low, of Ulnswalton, *vid:*	"	18
Elizabeth Heald, of Leyland, *vid:*	"	21
Roger, ye S. of Thomas Croft, of Whittle	"	23
Alice Taylor, of Whittle, *vid:*	"	29
Ralph Eves, of Cuerden	"	30
Jane Waring, of Farington, *vid:*	Feb.	2
William, ye S. of John Garstang, of Whittle	"	18
William, ye S. of William Roscow, of Whittle	"	24
Henry, ye S. of John Kirkham, of Farington	"	25
William, ye S. of Thomas Westby, of Cuerden	March	5
Jane, ye D: of John Bury, of Withnel	"	7
John, ye S. of Thomas Silcock, of Clayton	"	10

[1] Otherwise Heath-Charnock.

1704, Burials.

Elizabeth, yᵉ W: of John Giller, of Farington	April	5
Mary Calderbank, of Euxton, *vid:*	„	8
John Riding, of Clayton, & ... ... ⎫		
A child of John Slaytar & Mary Sagers, of Euxton ⎬	„	11
Ann Hodson, of Euxton, *vid:*	„	12
William Cowling, of Leyland, & ... ... ⎫		
Christofer, yᵉ S. of Henry Garstang, of Wheelton ⎬ May		1
Hannah, yᵉ D of John Piper, of Whittle	„	6
Elizabeth, yᵉ W: of Richard Crook, of Euxton	„	7
Isaac Sharrock, of Whittle	„	8
Roger Brining, of Whittle ... ... ⎫		
Edith, yᵉ D. of Robert Marsh, of Farington ... ⎬	„	12
Elizabeth, yᵉ D: of Thomas Sumner, of Euxton ...	„	15
Christofer Nowel,¹ of Leyland	„	19
William Anderton,² of Euxton-Hall, Gentleman ...	„	22
Alice Armetriding, of Euxton, *vid*	„	28
Henry, yᵉ S of Henry Catterall & Ellen Cocker, of		
Clayton	„	29
John Brown, of Farington	„	31
John, yᵉ S: of William Wright, of Euxton	June	2
Dorothy, yᵉ D: of Richard Leaver, of Leyland	„	3
Roger Lockwood, of Owlerton [Ollerton in Withnel]...	„	5
John Walmsley, of Whittle	„	16
John, yᵉ S. of Andrew Waterworth, of Leyland	„	20
Mary, yᵉ D: of Roger Blackburn, of Cuerden	„	21
William, yᵉ S: of Robert Blackledg, of Heapy	„	26
Isabel Fish, of Whittle, *vid:*	July	2
Alice, yᵉ D: of Henry Tod, of Leyland	„	9
Richard, yᵉ S. of Mary Rothwel, Traveller	„	11
Henry, yᵉ S. of Hugh Smith, of Euxton	„	16

¹ See note on entry Jan. 31, 1694 (Burials).

² This is probably the William Anderton, of Euxton, who was aged 26 years at the Herald's Visitation in 1664. See note page 136, also on March 1, 1702 (Burials). It is very difficult, however, to be sure of the identity of the different members of this extensive family, for there is great confusion in the various notices of them, and some errors in the dates. The Andertons of Clayton, of Euxton, and of Lostock are not clearly distinguished. The Preston Guild Rolls are entirely silent as to any "Anderton of Euxton." At the Guild of 1582, James Anderton, of Clayton, Ar., and his sons are entered, and the head of the family and his heirs appear among the Foreign Burgesses down to 1682. The fact seems to be that the Euxton and Clayton estates went together until the settlement of a younger branch at Euxton. The Clayton branch had the lordship of their manor of Clayton, which was not the case with Euxton until recent times. By the end of the 17th century the Andertons, of Clayton, had died out, whereas the Euxton branch became gradually more wealthy and better known, and has continued in possession down to the present time.

Evan, yᵉ S: of John Withnel, of Withnel Fold[1]	July	17
George Farington,[2] of Shaw: Hall, Gentleman ...		
Elizabeth Park, of Leyland	„	24
James, yᵉ S. of William Physakerley, of Whittle...		
John Withnel, of Withnel	„	26
Ellen, yᵉ D: of Peter Barton, of Cuerden, & ...		
Ellen, yᵉ D: of Gilbert Roscow, of Euxton	Aug.	7
William Farnworth, of Wheelton	„	10
Mrs Elizabeth Farington,[3] of Shaw-Hall, *vid:*	„	18
John Scot, of Whittle	„	18
Thomas, yᵉ S. of Thomas Porter, of Ulnswalton... ...	„	22
Richard Whittle, of Withnel		
Alice Biggins, of Whittle, *vid:* &	„	28
Alice, yᵉ D: of John Serjant, of Leyland		
Margret Leigh, of Ulnswalton ... ... Oct.		18
Elizabeth, yᵉ D: of Thomas Croft, of Whittle	„	19
Jane, yᵉ W: of George Dawson, senʳ, of Leyland ...	„	20
Grace, yᵉ D: of James Richmond, of Withnel ... ... Nov.		4
Mary, yᵉ W: of Peter Walkden, of Heapey	„	9
Jonie Hodson, of Cawbeck, in Euxton, *vid:*	„	11
Lawrence Biby, of Heapy	„	18
William Hardacre, of Clayton	„	22
Thomas, yᵉ S: of Thomas Ditchfield, of Euxton ...	„	24
Jennet, yᵉ D: of William Sharrock, of Euxton	„	25
William, yᵉ S. of Thomas Withington, of Clayton ...	„	28
Henry, yᵉ S. of John Yate, of Heapey ... ... Dec.		7
Elizabeth, yᵉ W. of Henry Tod, of Leyland	„	12
Alice Garstang, of Whittle, *vid:*	„	16
Margery, yᵉ W: of William Slaytor, Junʳ, of Leyland...	„	19
Elizabeth, yᵉ W: of John Briers, of Wheelton	„	23
Ralph Pierson, of Windie Harbor, in Wheelton	„	30
Richard Almond, in Leyland ... ... Jan.		3
John Milner, Junʳ, of Ulnswalton	„	6
Henry, yᵉ S. of William Charnock, of Whittle	„	12

[1] This is situated at the extreme north-eastern corner of the township.

[2] Mr. George ffarington, of Shaw Hall, was the second son of William ffarington, Esq. (the proposed Knight of the Oak), and his wife Katharine (ffleetwood). He married in 1672, Elizabeth, daughter of Valentine Whitmore, of Thurstaston, co. Chester. The eldest son of this marriage, William (baptised at Leyland, June 10, 1675), ultimately succeeded to the Worden estates. The other son, Valentine, was an M.D. in Preston. The two daughters, Elizabeth and Margaret, both died childless. Mr. George ffarington was entered as a Foreign Burgess at the Preston Guild of 1662, with his father and elder brother Henry. Also in 1682 with own sons William and Valentine.

[3] Mrs. Elizabeth Farington, of Shaw Hall, was the relict of Mr. George Farington, buried on July 24th, 1704 (see note). She survived her husband less than a month.

Alice Euxton, of Over-Hilton, in Dean P^{rish} ...	
Sarah, ye D: of Thurstan Phishwick, of Raddlesworth	Jan. 18
Mary, ye D. of Hugh Waterworth, of Farington-Hall[1]..	„ 20
Eleanor, ye D: of James Hall, of Euxton	„ 21
Thomas, ye S. of Ralph Walmsley, of Whittle	„ 26
Mary, ye D: of James Hall, of Euxton ... ... Feb.	6
Elizabeth, ye W: of William Tootel, of Heapey, Slaytor	„ 7
Mary, ye D. of Thomas Hey, of Heapey	„ 9
Jennet, ye D: of William Simmons, of Cuerden	„ 12
Margaret, ye w: of James Shakerley, of Euxton, &	
John Taylor, of Whittle	„ 17
Leonora, ye w: of Mr Farrond Hodgson,[2] of Leyland...	„ 18
Thomas, ye S: of George Porter, of Leyland	„ 27
John Riding, of Leyland ... ... March	3
Alice, ye D: of Robert Welch, of Leyland	„ 4
John Brindle, of Whittle	„ 9
John Taylor, of Cuerden	„ 20

Burials, 1705.

Thomas Jackson, of Cuerden ... ... April	6
Henry Breckall, of Leyland	„ 10
Henry Blackledg, of Wheelton	„ 13
Margret Hilton, of Clayton	„ 18
Richard Clough, of Leyland	„ 19
Ann, ye D of John Moulden, of Heapey	„ 21
Catherine, ye D. of William Sherd, at Clayton Hall[3]...	„ 23
Alice, ye D. of John ffishwick, of Withnel	„ 27
Henry, ye s: of Henry Breckall and Ann Moulden, of	
Leyland ... ... May	3
Ellen, ye D. of Adam Clayton, of Farington, in Pen-	
wortham P^{rsh}	„ 7
Sarah, ye w: of John Anderton, of Leyland	„ 12
Robert Turner, sen^r, of Leyland, &	
William, ye S. of William Porter, of Leyland ...	„ 16
John Low, of Euxton	„ 23
James, ye S. of Thomas Worthington, of Heapey ...	„ 31
Mary, ye D. of Robert Bradshaigh, of Farington, in	
Penwortham P^{rish} ... ... June	13
George Parkinson, of Leyland	„ 17
Catherine, ye W: of Evan Eastham, of Farington ...	„ 21

[1] See page 83.

[2] Mr. Farrand Hodgson was Master of the Leyland Grammar School. See also note on page 165. [3] See notes on page 89.

James, yᵉ S: of Thomas Withington, of Clayton ... June 23
Edward Sumner, of Leyland ... ... July 3
John, yᵉ S: of Thomas Withington, of Clayton ... ... „ 12
Elizabeth, yᵉ w: of William Tootel, of Euxton ... ... „ 17
Henry, yᵉ S: of Thomas Eastham, of Leyland ... ... Aug. 4
John Bilsburrow, of Wheelton, buried at Blackburn ... „ (*sic*)2
Alice, yᵉ D. of William Croston, of Ulneswalton ... „ 11
Thomas, yᵉ S: of John Farnworth, of Wheelton ... ... „ 17
Agnes, yᵉ D: of John Kirkham, of Farington ... ... „ 29
Alice, yᵉ D. of Thomas Cooper, of Leyland ... ... „ 30
Jane, yᵉ D. of Thomas Silcock, of Clayton ... ... „ 31
William, yᵉ S: of Gilbert Cowling, of Leyland ... ... Sept. 8
Edward, yᵉ S. of Henry Moulden, of Leyland ... ... „ 14
Richard Jackson, of Cuerden ... ... „ 18
Richard Whittle, of Leyland ... ... „ 25
Alice, yᵉ D. of George Asley, of Whittle ... ... Oct. 5
Jane Hodson, of Leyland, *vid:* ... ... „ 6
Thomas, yᵉ S: of William Bolton, of Withnel, &·⎫
John Pilkington, of Euxton ... ... ⎬ „ 19
Thomas, yᵉ S. of William Dewhurst, of Withnel ... „ 23
John Thornley, of Leyland ... ... „ 25
George Dawson, Senʳ, of Leyland ... ... „ 15
Richard Tootel, of Whittle ... ... „ 16
Thomas Gerrard, of Andlesark, in Bolton Pˢʰ ... ... „ 22
Robert Martin, of Heapey ... ... „ 29
John Hilton, of Leyland ... ... Dec. 2
Margret ffishwick, of Euxton, *vid:* ... ... „ 23
Thomas, s: to Thomas Morris, of Heapey ... ... Jan. 3
Henry Tising, of Ulnswalton ... ... „ 6
Elizabeth Turner, *vid:* of Charnock Ri: Stand. Pˢʰ ... „ 10
Dorothy, yᵉ W: of Edward Rawsthorn, of Farington ... „ 28
Mary, yᵉ D. of Richard Biccursteth, of Whittle ... ... „ 30
Andrew Cooper, of Euxton ... ... Feb. 10
Thomas, yᵉ S. of Thomas Breckall, of Mawdesley, in
Croston Pʳⁱˢʰ ... ... „ 18
Alexander Briers, of Whittle ... ... „ 19
Richard, yᵉ S. of Richard Almond, of Leyland ... ... „ 23
Jane, yᵉ D. of William Watson, Traveller ... ... March 9
Henry Jackson, of Euxton ... ... „ 23
Elizabeth, yᵉ D. of Thomas Silcock, of Clayton ... ... „ 24

[Written at the bottom of the page, immediately under the last entry, and in the same handwriting.]

Elizabeth, yᵉ D: of Thomas Silcock, of Clayton, Septembʳ
yᵉ 20, 1708.

Burɣals, 1706.

Margaret, yᵉ D. of William Shaw, of Leyland ... ...March 25
Ralph, yᵉ S: of Samuel Duncalf, of Heapey ... ... April 3
Ellen Clough, of Leyland, *vid:* & ... ... ⎫
Alice, yᵉ W: of Edward Longton, of Whittle ... ⎬ „ 5
John Okenshaw, of Euxton ... ... „ 6
Elizabeth, yᵉ W: of Ralph Cross, of Leyland ... ... „ 10
Henry,¹ yᵉ Son of Mr. William Farington, of yᵉ Shaw:
  Hall, in Leyland ... ... „ 20
Ellen Low, of Hutton, in yᵉ Pʳˢʰ of Penwortham, *vid:*.. May 3
William, yᵉ S: of Henry Kilshaw, of Burscow, in Orms:
  Church Pʳˢʰ ... ... „ 7
William, yᵉ S. of George Porter, & ⎫of Leyland ... „ 8
Elizabeth Leach ⎭
Jane, yᵉ D. of Ralph Pincock, of Whittle ... ... „ 9
John Charnock, of Cuerden ... ... „ 21
Margaret, yᵉ W: of William Garstang, of Charnock
  Richard, in Standish Pʳⁱˢʰ ... ... „ 22
Isabel, yᵉ W: of Thomas Jackson, of Cuerden ... ... June 6
Alice, yᵉ D. of William Croston, of Ulnswalton ... ... July 13
Agnes, yᵉ D: of Richard Tomlinson, of Farington ... Aug. 3
Geffrey Taylor, of Heapey ... ... „ 5
Ellen, yᵉ W: of Henry Moulden, of Leyland ... ... „ 10
Cicely, yᵉ W: of William Farington, Junʳ, of Farington,
  in Pen[wortham] Pʳⁱˢʰ ... ... „ 16
Grace, yᵉ D: of Richard Clarkson, of Euxton, & ⎫ „ 19
Richard, yᵉ S: of Henry Moulden, of Leyland ... ⎭
Henry, yᵉ S: of Thomas Crichlow, of Euxton ... ... „ 22
Alice, yᵉ W: of William Hawworth, of Clayton ... ... „ 29
Elisabeth, yᵉ W: of Oliver Martin, of Wheelton ... ... Sept. 2
Thomas, yᵉ S: of Robert Welch, of ffarington ... ... „ 6
Richard Gorton, of Leyland ... ... „ 9
Catherine, yᵉ D: of John Stephenson, of Leyland ... „ 19
John, yᵉ S: of Roger Crook, of Whittle ... ... „ 22
Thomas, yᵉ S: of Roger Walton, Junʳ, of Leyland ... „ 28
Ann, yᵉ W: of Richard Clarkson, of Euxton ... ... Oct. 11
Alice, yᵉ D: of Ralph Pierson, of Whittle ... ... „ 13
William Hawworth, of yᵉ Waterland, & ⎫of Whittle ... „ 19
Elizabeth, yᵉ D: of John Taylor ⎭

¹ This infant son of Mr. Wm. Farington and his wife Elizabeth (Rufine) was baptised at Preston, Sept. 14, 1705. See the entry of that date in the Leyland Register. Another son Henry was born in 1715. The marriage referred to on page 109 was that of the second Henry, and not of the one there named, who died an infant, as this entry proves.

Ann Pemberton, of Wheelton ... ... }
James, yᵉ S: of John Tyrer, of Heapy ... ... } Oct. 27
Margaret, yᵉ W: of Thomas Garstang, of Whittle ... Nov. 13
Nicolas Whittle, of Leyland ... ... „ 16
Robert Cooper, of Ashton-Bank, in Preston Parish ... „ 20
William, yᵉ S: of John Pincock, of Euxton ... ... „ 28
Jane Taylor, of Whittle, *vid:*... ... ... Dec. 5
Robert Lyne,[1] of Leyland ... ... „ 21
William Boydal, senʳ, of Euxton ... ... „ 27
Elizabeth, yᵉ W: of George Crook, of Withnel ... ... Jan. 2
Jane, yᵉ D: of Henry Wadington, Junʳ, of Hoghton ... „ 8
Mary Jackson, of Whittle, *vid:* & ... ... }
Alice Hall, of Euxton, *vid:* ... ... } „ 14
Mary, yᵉ D: of William Baxenden, of Euxton ... ... „ 27
Robert Blackburn, of Cuerden ... ... „ 29
Thomas yᵉ S: of Robert Sumner, of Ulnswalton ... Feb. 7
Elizabeth Marsden, of Whittle, *vid:* ... ... „ 11
Alice, yᵉ D: of Richard Crook & Elizabeth Kellet, of
  Euxton ... ... „ 23
Elizabeth, yᵉ D: of Thurstan Leyland, of Leyland ... March 3
Margaret, yᵉ D: of John Clough, of Leyland ... ... „ 8
Mary Marsh, of Leyland, *vid:* ... ... „ 10
John Marsh, of Leyland ... ... „ 11
Mary, yᵉ W: of James Andlezarck, of Duxbury, in
  Standish Parish ... ... „ 13
Ellen, yᵉ D: of John Slaytor, Junʳ, of Euxton ... ... „ 14

[Burials] 1707.

Thomas, yᵉ S: of William Cooper, of Leyland ... ... March 27
Isabel, yᵉ D: of Richard Wigans, of Whittle ... ... April 5
Margaret Unsworth, of Euxton, *vid:* ... ... „ 8
Andrew Stones, of Leyland ... ... „ 11
Richard, yᵉ S: of John Tootel, Junʳ, of Whittle ... ... „ 17
Edward Crane, of Clayton ... ... „ 19
John Farnworth, of Wheelton ... ... „ 25
Simon, yᵉ S: of Hugh Brown, of Heapey ... ... „ 30
Margaret Burscow, of Eccleston ... ... May 11
Jane, yᵉ D: of James Hornby, of Clayton ... ... „ 12
Frances, yᵉ D: of John Clough, of Leyland ... ... „ 16
William, yᵉ S: of Richard Liptrot, of Euxton ... ... „ 23
Ellen, yᵉ D: of John Gerrard, of Leyland ... ... „ 27

[1] This name does not occur elsewhere in the Register.

Alice, yᵉ D: of George Slaytor, of Auston [Alston],
    in Ribchester Parish ... ... May 30
Margaret Waterworth, of Leyland ... ... June 6
Richard, yᵉ S: of James Gerrard, of Euxton, & ... ⎫
Hugh, yᵉ S: of William Mackeril, of Farington ... ⎬ „ 14
Alice, yᵉ D: of John Woodcock, Junʳ, of Cuerden ... „ 20
Richard, yᵉ S: John Gerrard, of Leyland ... ... July 9
John Goulding, of Leyland ... ... „ 15
Thomas, yᵉ S: of William Croston, of Ulnswalton ... „ 17
Jennet, the W: of Richard Williamson, of Leyland ... „ 31
Ellis, yᵉ S: of Michael Taylor, of Whittle ... ... Aug. 5
Eller., yᵉ W: of James Nightingale, of Clayton ... ... „ 11
John Blackburn, of Euxton ... ... „ 12
Hugh yᵉ S: of John Sim, of Euxton ... ... „ 16
Martha Atkison, of Whittle ... ... „ 27
Isabel James, of Leyland ... ... Sept. 27
Ann, yᵉ D: Thomas Barton, of Leyland ... ... Oct. 12
Thurstan Sharrock, of Euxton ... ... „ 14
William Worden, of Clayton ... ... „ 28
Ellen, yᵉ D: of Hugh Brown, of Heapey ... ... Nov. 16
Ellen Hoghton, of Charnock Richard, in Standish Pʳⁱˢʰ „ 21
Elizabeth Whittle, of Withnel, *vid:* ... ... „ 25
James Nightingale, of Clayton ... ... „ 26
Agnes, yᵉ Wife of Geo: Porter, of Leyland ... ... „ 27
Elizabeth, yᵉ W: of Thomas Eastham, of Farington ... „ 30
Margaret, ye D: of John Dewhurst, of Withnel ... ... Dec. 3
Margaret Martin, of Heapey, *vid:*... ... ... „ 14
William, yᵉ S: of Thomas Garstang, of Whittle ... ... „ 15
Jennet, yᵉ W: of Henry Phizakerley,[1] of Leyland, & ⎫
John Slaytor, of Euxton, Blacksmith ... ... ⎬ „ 20
Robert Parker, of Leyland ... ... „ 26
Ann Taylor, of Cuerden, *vid:* ... ... „ 30
George Moonk, of Leyland ... ... ⎫
Ann, yᵉ D: of Robert Cocker, of Leyland ... ... ⎬ „ 31
John, yᵉ S: of John Kirkham, of Farington ... ... ⎭
Alice, yᵉ D: of John Cooper, of Leyland ... ... Jan. 3
Catherine Yate, of Heapey, *vid:* ... ... „ 6
Elisabeth, yᵉ D. of Thomas Ugnall, of Wheelton ... „ 10
Ann Marsden, of Withnel, *vid:* ... ... „ 12
Elizabeth Balshaw, of Leyland, *vid:* ... ... „ 15
Ellen, yᵉ W: of William Marsden, of Whittle ... ... „ 21
John fforshaw, of Leyland ... ... ffeb. 9
William Dewhurst, of Withnel ... ... „ 14

---

[1] Otherwise and more commonly Fitz-ackerley or Fazakerley.

Thomas, yᵉ S: of James Gerrard, of Wheelton	ffeb. 15
John Livesay, of Withnel	„ 17
Charles, yᵉ S: of Charles Rothwel, of Leyland	„ 19
Jennet Bancroft, of Leyland, *vid.*, & ... ... Joan Briers, of Euxton, *vid.*	} March 5
Ellen, yᵉ W: of James Garstang, of Ulnswalton	„ 15
John Sherdley, of Farington, & ... ... Elizabeth, yᵉ W: of Thomas Parker, of Wheelton	} „ 16
Richard Richmond,¹ of Withnel	„ 17

1708, Buryals.

William Garstang, of Charnock Richard, in Standish Prish	April 13
Ann, yᶜ D. of James Hornby, of Clayton, & ... John, yᵉ S. of William Marsden, of Whittle... ...	} „ 18
Ellen Blackledg, of Whittle, *vid:*	„ 22
Ann Martin, of Heapey, *vid:*	„ 29
Ellen, yᶜ W: of William Sharrock, of Clayton	May 6
William, yᵉ S: of William Garret, Traveller	„ 30
Jane Martin, of Leyland...	June 14
Ellen, yᶜ D: of William Cooper, of Leyland	„ 25
Catherine Withnel, of Withnel	July 20
Jennet, yᶜ D: of William Porter, of Leyland	„ 27
Isabel, the wife of Richard Wiggins, of Whittle	Aug. 2
James, yᶜ S: of Robert Cocker, of Leyland	„ 18
Ann, yᶜ W: of William Wilson, of Lealand...	„ 23
John Withnel, of Withnel-fold²	„ 27
³[Elizabeth, yᶜ D: of Thomas Silcock, of Clayton	... Sept. 20]
William Jackson, of Cuerden, Webster...	„ 22
Jane, yᵉ W: of William Crichlow, of Euxton	„ 24
Jane, yᵉ D: of Widow Garstang, of Heapey	Oct. 6
Ellen, yᵉ W: of Robert Welch, of Farington, & ... Ann, yᶜ W: of John Arthrick, of Farington... ...	} „ 12
Elizabeth Pincock, of Euxton, *vid:*	„ 22
Mary Briers, of Whittle, *vid:*...	„ 28
John Wigan, of Andlezark, in Bolton Prish	Nov. 5
Ellen, yᵉ W: of John Gabbot, of Withnel	„ 12
Ann, yᵉ D: of Robert Illridge, Traveller	„ 14
Elizabeth, yᶜ D: of Ralph Pilkington, of Leyland ...	„ 15
Thomas, yᵉ S: of John Halliwell, of Whittle	„ 16

¹ There is a farm, situated about the middle of the township of Withnell, which still goes by the name of "Richmond's."

² This farm lies in the extreme north-east corner of the township of Withnell.

³ Entered under the year 1705 (see p. 276).

Lawrence, yᵉ S: of Alexander Briers, of Whittle ... Dec. 11
Thomas, yᵉ S: of Thomas Hey, Junʳ, of Heapey ... „ 14
Ann, yᵉ D: of John Clough, of Leyland ... ... „ 15
Jane Bank, of Leyland, *vid:* ... ... „ 23
Ambry,¹ yᵉ D: of Thomas Abbot & Ann Hey, of⎫
 Heapey, & ... ... ⎬ „ 27
Peter Clayton, of Farington ... ... ⎭
Elizabeth Sumner, of Leyland ... ... Jan. 10
Ellen, yᵉ W: Edward Park, in Leyland ... ... „ 14
Thomas, yᵉ S: of William Dewhurst, of Raddlesworth. „ 17
Margery, yᵉ D: of John Tomson, of Leyland ... ... „ 18
John, yᵉ D: of Richard Crook, of Euxton ... ... „ 25
Alice, yᵉ D: of John Walmsley, of Heapey... ... ... „ 26
Francis, yᶜ S: of John Smith, of Leyland ... ... „ 27
Thomas Whitehead, of Farington... ... ... ⎫ „ 28
Ann, yᵉ D: of John Beardsworth, of Farington ... ⎭
Thomas Clarkson, of Bretherton, in Croston Pʳⁱˢʰ ... Feb. 5
George Charnley, of Euxton... ... ... „ 7
Henry, yᵉ S: of Henry Wadington, Junʳ, of Hoghton, &⎫ „ 10
Alice, yᵉ D: of Roger Bolton, of Euxton ... ... ⎭
John, yᵉ S: of Thomas Mackeril, of Leyland ... ... „ 15
Agnes, yᵉ W: of Thomas Withnel, of Heapey ... ... „ 20
Elizabeth, yᵉ W: of Richard Briers, of Withnel ... ... „ 21
Thomas Hey, senʳ, of Heapey ... ... „ 25
William Abbot, of Chorley,² in Croston Parish ... ... „ 28
Ann, yᵉ W: of James Pilkington, of Whittle ... ... March 1
Ralph Whittle, of Whittle ... ... „ 3
Cicely Walton, of Leyland ... ... „ 4
Thomas, yᵉ S. of Thomas Longton, of Whittle ... ... „ 13
James Garstang, of Tock-Holes, in Blackburn Pʳˢʰ ... „ 20

Burials, 1709.

Ann Briers, of Withnel, *vid:* ... ... ⎫March 26
Ellen, yᵉ W: of Henry Ainsworth, of Withnel ... ⎭
Jennet, yᵉ W: of William Woodcock, of Leyland ... April 7
Mary, yᵉ W: of Robert Clayton, of Farington ... ⎫
Robert, yᵉ S: of Thomas Withington, of Clayton ⎪
Ann, yᵉ D: of Henry Smith, of Cuerden, & ... ⎬ „ 11
Mary, yᵉ D: of James Tomson, of Eccleston ... ⎭

¹ This is a curious Christian name. The fields near to the glebe land used to be called the Ambrye Meadows.

² Chorley, which is now a rectory and a corporate town, was a chapelry of Croston down to the year 1793, when it was severed by Act of Parliament.

Henry, yᵉ S: of Richard Clarkson, of Euxton ... ... April 14
John Gorton, of Withnel... ... ... May 4
Oliver, yᵉ S: of Ralph Pierson, of Whittle ... ... „ 5
Richard Wiggins, of Whittle ... ... „ 11
John Haughton, of Clayton ... ... „ 14
Thomas, yᵉ S: of William Wiggins, of Leyland... ... „ 21
William, yᵉ S: of Richard Clough, of Little-Hool¹ ... „ 22
Jane, yᵉ W: of Thurstan Leyland, of Leyland ... ... „ 31
Ellen, yᵉ W: of Roger Harrocks, of Euxton ... ... June 9
Henry, yᵉ S: of Henry Kirkham, of Farington ... ... „ 20
John Woodcock, of Leyland ... ... July 5
Thomas Dewhurst, of Cuerden ... ... „ 10
Elizabeth, yᵉ D: of William Jackson, of Cuerden ... „ 27
Ann, yᵉ D: of Robert Wilding, of Leyland... ... ... Aug. 3
Ellen, yᵉ D: of John Waln, of Cuerden ... ... „ 4
Richard Clarkson, of Euxton, & ... ... ⎱
Margaret, yᵉ D: of John Smith, of Whittle ... ... ⎰ Sept. 6
Margaret, yᵉ W: of Thomas Smith, of Ulneswalton ... „ 25
Ellen, yᵉ W: of John Sumner, of Cuerden ... ... Oct. 1
John Walmsley, of Heapey ... ... „ 10
Sylvester Hilton, of Lealand... ... ... „ 27
Catherin, yᵉ D: of Richard Leaver, of Lealand ... ... „ 30
Jane, yᵉ D: of James Jackson, of Farington ... ... Nov. 4
Thurstan, yᵉ S: of Thurstan Sharrock, of Euxton ... „ 14
Hugh Waterworth, of Farington ... ... Dec. 7
John Gardiner, of Lealand ... ... „ 15
Mary, yᵉ D: of Thomas Croft, of Whittle ... ... „ 18
John, yᵉ S: of Thomas Smith, of Ulnswalton ... ... „ 21
Alice, yᵉ D: of Robert Stones, of Euxton ... ... „ 22
Cicely, yᵉ D: of James Walton, of Leyland, & ... ⎱
Jane, yᵉ D: of William Leyland, of Cuerden ... ⎰ Jan. 11
Dennis,² yᵉ W: of Thomas Smith, of Leyland ... ... „ 16
Richard, yᵉ S: of John Waln, of Cuerden ... ... „ 21
Elizabeth, yᵉ W: of Henry Catterall, of Clayton ... „ 25
Jane, yᵉ D: of Thomas Eastham, of Leyland ... ... „ 27
Catherine, yᵉ D: of Mʳ Farrand Hodgson,³ of Ley-
land ... ... „ 31
Elizabeth, yᵉ W: of John Whalley, of Leyland ... ... Feb. 3
Jane, yᵉ D: of Ellis Sumner, of Leyland ... ... „ 10

---

¹ A township formerly part of the ancient parish of Croston. Much (or Great) Hoole and Little Hoole became a separate parish in 1641, by Act of Parliament of that date.

² An unusual name for a woman.

³ See Baptisms, page 112; also Marriages, page 165 (note).

Jane Lee, of Euxton, *vid:* ... ... ⎫
Jane, yᵉ D: of George Woods, of Euxton, & ... ⎬ Feb. 13
John, yᵉ S: of James Brown, of Farington ... ... ⎭
John Sim, of Euxton ... ... „ 14
Ann, yᵉ D: of Robert Cocker, of Leyland ... ... „ 15
Miles, the son of Ellis Sumner, of Leyland ... ... „ 21
Elizabeth Biby, of Heapey, *vid:* ... ... „ 22
Mary, yᵉ D: of Thomas Jackson, of Cuerden ... ... „ 27
Alice, yᵉ W: of Hugh Rigby, of Heapey, & ... ⎫ March 3
Oliver Garstang, of Clayton ... ... ⎭
John, yᵉ S: of John Jackson, of Cuerden ... ... „ 22

Buryals, 1710.

William, yᵉ S: of George Asley, of Whittle ... ... April 8
Frances, yᵉ D: of Robert Whittle, of Withnel ... ... „ 10
William, yᵉ S: of John Woodcock, Junʳ, of Cuerden ... „ 11
Elizabeth, W: of Robert Bradshaw, of Walton-in-le-⎫
Dale ... ... ⎬ „ 18
Margaret, yᵉ D: of John Scot, of Whittle ... ... ⎭
Elizabeth, yᵉ W: of John Pierson, de Hole in Wheelton „ 25
Alice, yᵉ D: of Thomas Eastham, of Farington ... ... May 7
Ann, yᵉ D: of John Hawworth, of Whittle ... ... „ 12
Elizabeth, yᵉ D: of Henry Catterall, of Clayton ... ... „ 22
Jennet, yᵉ D: of William Man, of Euxton ... ... June 2
Richard, yᵉ S: of Robert Bradshaigh, of Cuerden ... „ 9
Robert Foster, of Euxton ... ... „ 15
William, yᵉ S: of Thomas Crook, of Farington ... ... „ 19
Lawrence Whittle, of Leyland ... ... „ 26
Ann Abbot, of Whittle, *vid:* ... ... July 2
Ellen, yᵉ D: of William Roscow, of Charnock Richard „ 18
Mary, yᵉ D: of John Halliwell, of Whittle ... ... „ 20
Alice, yᵉ D: of William Wright, of Euxton... ... ... Aug. 19
Elizabeth Farington, of Farington, *vid:* ... ... „ 26
William, yᵉ S: of Roger Walton, Junʳ, of Leyland ... „ 30
Mary, yᵉ D. of Robert Cooper, of Cuerden ... ... Sept. 7
Ralph, yᵉ S: of John Hunt, of Cuerden ... ... „ 10
Elizabeth, yᵉ D. of Thomas Trigg, of Heapey ... ... „ 15
Richard Parker, of Charnock Richard, in Standish Pᵣⁱˢʰ „ 19
Thomas, yᵉ S: of John Ditchfield, of Leyland ... ... Oct. 12
James, yᵉ S: of Robert Hey, of Heapey ... ... „ 14
George Bury, of Withnell ... ... „ 19
William Tootel, of Heapey ... ... Nov. 28
Ann, yᵉ D: of Henry Smith, of Cuerden ... ... Dec. 5
John Morrow, a Traveller ... ... „ 6

Margaret, yᶜ W: of William Holland, of Euxton ... Dec. 11
John Barker, of Withnel... ... ... ,, 16
John, yᵉ S: of John Whittle, of Withnel ... ... ,, 27
Alice, yᵉ D: of James Asley, of Whittle ... ... Jan. 4
William Withnel, of Withnel ... ... ,, 23
Ellen Blundel, of Farington ... ... ,, 24
Hugh Pilkington, of Euxton ... ... ,, 27
Matthew, yᵉ S: of John Moulden, of Heapey ... ... ,, 30
Sarah, yᶜ W: of Thomas Cooper, of Leyland ... ... Feb. 1
Isabell, yᵉ W: of William Atherton, of Leyland ... ... ,, 2
John Jackson, of Farington ... ... ,, 6
William Cooper, of Leyland ... ... ,, 7
Thomas Frekleton, of Euxton, & ... ... ⎫
Alice, yᵉ D: of John Waln, of Farington ... ... ⎭ ,, 11
John Critchlow, of Clayton ... ... ,, 12
Jane Slaytor, of Euxton, *vid:* ... ... ,, 13
Mʳ John Farnworth,¹ of Walton-in-le-Dale ... ... ,, 16
Alice Johnson, of Whittle, *vid:* ... ... ,, 18
Robert, yᵉ S: of John Livesay, of Withnel ... ... ,, 20
Thomas, yᵉ S: of William Cuerden, of Clayton ... ... ,, 22
John, yᵉ S: of Edward Hawet [? Heywood] ... ... ,, 24
Richard Simpson, of Wheelton ... ... ,, 26
Cicely, yᵉ W: of Richard Liptrot, of Euxton ... ... March 6
Adam Plat, of Euxton ... ... ,, 18
Henry, yᵉ S: of Henry Whaley, of Leyland ... ... ,, 23

¹ Probably a member of the family noted on pages 58, 62, &c. This may perhaps be the brother of Mr. Edward Farnworth, of Runshaw in Euxton, entered with him at the Preston Guild of 1682 as a Foreign Burgess.

[*End of Burials in earliest extant Register.*]

Index of Names and Places.

T

Hand James 38, Jane 38
Hargreaves Alice 141, George 83
Harper Elizabeth 51, John 51
Harrison (Alice) 50 129 152 218 225
234, Ann 74 107, Cicely 146 170,
Elizabeth 58 71 95 234 256, Ellen 83,
Grace 146 251, Henry 47 107 251
257, James 100 106 111, Jane 188,
Jennett 28, John 71 74 77 83 88 *bis*
100 101 103 106 170 188 199 226 238
251 256, Lawrence 88, Margaret 5 53
242, Mary 226 238, Robert 9 58 77
81 129 141 146 197 218 225 234 251
254, Thomas 5 77 81 95 101 106 152
170 256, William 28 47 50 53 170 234
246 249 257
Harrock 205n
Harsnipp Elizabeth 133
Hartley Henry 159, James 111 116,
John 116, Katharine 130, Margaret
111, Mary 159 William 159
Harvey (Haruey) Hannah 128, Joan 148,
John 128
Harwood 139 166 *bis*
Haslam (Haslom) Mary 137, William 34
bis 137
Haslingden 141n
Hasminough Ellis 76, Katharine 76
Hatch (Hach) Annice 179, Cicely 149
150, Ellen 134, George 134 150 161,
James 179, Mary 161
Haukshead Anne 137, Margaret 26,
William 26
Haulgh Elizabeth 197, Thomas 214
Hawet (? Heywood) Edward 284, John
284
Haydock (Haddock) Alice 247, Eliza-
beth 131 190, Emma 178, Evan 102
257, Giles 172, Henry 29 *bis*, Isabel
159, James 26 131 180 190 248, Jane
67 265, Jennett 160 180, John 16 20,
Margery 6, Oliver 26 191, Richard
102 159 249, Thomas 16 20 67 94 188
261, Widow 204, William 18 94 175
178 184 261
Heald Alice 127, Anne 11, Cicely 182,
Elizabeth 48 272, Evan 101 105,
Henry 24 26 *bis* 30 39 178 197 220,
James 105, Jane 220, Jennett 101,
John 18, Richard 39, Thurstan 48,
William 182 198
Heapy Chapel 43n 114n 160n
Heapy (township of Leyland parish)
frequently
Heel Helen 146
Helme Elizabeth 136
Hemming Alice 250
Hesketh (Hesket) Alice 12 164, Andrew
68, Ann 134, Elizabeth 132 243, Ellen
137, Grace 158, Henry 147, Jane 132,

John 13 49 51 56 61 68 91 132 238,
Margaret 56 147, Robert 13 197,
Simon 257, Thomas 51 137, William
15 49 91 100 270 272
Hesketh Bank 135n 142
Hesketh-with-Becconsall 135n, *township*
138n
Heskin 27 28 30 138
Hesmonall Anne 167
Hey (Heyes) Alice 92 141 261, Ambry
281 281n, Amery 241, Amy 113, Anne
167 281, Cicely 164, Ellen 151 259,
George 164, James 283, Jane 93 195,
Jennett 92, John 93 141, Margaret
116 153, Mary 118 275, Nicholas 87
250, Ralph 101, Robert 113 153 283,
Thomas 87 116 118 151 167 195 249
250 259 261 275 281 *bis*, William 249
Heysham 36n
Heywood (Hewitt, Hawett) Anne 169,
Edward 284, James 260, Jane 270
270n, John 284, Thomas 169
Higginson (Higgison) Alice 115, Anne
115, Christopher 116, Elizabeth 164,
James 67 111 116 164, Margery 57,
Ralph 111, Richard 57 61 67 106 111
140 255, William 61 102 106 111 115
Higham (Hicham) Anne 151, Elizabeth
151, Thomas 112 151
Highfield Hall 7n
Hilton (Hulton) Alice 74 76 116, Anne
49 242 245 273, Edmund 15, Elizabeth 20 44 145 153 217 220 232 268,
Ellen 159 223, Evan 52, George 27
74 90 96, Isaac 86 94, Jacob 86 94
263, James 191, Jane 26, John 17 26
27 29 34 39 40 44 *bis* 59 86 94 96 170
176 193 203 210 223 228 230 232 242
242n 251 257 263 *bis* 276, Katharine
241 260 261, Margaret 39 252 275.
Margery 40 256, Mary 90 154, Oliver
52, Ralph 228, Richard 59 64 68 69
74 76 209 230 233 246, Robert 64 69
116 233, Roger 34, Sylvester 282,
Thomas 44 49 52 79 170 217 219 263
268, William 17 68 154 223 241 245
246 252 254 260
Hind Margaret 172 189, Richard 172
Hindle Alexander 91 148, Civil 148,
Ellen 269, Margaret 148, Robert 91
263
Hindley Anne 163, John 163, Robert
87, Thomas 87
Hindley 186
Hitchen Jane 138
Hodges Christian 130, Jane 139 144
Hodgkinson (Hodkison) Anne 134 167,
Elizabeth 149, George 8, Henry 152,
Jane 135 157, Jennett 8, John 134
149, Thomas 135 212n

U

End of Volume XXE.

EXAMINER PRINTING WORKS, MANCHESTER.